THE COMPUTER COOKBOOK®

HOW TO CREATE SMALL COMPUTER SYSTEMS THAT WORK FOR YOU

WILLIAM BATES

A SPECTRUM BOOK

Prentice-Hall, Inc., Englewood Cliffs, New Jersey 07632

Library of Congress Cataloging in Publication Data

Bates, William.
    The computer cookbook.

    "A Spectrum Book."
    Includes index.
    1. Microcomputers.   I. Title.
QA76.5.B323 1983   001.64   82-23104
ISBN 0-13-164558-7
ISBN 0-13-165167-6 (pbk.)

This book is available at a special discount when ordered in bulk quantities.
Contact Prentice-Hall, Inc., General Publishing Division,
Special Sales, Englewood Cliffs, N.J. 07632

10 9 8 7 6 5 4 3 2

ISBN 0-13-164558-7
ISBN 0-13-165167-6 {PBK.}

The *Computer Cookbook*® is a registered trademark of William Bates, Publisher.

Editorial/production supervision: Kimberly Mazur
Cover design: Honi Werner
Manufacturing buyer: Cathie Lenard

Prentice-Hall International, Inc., *London*
Prentice-Hall of Australia Pty. Limited, *Sydney*
Prentice-Hall Canada Inc., *Toronto*
Prentice-Hall of India Private Limited, *New Delhi*
Prentice-Hall of Japan, Inc., *Tokyo*
Prentice-Hall of Southeast Asia Pte. Ltd., *Singapore*
Whitehall Books Limited, Wellington, *New Zealand*
Editora Prentice-Hall do Brasil Ltda., *Rio de Janeiro*

To My Parents

A

Accounting

Accounting is one of those boring things in life better left to computers. Many people who complain about what computers are doing to the modern world should read their history books, to see how much time people in the past spent adding up long columns of figures in their heads or by hand. A wonderful play about this sort of work, "The Adding Machine", opened in New York in 1923, well before there were digital computers - although there had been punched "IBM" cards to fold, bend, spindle, and mutilate for over 30 years. These were invented by Hermann Hollerith in 1890 to cope with the large amount of data collected in the census of that year.

Although accountants tend to like computers, people trained in math or computers sometimes have difficulty with accounting. To people trained in math, accounting seems like it should be an exact science. Transactions are objective things: money comes in here and goes out there. If all transactions can be put on the computer, everything else, or so it seems, should be a matter of addition and subtraction.

This way of thinking confuses accounting with bookkeeping. Accurate records of transactions are the raw material of accounting, but the end product is something else - the report. There are traditions, which vary from country to country, and evolve slowly over time, about what reports should contain and just how they should look. The most important thing, however, is that reports must be useful - and that producing useful reports, whether by hand or by computer, can be something of an art.

[Personal Finances]. On the theory that one must creep before one can crawl, accounting problems are best introduced in low finance rather than high. In any accounting system, whether personal or business, records must be kept of transactions. When money is spent, it is typical to record the date and amount; the place it was spent and a description of the reason or item; and the method of payment, i.e., cash, check, credit card. A notebook in which this sort of information is kept is called a journal, which is a basic, daily record of transactions.

[Journals and Registers]. On a given day an adult might pay cash for something, write a check for something else, and use a credit card to charge another item. When someone writes a check, information about that check is usually written down in a part of the checkbook called the register, whose entries look like:

No. 256   7/1   Landlord   Rent $450   Balance: $754.34

A register is a list of transactions organized by account and by date. An individual might keep a register for the following sorts of accounts:

> a cash account;
> a checking account;
> a savings account;
> a MasterCard or Visa account;
> a mortgage account;
> various loan accounts;
> informal "tabs" involving
>   spouses, roommates, etc.

In general, it is easier to keep transactions organized by account than in a daily journal, because other institutions - like banks - do. A register can be reconciled against the bank's version of it. Note, however, that personal accounts do not necessarily involve cash transactions. For example, a "fixed asset" account might be established for a car or equipment like a computer, where an annual depreciation amount is deducted from the original value.

[Net Worth]. If a individual sets up an exhaustive list of accounts, the sum of the balances in all accounts will yield the net worth of an individual. Note that in this set-up, accounts can have positive and negative balances. A checking account will be positive unless overdrawn; a MasterCard account will be either negative or zero. Transfers between accounts do not affect net worth or equity; paying a MasterCard bill with a check is not an expense but rather a transfer from the checking account to the MasterCard account.

On a computer, an individual might keep a floppy disk file for every account. A simple but useful program might keep a running balance of each account. With some additional information kept on each transaction, however, it is possible to check on income and expense patterns.

In the real world, reports should be generated as summaries across all accounts. Consider a couple worried that they are spending too much money eating in restaurants: sometimes they pay cash, once in a while they write a personal check, and sometimes they charge dinners. Clearly, all of these transactions should go into the "dinner" pot. Items for company expense accounts, and tax deductions, can be likewise flagged.

In computer terms, such a report generating system is a database manager, and the database is the total of transactions however organized. Each transaction is a record, and each record has the following structure:

DATE   ID   VENDOR   DESCRIPTION   CATEGORY   ACCOUNT   AMOUNT

DATE is the month/day/year of the transaction; ID might be some additional identification of the transaction, perhaps a check number; the VENDOR is to whom a check was written or where a purchase was made; the CATEGORY is an expense or income category; and so on.

Various useful reports can be defined as SORT, MERGE, and EXTRACT operations on this transaction database. A "raw" transaction journal can be created with a MERGE individual account files and SORT of the resulting monster file by DATE. In the universe of all transactions, the checkbook or individual account register is an EXTRACT of all transactions for which ACCOUNT=CHECK, with the selected records SORTed by DATE. Expenses by category can be had by EXTRACTing transactions by CATEGORY and SORTing by DATE. Sorts by vendor — how much was spent at a particular store — are also useful.

In the real world, various modifications must be made. Cash expenses are often unrecorded; a system usually needs "unaccounted for" as an expense category, and a technique to force balances to a given amount, such as the amount of cash actually on hand, as opposed to what the computer says should be on hand. Individual transactions can have dual personalities: a man goes to dinner with friends, collects cash from the group, and uses a credit card to pay the total bill. This needs to be split into (1) a dinner expense, and (2) a transfer from the credit card account to cash. Finally, categories can change, or one may want multiple sets. On its Schedule C for self-employed professionals the IRS, for example, puts telephone expenses under "utilities"; other people might want to break out telephone expenses in a category separate from the electric bill.

[Business Transactions]. Consider a simplified model of a business. A business has customers that buy its goods and services. In a typical transaction, a customer calls the business and places an order, giving his company's purchase order number at the same time. The business makes a decision to serve the customer and ships him the items. The business sends the customer an invoice, and, if it is a regular customer, a statement of his account. After receiving the invoice, the customer sends a check to pay for the items.

This simple scenario is complicated enough, but consider other problems:

(1) A would-be customer may not be right for the business. The idea of a customer implies a regular, repeat relationship. Some businesses may only sell to certain classes of customers — for example, a wholesaler may sell only to operators of retail stores, not to the general public. A business may go through a general process of qualifying potential customers to see if they should take their money at all. Taking on bad customers or wasting time on non-customers can be a serious expense.

(2) The items the customer wants may not all be at hand. If an item is not in stock, it can be back ordered if the customer will wait; otherwise, there is a danger of losing the customer to a competitor who can deliver the item immediately. If a business keeps a large inventory customers are likely to get want they want immediately; however, it costs a business money to carry an inventory. Some types of items cannot be put in inventories at all. Others, including perishable goods such

as fruit, or items that go out of style such as dresses or last year's computer, will need to be thrown away or written off if not sold in time, and the business absorbs the cost.

(3) The business may have the items but not trust the customer to pay for them. A COD - cash on delivery - means that the item and the cash trade hands at the same time. If a business gives a customer time to pay for an item, it is essentially extending credit - operating somewhat like a bank. A business that always insists on being paid in cash may lose sales, whereas a business that sends goods to a customer who never pays has a bad debt and takes a loss for the value of the goods. A business may have a formal or informal credit limit for a customer and may not want to ship to customers who owe too much, or have taken too long to pay.

(4) Even when customers pay, they may pay in part or in full. Customers might pay by cash, check, or credit card, or even with other goods, in what is called a trade out.

This basic model is for a business dealing in tangible goods. A service business has other problems. Services can't be inventoried - if time passes when no service is performed, that time is lost. Although payment can be demanded in advance for services, if it is not, and the service is performed, there is no tangible object to take back if an account goes bad.

[Computer Accounting]. Five generic types of software packages make up most of all business software:

>   Accounts Receivable (A/R)
>   Accounts Payable (A/P)
>   Inventory
>   Payroll
>   General Ledger (GL)

In all of these functions, except perhaps the general ledger program, the computer is taking over things already done by some system in the day-to-day operation of a business. Switching to a new system - doing things the computer's way - is almost always a headache. The question is whether the headache is worth it. Typically, computers help in rapidly growing businesses where things are going well but are slightly out of control. A business may be booming, for example, but have no idea where its receivables stand, or even if it's selling to a bad account that isn't paying. Likewise, there may be no idea of what is in inventory or if things have been reordered or not, causing delays or wasteful overstocking.

[Accounts Receivable]. Receivables are the proceeds of sales made to customers who are given a period of time in which to pay. Giving customers time in which to pay a bill, instead of demanding cash in advance or cash on delivery (COD), is traditional when customers are known and also encourages sales. In the U.S.A., sales on account are typically made on a 30-day basis.

A business selling on terms is essentially acting like a bank and making a short-term loan to the customer. Like any loan, a receivable can go bad, that is, the goods can be delivered or used, and the customer be unable to pay. A going business often has expenses involved with creating the item delivered, and then must wait to be paid, leading to a drain on its cash. A business that has accounts receivable but little cash has a choice of either speeding up its collections or getting a short-term loan to bridge the gap until the receivables are collected (a practice known as factoring when the loan is secured against the receivables themselves).

Most accounts receivable systems are built around the concept of the invoice. Oddly, although invoices are a fundamental part of business culture, there is some confusion about what invoices are and even what the word means. Since an invoice is a type of bill, many people believe that it has to do with one's conscience calling - an inner voice. Actually, like the diplomatic term envoy, the word derives from the French envois and merely means that things have been shipped or conveyed.

The sum total of invoices sent out but not yet paid are the accounts receivable of a business. Accounts receivable are technically an asset but not one most businesses like to have. A computerized accounts receivable system has the following goals: (1) speed up invoicing and (hopefully) collections, so that receivables are converted faster into cash; and (2) catch bad accounts that are either behind in their payments or over a credit limit.

A common report generated by a computer A/R system is an "aged" report of receivables, which shows how many unpaid invoices have been out (1) under 30 days, (2) between 30 and 60 days, (3) between 60 and 90 days, and (4) over 90 days. Accounts where a customer has had over 90 days to pay often go into collection, meaning that some special in-house department tries to get the customer to pay, or the receivable is sold at a deep discount to a collection agency, which then tries to collect the debt.

[Accounts Payable]. Accounts payable - bills to pay - are the opposite side of the coin from accounts receivable. With accounts receivable, the point is to speed up collection; with accounts payable, the point is to delay it as much as possible. The money a business can use by building a gap between its receivables and its payables is called float. Travel agents, for one example, often collect for tickets several months before they must pay for fares; hence they usually have a large float. Many banks and large financial institutions would like to get their hands on small business and consumer float; this desire is one of the moving forces behind electronic funds transfer (EFT).

A computerized accounts payable (A/P) system has several goals. The first is to project and anticipate cash needs: if the computer is told when bills should be paid, it can easily compute, for example, the total cash needed to get to the end of the month or the end of the quarter. (This is one-half of a cash flow analysis; the other half needed is a projection of expected income.) Many A/P programs allow for bill juggling, which is a polite way of saying that some people get paid on time, and others don't. Delayed payments are a fact of life in both small and big businesses. A realistic payables system can't assume that a business can always pay cash for everything on time.

Aside from planning purposes, an accounts payable program can also write checks and perform other clerical work. In a typical system, a payable - usually an invoice from a supplier - is received. It must then be approved for payment, and a date established on which it is to be paid. Often a payment voucher is attached to the original invoice at this point. The vouchers are then entered into the computer system.

Naturally, some setting up of the computer is required. Usually vendors - the people a company buys from - have been assigned a number or code. If a company buys from relatively few vendors, setting up a vendor file is no problem. If vendors change constantly, it can be. Other set-up information might include the various general ledger account numbers to which expenses are to be posted.

Giving a computer the ability to write checks can be disconcerting. Usually, a payables system allows vouchers to be marked PREPAID, HOLD, or RELEASE when they are entered: prepaid means those already paid, like CODs, but entered into the system anyway to keep the books straight; HOLD means those for which checks should not be written automatically; and RELEASE means those for which the computer should go ahead and write checks when the current date hits or passes the payment date. Having a few other controls over the computer - like not letting it overdraw the checking account - makes for a nice touch.

[Payrolls]. Payrolls are a special case of accounts payable. Unlike accounts payable, payrolls are rarely fiddled with or postponed (such actions on the part of management being rightfully viewed as a source of concern to employees). However, payrolls do require considerable calculation and deduction of taxes, making them a prime candidate for computerization.

In general, a payroll program will maintain a file of data on employees, including such items as the number of exemptions declared by each, social security numbers, and mailing addresses. For firms with lots of turnover or casual labor, maintaining this employee file can be a difficult chore.

Every pay period, whether weekly, bi-weekly, or monthly, additional information is usually posted to the system. For some types of operations, data on every employee needs to be put in every time; for others, default values can hold, and only exceptions be entered. Posting data off time cards is equivalent to posting payment vouchers in an accounts payable system.

Once posted, proofed, and corrected, a payroll system calculates tax and other deductions, putting these on a statement attached to each employee's check, and then prints a check for the employee's net pay. An important part of the payroll program's job is to keep year-to-date figures for tax reporting. In the U.S.A., these must be sent by employers to the Internal Revenue Service in January, and a copy, the W-2, is sent to the employee. The long life of payroll records means that back-up procedures for disks and tapes is particularly important.

As with an accounts payable program, a payroll program can be integrated into a general ledger system, and automatically post the payroll information into the general ledger accounts. A payroll program that does this will, of course, need to be told the account number of accrued taxes, and so on, during a set-up period.

[Inventory Control]. In a time of high interest rates, tight control of inventories has moved from being merely desirable to being absolutely necessary. Both manufacturers and retailers spend money to put items into inventory - a manufacturer spends money producing the item, a retailer spends money to buy it.

In all but the most exceptional circumstances, there is a gap between the time the item is paid for and the time it is sold and its price collected. During this time therefore, cash is tied up in inventory. Tying up too much money in inventory can leave a business illiquid and may force it to dump inventory to raise cash. In theory, a business could get a loan for an amount equal to what it has tied up carrying the inventory. The interest on this theoretical loan is the carrying cost of the inventory. The higher the general interest rate, the more expensive it is to carry inventory.

The goal of automating inventory control is to speed the average turnover of items, so that carrying costs are reduced without compromising service to customers (i.e., without increasing situations where ordered items are out of stock). The basic inventory control procedure is simple. As an item is sold or taken out of stock, a count - the number on hand - associated with the item is decreased by one. If the number of items on hand drops below a threshold level, the reorder point, a purchase order is issued to its supplier for more. Often a purchasing lead time is factored into the reorder decision. Once items are received, the count of the inventory is increased.

The problems with implementing inventory control are not so much conceptual as practical. A distributor, for example, might carry many thousand different items in an inventory. In changing over to an automated system, these must all be given unique part numbers, and then a great deal of data - the part numbers and their counts - must be entered into the computer system. It might take several months to enter this amount of data and then several more months to weed out all of the typos and mistakes. In the meantime, day-to-day business can suffer badly - yet another example of computer conversion trauma.

One important offshoot of an automated inventory control system is be better sales analysis, where carrying costs are taken into account in evaluating the profitability of one item against another. Consider a toy company that sells one stuffed white elephant every two years at four times the price it paid for it. It also sells several dozen ordinary panda bears a month at 30% over their cost. The white elephant may look like a big profit item but not if the cost of keeping it around is figured.

[General Ledger]. A accounts receivable, accounts payable, inventory and payroll programs are designed to improve the day-to-day operations of a company. General Ledger programs are concerned with a more abstract entity, the balance sheet. General Ledger and the Balance Sheet are often treated with mysterious dignity as if they were some kind of Holy Book on which the essential secrets of a business were inscribed. Actually, the balance sheet is only a sort of snapshot, often blurry, of what a business looks like at a given time.

Put most simply, the net worth of a company is what is has minus what it owes - that is, its equity equals assets minus liabilities. Note that there is no reason why a net worth cannot be negative. However, accountants traditionally dislike working with negative numbers, so this equation is usually stated as:

$$Assets = Liabilities + Capital$$

In this form, it is called the accounting equation.

Within the general categories of assets and liabilities, there are subcategories. Current Assets are those assets that can be quickly converted into cash or which will turn into cash in the normal course of business in less than a year. Accounts receivable are current assets. Money lent for a short time is a current asset, as are inventories and pre-paid expenses. Fixed Assets are items like real estate, houses and buildings, and equipment, including computers. Most fixed assets decline in value along a sort of curve. This decline in value is called depreciation. There are a number of formulas for computing depreciation that attempt to approximate this curve.

Current liabilities, as with current assets, are those items that will be paid for by cash within a year. Current assets typically include accounts payable, debts due within a year, accrued taxes, and dividends to be paid out. Several useful indicators of a company's financial health can be defined in these terms. The quick ratio is the ratio of cash and receivables to current liabilities. A 2-to-1 ratio is considered average. The current ratio is the ratio of current assets to current liabilities. A 3-to-1 ratio is typical. Both these ratios actually are indicators of future cash flow.

The complete listing of categories and subcategories used by a business is called the chart of accounts - a list of all the various accounts used in a business. These usually form a tree structure:

```
                         general ledger
       /                 /            \              \
  asset accounts   liability accounts   equity accounts   operating accounts
   (begin with 1)   (begin with 2)     (begin with 3)      (begin with 4)
```

This numbering convention is peculiar to the U.S.A. Miscellaneous accounts often begin with a 5 or 6.

When a General Ledger program is run, it usually produces what is called a trial balance, meaning a draft balance sheet for the business. The balance sheet is based on the idea of the accounting equation, namely, assets equals liabilities plus equity. If the trial run is out of balance, the various accounts need to be fiddled with to correct it. This may sound bad, but in practice books never balance on the first run. Juggling books is a crime; balancing them is what accountants are paid to do.

The second type of report generated by most general ledger programs is the Income Statement, also called the profit and loss statement, or P&L. The balance sheet is a static snapshot of a business's financial condition at any one time. The P&L, by contrast, concerns a recent, fixed period of time, such as the last month, last year, or last quarter. The general equation for profit and loss is simple: profit results if income minus expenses is positive, whereas there is a loss if expenses exceed income. Part of the intricate nature of accounting comes from decisions as to how to allocate income and expenses over time so as to produce a true report of profit and loss.

[Business Software]. The problem with business software is that there is too much of it, or rather too many vendors offering A/R, A/P, and so on - programs that seem to differ very little from one another.

Most packaged business software runs under the CP/M operating system or on one of the larger selling computers like the IBM PC or the Apple II. Buying a package is not always the best thing to do, especially for companies with unusual requirements. Very often packages will either need customizing by a programmer or a change in accounting procedures. Most small businesses, being unwilling to deal with programmers, will opt for the latter.

Of the suppliers of business software, the "big 3" are Peachtree Software Inc., (3445 Peachtree Rd., N.E., 8th floor, Atlanta, GA 30326, 404-266-0673), whose programs are sold by IBM for its personal computer (Peachtree software also runs on other computers); BPI Systems (3423 Guadalupe, Austin, TX 78705, 512 454 2801), whose programs are sold by Apple; and Structured Systems Group (5204 Claremont Ave., Oakland, CA 94618, 415-547-1567), which is the leading vendor of CP/M software, with over 50,000 packages installed in 5 years.

In evaluating a software package, it is important to determine whether the manufacturer (or author), distributor, or retailer is responsible for training and support. Lifeboat Associates (1651 Third Ave., New York, NY 10028, 212-860-0300), for example, is a large distributor of CP/M software written by other manufacturers, and it divides support responsibilities with them.

"Accounting Plus II", for example, is an Apple II software package that can be purchased from local computer stores, but was written by a company called Software Dimensions and is distributed by Systems Plus (1120 San Antonio, Palo Alto, CA 94303). This is a $1,250 package; one should know who to call if it can't be made to work. Another Apple II business software company is The National Software Co. (Chamber of Commerce Bldg., Suite 117, Baltimore, MD 21202, 301-539-0123, 800-638-7563).

Some of the larger vendors of accounting software, mostly CP/M based, include: Dakin 5 Corporation (7000 Broadway, Suite 304, Denver, CO 80221, 303-426-6090); Advanced Operating Systems (450 St John Road, Michigan City, IN 46360, 800-348-8558, 219-879-4693); Definitive Systems, Inc. (3156 University Drive, N.W., Huntsville, AL 35805, 205-536-2625); Star Computer Systems, Inc. (18051 Crenshaw Blvd., Torrance, CA 90504, 213-538-2511); Open Systems, Inc. (430 Oak Grove, Suite 409, Minneapolis, MN 55403, 612-870-3515); International Micro Systems (6445 Metcalf, Shawnee Mission, KS 66202, 913-677-1137); American Business Systems, Inc. (3 Littleton Rd., Westford, MA 01886, 617-692-2600); TCS Software (3209 Fondren Rd., Houston, TX 77063, 713-977-7505); Microcomputer Consultants (PO Box T, Davis, CA 95617, 800-824-5952, 916-756-8104); Starsoft, Inc. (4984 El Camino Real, Suite 125, Los Altos, CA 94022, 415-965-8000, 800-882-8000); and Solid Software (Suite 501, 5500 Interstate North Parkway, Atlanta, GA 30328, 404-952-7709). Some of these sell only to dealers, and not directly to the public.

[Business Forms]. Any serious user of a business computer will want to buy special forms that allow the computer to fill out checks, invoices, and so on. A printer on a business computer system should have a tractor feed - namely, little sprocket wheels on each side of the platen that pull paper through. A number of companies make continuous forms designed to feed through computer printers. In general, payroll checks, invoices, statements, and so forth are easily available. MasterCard and other specialized forms are harder to find. A cost-effective trick for small business is to buy blank invoices or other forms and to let the computer customize them by printing the company name and logo. Aries Computer Products (PO Box 7932, Eugene OR 97401, 503-687-0625) sells such "generic" business forms in small quantities (e.g., 200) at very reasonable prices. Checks To Go (8384 Hercules St., Box 425, La Mesa, CA 92041, 714-460-4975) and GoForms (Box 55247, Valencia, CA 91355) sell blank three-part invoice forms for about $80 per 1000.

For a large business, an investment in preprinted forms is undoubtedly worthwhile in terms of cost and professional look. Custom forms can be designed and printed locally, which has the advantage of giving the business control over the process. Several firms, however, do quick, low-cost customizing by mail. The largest and most aggressive of these is NEBS Computer Forms (78 Hollis St., Groton, MA 01471, 800-225-8560), which promises 6-day turnaround of orders. Another firm specializing in computer mailing labels is Commercial Mailing Accessories, Inc., (1335 Deimar, St. Louis, MO 63108, 314-231-6006). Both of these firms print invoices, checks, and statements to order. Note that checks require a sample check from your bank with the funny numbers (MICR coding) on the bottom. Sending check printers a MICR permission sheet from the bank is also a good idea. The following table lists business form products:

SYSTEM	MANUFACTURER	DESCRIPTION/IDENTIFICATION	LIST	DISCOUNT
Forms	Aries	0101 invoice/point of sale (500)	65.00	
Forms	Aries	0102 stmt w/return payment (200)	39.00	
Forms	Aries	0901 personal check (500) MICR	79.00	
Forms	Aries	0931 business check w/stub (500)	95.00	
Forms	Aries	8001 statement (1000)	117.00	
Forms	Goforms	1013 3-part invoice 8 1/2 x 11	79.00	
Forms	Goforms	1023 3-part statement	79.00	
Forms	Goforms	1033 3-part purchase order	79.00	
Forms	NEBS	1208-1 1st class mail label (500)	21.50	
Forms	NEBS	1209-1 Ret Postage label roll	21.50	
Forms	NEBS	1210-1 Blank Lower Panel label	21.50	
Forms	NEBS	710-1 return envelope for 9051	16.00	
Forms	NEBS	770 Return envelopes (500)	16.00	
Forms	NEBS	771 Window envelopes f/9050(500)	14.75	
Forms	NEBS	775 Window envelope for 9022	17.95	
Forms	NEBS	9022-1 single checks (500)	32.50	
Forms	NEBS	9022-2 duplicate checks (500)	43.50	
Forms	NEBS	9022-3 triplicate checks (500)	49.95	
Forms	NEBS	9024-1 Continuous checks		
Forms	NEBS	9050-1 1 part stmt/invoice (500)	32.50	
Forms	NEBS	9050-3 3-part stmt/invoice (500)	49.95	

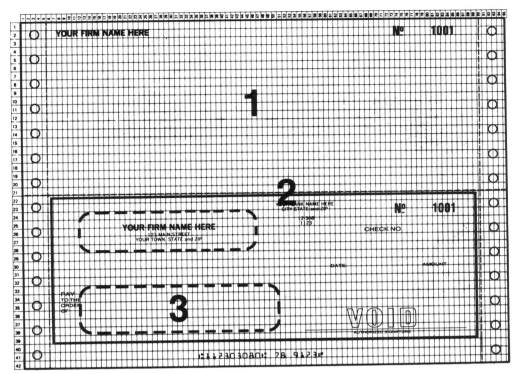

Programmer's Guide to NEBS checks, 53% actual size

Ada

Ada is a new programming language, the specifications for which were first made public in September 1980. "Ada" is a trademark of the US Department of Defense (DOD), which developed the language.

[Ada Herself]. Ada, the programming language, is named for Augusta Ada, Countess of Lovelace. Ada was the assistant of Charles Babbage, inventor of an analog calculating machine that is sometimes considered the first computer. Ada came from a distinguished if troubled family. Her father was Lord Byron, already a notorious celebrity at the time of Ada's birth in 1815. Ada's mother, Lady Annabella Byron, left her father shortly thereafter, never permitting the poet to see his daughter again.

Ada's mother, herself something of a nonconformist, encouraged all of Ada's intellectual interests, including her interest - unusual for women of the time - in mechanics and mathematics. Ada's first math tutor was William Frend, also known as an astronomer. In 1834, at the age of 19, Ada married William King, later the First Earl of Lovelace, eventually bearing him three children. Ada's work, however, was not hampered excessively by motherhood. Introduced to Babbage, she translated his treatise on the "analytical engine," eventually added her own notes that were themselves the first description of what in the 20th century is called computer programming.

Like many mathematicians, Ada was fascinated by gambling and carried on a passionate correspondence with Babbage in an effort to work out a foolproof method of betting on horses, evidently without success. In her 30s, Ada gambled heavily, borrowing from her mother to hide her losses from her husband. She died young, at age 36, in 1852, a hundred years before her time.

[Modern Ada]. In 1975, the US Department of Defense started a study of its large-scale software projects. What it found was not surprising: software development projects had serious problems in meeting deadlines, in programmer productivity, with software reliability, and, of course, with cost. The Defense Department then decided to do something about it and, in a military maneuver straight from a John Wayne film, appointed four teams, GREEN, RED, YELLOW, and BLUE, to design a new common programming language. There was, of course, precedent for this action: COBOL came about in much the same fashion in the late 1950s.

Ada is a step beyond Pascal, just as Pascal was a step beyond Algol 68. This line of evolution in the family of computer languages, generally favored by scientific and mathematical circles (as opposed to FORTRAN, more of an engineering language, and COBOL, a business language), has always emphasized the independence of procedures and functions, recursion (functions that can call themselves), and abstract data types. Thus in Pascal the program:

```
program main;
var i,j,k: integer;
...
procedure inner;
var i,j,k: integer;
...
```

defines two sets of variables i, j, and k, with the outer or "global" set protected from changes made to the variables of the same name within the procedure inner. If well constructed, or "structured" a tested Pascal procedure can be added into a program with no ill effect on its environment.

Ada takes this principal of structure a step further in rigor. In Ada, the idea of the parameter carefully defined and passed between procedures has been extended into the concept of an "object". An object is not only some sort of data type, like an integer or floating point number, but can also be a program or procedure. When objects can be passed around like parameters, the computer language takes on many properties of an operating system. Thus part of a typical Ada program might look like:

```
package BOX is
i,j: integer;
procedure INNER(..)
...
end BOX
```

This part of the program is publicly visible, but implementation details are hidden. (The nearest thing to this in Pascal is the DECLARATION and IMPLEMENTATION part of library UNITS.) This is defined by further code:

```
package body BOX is
```

```
procedure INNER (..) is
begin
...
end INNER
```

This part of an Ada program is akin to the 9/10s of the iceberg below water. Ada's claim is that it increases productivity on large projects by allowing the interfaces to be agreed upon in public, leaving the actual implementation details hidden, or subject to maintenance and revision, from the other programmers in the project. As long as a programmer takes an "object" and does what he is supposed to do with it, his module can be treated as a black box by the rest of the effort.

[Critics of Ada]. Ada is not everybody's darling. Critics of Ada claim that the language is too complicated, lacks symmetry, and is ambiguous. Part of the problem with Ada is that it was designed by committee: no fewer than 130 military and private sector groups were involved in its selection. Its development was by both Cii-Honeywell Bull, of France, and Honeywell, Inc., of the USA.

As a result, Ada seems to be a core language much like Pascal but with a large body of confusing, extra features. A simple Ada fragment:

```
type            real_array is array
                    (integer range <>) of float;
procedure       array_sum (
    a:              in real_array;
    sum_x:          out float;
    sum_indexes:    out float;
    sum_squares:    out float)
is

begin
    sum_x := 0.0;
    sum_indexes := 0.0;
    sum_squares := 0.0;
    for i in a'range loop
        sum_x := sum_x + a(i);
        sum_indexes := sum_indexes + (a(i) * float(i));
        sum_squares := sum_squares + (a(i) ** 2);
    end loop;
end array_sum;
```

[The Intel 432]. Ada might be just another programming language if not for the Intel 432 processor. The Intel 432, the first 32 bit microprocessor, is essentially an "Ada machine". A board level Multibus (IEEE standard 769) version of the 432 became available from Intel in April 1982. Although National Semiconductor announced a 32-bit processor in May 1982, Intel has a definite lead in the 32-bit race, and a unique design putting software onto silicon.

With the 432, Intel is essentially designing a mainframe computer. There are actually two types of 432 chips: a General Data Processor, or GDP, and an Interface Processor, or IP. An Intel "mainframe" has a familiar architecture:

a star pattern of IPs surrounds the central core of GDPs. The Interface Processors handle all I/O, taking much of the burden off the central GDPs.

Where Intel's mainframe architecture deviates from tradition is that it allows any number of GDP's to be used. In short, the 432 is designed for parallel and concurrent processing. GDPs share common memory, up to 2^{24} (16 megabytes) of real, physical memory, or 2^{40} bytes of virtual memory. 432 processors send variable length "packets" of information to memory and thus operate on different sized buses. The 432 is thus slightly similar to a local network architecture: the basic idea is that processors can be added until enough processing power is there.

Since the 432, as a silicon chip, will still be relatively slow compared to mainframes, concurrent processing will be a necessity for 432 designs competitive with mainframes in speed. Coprocessing offers other advantages, however, such as reliability and fail-safe operation. All 432s have two 64-pin chips, one "shadowing" the other; they might be thought of as "little Tandems". 432 systems will be cluster computers, able to limp along even if a processor is dead. Since chip microprocessors are reliable anyway, 432 systems should approach zero down time, an interesting threshold in the development of machine intelligence.

[Ada Machines]. One of the attractions of developing software in Ada is that a large and powerful organization, the US Department of Defense, will eventually require all its software vendors to program in it. Ada compilers, which are being developed by a number of private companies in the USA, will need to be validated by the DOD.

As of this writing, no validated Ada compiler for microcomputers exists, although several tiny Adas or micro Adas do. Of these, the most interesting is Western Digital's MicroAda. Western Digital is originally a semiconductor company and maker of DEC's microcoded LSI-11 16 bit processor.

In 1979, WD introduced a "Pascal Engine", which used the microcoded LSI-11 to directly run UCSD Pascal P-code. This machine is extremely fast for a Pascal machine. In mid-1982, Western Digital introduced, on the same pattern, an Ada machine called the "SuperMicro". This machine runs a subset of full Ada, and Western Digital has confidently announced plans to upgrade users to full, validated Ada as soon as possible.

An S-100 based Ada machine is offered by Digicomp Research (Terrace Hill, Ithaca, NY 14850, 607-273-5900), which also offers a Pascal version. The Delphi-100 uses a Motorola MC68000 microprocessor, Z-80 coprocessor, and several other special S-100 boards. The software supplied with the machine is from TeleSoft and includes the TeleSoft-ROS operating system, which is single user but multitasking; a screen editor; TeleSoft Ada, which generates Pascal-like P-code; TeleSoft Pascal; and a MC68000 P-code to native-code translator. The Digicomp Research machine can use Quantum hard disks and is IEEE-696 standard. TeleSoft also plans an Ada compiler that will pass the DOD Ada Compiler Validation Suite.

[Tiny Adas]. An Ada compiler for microcomputers is offered by Digital Electronic Systems (Box 5252, Torrance, CA 90510, 213-539-6239). "Ada/M" is a compiler that runs in a CP/M environment and produces intermediate code similar to Pascal P-code. This intermediate code is then interpreted by a set of run-time routines called CAPSE, an acronym for Compiler Ada Programming Support Environment. These two programs are sold by Digital Electronic Systems for $495. A version that operates with "C" is $995.

A mini-Ada called Janus is available for CP/M computers from RR Software (PO Box 1512, Madison, WI 53701, 608-244-6436) for the IBM PC, the North Star computers, and the Apple II using the Microsoft CP/M Softcard. The 8080/Z80 versions require 56K machines and cost $300. The 8086/8088 versions use 64K and cost $400.

APL

When computers were first invented during World War II, they were immediately put to work doing all kinds of boring things, like computing artillery firing angles. These sorts of numerical computations led to the giant brain concept, the first of many myths about computers. Throughout the 1950s, much of the public believed that numbers were fed into computers and, after much whirring and clicking, an answer printed on a single slip of paper fell out of a slot.

Although the giant brain myth misses most of the fun of computing, it is at times wise to recall the origins of the computer as a calculator. In the 1950s there were two types of computers: scientific machines, like the IBM 7094, designed for number crunching and calculation, and business machines, like the IBM 1401, designed for printing bills and reports. Much to its profit, IBM forever obliterated this distinction in 1963 with the introduction of the System 360, which it sold as an all-in-one (even the name, 360, suggested a wholistic full circle of 360 degrees) computer capable of both business and scientific data processing.

In software, the highest evolution of the computer as calculator is APL, which stands simply for A Programming Language. APL was developed by Kenneth Iverson of IBM in the early 1960s. IBM never intended to let APL out of the house but made an admirable concession to good sense when the company's managers discovered its scientists becoming converts to a difficult language that IBM managers could not understand but figured they could sell. Iverson and his wife, Jean, were not above proselytizing for the new language, even starting a small press to further their mission. Today, APL is firmly entrenched on most large computer systems and increasingly, on desktop machines and micros like the IBM 5110.

What APL provides is an extremely compact mathematical language that, if used skillfully, can reduce huge FORTRAN (or equivalent language) programs to short screenfulls of code. The bad news is that APL does this by using a special character set - a sort of computer Greek. Thus an APL program to (a) read a list of values into an array, (b) sort them into ascending order, and (c) print the results, looks like this:

$$\square \leftarrow A[\text{\ding{115}} A \leftarrow \square]$$

The time saved in typing is almost enough to make APL worth learning!

[APL Syntax]. APL packs so much processing into its functions that the syntax of the language is relatively simple to learn. On most systems, an APL program starts with an upside-down delta or del, followed by a short, all-caps name for the program. Each line in the program has a number written in square brackets in the right-hand margin. Except when editing and inserting lines in a program, the numbers ascend by 10. The very last line in a program is marked by another del.

Within a program, there are only three types of statements, each made up of expressions. The trick here, or rather the beauty of APL, is that these expressions can be extremely complicated functions made up of APL's various special symbols and operators. The first type of statement possible in an APL program shows the calculator function of the language: if an expression appears on a line alone, the expression is evaluated by the APL interpreter, and the result is printed on the video screen. In this, the action of the APL interpreter is similar to that of many microcomputer BASIC interpreters in direct mode, where typing in a statement without line numbers results in its immediate execution.

APL has an assignment statement similar to BASIC and FORTRAN that uses a left arrow. The left arrow assigns the value of the expression on the right of the arrow to the variable named on the left. APL's third type of statement uses a reverse or right-pointing arrow. This statement is a clever computed GOTO, comparable to the ON N GOTO 100,200,300,400 of most BASICs. The right arrow causes a branch to the statement number that results from evaluating the expression it points to. Again, this expression can be extremely complicated, providing this one statement all the power of the branching instructions (e.g., "IF...THEN", "CASE", etc.) of other languages.

[APL Functions]. Although APL's syntax is relatively simply, its character set and built-in functions are not and require some math background to fully understand. This aspect of APL can be intimidating but is really not so bad. Many features of APL can be found in computer languages like BASIC but have more imposing names in APL. Thus a "scalar" in APL can be thought of as a simple variable or constant. A "vector" in APL is just an array; an APL "matrix" is simply a two-dimensional array. A "3-array" is a three-dimensional array, and so on. Most APL implementations allow n-dimensional arrays.

Likewise, APL functions are relatively straightforward, even if complicated at first encounter. Monadic functions (Greek monados, one, alone, single, as in "monotone", etc.) take one item and change its value. A familiar monadic function is the minus sign: "-A" takes one variable, A, and changes its value. Dyadic functions need two variables to work on. Simple dyadic functions are addition (+), multiplication (X), division (/), and so on - nothing complex.

Where APL gets powerful is in the range of advanced mathematical functions that are built into the language and in the fact that users can define their own functions using these already powerful primitives. For example, the function "/", called compression, is a dyadic function that operates on two vectors, the first full of either 1's or 0's, and selects into a third vector the elements of the second that correspond to the 1's in the first (or logical) vector. Simple operators exist for producing the inner product and outer product of matrices and for performing other calculations that would require subroutine packages in other languages.

[Microcomputer APL]. The primary difficulty in implementing APL on a microcomputer involves the character set. A standard APL keyboard, with the APL characters above it, looks like this:

There is a standard ASCII multiletter translation for APL symbols. However, most APL systems require special video character generators, which in turn means that the systems must be built from the "ground up" for APL operation.

IBM, of course, is the original APL company. In March 1980, IBM announced its "5120" computer system, a number of whose models come standard with APL character sets. The 5120 Computing System is built around the 5110 Model 3 Computer, and can add one of two printers, a 1.2- or 2.4-megabyte floppy disk system, and a variety of communications options. Although the 5110 computer has a small (16 lines by 64 character) screen, it has a composite video adapter that is extremely nice for classroom use; a large monitor can be attached for students to watch, while the instructor is free to type while looking at the 5110 screen. The following price schedule was announced for the 5120 series:

IBM5110	IBM	A31 16K main storage memory	9990.00
IBM5110	IBM	A32 32K memory	10775.00
IBM5110	IBM	A33 48K memory	11560.00
IBM5110	IBM	A34 64K memory	12345.00
IBM5110	IBM	C31 16K w/BASIC and APL	10820.00
IBM5110	IBM	C32 32K version of C31	11605.00
IBM5110	IBM	C33 48K version	12930.00
IBM5110	IBM	C34 64K version	13175.00

[Vanguard Systems Corporation]. Vanguard Systems (6812 San Pedro, San Antonio, TX 78216, 512-828-0554) is a specialized supplier of APL microcomputer systems. Vanguard is a privately held Texas corporation that was founded in September 1976 and has close ties to Trinity University. In the past, Vanguard has offered other APL products, including a S-100 character generator based on the Processor Technology VDM-1 board. Vanguard's primary interest now seems to be in selling complete, packaged systems. However, some of these early component products may still be available.

Vanguard currently offers a system called the APL/DTC, which is built around the Vector Graphic MZ computer and Flashwriter board. The MZ uses a Z-80 microprocessor running at 4 MHz and has Micropolis disks with a total of 630 kilobytes of storage. Vanguard sells it with 64K bytes of RAM. The special terminal supplied has APL keytops, and the system has a RS-232 interface designed for a Diablo printer that can use an APL daisy wheel. Vanguard's APL/DTC sells for $7995, FOB, San Antonio.

A version of Vanguard's APL interpreter that runs under CP/M is available "unbundled" for $350. It requires 44K of RAM memory and uses overstrikes to create APL characters from the standard ASCII set. This product is called APL/Z80. The manual for APL/Z80 is available for $25.

[APL under CP/M]. Softronics (36 Homestead Lane, Roosevelt, NJ 08555) sells a version of APL using ASCII memonics for APL characters. Softronics microAPL costs $350 on a CP/M disk; the manual alone is $50.

[The APL Press]. The APL Press (220 California Ave., Palo Alto, CA 94306, 415-327-1700) is a excellent institution that publishes tutorials and programs on and in APL. Their introductory books on APL feature several low-cost pamphlets suitable for use in schools, including: "Introducing APL to Teachers" (25 pages, 95 cents), "An Introduction to APL for Scientists and Engineers" (26 pages, 95 cents), "APL in Exposition" (61 pages, $1.15), and "A Source Book in APL" (139 pages, $10.35). These books are most useful to those with access to an APL machine or terminal.

Several interesting applications programs written in APL are also published by the press. "Resistive Circuit Theory", by R. L. Spence, uses APL to model resistive circuits using node-branch incidence matrices. "Starmap", by P. C. Barry and J. C. Thorsensen is a simple model of the solar system written in APL with tables.

The Apple][

During 1981, the Apple II computer became the single best selling personal computer with a price over $500. More Apple IIs, some 300,000, were sold in 1981 than existed in December 1980.

Apple clearly deserved this success. The Apple II is a very well designed computer, one of the best of its generation. Further, Apple Computer Company has been different; many microcomputer companies reproduced, in micro, all of the flaws of the computer giants, from unreadable documentation to "user hostile" design. Apple cared about its users, took them seriously, and laughed all the way to the bank.

Unfortunately, for all its success, Apple has remained a one-product company, and still relies heavily on the Apple II. In 1982, the II finally showed its age, with sales flattening out in the early part of the year. Further, several Apple clones appeared that year, notably the Franklin Ace (7030 Colonial Highway, Pennsauken, NJ 08109) which runs all Apple II software, but comes standard with such features as 64K of RAM, heavy-duty power supply, numeric pad , and full keyboard with upper and lower case.

To meet such competition, Apple not only sued Franklin (losing the early rounds, however) but also readied for 1983 release the "Super II", a low-parts count, low-manufacturing cost version of the II.

The Super II, however, is merely more (or rather less) of a proven thing. Apple's attempts to introduce big computers, notably the Apple III, have thus far been failures. "Lisa", a machine using the Motorola MC68000 16-bit chip, is currently sucheduled to be announced in January 1983.

[History of The Apple II]. Steven Jobs met Steve Wozniak ("Woz") when Jobs was 13, in the garage of a mutual friend. "Woz was the first person I'd met who knew a lot about computers and electronics," Jobs said in an interview with InfoWorld magazine in 1982. By 1975, Jobs was working at Atari repairing video games, and Wozniak was working at Hewlett-Packard.

When the Altair came out, it was featured on the cover of Popular Electronics in January 1975, Wozniak and Jobs designed their own kit computer and built it with parts "Liberated" in Jobs's words from Atari and Hewlett-Packard. Jobs sold a Volkswagen and Wozniak a HP calculator, and the two raised $1,300. This money went to have a printed circuit (PC) board professionally laid out. The two expected to sell 100 PC boards at $50, leaving a $2500 profit.

This kit eventually became the Apple I. The Byte Shop of Mountain View, CA, ordered 50 of them but wanted them assembled. Jobs and Wozniak managed to build 100. They continued to build and sell the Apple I in late 1975 and early 1976. A total of 200 were sold. By fall 1976 they had a new design, the Apple II, more or less complete. The Apple II differed from existing computers in that it had a lightweight plastic case and used 4K dynamic RAMs. At that time, 8K of memory for Altair-type systems was thought a lot; Wozniak and Jobs proposed to increase this by using the new, low-cost dynamic parts.

Needing capital, the prototype of the Apple II was shown around in the fall of 1976, first at the Home Brew Computer Club, which used to meet at the Stanford Linear Accelerator. The Apple II was also shown to Commodore, then making calculators, which wanted to acquire it, and to Hewlett-Packard, which didn't. When the computer was announced, orders poured in. Like many small concerns with a hot product, Jobs and Wozniak had trouble keeping up with orders, having special headaches with the Apple II's plastic case.

In 1977, Wozniak and Jobs, still looking for help, were introduced to Mike Markkula. Markkula's role in the Apple success story has been generally overlooked by the popular media, which has been more comfortable with garage shop engineers Wozniak and Jobs. Without Markkula, however, Apple may have gone the way of the Altair, Sol, IMSAI, or other computers of its design generation. Markkula had been an engineer at Hughes and in marketing at Fairchild Semiconductor and Intel. Later Apple's president, Markkula wrote a business plan that attracted investment for Apple from Arthur Rock's Venrock Associates, dean of the Silicon Valley venture capitalists. With that money, and aided by excellent, consumer-oriented advertising starting in 1977, Apple was on its way.

[The Apple II]. Over a number of years, Apple has continued to evolve the II. The Apple II+ is now the standard Apple. The Apple II+ differs from the plain Jane Apple II by coming standard with Applesoft BASIC, an advance over Apple's old Integer BASIC, which is now something of a special order item (Integer BASIC comes on disk with the Language Card; many of the better games for the Apple are written in Integer). The Apple II+ is designed to work easily with a disk drive, and comes with an Autostart ROM to allow a disk to be put in the drive, the computer to turn on, and everything to work.

Much of the success of the Apple II, however, has had little to do with Apple Computer Company. Apple was the first example of an "open" computer system, a system in which the hardware and operating software were no secret, and which allowed third party developers to get in on the act. As a piece of hardware, the Apple II is now a sort of platform for all sorts of devices ranging from 8088 coprocessors to piano keyboards to logic probes. And no other system has had more software written for it than the Apple II.

Technically, what made this possible was the fact that Wozniak and Jobs reserved large chunks of the Apple's address space for system use in the machine. The 6502 microprocessor can address up to 64K bytes of memory at one time. In the Apple, users are effectively limited to 48K, with the remaining 16K of memory, starting with hex address C000, reserved by the Apple system.

Unlike other manufacturers, however, Apple made a virtue of this necessity. From the beginning, for shrewd copyright reasons as well as convenience, Apple placed much of its software not on tape or disk (where it could be copied) but in ROMs that plugged into the reserved region.

Further, the Apple gave each peripheral device its own space in memory in the C000 address block. This allowed standardized driver routines to be placed in ROM on the peripheral cards themselves, rather than being patched into the operating system later. The result was a system where the inflexibility of ROM actually helped, not hurt, as it did in most other systems. Apple's use of ROM, helped standardize the system, made it more reliable, and eliminated much of the bother of loading tapes and disks.

At the same time, such stable system software created an ideal environment for independent programming, since programs developed on one Apple could be counted on to run on other Apples. Compatibility among Apples is not a serious problem as it is, for example, among S-100 bus machines.

[Apple Graphics]. Much of Apple's difference has been in its color video graphics. With an inexpensive (if dubiously legal) device called an RF modulator (available at most stores that carry the Apple, or by mail from various vendors), the Apple can feed its video signal into a home color TV. The Apple II has three video display modes:

* Text. In the text mode, the Apple displays 24 lines of 40 characters each on the video screen. Text mode is used for programming and typing into the computer.

* Low-Resolution Graphics. In the low-resolution (lo-res) graphics mode, the screen is divided into 1600 relatively large blocks - 40 across the screen and 40 down. This mode is

commonly used for bar charts and other similar displays. 16
colors are available in lo-res mode if a color TV or monitor
is being used.

* High-Resolution Graphics. In the high-resolution (hi-res)
  graphics mode, the Apple screen is made up of many fine dots,
  280 across the screen and 192 down, for a total of 53,760
  points. The hi-res graphics mode is used for charts, graphs,
  and by most games. Only seven colors are available in hi-res
  graphics mode, and there are restrictions on the way they can
  be combined. There are two hi-res pages in the Apple's
  memory, allowing one page to be built up by the processor
  while the other is displayed.

Applesoft BASIC (a special version of Microsoft BASIC written for Apple) has a
number of special commands designed for graphic manipulation.

Low-resolution graphics mode, for example, is entered by the command GR. In
low-resolution mode, the command PLOT X,Y sets a colored square at point X,Y.
(0,0 is top left, 39,39 is bottom right). COLOR=X, where X ranges from 0 to
15, sets the current color on the display. SCRN(X,Y) sets the current color
to the color of the point X,Y on the screen. Several commands make it very
simple to draw charts and graphs without complicating programs with loops.
HLIN X1,X1 AT Y draws a horizontal line between points X1 and X2 on screen
line Y. VLIN Y1,Y2 AT X draws a vertical line between Y1 and Y2 at row X.

In high-resolution mode, the Apple has even more sophisticated commands in
BASIC, including the ability to define, store, and draw shapes on the screen.
These shapes can also be rotated at various angles and scaled up from a stored
template.

[Apple's Price Codes]. Apple's products are coded as follows: the first two
letters ("A2") stand for the system. The next letter tells the type of the
product, as follows: "B" stands for "board" or card, as with the Applesoft
firmware card A2B0009; "M" stands for "module," as with the graphics tablet
A2M0029; "L" stands for literature, as with the 6502 Hardware Manual, A2L0002;
"T" stands for software distributed on cassette tape; and "D" stands for
software distributed on disk. "S" is used to signify packaged systems. The
designation "C" once stood for components, which Apple no longer sells
individually. So-called EUROMOD versions of the Apple II run at 220/240 volts
AC and generate CCIR (625 line) video for European TVs.

[The Apple Computer]. The Apple mainframe is a light, attractive off-white
plastic case with keyboard on the front. When opened, the power supply is on
the left, and the eight expansion slots are along the back.

The brains of the Apple, the 6502 microprocessor (the same used in the Atari
and the PET), is the long black chip mounted horizontally on the motherboard
just below the slots. Three rows of eight memory chips are in a boxed area in
plain sight. Most Apples sold after 1981 were 48K. Adding memory to the
Apple is a relatively simple operation involving the plugging 2114 chips into
the motherboard. (Naturally, the power should be off when this is done, and
the installer should ground himself frequently by touching the power supply to
prevent damaging the chips with static electricity.) Memory chips slower than

-21-

Apple II system with modem, monitor, floppies and printer

250 nanoseconds should not be used.

On the back of the Apple is a RCA jack for output video. This runs to a video monitor (a TV can't be used without an RF modulator). A socket on the motherboard is a plug for game paddles, once standard equipment with the II and now an option. A cassette recorder jack, now rarely used, is also on the back.

After April 1, 1981, all Apple IIs sold in the United States had a number of new features designed to bring the computer in line with the FCC's guidelines on radio frequency (RF) emissions for personal computers. "New" Apples sold after this date have a gray coating inside the case and have short cables for the disk drives. The new Apples have a redesigned motherboard, which has at location F on the far left of the board (as one faces the computer) a nine-digit number 820-0044-xx, where xx is the revision level of the board.

The following changes went into effect with these boards: (1) The board no longer has RAM configuration blocks; this means that it must be expanded in units of 16K, using 2114 chips, which has been the de facto practice for several years anyway; (2) the 2513 character generator ROM has been replaced by a 2316B, which has additional capacity; it can be replaced by a user-programmed 2716 for custom character sets; (3) several improvements have been made in the "color killer" video circuitry to kill the red-and-blue smears seen around text on color TVs and monitors and to improve performance with digital sync monitors.

[Apple Video]. The Apple produces a somewhat nonstandard color video signal as an output. This signal can be fed directly into either a black-and-white or color monitor. (Video monitors are like televisions but do not have receiver circuitry; they are used, for example, for closed circuit TV but not for receiving TV pictures off the air.) A color television can be used with the Apple with a RF modulator, but monitors will provide better images.

Apples generate 524 horizontal scan lines, not the 525 of the usual US TV picture. Further, the color generation method developed by Wozniak may be low-cost, but it develops a "halo" effect around text when displayed on color monitors, and it generates unusual artifacts. On early Apples, the color output could not, for example, be recorded on a home VCR or Betamax. Apple's improved machines can be recorded. Adwar Video (100 5th Ave., New York, NY 10011 / 212-691-0976)) makes a "Proc Mod" board for cleaning up Apple II video to the point where it can be edited on VCRs. This board usually goes in slot 7. Adwar also sells an expensive ($2150) genlock system that gets NTSC standard video out of the Apple and allows it to be integrated with professional video equipment.

In general, for any kind of text processing or extended desktop use, a black-and-white or green phosphor video monitor is best. Apple for years has sold a 9" Sanyo black-and-white monitor. Amdek, which has both a black-and-white and a green phosphor, is extremely popular for use with the Apple II. Zenith also has a low-cost ($120) green phosphor with a switch on the back for 40- or 80-column operation. Apple has recently been selling its "Monitor ///" with an attractive stand that fits over the II.

To use a home TV with the Apple, the video output from the computer must be "modulated" and fed into the TV through the antenna in such a way that it looks like an off-the-air signal to the TV. Like a VCR, the computer needs an unused channel in the local area. Most RF modulators are tuned to one of the low VHF channels, like 2 or 3, although some use UHF channels.

RF modulators are really tiny TV transmitters. Like CB radios, they can interfere with neighboring TVs, one reason the FCC has frowned on their sale in assembled form. Technically, the FCC requires assembled RF modulators to be certified but does not impose this restriction on kits. Almost all VCRs have FCC approved RF modulators built-in, as do newer home computers like the Atari 400 and TI 99/4.

Some care should be taken to get good quality pictures from an RF modulator and to prevent interference. Coaxial cable (RU/59) should be used to connect the modulator and the TV set, if possible directly to a 75-ohm cable TV jack on the back of the set, using an "F" type video connector. To prevent interference, the RF modulator can be shielded in a metal box (e.g., Pomona #2428). Alternately, the coax cable can be wound around a Ferrite toroid to reduce spurious RF from the modulator.

Of the RF modulators on the market, the best are by ATV Research, UHF Associates, and M&R Enterprises. ATV Research makes three different RF devices: the Pixi-Verter, available only in kit form, which uses a blank channel from 2 to 6; the $35 "Micro-Verter," ATV's assembled RF modulator designed for use on computers, which uses any UHF channel above 14 and wires direct to UHF tuner input; and the "Pixe-Plexer," an experimenter's RF modulator kit sold for $24.50. UHF's kit, a fine, high-quality model, uses

any channel between 2 and 6.   M&R's "Sup'R'Mod II" is an assembled and tested
unit complete with coaxial cable and shielding.   It is perfect for the
nonelectronics buff who merely wants to get his Apple running.

[Apple Peripherals].   There are at least several hundred peripheral boards
available for the Apple II, and no one could possibly keep track of them all.
In general, boards available for the Apple fall into various categories, and
there is a rough consensus about "standard" slot assignments for each.

In general, the slot assignments for the Apple II are:

> 0 - language card or Integer ROM card
> 1 - printer card
> 2 - modem or serial card
> 3 - 80 column card
> 4 - disk slot for drives 3 and 4
> 5 - miscellaneous
> 6 - disk controller card, drives 1 and 2
> 7 - clock or video card

Of these, only the disk card (slot 6) is almost mandatory. Apple has always
had problems with its floppy disks.   In the beginning, Apple took standard
single-density Shugart minifloppy drives and added custom electronics, putting
13 sectors on each track for a capacity to 116K bytes.   Since then,
double-density disks have leapfrogged those of the Apple, giving it less disk
storage for the money than other systems.   In 1980, Apple brought out DOS 3.3
and began a painful (for Apple II users) changeover to a 16-sector per disk
system, now the standard.   In the 16-sector system, each disk has 143K of
memory.

Apple's disk controller is a card that plugs into slot 6.   One card will run
two drives.   The controller card and first disk (part number A2M0004) list at
about $650; an additional drive, which can be run from the same controller
card, lists at $495 (part number A2M0003).   Several third party vendors offer
cheaper replacement plug-compatible drives.   Hard disks for the Apple use the
same slots and controller system as for floppies; however, Corvus Systems, of
San Jose, CA, offers a 10-megabyte Winchester for the Apple that looks like 82
floppies online at once.

[Slot 0 - Language Card].   Apple has more or less reserved slot 0, the
left-most slot, for one of two language cards. Apple's Integer ROM card is
something of an antique and is important only to those who must use the
Integer BASIC and who can't be bothered loading it from a disk. Apple's other
card for this slot, which it sells as a "language card", is something of a
misnomer: it is actually a 16K RAM card that allows various languages, like
Integer BASIC, Applesoft BASIC, Apple Pascal, or Apple FORTRAN, to be loaded
into its RAM from floppy disk.

The Language Card gives the Apple II its full complement of 64K, the maximum
that can be addressed by the 8-bit 6502 processor at one time, although it
actually bank switches two 4K blocks in and out of the D000 space rather than
use the C000 block. A number of independent vendors, notably MicroSoft, offer
cards identical to the Language Card in function and about 20-30% cheaper. In
the early days, these cards required users to illegally copy Apple Pascal,

which for a time was sold only with the official Apple card. Later, Apple "unbundled" Pascal and FORTRAN from the card, allowing users of other cards to buy legal system software. Andromeda, one of the first to introduce a RAM card, recently cut its prices to $95 per card.

[Slot 1 - Printers]. Apple sells a parallel board that usually plugs into slot 1 and that has driver firmware in ROM on the board. This Centronics Card (Apple part A2B0007) is prewired to use data bit 8 as a strobe and includes a ribbon cable with an Amphenol 57-30360 connector that plugs into the back of either printer.

Other Centronics compatible printers can be used with the Centronics interface card. Any parallel printer can, in theory, be run from the Apple using the general purpose parallel interface card (Apple part A2B0002), which can be jumpered to handle various strobe and acknowledge options.

CCS's 7720 ($120) is a low-cost parallel interface for the Apple. This board is difficult to interface, making the Apple's simpler parallel board a better choice, unless exact cable and wiring diagrams are known.

Normally, the Apple II has no need for a serial interface of any kind. Unlike many larger computers that use video terminals, the Apple generates its own video internally and needs only a video monitor on which this output can be displayed. However, there are reasons why a user might want to add a serial interface to the Apple: to use a letter quality printer; to connect a modem or CRT; or to allow the Apple to communicate with another computer.

High-quality daisy wheel printers, like those made by Diablo (Xerox), Qume, or NEC, require serial interfaces, typically at 1,200 but sometimes at 300 baud. Serial cards for printers, like parallel cards, are usually placed in slot 1 of the Apple. For connecting a letter quality printer to an Apple, The Computer Cookbook recommends Apple's Serial Interface Card (A2B0005). This serial interface card should not be confused with the Communications Interface Card (A2B0003), which is a 300-baud card intended for use with a modem.

For use with a serial printer, the A2B0005 should be obtained with the P8A replacement ROM, which implements an ETX/ACK protocol allowing connection of Qume-type printers at 1,200 baud. Although the Qume and other printers can receive text at a rate of about 120 characters per second (cps), they can only print at about 45 cps, meaning that the computer can easily overrun the small (typically 157-character) buffer of the printer.

In the ETX/ACK protocol, the computer periodically sends an ETX (03H, or control C) to the printer, usually at the end of every line. When the ETX is removed by the printer from the print buffer (like a NUL, it has no effect on what appears on the page), the printer sends back, over the serial interface, an ACK (06H), which is a signal to the computer that the printer once again has room in its buffer. Note that the return lines to the printer must be in place for this system to work; the printer, which we normally think of as a receive only device, is sending input to the computer.

[Apple's "Silentype"]. Apple Computer introduced a low-cost thermal printer for the Apple II in March 1980 called the "Silentype" - so named because thermal printers are much quieter than impact printers. Actually, the

Silentype is an Apple version of the Trendcom printer, which during 1979 found a strong following among Apple users. Currently, the Silentype, discounted as low as $300, competes primarily with the Epson MX-80, which offers better, near-letter-quality dot matrix printing for about $700.

The Silentype, as sold by Apple, has the major advantage of being expressly designed to work with its computer (the Silentype also works well with the Apple III, which has a special jack for it on the back). The Silentype can dump an Apple high-resolution graphics screen to the printer with a single keystroke command. With other printers, this type of graphics screen dump takes a special interface card ("The Grappler", from Orange Micro, is one).

Many important features of the Silentype are implemented in firmware on the interface card. The Silentype has the following print features that can be set under program control: (1) a form feed can be simulated by moving 40 paper steps, about 1 inch (default), up to 255 steps maximum; (2) line spacing can be varied from one paper step to 252, with two steps between lines the default; (3) the print directioncan be either unidirectional or bidirectional.

Unidirectional printing is slower but higher quality. To continue the list: (4) the print intensity can be varied from 0 (very light) to 7 (very dark), with default level 5; (5) the left margin and right margin can be set between 0 and 82, with default settings 2 and 81 (80 character line); (6) either high-resolution page can be selected by the card firmware, and the selected page can be dumped to the printer with a single command. An inverse graphics mode that produces a "negative" of the screencan be selected.

These parameters are controlled by the values of the following locations:

form feed	CF0D	-12531	0-255
line inc	CF0E	-12530	0-255
direction	CF0F	-12529	0(bi) or 128(uni)
intensity	CF10	-12528	0 to 7
left margin	CF12	-12527	0 to 82
right margin	CF13	-12526	0 to 83
hi-res page	CF13	-12525	page 1=32,page 2=64
hi-res inverse	CF14	-12524	255=normal,0=inverse

In addition to these parameters, the Silentype responds to the following control codes when sent by a program:

control C	cancels a hi res dump
control F	force out buffer
control H	backspace
control J	linefeed
control L	formfeed (3" space)
control M	carriage return (CR)
control Q	dump hi-res screen
control T	toggle screen echo

From Pascal, a PRINTSTUFF unit, described in the Silentype manual, provides a number of useful functions and procedures for the machine.

One of the infrequent types of repair needed on the Silentype is changing the thermal printhead, which can burn out with age or bad luck. To change the printhead, turn the printer over, and remove five small screws from the front of the Silentype case and two from the sides. Turn it back around, and the main printer mechanism should still be mounted to its base. However, the printhead should slip easily out of its slot and be replaced.

[Slot 2 - communications]. Slot 2 of the Apple is generally reserved for a card that allows computer to computer communications - either a serial card or a modem.

ASCII and RS-232 are the standards for communication in the microcomputer world. The easiest way to talk to a nearby computer is through a serial interface. Since telephone lines are not used, no modem is required. On the Apple, in Pascal, the serial card to do this would normally go in slot 2 (REMIN and REMOUT).

The Computer Cookbook recommends using the California Computer Systems (CCS) 7710 card for computer to computer communication. Unlike the Apple boards, the CCS 7710 has a hardware UART - a Motorola 6850 ACIA - which allows buffering of incoming characters and which will also generate interrupts to the Apple when enabled. The 7710A is configured as a DCE - that is, it looks like a modem - so that it will work with a simple, straight-across serial cable to a terminal or printer.

For use with an external modem, the CCS 7710 requires a so-called null modem cable - that is, one crossing pins 2 and 3. The 7710A has one other minor annoyance, in that pins 4 (RTS) and 20 (DTR) must be kept high for operation. To make a simple three-wire cable for this card, jumper pin 4 to 5 and pin 6 to 20.

Most serial interfaces used with small computer systems are asynchronous, meaning that characters can be sent whenever they are ready - as when, for example, someone is typing. For high-speed data communications, however, mainframe computers, especially IBM equipment, use synchronous data transmission.

Synchronous transmission means that several special characters (usually the ASCII SYN code) are sent to synchronize the sending and receiving computers, then a high-speed burst of information follows. Synchronous transmission is more efficient for high-volume data transfer because the start and stop bits sent with each and every character in asynchronous transmission are not used. Consequently, more data can be sent in their place. California Computer Systems' synchronous serial interface (7712A) allows an Apple to be tied to an IBM mainframe.

[Modems]. There are three basic options for putting a modem on the Apple II: using a Communications Card with an external modem; using the Hayes Micromodem II; or using the Novation Apple CAT. Each approach has some advantages.

Most serial cards can be used with external modems, including California Computer Products 7710. However, that Apple's Serial Interface Card (A2B0005), as opposed to the Communications Card (A2B0003), is not suitable for use with an acoustic coupler, since it does not implement the necessary modem control signals Data Terminal Ready (DTR) and Clear to Send (CTS).

When attached to a modem, the Communications Interface Card allows the Apple to be used as a timesharing terminal, at either 110 or 300 (but not 1200) baud. Apple sells the Novation 4100 modem for use with the communications card. This is a better quality but more expensive modem than the familiar $150 Novation CAT.

A highly popular and almost standard alternative to this Apple product is the $325 Hayes Micromodem II, which combines RS-232 and modem functions on a card. The Micromodem II plugs into an Apple slot and connects directly to a modular (RJ-11C) phone plug. This direct, not acoustic, coupling to the phone system produces a better connection. The Micromodem works at either 110 or 300 baud, with a variety of programmable settings for parity, start and stop bits, etc.

The Apple II is not really fast enough to communicate at 1,200 baud, and The Computer Cookbook recommends being satisfied with 300-baud communications or buying a faster computer. However, Novation sells a two-board modem set - its Apple-CAT II, plus a second 212 board - that turns the Apple into a Bell 212-compatible terminal. Note that the Apple-CAT II, while in fact being a 1200-baud modem, is Bell 202-compatible, which means that it cannot connect by itself to the 1,200-baud ports of most timesharing services.

[The Hayes Micromodem II]. The Hayes Micromodem II for the Apple is one of the better boards designed for microcomputers. Although for advanced programmers it has some hardware limitations, the Hayes board has on it onboard firmware that turns the Apple II into a convenient intelligent terminal for novice computer users who want to access The Source, CompuServe, Dow Jones News Retrieval Service, or other online service. Further, the Hayes board, which has the ability to answer incoming calls, can with the right software package be used in local networks and community bulletin board systems.

Consider this actual dialogue with a timesharing computer. To simplify booting the Apple, the Hayes board was placed in slot 2 of an Apple II+ and the disk controller was card removed. The computer came up with the Applesoft prompt:

]

To this, IN#2 <return> was typed, instructing the Apple to echo all input to slot 2, the Hayes card slot. Then, the following sequence is typed:

<control-A> <control-Q>

At this point, the Hayes firmware responded:

MICROMODEM: DIALING:

Then, the number of the CBBS system, this one in Phoenix, AZ, was typed slowly:

MICROMODEM: DIALING: 16029969709

After about 20 seconds, while the call was going through, the board replied:

and suddenly the conversation with the CBBS system was on.

[Micromodem Firmware]. The secret to this ease of operation is in the Hayes Micromodem's firmware. This firmware responds to the following keystroke sequences:

> <control-A> <control-H>. Control-H sets the terminal to operate in half-duplex mode. <control-A> <control-F> sets the terminal to operate in full-duplex mode. Full-duplex is the usual and default setting.

> <control-A> <control-Q>. Control-Q tells the Micromodem II to pick up the phone and start dialing. It waits two seconds and assumes after that amount of time that it has a dial tone. The modem then accepts digits, one at a time, until RETURN is typed. The board then listens 30 seconds for the carrier of the answering computer. If no carrier is detected in 30 seconds, it hangs up.

> (Warning - the time required to get a dial tone varys with the load on the exchange and with a number of other factors. In an auto-dial program, make sure ample time is allowed or that the dial tone is positively detected - as it can be with some units, like the Novation Apple-CAT II, but not the Hayes).

> <control-A> <control-S>. Control-S on the Apple II keyboard simulates sending a BREAK signal to the remote computer. Break is used by some timesharing services to turn off output (cancel long listings, for example).

> <control-A> <control-1>. Control-1 sets the rate of the Hayes board to 110 baud. <control-A> <control-3> sets the rate to 300 baud. 300 baud is normal and default.

> <control-A> <control-Z>. Control-Z tells the Micromodem to hang up the phone.

Note that control-A gets the attention of the Hayes board. It is essentially a lead-in character, similar to the commonly used ESC, for Hayes board.

The Hayes board can also be used from a remote terminal, turning the Apple into a device run by remote control. The board does this by routing the characters that would normally go to the Apple's keyboard to the remote keyboard. The Hayes board will be set up in an auto-answer mode when the following conditions hold: the board is enabled (by the usual slot number control-K return sequence); the phone has not been dialed; and keyboard input is expected by the Apple.

In this state, the Hayes board will check to see if the phone is ringing. If it is, it answers and routes the expected keyboard input and output characters over the phone line to the remote terminal. In this remote mode, the Hayes firmware responds to the additional control characters:

<control-A> <control-S>. Control-S causes the Hayes to
    temporarily stop sending output. It is used when the Apple is
    overrunning the remote terminal (e.g., to stop and look at a
    program listing, etc.). Sending any other code causes output
    to resume.

<control-A> <control-Y>. Control-Y simulates a reset of the
    Apple. It does not disconnect the Hayes board, as would a
    true hardware reset.

<control-A> <control-R>. Control-R disables the Apple's
    keyboard. <control-A> <control-T> reenables the Apple's
    keyboard.

<control-A> <control-Z>. As in the terminal mode, Control-Z
    tells the Micromodem to hang up the phone.

From Apple BASIC, the Hayes board can be used in PR and IN statements just as
any other device attached to one of the numbered slots can be. Thus, the
following statement dials a phone number from BASIC:

                PR#n:PRINT<control A><control-Q>;"212-976-3838"

where n is the slot number of the Hayes board.

Memory location 1656 + n contains the status register of the Hayes board in
the Apple implementation. Since bit 7 of this register tells if a carrier
tone is being received, the value PEEK(1656 + n) will be greater than 127 if
the carrier has been detected. Additional control of the Hayes board can be
gained by PEEKing and POKEing various memory locations.

[Slot 3 - 80 Column Cards and CRTs]. Although it is somewhat extravagant in
terms of hardware, attaching an ASCII video terminal like a a Hazeltine or
SOROC to the Apple is probably the best (and most expensive) method of doing
word processing on the machine. A serial card would be plugged into slot 3 of
the Apple. Apple Pascal automatically checks slot 3 to see if a serial card
is there; for CP/M, MicroSoft's Z-80 SoftCard card does the same. The
Computer Cookbook recommends using the CCS 7710 for a slot 3 serial card.

The Apple was designed as a 40 column display computer, but since 1980 at
least six plug-in boards have become available for it that double this to an
80-column wide display, which is the standard in the computer industry for
like ASCII terminals and printers. The most important 80-column cards are:

            VISION-80   VISTA COMPUTER PRODUCTS
            SMARTERM   ADVANCED LOGIC SYSTEMS
            FULL-VIEW 80   BIT 3 COMPUTER CORP.
            SUPE'R'TERM   M&R ENTERPRISES
            VIDEOTERM   VIDEX
            DOUBLEVISION   THE COMPUTER SHOP OF LAWNDALE

Although home television sets have adequate quality for 32- or 40-column wide
lines, ordinary TVs have insufficient bandwidth to display 80 columns of text.
The concept of bandwidth has a precise technical definition to video engineers

(and is also, unfortunately, becoming something of a buzzword to future-thinker media experts.)

In the context of screen displays, bandwidth is the measure of the ability of a video tube to display individual horizontal dots along a line. Since alphabetic characters on a video screen are, in fact, made up of closely spaced dots, good bandwidth is vital in creating readable text. When the bandwidth of a monitor is exceeded, it will typically produce horizontal streaks rather than legible text.

Bandwidth is measured in megahertz (MHz). A home TV has a bandwidth of about 3.5 MHz; a typical quality black-and-while video monitor used with the Apple II, like the Sanyo or Amdek (formerly Leedex), has a bandwidth of 10 or 12 MHz. Using an 80-column boards with the Apple requires using a video monitor, not a TV. Even with a high-quality monitor, some of the 80-column boards will have a "squished" look. On some, the right edge of the display may disappear off the edge of the screen around column 72. Moral: don't buy an 80-column board sight unseen.

[The Pascal Heritage]. Although 80-column boards are now commonly used by people programming the Apple in BASIC, or running word processors, it must be remembered that 80-column boards were originally designed to be used with the Apple Pascal system. UCSD Pascal, as implemented on the Apple, keeps an 80-column "internal" format but displays only 40 columns on the screen, requiring a toggle of the control-A key to reach the "back 40", as a farmer might say.

This is not a desirable situation, particularly since many Pascal programs, which use indents to clarify structure, rapidly head across the page, viz.:

```
FOR I:= 1 TO 100 DO
        BEGIN
              WHILE J>1 DO....etc.
```

With this problem in mind, Apple Pascal was designed to look, while booting, for a communications or serial card in slot 3 and, if it finds one, to use it as the programmer's terminal device (CONSOLE:).

Using a serial card and ASCII terminal is wasteful of hardware, since the Apple already has a video screen and a keyboard (unless one wants to use the Apple's monitor full-time for graphics, another situation entirely). Apple 80-column boards essentially are naked terminal boards designed to create a ASCII terminal device by taking advantage of the video monitor, keyboard, and computer RAM already in the system. (Such naked terminals are also used by Vector Graphic and other S-100 computer manufacturers.)

[Compatibility with BASIC]. Although originally designed to be used with Apple Pascal, the various 80-column boards are not always fully compatible with Apple BASIC, either Integer or Applesoft. A quick summary of the Apple BASIC features not supported by the various boards:

> VTABS: Full-View 80
> INVERSE: Videoterm and Full-View 80
> HOME: all but DoubleVision

These incompatibilities may require rewriting programs in BASIC, and that copy-protected and unalterable games may not work properly with the board installed.

[The Dual Monitor Problem]. All of the Apple 80-column boards carry a video output jack that is used for the "substitute" video display. Unfortunately, this means disconnecting the monitor from its usual outlet at the back left of the Apple. The problem then is this: Can the board display the Apple graphics, which are normally generated on the other connector? The Full-View 80 and the Smarterm have electronic switching between the two displays, which allows software or keyboard control of a (single) display monitor. Three other boards require manual switching between text and graphic displays. Videx, manufacturer of the Videoterm, makes a switchplate that mounts on one of the back cutouts of the Apple. The Videx switchplate can be used unchanged by the DoubleVision Board and, with a minor change, by the Supe'R'Term.

Dual monitors, of course, are a happy but expensive solution. In particular, the ability to write a program on the text page and see the results on the graphics page is very useful while programming. A sharp black-and-white monitor on the text page (80-column board jack) and a color monitor for graphics (Apple rear jack) is an ideal, cost-is-no-object solution.

[Shift Key Problem]. Nearly all Apple 80-column boards require wiring a jumper between a pad on the keyboard and one of the game I/O connectors at the right rear of the Apple motherboard. This jumper should be 30-gauge (thin, "wire wrap") wire and typically connects to pin 4 on the game paddle connector. (As on most sockets, pins are numbered counterclockwise, starting with pin 1 in the upper-left-hand corner, which is marked by a white dot, slashed corner, etc.) This is close soldering and should be attempted only with a good, thin soldering iron and steady hand. Note that the shift key modification voids the Apple warranty.

Also note that enabling the shift key removes a standard feature of the Apple - namely, that shift M is "]", shift N is "^", and shift P is "@". On all boards but the Smarterm, these can only be typed by toggling the 80-column board in and out of operation - quite a pain. In short, all the boards can display a full 128-character ASCII set, not all have keyboard setups to input it (the source of the problem, of course, being the Apple's limited number of keys).

"Vision 80" (Vista Computer Products, 1317 E Edinger Ave., Santa Ana, CA, 714-953-0523 / 800-854-8017). Vision 80 was designed by two Australians, Harry Harper and Ken Thompson, and introduced at the 1981 West Coast Computer Faire. The board is distributed in the USA by Vista Computer Products, the Orange County-based firm best known as a distributor of low-cost floppy disks. Vision 80 retails for $350.

Although most Apple 80-column boards were designed to work with Apple Pascal, Vision 80 is also fully compatible with Apple BASIC. Various commands like VTAB, NORMAL, INVERSE, and HOME all work properly within the 24-line by 80-column environment, as do the editing diamonds A,B,C,D and I,J,K,M. Visual qualities of the board's characters are excellent, with good descenders on lower-case letters. In addition, various special characters are available in upper-case, including underscore, square root sign, and a tiny apple. A graphics or alternate language set is built in and can be toggled in and out with a single control code.

In Pascal, Vision 80 boots automatically when placed in slot 3. The card switches automatically to the high- and low-resolution screens for graphics and can be used with two monitors, one connected to the regular video jack on the back of the Apple, the other to the "Vision 80" card, to allow simultaneous display of Turtlegraphics and text.

Finally, "Vision 80" comes with a communications program ROM that allows its use with any modem that will work with either the Apple Communications Card or California Computer Products 7720 serial card, and speeds up to 1,800 baud. This is effectively a bonus serial card and makes the implementation of a communicating word processor using the "Vision 80" an attractive project. For communications, "Vision 80" requires a 48K.

"Smarterm" (Advanced Logic Systems). Smarterm is a cleanly designed board that requires a minimum of jumpers and hardware modifications to the Apple, at the price of some programming flexibility. A short video cable supplied with the Smarterm loops from the Apple's output jack into the card, with another connector available for the final, composite output. This allows the card to switch, in software, between the Apple graphics screens and the 80-column text screen.

Smarterm uses control-A for shifting rather than requiring a hardware modification. This preserves the Apple's warranty but is a potential source of incompatibility with some software. Smarterm, as mentioned above, generates the full ASCII character set. However, characters are made up of a 5 by 7 dot matrix without descenders and visually take some getting use to. Smarterm uses about the same screen area as the Apple 40-column display, eliminating problems with edge distortions and lop-off, but making the characters quite small. The Smarterm lists for about $360.

"Full-View 80" (Bit 3 Computer Corp., 1890 Huron St., St Paul, MN 55113, 612-926-6997). Full-View 80 also loops the Apple's video through its rather large card and allows software or keyboard selection of text or graphics screens. Full-View 80 requires the standard soldering shift key modification. Its normal character set is 5 by 7, without descenders. However, Bit 3 offers as a $62 option a ROM character set (manually selectable by dip switches on the board) that is 7 by 9, with descenders.

One useful extra feature is a "transparent" mode, found on some advanced ASCII terminals, that lists control codes (CR, LF, etc.) as single characters. Some additional features include: a 60-Hz clock signal that can be used to trigger the NMI (nonmaskable interrupt) on the Apple (and can conveniently drive a software clock), and special "function" keys for CATALOG, LOAD, and RUN, used of course with Apple BASICs. Full-View 80 lists at $395.

"Supe'R'Term" (M&R Enterprises, San Jose, CA). One of the earliest 80 column boards for the Apple, the Supe'R'Term has been adapted to more Apple word processing software than many of the other boards. Its features are now somewhat limited compared to the other boards on the market, although it has one specific advantage - namely, several video level and brightness controls, which can be adjusted to produce excellent image quality on most monitors.

Lastest revision as of this writing is 2.2. Installation of the Supe'R'Mod requires installation of a piggy-back board in place of a chip on the Apple motherboard, which is then connected to the board in its slot. List price is $375.

"DoubleVision" (The Computer Stop, 16919 Hawthorne Blvd., Lawndale, CA 90260, 213-371-4010). The least expensive of the 80-column boards, DoubleVision does not come with firmware in ROM; rather, it needs to have its routines loaded into RAM each time the Apple is booted up. (DoubleVision requires an Apple with 32K of RAM.) It is compatible with the "Apple-PIE 2.0" text editor. Special Pascal routines are available for $25. DoubleVision uses the escape key for its shift. List price is $295.

"Videoterm" (Videx, 3060 NW Thistle Pl., Corvallis, OR 97330, 503-758-0521). Version 2.0, $345. The Computer Cookbook recently had a Videx card on an Apple II in its lab and offers these observations.

[Using the Videx board]. Using Pascal with the Videx board is no problem. If the board is in slot 3, Pascal recognizes the presence of the board, as if it were a serial terminal, and directs its CONSOLE output to it. This means that the Pascal prompt comes up on the screen (in upper and lower case, to boot), and away you go. Microsoft's CP/M board also looks for a terminal in slot 3 and uses it if found.

From BASIC, either Applesoft or Integer, the situation is a bit more difficult. To turn on the board, it is necessary to select slot 3 (assuming, which we will for now, that that is where the board is installed) with the usual command:

PR#3

Note that this command must be typed blind: if the monitor is connected to the Videx card, not to the Apple's rear video output jack, no video will go to the monitor until the board is turned on. This can be quite disconcerting when using the board for the first time, since it will be uncertain whether or not the board is connected right. If Pascal is available, boot it (disk "APPLE1:") to eliminate some doubt.

[Control of the Videx board]. The Videx board should be thought of as something like an ASCII terminal in the way that it responds to control characters. Most terminals, like the SOROC or Hazeltines, respond to escape sequences like ESC Y, which in the case of the SOROC homes the cursor. The Videx board responds to the following control sequences, which begin, however, not with the escape code, but with control-Z:

        control-Z 0: clear screen, set to 24 lines
        control-Z 1: clear screen, set to 18 lines
        control-Z 2: select standard set or normal video
        control-Z 3: select alternate set or inverse video

In addition to these control sequences, the Videx card displays something for every one of the 128 ASCII codes sent to it, including control characters:

        control-@ to control-G: display low res graphic chars

control-H to control-O: display "transparent" control chars
control-P to control-SHIFT-O: display line draw chars

The eight lo-res graphics characters available on the Videx are simple 1 across by 3 high cells of solid color. The 16 line drawing characters are a set of rules and boxes useful for form design. In a version of what is often called "transparent" mode on expensive terminals, the Videx displays a tiny abbreviation of the eight- key control characters from backspace (control-H) to shift in (control-O). This is quite useful for debugging troublesome texts (for example, those captured off timesharing services) that are frequently spiked with such control characters and that often drive printers, terminals, and programmers crazy.

There are two important accessories for the Videx board: the Videx Keyboard Enhancer (a shift key modification) and the Videx Switchplate Assembly. The Computer Cookbook strongly suggests that both of these be ordered along with the Videx, since using the board without the shift key modification is likely to drive one crazy. Without the shift key mod, upper-case and lower-case are toggled by typing control-A, a lot of extra keystrokes.

[Slot 5 - Coprocessors]. Although the use of slot 5 is probably most open to variation on the Apple, various cards using other processors are an important subset of available Apple peripherals.

Microsoft introduced the "SoftCard" in early 1980, and it became widely available in the latter part of that year. The device was the first multiprocessor card for the Apple and was a truly innovative product. What the MicroSoft card did was acknowledge, in a way, a new order in the relative importance of hardware and software. The Z-80 used on the MicroSoft card costs under $5, although software - especially the type of business software that exists under CP/M - is far more expensive. MicroSoft's answer was to leave the software alone and change the hardware. At the time, it was a radical idea; of computers announced in 1981 and 1982, at least half seem to have coprocessors of one type or another, including 8/16 bit combinations.

Although the MicroSoft card adds flexibility to the Apple, it does not really speed up the computer. By contrast, the "Mill" from Stellation Two (Box 2342, Santa Barbara, CA 93120, 805-966-1140) is a Motorola 6809 add-on processor board that makes the Apple run about 25% faster. A Pascal patch for the Mill is available. The Mill lists at $275, and its manual alone costs $25.

Another board that can speed up the notoriously slow Apple, at least in number-crunching applications, is the CCS Floating Point Board (of which a clone is now sold by Applied Analytics as microSPEED). These boards use the Advanced Micro Devices 9511 Arithmetic Processing Unit for floating point calculations. Use of this board can speed up the Apple in number crunching by a factor of ten, although there are some tradeoffs.

The AM9511 has only seven decimal digit precision, compared with nine digits in Applesoft BASIC. Numbers in the AM9511 can range between plus and minus ten to the 20th power; in Applesoft they can range between plus and minus ten to the 40th power. However, with CCSOFT, a software patch to Applesoft BASIC provided by California Computer Systems, the AM9511 can achieve the following benchmarks (seconds per 5,000 repetitions) compared to Applesoft BASIC:

```
MUL       17.6    22.3
FDIV      17.6    27.3
EXP       25.4   130.6
SQR       17.1   248.9
RND       18.4    29.9
LOG       26.4   114.3
COS       26.6   135.2
PWR       41.1   153.9
TAN       28.7   244.8
ATN       29.2   222.4
ACOS      30.6   554.8
ASIN      30.4   472.3
LOG(10)   26.8   325.6
PI        14.8    53.7
INV       16.6    29.6
SINH      37.7   266.5
COSH      37.4   265.4
```

Computer Station, of St Louis, MO, is said to have a Pascal TRANSCEND unit that takes advantage of the CCS card. This would be a useful speedup in Pascal graphics applications.

[GPIB Bus Controller]. This interesting $300 product, CCS 7490A, allows the Apple II to be used as a monitor of laboratory test instruments that use the General Purpose Instrument Bus (GPIB), IEEE standard 488 (sometimes called the Hewlett-Packard bus because of that company's importance in gaining its acceptance). Basically, this bus connects various devices that can be either listening (to the other devices on the bus), talking (to other devices on the bus), or controlling. The protocol for talking on the bus is fairly complicated and should be attempted only by experienced programmers. Another item of interest to labs is CCS's 7470A, which converts DC voltage levels into a stream of BCD digits.

[ROM boards]. The CCS 7114A ROM board allows the firmware of the Apple to be overlaid. It is for the knowledgeable hobbyist only. ROMPLUS+, from Mountain Computer, is a board that allows six 2K ROM or EPROM chips to be added to the Apple. These can provide important programs in firmware. The first in firmware, which comes with the board, is a "Keyboard Filter" that gives the Apple upper- and lower-case letters using hi-res graphics; it also allows user-defined character sets.

[Graphics Tablet]. Apple's graphics tablet was introduced in late 1979. The graphics tablet is similar to the Summagraphics Bit Pad One or Houston Instrument's HI-Pad. It allows such items as drawings and blueprints to be traced and input into the Apple in digital form. The Graphics Tablet is somewhat expensive ($795) and requires 48K and the Disk II to use. Unfortunately, it is not supported from Apple Pascal.

[Slot 7 - Clock Cards]. The oldest and best established clock card for the Apple II is the Mountain Computer Apple Clock, a card that is sold also by Apple. Since 1980, the Thunderclock has also gained in popularity, as has the Mountain Computer multifunction card, which combines the old clock card with a serial and parallel port.

The Mountain Computer product is a long card that includes a Ni-Cad transistor radio battery. When the computer is on, the card draws power from the Apple bus and charges the battery. When the computer is off, the clock update circuits feed off the battery, keeping the correct time for 3 or 4 days. A 12-volt adapter supplied with the unit will keep it running indefinitely off of house current; The Computer Cookbook strongly recommends its use. The clock works in 1 millisecond intervals and can be set to allow interrupts.

The clock counts seconds in binary and milliseconds in BCD and makes them available in a series of registers. Time up to 2^{24} seconds can be read from ten memory locations C0n0-C0n9, where n is the Apple slot number + 8 of the card. Thus, if the clock is in slot 4 of the Apple, the following memory locations are significant:

C0C0	2^{20} - 2^{24} times bits
C0C1	2^{12} ^ 2^{19} time bits
C0C2	2^{4} ^ 2^{11} time bits
C0C3	left nibble: 100ms in BCD; right nibble: 2^{3} bits
C0C4	left nibble: 1ms in BCD; right nibble: 10ms in BCD
C0C5	starts clock when read
C0C6	stops clock when read
C0C7	advance clock one bit; clear IRQ
C0C8	advance clock two; clear INT-OUT
C0C9	set interrupt

These locations can be PEEKed at from BASIC or can be read with a LDA in 6502 assembly language programs. However, the firmware ROM on the Mountain Hardware board makes conversion of seconds and milliseconds much easier. The ROM returns a string in the following format:

XXX.SS;MM;HH DD/MM

where XXX is the count in milliseconds, SS the seconds, MM the minutes, HH the hours, and DD/MM the day and month. The following Applesoft BASIC code will read the clock into string variable T$:

```
PRINT D$;IN#;SLOT : REM D$=CONTROL-D
PRINT D$;PR#;SLOT
INPUT  ;T$
PRINT D$;IN#0
PRINT D$;PR#0
```

The correct time is given, of course, only if the clock has at some time be set using the Mountain Hardware software. This software zeros the second count at a base date used by the ROM firmware.

For interval timing, the CCS card can be polled with resolution of about 1 ms. For other applications, the CCS 7740A Programmable Timer is a better choice. It uses a MC 6840 that has three automatic built-in timers. When properly programmed, which is not a simple matter, the $120 timer can generate interrupts for various time sequences.

[Pascal Clock]. Mountain Computer's clock can also be used from Pascal. Owners of the clock can write Mountain Computer with their serial number and receive a free Pascal disk with a CLOCKSTUFF unit similar to the APPLESTUFF and TURTLEGRAPHICS units distributed by Apple. The disk has several stand-alone programs as well as the CLOCKSTUFF procedures, which are intended to be incorporated into user programs that require the clock. Slot 7 is the usual Pascal assignment for the clock.

One of the more interesting uses of the Apple Clock is as an interrupt generator for a sophisticated foreground and background processing system for the Apple II, which is otherwise a non-concurrent machine. As it comes from the factory, the Apple Clock, if enabled, generates interrupts every second. If this interrupt rate is speeded up, the Apple can do something like constantly read a low-speed (134.5 baud) data line, yet still be available for other functions.

For the sake of an example, assume that the data line requires no processing other than to display a running tape across the bottom of the screen. The following software and one hardware modification is needed to accomplish this:

> an initialization routine that enables the clock for interrupts, clears the serial port, and sets the interrupt vector (memory locations FFFE-FFFF) on the Apple at the polling routine;

> an interrupt routine for polling that (a) saves all registers, like a good interrupt routines, (b) checks the serial status port for an incoming character, and (c) if a character is ready, reads it, and finally (d) restores the registers and returns.

The hardware modification involves changing the interrupt frequency on the board to be faster than the 134.5-baud line. A quick calculation shows that 15 characters will come in per second. An interrupt every 10 milliseconds (100 per minute), available by cutting some traces and jumpering the board, is more than adequate to poll the line for incoming characters, and will not appreciably slow down the Apple. The Computer Cookbook has used such a system to read the low-speed UPI newspaper wire service line into an Apple II.

[Survey of Apple Hardware]. The following table is an attempt to be a useful (but incomplete) survey of Apple II hardware. The left-hand column is the generic name of the product (e.g., video monitors) or the target system (Apple II, TRS-80 Model III). The second column is the actual manufacturer; note that for some systems (e.g., the IBM), there are many non-IBM vendors of compatible products. The third column provides as much identifying and descriptive information about the product as space permits, including the manufacturer's part number, if available. The first price given is the suggested list price; the second price is the lowest observed discount price, or sometimes the dealer or wholesale price. These should be used together to establish a high and low range for actual prices.

SYSTEM	MANUFACTURER	DESCRIPTION/IDENTIFICATION	LIST	DISCOUNT
Apple II	ABT	Bar Code Wand	199.00	
Apple II	ABT	Numeric Key Pad	125.00	100.00
Apple II	ALF	Music board, 9-voice		159.00

Apple II	ALS	16K RAM "addram"		119.00
Apple II	ALS	Smarterm	269.00	
Apple II	ALS	Z80 card, "Z-card"		209.00
Apple II	Andromeda	RAM 16K card	195.00	95.00
Apple II	Apple	Disk Drive w/controller	650.00	
Apple II	Apple	Disk Drive w/o controller	575.00	459.00
Apple II	Apple	FORTRAN	175.00	
Apple II	Apple	Firmware - Applesoft	200.00	170.00
Apple II	Apple	Firmware - Autostart ROM	65.00	55.00
Apple II	Apple	Firmware - Integer	200.00	170.00
Apple II	Apple	Graphics Tablet	795.00	675.00
Apple II	Apple	II+ Computer, 16K	990.00	
Apple II	Apple	II+ Computer, 48K	1449.00	
Apple II	Apple	Language System	469.00	
Apple II	Apple	Printer IF Centronics	225.00	191.00
Apple II	Apple	Printer IF parallel	180.00	153.00
Apple II	Apple	Serial IF high speed	195.00	165.00
Apple II	Apple	Serial IF low-speed comm	225.00	191.00
Apple II	Base2	Graphics Printer Driver	160.00	
Apple II	Bit 3	16K RAM card	149.00	
Apple II	Bit 3	80 col card 810	379.00	
Apple II	Bit 3	I/O 2S	239.00	
Apple II	Bit 3	Video Board	349.95	
Apple II	CCS	7114A Prom Module	79.95	
Apple II	CCS	7424 Calendar/Clock	125.00	
Apple II	CCS	7470A A/D Converter	111.95	67.17
Apple II	CCS	7490A IEEE-488 Interface	300.00	180.00
Apple II	CCS	7500 Wire Wrap Board	21.00	14.70
Apple II	CCS	7710A Asynchronous Serial	159.95	95.97
Apple II	CCS	7811A Arithmetic Processor	399.95	239.97
Apple II	CCS	A/D converter	112.00	95.00
Apple II	CCS	Arithmetic Processor	400.00	340.00
Apple II	CCS	Clock calendar 7424A	125.00	106.00
Apple II	CCS	Extender board 7520A	25.00	22.00
Apple II	CCS	Keypad	174.95	
Apple II	CCS	Parallel Interface 7720A	120.00	102.00
Apple II	CCS	Parallel card	94.95	
Apple II	CCS	Prom module w/o proms	80.00	68.00
Apple II	CCS	Synch serial IF 7712A	180.00	153.00
Apple II	CCS	Timer unit 7440A	115.00	97.00
Apple II	Coprocessors	8088 + 16K RAM + CP/M-86		899.00
Apple II	Corvus	IF card		179.00
Apple II	Epson	Cable to printer 8230	30.00	22.50
Apple II	Epson	Printer IF card 8131	80.00	60.00
Apple II	Franklin	ACE look-alike computer		1195.00
Apple II	Hayes	Micromodem	379.00	
Apple II	Lobo	Floppy Drive w/controller	565.00	510.00
Apple II	Lobo	Floppy Drive w/o controller	465.00	405.00
Apple II	M&R	80 col. SuperTerm	395.00	300.00
Apple II	M&R	Superfan II	74.95	
Apple II	MISC	Memory Upgrade 4116 chips	49.95	35.00
Apple II	Micro-Sci	Floppy controller bd, A2	95.00	
Apple II	Micro-Sci	Floppy controller, A70 or A40	79.00	
Apple II	Micro-Sci	Floppy drive, A2	395.00	

Apple II	Micro-Sci	Floppy drive, A40, 160K	369.00	
Apple II	Micro-Sci	Floppy drive, A70, 286K	489.00	
Apple II	Microsoft	16K Ramcard	165.00	
Apple II	Microsoft	Z80 Softcard & CP/M	349.00	
Apple II	Mountain	CPS Multifunction	209.00	
Apple II	Mountain	Clock Calendar	195.00	
Apple II	Novation	Apple-Cat II modem	329.00	329.00
Apple II	Orange Micro	Printer IF "Grappler"		129.00
Apple II	SEC	A/D interface	99.50	
Apple II	SSM	I/O 1P 1S	225.00	191.00
Apple II	SSM	I/O serial/parallel		159.00
Apple II	Saturn	128K RAM card		509.00
Apple II	Saturn	32K RAM card	239.00	
Apple II	TG	Expand-a-port	59.95	
Apple II	TG	Joystick	59.95	
Apple II	TG	Paddles	39.95	
Apple II	Thunderclock	BSR Interface	49.95	
Apple II	Thunderclock	Clock card	139.00	
Apple II	Videx	80-column card	345.00	
Apple II	Videx	Keyboard Enhancer	129.00	108.00
Apple II	Videx	Switchplate	19.00	15.00
Apple II	Vista	Floppy Drive 80-track	459.00	

[Apple Software]. The problem with Apple II software is that there is just too much of it for any one person to keep track of. A summer 1982 issue of Ben Rosen's "Rosen Electronics Letter" counted 89 vendors of 659 programs in the Sofsel Software (a major distributor) catalog alone. Naturally, many programs for one reason or another don't make it onto the Sofsel list. Vital Information, Inc. (350 Union Station, Kansas City, MO 64108, 913-384-3860) published a several hundred page guide to Apple II and III software in 1981. The Computer Cookbook has not seen a later edition of this book, but presumably one exists.

The best source of information about new Apple software is Softalk magazine (Box 60, North Hollywood, CA 91603, 213-980-5074, $24/year). Softalk at one time concentrated on game software but has spun off a new all-game software magazine, Softline, to allow the parent to cover other things. The larger Apple software companies also advertise, of course, in InfoWorld and Byte.

The following impressions of Apple II software are entirely subjective. The Computer Cookbook is in the position of being a software deejay: it may not know art, but it knows what it likes.

[Diagnostics]. Just as every automobile owner should know how to change his or her own oil, every personal computer owner should know how to test the RAM of their computer and (for Apple owners, at least) calibrate the speed of flakey floppy disk drives. To do this, however, requires a diagnostic disk. To date, it took a friendly dealer to pirate these for you. Now a disk called "Master Diagnostics" from Nikrom Technical Products (25 Prospect St., Leominster, MA 01453, 800-835-2246) is being sold openly for $55, and with a disk head cleaning kit for $75.

[System Software]. System software for the Apple II is best bought from Apple itself (10260 Bandley Drive, Cupertino, CA 95016, 406-996-1010). Apple's manuals are generally very good. In addition to two flavors of BASIC, Apple sells the UCSD P-system, which runs Apple Pascal and Fortran. In 1982, Apple introduced LOGO, a graphics language for children; two other LOGOs are on the market for the Apple II from Terrapin and Krell Software. Apple also sells PILOT, a course authoring language for teachers that has been something of a disappointment. Just about every higher-level language except Ada is available for the Apple II if one looks hard enough.

MicroSoft's Z-80 implementation of CP/M opens up the Apple II to a wide variety of software running under that language. SoftCard CP/M, however, can be somewhat odd in its use of I/O devices and disks, since it must cooperate with the Apple 6502 for this.

[Terminal Software]. A modem is just as good as its terminal program. Whereas both Hayes and Novation supply minimal programs with their products (Hayes has recently unbundled its software to make a pseudo price reduction of its hardware), the best communications software comes from Southwestern Data Systems (PO Box 582, Santee, CA 92071, 714-562-3670). Southwestern sells "ASCII Express II" ($79.95) and one of the few packages known to The Cookbook that can use the Novation Apple-CAT II at 1200 baud (from Pascal, no less), P-Term "The Professional" ($129.95).

A company with a similar name, Southeastern Software (6414 Derbyshire Drive, New Orleans, LA 70126, 504-246-8438), sells a terminal program "Data Capture 4.0" that is adequate, but not as easy as Southwestern's to use.

SSM Microcomputer Products, Inc. (2190 Paragon Drive, San Jose, CA 95131, 408-946-7400), primarily a hardware maker, has a very popular terminal program for the Hayes modem, "Transend". Other terminal software is sold by Computer:applications, Inc. (13300 SW 108 Street Circle, Miami, FL 33186, 305-385-4277); Context Management Systems, Inc. (23864 Hawthorne Blvd., Suite 101, Torrance, CA 90505, 213-378-8277); Datamark Business Systems (279 South McKnight Rd., St Paul, MN 55119, 612-738-9111); and Ferox Microsystems, Inc. (1701 North Fort Meyer Drive, Arlington, VA 22209, 703-841-0800).

A community or club bulletin board system can be put up on the Apple using "ABBS", for Apple Bulletin Board System, from Software Sorcery, Inc. (7927 Jones Branch Dr., Suite 400, McLean, VA 22102, 703-385-2944). Microcom (89 State Street, Boston, MA 02109) sells a package that allows the Apple II to be used as a Telex machine or Western Union Mailgram terminal.

[Business Software]. Every discussion of business software for the Apple II must begin with VisiCalc, a spreadsheet program sold by VisiCorp (2895 Zanker Rd., San Jose, CA 95134). Some people prefer SuperCalc, by Sorcim, to VisiCalc. Advanced Logic Systems (1995 E. Arques Ave., Sunnyvale, CA 94086, 408-730-0306) sells a hardware/software package called the Synergizer consisting of a Z-Card (Z-80 card, a SoftCard clone), Smarterm 80-column card, Add-Ram 16K memory card, and SuperCalc thrown in, all for $749.

Beyond spreadsheets, there are data base managers like Personal Filing System (PFS), from Software Publishing, and DB Master, from Stoneware (50 Belvedere St., San Rafael, CA 94901). PFS is easier to use; DB Master is more flexible.

Word processors present a special problem for the Apple II, which was designed to be an upper case only, 40-column across machine. No one should buy an Apple II for word processing; try the Osborne, TRS-80 Model III, or IBM instead. "Apple Writer", sold by Apple, is probably the most popular Apple word processor simply because it is sold by Apple. "Easywriter", introduced in 1979, was originally an Electric Pencil clone written in FORTH and has now wandered over to being the IBM PC standard. With the SoftCard, "WordStar" from MicroPro International can be run; this settles the question for many people - WordStar has a strong following. It should also be pointed out that Apple Pascal has a good text editor as part of the P-system, and the price is right (free) if buying Pascal anyway.

[Game Software]. The Apple II has hundreds of games available, most on floppy disk (a few are still distributed on cassette tape). The software publishing industry is new and growing rapidly; in the next few years, we can also expect to see large traditional publishers, such as Dow Jones, Time-Life, and CBS, get into the business. One traditional publisher, Hayden Book Co., Inc. (50 Essex St., Rochelle Park, NJ 07662, 201-843-0550, TWX 710 990 5071 HAYDENPUB ROPK) has been involved since 1979 and publishes "Sargon II", among other

Of the upstarts, On-Line Systems (36575 Mudge Ranch Rd., Coarsegold, CA 93614, 209-683-6858) is one of the most professional in the game field, even licensing arcade titles a la Activision and the other heavies. Sirius Software (10364 Rockingham Dr., Sacramento, CA 95827) and Quality Software (6660 Reseda Blvd., Suite 105, Reseda, CA 91335) are among the other blossoming small companies. Edu-Ware (Box 22222, Agoura, CA 91301, 213-706-0661) is one of the best of the educational software publishers.

[Board Games]. Kathy and Dan Spracken, who live near San Diego, CA, are the authors of the Sargon chess program published by Hayden, and they have been affiliated with the University of California at San Diego. Sargon was originally written in Z-80 assembler code (the source code was published in book form by Hayden) and was adapted to run on the 6502. Peter Jennings is a chess master and author of several chess programs for microcomputers, including the TI 99/4 program, and "Microchess," for the Apple II, which was once sold by Personal Software (now VisiCorp) but has apparently been discontinued.

[Adventure Games]. Scott Adams, of Florida, is certainly the dean if not the creator of Adventure games. Actually, Adventure was developed in the 1970s as a diversion on time-sharing systems, with text-only version by Will Crowther and Don Woods, based on D&D themes, being one of the first. This classic version is available from MicroSoft as "Adventure" in Apple II disk format. Like an old black-and-white movie, it has been technically surpassed, but has a great plot.

Scott Adams is the founder of Adventure International (Box 3435, Longwood, FL 32750), a software house specializing in Adventure games. Recently, Adams has been moving toward longer and longer playing versions and has a boxed set of disks that apparently takes a year or more to play (ideal for Christmas - give the gift that keeps on giving, and you might not have to give anything next year).

On the Apple II, with its high-resolution graphics capability, it was a matter of time before someone thought to illustrate text Adventure games with graphic "slides". Credit for this innovation generally goes to Ken and Roberta Williams, programmers for On-Line Systems. "Beneath Apple Manor" and "Temple of Apshai" are early Apple II versions of Adventure, "Beneath" being in lo-res graphics, "Temple" in hi-res. The next stage in "Adventure" was use of hi-res graphic pictures as substitutes or at least supplements for verbal descriptions ("you are in a house...").

David Mullich has programmed "The Prisoner," a game based on the BBC series staring Patrick McGohan. "The Prisoner" is an Adventure-type game but with an adversarial feel added by the fact that the computer is constantly attempting to trick the user, adding a grain of paranoia absent from other Adventure games. "The Prisoner" is published by Edu-ware.

[Arcade Games]. One of the best and most prolific authors of arcade style games for the Apple II is Nasir, a (Bombay) Indian who has a cult following among Apple II graphics freaks, who was primary programmer for Sirius Software before starting his own company.

Most popular arcade games - "Space Invaders", "Galaxian", "Pac-Man", "Donkey Kong" - were developed by Japanese companies Taito and Namco. Minoru Nakazawa heads a company called Star Craft in Japan. In Fall 1980 Nakazawa's company came out with a version of the Namco "Galaxian" for the Apple II computer; called "Apple Galaxian" it was shown at the Boston Computer Fair that year.

Broderbund (1938 4th St., San Rafael, CA 94901, 415-456-6424) distributes "Snoggle", an Apple version of "Pac-Man", written by Jun Wada (a woman) and Ken Iba. Tony Suzuki is the author of "Alien Rain", a "Space Invaders" game.

Mark Turmell is the author of "Sneakers," another clever variant of the "Space Invaders" game. In "Sneakers," the invading creatures have smiles and big feet. Turmell traces the influences on him to "Gorf" and "Astro Blasters". Bob Bishop is the author of several advanced Apple graphics and animation programs once published by Softape. Apple's use of his "AppleVision" program on its system disk has made his name very familiar to Apple owners.

Bill Budge was a programmer for California Software before starting BudgeCo (428 Pala Ave., Piedmont, CA 94611, 415-658-8141), to publish "Raster Blaster", a pinball game. The success of "Raster Blaster" has made Budge an instant spokesman for game programmers. In an article in Softline (Vol. 1, No. 2; 11021 Magnolia Blvd., North Hollywood, CA 91601, $6/year), speaking of authoring programs, he says, "Most people don't have the combination of skills . . . it's kind of specialized. To write a good game, you have to know assembly language, which rules out quite a lot of people; you have to like to play with graphics, which rules out more people; and in the end, there aren't that many people left who can write games. And the number who can finish a program is another small fraction."

[Fantasy Games]. Richard Garriott is perhaps the only personal computer program author to use a pseudonym ("Lord British"). Garriott has a definite high-tech pedigree: his father is Owen Garriott, one of the astronauts that was on Skylab I. Garriott lives in Houston, is a student at the University of Texas, and works at a computer store. He writes Adventure-type games, including "Akalabeth", "Ultima I", and "Ultima II". "Ultima III" will be available soon. "Ultima" is published by California Software.

Doug Carlson, author of "Galactic Saga" and a founder of Broderbund Software, is a Harvard-trained lawyer. Like a number of attorneys, Carlson quit a "good corporate job" in Chicago to work in rural Maine. There he took up programming on a TRS-80 as a hobby, his first product being the trilogy of strategy games with philosophical overtones. This program was purchased for distribution by Scott Adams, the Adventure man, and then translated for the Apple II in time for display at the 1980 West Coast Computer Faire.

[Simulations]. Strategic Simulations, Inc. (465 Fairchild Dr., Suite 108, Mountain View, CA 94043, 800-227-1617, 800-772-3545 in CA) is a software house run by a stable of war-game buffs. SSI was founded in 1979 in Campbell, CA by Joel Billings and John Lyon. Its first product was "Computer Bismark", written by Ed Williger, which was also a notable advance in packaging for personal computer programs, including in a book-sized box a plastic movement chart, maps, grease pencil, and other items.

Finally, no parent should be without "Rubik's Cube Unlocked", by Double Gold Software (13126 Anza Drive, Saratoga, CA 95070, 408-257-2247) to assist with bothersome questions asked by children.

[Graphics Tools]. Both Penguin Software (830 4th Ave., Geneva, IL 60134, 312-232-1984) and SubLogic (713 Edgebrook Dr., Champaign, Il 61820) sell programs to develop graphics applications on the Apple, as does Insoft (10175 SW Barbur Blvd., Suite 202B, Portland, OR 97219, 503-244-4181) with its GraFORTH graphics language.

Finally, rather than junk your Apple, you can turn it into an oscilloscope to debug your next computer. "Applescope Interface" from RC Electronics, Inc. (7265 Tuolumne Street, Goleta, CA 93117, 805-968-6614) uses a 2-board $595 set. It also has an Apple II logic analyzer called "Bus Rider".

SYSTEM	MANUFACTURER	DESCRIPTION/IDENTIFICATION	LIST	DISCOUNT
Apple II	Apple	Apple Logo - 1 of 3	175.00	
Apple II	Apple	Apple Writer - word processor	75.00	
Apple II	Apple	DOS toolkit - text fonts, etc.	75.00	
Apple II	Apple	Dow Jones News Quote Reporter	95.00	
Apple II	Apple	Goodspell - checker for Apple Wr	60.00	
Apple II	Ashton-Tate	dBase II - relation dbm;Softcard	700.00	
Apple II	Broderbund	Alien Rain - version of Galaxian	24.95	
Apple II	Broderbund	Apple Panic - Donkey Kong	29.95	
Apple II	BudgeCo	Raster Blaster - pinball game	29.95	
Apple II	Cal Pacific	Super Invader - oldie but goodie	19.95	
Apple II	Cal Soft	Ultima - by Lord British	39.95	
Apple II	Cavalier	Bug Attack - medfly madness	29.95	
Apple II	DataMost	Snack Attack - eat the dots	29.95	
Apple II	Edu-Ware	The Prisoner Adventure	29.95	
Apple II	Epyx/AS	Temple of Apshai - prize winner	39.95	
Apple II	Hayden	Sargon II - best chess game	34.95	
Apple II	IDSI	Pool 1.5 - ins replay & slo-mo	34.95	
Apple II	Infocom	Zork - English-speaking text Ad	39.95	
Apple II	Infocom	Zork II - yet more Zork	39.95	
Apple II	Insoft	GraForth - graphics FORTH	75.00	
Apple II	Lightning	MasterType - fun typing tutor	39.95	

Apple II	Link Sys	Datafax - unstructured text dbm	199.00
Apple II	Microcom	Micro-Courier - EMAIL system	250.00
Apple II	Microsoft	Crowther/Woods text Adventure	35.00
Apple II	Muse	Castle Wolfenstein	29.95
Apple II	Muse	Robot War - strategy game	39.95
Apple II	On-Line	Mystery House Adventure #1 w/pix	24.95
Apple II	On-Line	Wizard & Princess Hi-Res Ad #2	32.95
Apple II	Penguin	Above for Apple graphics tablet	119.95
Apple II	Penguin	Complete Graphics System - tools	69.95
Apple II	Quality	Beneath Apple Manor fantasy gm	40.00
Apple II	Quality	Meteroids in Space - guess what?	19.95
Apple II	Sensible	Sensible Speller - w/85,000 words	75.00
Apple II	Sierra	LISA 2.5 - best 6502 assembler	79.95
Apple II	Sirius	Epoch - space odyssey	34.95
Apple II	Sirius	Gorgon - Nasir authored space gm	39.95
Apple II	Sirius	Sneakers - Adidas Invaders	29.95
Apple II	Softape	Microgammon II - backgammon	19.95
Apple II	Software Pub	PFS, Personal Filing System dbm	95.00
Apple II	Software Pub	PFS:Graph from PFS or VisiCalc	125.00
Apple II	Software Pub	PFS:Report generator from PFS	95.00
Apple II	Southeastern	Data Capture 4.0 - terminal prog	65.00
Apple II	Southwestern	ASCII Express - terminal program	79.95
Apple II	Southwestern	Z-Term - CP/M terminal prog	99.95
Apple II	Stoneware	DB Master Utility Pak II	99.00
Apple II	Stoneware	DB Master data base manager	229.00
Apple II	SubLogic	Flight Simulator	33.50
Apple II	Synergistic	Odyssey - extended fantasy game	30.00
Apple II	Synergistic	Wilderness Campaign fantasy gm	17.50
Apple II	VisiCorp	VisiCalc - classic spreadsheet	250.00
Apple II	VisiCorp	VisiFile - db manager	250.00
Apple II	VisiCorp	VisiTrend/VisiPlot - plot data	259.95

The Apple ///

The Apple /// was announced at the National Computer Conference in Anaheim, CA in May 1980 - and nothing happened. The Apple /// was a shoe that everyone had waited to drop, but the silence after its introduction, if anything, was more nerve-wracking than the silence before.

In the fall of 1980, the Apple Computer - just before its public stock offering in December - began shipping Apple ///s to its dealers. Many of these didn't work, and the /// developed a reputation it had difficulty living down. In late 1981, Apple reintroduced the ///, this time along with the ProFile, a mini-Winchester hard disk. The reintroduction of the /// worked, in the sense that most of the earlier worries about the reliability of the machine were erased.

The problem with the reintroduction was that it came too late; the IBM PC had been introduced in August 1981. Like the PC, the Apple /// is a hybrid 8/16-bit machine, competing in an increasingly 16-bit world. It is slow (its real problem) and has simply never attracted the attention of software developers the way the Apple II or IBM PC have. In mid-1982, a count by industry consultant Ben Rosen showed only seven non-Apple vendors offering software for the III, with a total of 13 programs. The Apple II, by contrast, had 89 different vendors with 659 programs!

In one sense, the machine is Apple's first computer, because Apple Computer is hardly the same garage-shop operation that designed the Apple II. (Apple has about 150 people in R&D who have supposedly designed their way to the Apple V and beyond.) Designing computers is far different from selling them, however, and the results on the Apple ///, though not fully in, are mixed. The Apple /// was built not to replace the successful Apple II but rather to add a business computer to Apple's product line at the high end of the spectrum.

There are some who would say that this is a wrong-headed move for Apple in the first place. The small business computer market is crowded with machines like Tandy's TRS-80 Model II, the IBM PC, and others. Apple has been very eager to shed its game-computer image but it is unclear what competitive advantage Apple brings to the small business computer field.

Nevertheless, the Apple /// has been designed by an interesting and intelligent computer company. Here are its major features:

* Additional memory. While bank-switching schemes have been available on S-100 bus computers for some time, small personal computers like the Apple II and TRS-80 series have been limited to the 64K address range of the 8-bit microprocessors. The Apple /// uses a memory manager that fools the ///s 6502 CPU into believing it has up to 128K of RAM.

* Upper- and lower-case. One of the Apple II's serious limitations was in word processing, which it could do with only poor surrogates for true upper and lower case. The /// comes standard with a full ASCII terminal style screen: 24 lines down by 80 columns across. In color, 40 by 24 lines are possible.

* Extended graphics. Perhaps the Apple ///'s most interesting features lie in its extension of Apple II graphics. The /// has four graphics modes: 192 lines of 280 dots in black and white (same as Apple II); 192 by with 280 dots in 16 colors with limitations on color combinations (same as Apple II but more colors); 192 lines of 140 colors, no limitations; and 192 by 560 dots in black and white. The video color signal is available as a composite NTSC signal or on separate red, blue, and green lines. (These require some minor mods before they can be fed to a stock RGB monitor.)

However, these differences between the Apple II and the Apple /// should not mask the similarities. Some of the Apple II's problems remain in the ///, notably processor speed. The Apple ///'s 6502 CPU operates at 1.4 MHz, not nearly fast enough for a small business machine. It can be sped up slightly, to 2 MHz, by disabling the video circuitry.

[Apple II Compatibility]. The Apple II, for all its PEEKs, POKEs, and CALLs, had a hardware structure many users could understand. The Apple /// operating system puts too much on its plate: a File Manager, Device Manager, Memory Manager, Utility Manager, and Interrupt Manager. The /// suffers from software over-engineering. However, the Apple /// will find some interesting applications in sophisticated, software-intensive systems (probably written in Pascal) that can use its graphics capabilities.

Although the /// has only one card designed especially for it, various Apple II cards will work in the ///. The following table shows card compatibility:

Disk Controller	No Problem, but no slot 5
Graphic Tablet	Works in slots 1-4
Silentype	Tight fit, but works in slot 1
Serial IF Card	No problem
Parallel IF card	No problem
Communications card	No problem, but not necessary
IEEE-488 card	No problem
Language card	Will not work. Emulates 48K Apple II+

These cards are by non-Apple manufacturers:

Microsoft Z-80 SoftCard	Will not work
Mountain Hardware Clock	Will not fit
Mountain Hardware CPS card	Will not fit
Mountain Hardware Music Sys	Will not work
Hayes Micromodem	Must modify connector to fit
Thunderclock	No problem
various 80-column cards	Forget it!

[Inside the Apple ///]. The Apple /// uses an ordinary 6502 processor, but one with additional circuitry (a black box incorporating two versatile interface adaptors, or VIAs, to be specific) watching it. These VIAs are responsible for bank switching memory to fool the 6502 into being able to access over 64K.

The memory map of the /// looks like this:

0000-1FFF	system bank
2000-9FFF	32K user bank
A000-FFFF	system bank

The bank used is determined by the low nibble of memory location FFEF. Up to 15 different banks can be selected (a 0F pattern as the bank nibble has a special interpretation). This gives the /// a theoretical maximum of 512K of memory (16 banks times 32K), even though the maximum implemented in hardware currently is 256K.

Bank switching can be slow, especially transfers between mutually exclusive banks. However, the /// uses a clever scheme by which the VIAs detect when the 6502 is doing zero page extended addressing and adds in a Xbyte from memory locations 1600 to 16FF. In effect, the /// turns part of its low system bank into base registers.

Several other clever tricks are involved in the ///'s addressing. Up to 8 zero pages, in fact, are allowed and, with each zero page, an associated stack page. There is relatively little time cost in this addressing, since much of the additional fetching and fiddling of the memory addressing takes place during the DMA cycle. Putting 8F in the Xbyte, however, turns the /// into a normal 64K 6502 machine and gives access to the system clock, which is in memory area FFD0 to FFEF and usually papered over by the VIA ports. This protection of the system clock explains why only a cold, power-off boot affects the system clock.

[Apple /// Price List]. In the following table, the left-hand column is the generic name of the product (e.g., video monitors) or the target system (Apple II, TRS-80 Model III). The second column is the actual manufacturer; note that for some systems (e.g., the IBM) there are many non-IBM vendors of compatible products. The third column provides as much identifying and descriptive information about the product as space permits, including the manufacturer's part number, if available. The first price given is the suggested list price; the second price is the lowest observed discount price, or sometimes the dealer or wholesale price. These should be used together to establish a high-low range for actual prices.

SYSTEM	MANUFACTURER	DESCRIPTION/IDENTIFICATION	LIST	DISCOUNT
Apple ///	Apple	A3B0001 - OEM Prototype Card	45.00	35.00
Apple ///	Apple	A3B0002 - Universal Parallel	225.00	140.00
Apple ///	Apple	A3D0002 - VisiCalc ///	250.00	165.00
Apple ///	Apple	A3D0003 - Mail List Manager	150.00	95.00
Apple ///	Apple	A3D0004 - Business Basic	125.00	80.00
Apple ///	Apple	A3D0005 - Pascal	250.00	162.00
Apple ///	Apple	A3D0009 - System Software	250.00	165.00
Apple ///	Apple	A3G0003 - Extended Warranty	395.00	275.00
Apple ///	Apple	A3G0005 - Profile Extended Warr	385.00	249.00
Apple ///	Apple	A3M0001 - Silentype Printer	350.00	234.00
Apple ///	Apple	A3M0004 - Disk ///	495.00	356.00
Apple ///	Apple	A3M0006 - Monitor /// 12" b/w	320.00	235.00
Apple ///	Apple	A3M0009 - Vinyl Carring Case	75.00	52.00
Apple ///	Apple	A3M0018 - 256K Memory Upgrade	800.00	
Apple ///	Apple	A3M0039 - Monitor /// 12" grn	320.00	235.00
Apple ///	Apple	A3M0305 - Profile Disk Drive	3499.00	2431.00
Apple ///	Apple	A3S0001 - Info Analyst	375.00	245.00
Apple ///	Apple	A3S1028 - 128K Computer	3495.00	2430.00
Apple ///	Apple	A3Z0001 - Mail List Traning Pak	20.00	
Apple ///	Apple	A3Z0002 - VisiCalc Training Pak	20.00	
Apple ///	Apple	C3B0001 - Apple Writer ///	225.00	146.00
Apple ///	Apple	C3B0002 - Business Graphics	175.00	113.00
Apple ///	Apple	C3B0003 - Access ///	150.00	97.00
Apple ///	Apple	C3B0004 - Script ///	125.00	81.00
Apple ///	Apple	C3Z0001 - Apple Writer Training	20.00	
Apple ///	Apple	C3Z0002 - Business Graphic Pak	20.00	

Computer Arithmetic

Computers are very good at adding and subtracting, as long as they get their own way about doing it. Their ways are not our ways. At times, as when 2 + 2 equals 3.99999999, these overstuffed adding machines seem exceedingly dumb.

This is the wrong approach. Computers have their own culture and need to be understood. A person can use a higher-level language on a computer for years and never be really bothered by how the computer does arithmetic, just as someone may speak to someone who speaks near-perfect English and never be bothered by their rare mistakes. True understanding of the computer, however, takes more work, including a look at the binary number system.

[Binary Numbers]. The simplest type of binary number is the unsigned integer. On microcomputers, unsigned integers will typically be 8, 16, or perhaps 32 bits long, giving them maximum values of 255, 65535, or 4,294,967,295 respectively. Bits are numbered from right to left, starting with 0 and on up. An 8-bit binary number might look like:

B7	B6	B5	B4	B3	B2	B1	B0
1	0	0	0	1	0	0	1

This number is 137 in decimal, since it is:

$$2^7 (128) + 2^3 (8) + 2^0 (1) = 137.$$

Likewise, 16 bit numbers are lettered B15 (leftmost) to B0, and so on.

[Negative Integers]. Representing negative numbers presents some minor problems on the computer. A first approach is to use the highest order bit (bit 7 in the case of an 8-bit value), and use the following rule: if bit 7 is 1, the number is negative; if 0, it is positive. Note that this effectively restricts the absolute value of numbers that can be represented to 127. Use of negative numbers always causes the loss of one order of magnitude, since the sign information takes up one binary bit. The number above would be -9 if this convention were being used.

Another technique of representing negative numbers is called the one's complement. The one's complement is formed by inverting the bits in the positive number. Thus, for the number 0110 0111, the one's complement is:

1001 1000

One's complement representation has some advantages over the signed binary representation, but is still not good enough. A third method of representing negative integers turns out to be best. Two's complement representation is a hybrid of the other two methods. In two's complement, as in signed binary, the leftmost bit of a positive number is 0. A negative number, however, is formed by taking the one's complement, then adding 1. Thus the two's complement of –3 is:

```
0000 0011        positive 3
1111 1100        one's complement
+0000 0001       plus 1
---- ----
1111 1101        two's complement
```

The great advantage of two's complement representation for microcomputers is that subtraction becomes a form of addition and can be accomplished with the same circuitry. Consider the following examples:

```
0000 0100        +4
1111 1110        -2
---- ----
0000 0010        +2

0000 0010        +2
1111 1100        -4
---- ----
1111 1110        -2
```

The maximum positive number that can be represented in two's complement is 0111 1111, or +127, while the largest negative number is –128:

```
0111 1111        +127
  ...
0000 0010        +2
0000 0001        +1
0000 0000        +0
1111 1111        -1
1111 1110        -2
  ...
1000 0001        -127
1000 0000        -128
```

[Overflow and Carry Flags]. If two positive numbers are added so that the result is greater than 127, or two negative numbers added so that the result is less than –128, an "overflow" condition is said to have occurred. Overflow is rather easily detected in two's complement notation: it is a carry from bit 6 to bit 7. Overflow will "clobber" the sign bit. Nearly every microprocessor provides hardware to detect overflow, usually called the "V" flag. Thus:

```
0111 1111        +127
0000 0001        +1
---- ----
1000 0000        -0
```

After this instruction, the "V" flag will be set (=1). Good programming practice would test for overflow after additions or subtractions where it might occur.

In the course of two's complement addition/subtraction, a carry often takes place from bit 7 out of the 8-bit range of the register. Unlike overflow, which if meaningful indicates an error, these carries are "good". They can be either ignored or used in multibyte arithmetic. For 16-bit numbers, bit 8 in the low-order byte is a data bit, not the sign bit, which is B15:

        1000 1100 0001 0000   a negative 16-bit number in 2's complement

Carry flags are usually called the C flag. When arithmetic is done between bytes on 8-bit computers, or between words on 16-bit computers, the carry flag "carries" the result of the operation from one column to another, just as a human might place a mark at the top of the column in decimal addition. Two 16-bit numbers are added as follows on the 6502 8-bit processor:

```
        CLD                     ; BINARY ARITHMETIC
        CLC                     ; CLEAR CARRY
        LDA     LOWA            ; LOAD ACCUMULATOR
        ADC     LOWB            ; ADD AND GENERATE CARRY
        STA     LOWC            ;  IF ANY, STORE RESULT
        LDA     HIGHA           ; LOAD 2ND BYTE, ADD WITH OLD
        ADC     HIGHB           ; CARRY GOES INTO HIGH WORD
        STA     HIGHC           ; AND STORE RESULT
```

Note that overflow means nothing in the low byte addition, but it means that the result has exceeded some 32,000 if it happens in the second addition.

Subtraction across byte boundaries has a slight twist. Most processors have a subtract operation, which does subtraction as described above, by forming the one's complement, and adding 1 to form the two's complement, then adding. However, in the subtraction operation, the processor usually complements the carry flag, so it can be used as a "borrow" in multibyte operations. Consider the following 16-bit subtraction, C=A-B:

        A = 0000 1000 0000 0001 = 2049
        B = 0000 0010 0000 0101 = 517

        C = 0000 0101 1111 1100   1532

The 6502 code required to do this correctly is:

```
            CLD                     ; BINARY ARITHMETIC
    (1)     SEC                     ; SET CARRY FLAG = 1
    (2)     LDA     LOWA
    (3)     SBC     LOWB
    (4)     STA     LOWC
    (5)     LDA     HIGHA
    (6)     SBC     HIGHB
            STA     HIGHC
```

At each step, the contents of the carry flag, the A register, and an intermediate adder in the microprocessor are:

    CARRY   A-REG   ADDER

```
(1)   1       XXXXXXXX       XXXXXXXX       SET CARRY FLAG SET TO 1
(2)   1       00000001       XXXXXXXX       FETCH LOW BYTE OF A

(3)   1       00000001         00000101     FETCH B
      1       00000001       V 11111010     FORM 1'S COMPLEMENT OF B
      1                      + 00000001
      1                      = 11111011     2'S COMPLEMENT OF B
      1                      + 00000001     NOW ADD A NOTE NO CARRY
      1                      = 11111100     INTERMEDIATE RESULT = A - B
      1                      - 00000000     SUB COMPLEMENT OF OLD CARRY
      0       11111100       = 11111100     CARRY FLAG NOW = 0

(4)           11111100       XXXXXXXX       STORE LOW BYTE OF RESULT

(5)   0       00001000       XXXXXXXX       LOAD A REGISTER

(6)   0       00001000         00000010     GET HIGH B
      0       00001000       V 11111101     FORM 1'S COMPLEMENT
      0       00001000       + 00000001     +1 FOR 2'S COMPLEMENT
      0       00001000       = 11111110     2'S COMPLEMENT
      0       00001000       + 00001000     PLUS A
      0       00001000       = 00000110     INTERMEDIATE RESULT
      0       00001000       - 00000001     SUB COMPLEMENT OF CARRY FLAG
      1       00000101       = 00000101     FINAL RESULT

(7)   1       00000101       XXXXXXXX       STORE HIGH BYTE OF RESULT
```

As with addition, multibyte subtraction can be extended over 3, 4, or any number of bytes, as long as carry operations are used correctly. One major advantage of 16-bit and larger microprocessors, however, is that integer addition and subtraction can take place between registers of the processor, without the need for repeated memory access. The Z-80 can perform 16-bit addition and subtraction between registers; the Motorola MC68000 can perform 32-bit addition and subtraction between registers.

[BCD Arithmetic]. Computers have problems representing fractions and, in particular, amounts of money. Many fractions are difficult to represent in decimal form. Two-thirds, 2/3, is 0.6666... decimal, and there are of course infinitely many other examples. It is equally difficult to represent fractions using binary numbers.

This problem manifests itself in penny-ante ways - namely when dollar and cents amounts are off, frustratingly, by a single cent and cannot be corrected. One solution to the problem, common with pocket calculators, is to implicitly multiply all dollar amounts by 100, and just use integers. Unfortunately, most computers use 16-bit words, with negative numbers represented in two's complement. Since the largest positive number that can be stored under this convention is 32767, interpreting this as cents gives a maximum range of $327.67 - a very low budget solution.

In general, for accounting, a decimal representation of numbers is desired. Over the years, circuitry has been added to computers to allow them to use binary coded decimal, or BCD, a kind of half-way compromise between the computer world and the human world. In BCD, each decimal digit takes 4 bits, or a "nibble" (1/2 of a byte):

```
0000        0
0001        1
0010        2
0011        3
0100        4
0101        5
0110        6
0111        7
1000        8
1001        9
```

BCD numbers are strings of these nibbles, usually packed two per byte. The North Star, whose BASIC works with BCD decimals, offers precision from 8 to 14 decimal digits. Note, however, that all bits of the nibble are needed for each BCD digit; there is no free space. Consequently, most BCD numbers require an extra byte for the sign. North Star's 8-digit BCD BASIC uses 5 bytes per number, while its 14 digit precision BASIC takes 8 bytes per number. A typical BCD number in memory might look like:

```
sign byte    6     6     4     0     9     8     2     3
SSSS SSSS  0110  0110  0100  0000  1001  1000  0010  0011
```

The problem now is how to add and subtract this stuff. Clearly, binary addition won't work: 1000 (8) plus 0111 (7) will equal 1111, not 0001 0101 (15).

Fortunately, most microprocessors have special BCD instructions. The algorithm for BCD addition is relatively simple: if the result of adding two binary nibbles is greater than 9, add another 6. Thus 1000 + 0111 + 0110 does in fact equal 0001 0101. Carries out of a byte containing 2 BCD digits work as they do in multibyte addition. A "carry" between the low-order nibble and the high-order nibble is called a half-carry and can be tested on some processors like the Z-80 but not on the 6502. The Z-80, however, requires a two instruction group for decimal addition. If the A and B registers in the Z-80 contain BCD digits (4 total, 2 in each), the following instruction adds them properly:

```
ADD     A,B          ; ADD W/O CARRY
DAA                  ; DECIMAL ADJUST
```

To add multibyte BCD numbers, the ADC (add with carry) should be used on subsequent bytes. The Z-80 DAA instruction works by the following algorithm if the last operation was addition:

```
if a half carry, add 6 to low BCD digit
if low digit>1001, add 6 to it
if a full carry, add 6 to high BCD digit
if high digit>1001, add 6 to it
```

BCD subtraction requires the formation of the ten's complement, which is formed by taking the nine's complement and adding 1. Fortunately, most microprocessors have automatic BCD subtraction. To subtract on the 6502:

```
SED                  ; SET DECIMAL MODE
```

```
              SEC                              ; SET CARRY
              LDA      BCD1                    ; LOAD A BCD BYTE
              SBC      BCD2                    ; SUBTRACT ANOTHER
              STA      ANSWER                  ; AND STORE ANSWER
```

On the Z-80, the DAA instruction also works for subtraction of BCD numbers. If the last operation was a subtraction, DAA uses the following algorithm:

    if half-carry, subtract 6 from low bcd digit
    if carry, subtract 6 from high bcd digit
    if both, subtract 6 from both bcd positions

[ASCII numbers]. Arithmetic is sometimes done directly on ASCII digits, and some newer processors, like the Intel 8086, have instructions facilitating it. However, ASCII strings are usually converted into binary or BCD before any arithmetic is done to them. Note, however, that ASCII was carefully designed to allow comparisons to work between numbers. The "collating" sequence established by the ASCII codes can be used to sort fixed field punch card images: "blank" collates before any digit (including 0), and so on.

The following Z-80 routines are useful output conversion routines. AHEX translates a byte into two ASCII characters 0 to F. BTOD translates a 16-bit binary number to a 5-digit string of ASCII digits. Suppression of initial 0s can be added without too much trouble to improve the look of the output:

```
;
; BHEX
;
; SUBROUTINE TO CONVERT BINARY TO HEX
;
;          called with a hex byte in C
;          calls COUT output routine
;            with ASCII hex digit in A-reg
;
BINHEX   LD       A,0F0H            ; MASK FOR LEFT PART
         AND      C
         RRCA                       ; SHIFT OVER
         RRCA
         RRCA
         RRCA
         CALL     CVERT
         CALL     COUT
;
         LD       A,0FH             ; MASK FOR RIGHT PART
         AND      C
         CALL     CVERT
         CALL     COUT
         RET
;
CVERT    ADD      A,30H             ; CONVERT 0-15
         CP       3AH               ; UNDER 10? (A)
         JP       M,LAB1
         ADD      A,7
LAB1     RET
```

```
;
; BTOD - CONVERTS A 16-BIT BINARY NUMBER
;         TO A 5 DIGIT ASCII DECIMAL NUMBER
;
; CALLED WITH BINARY NUMBER IN HL
; CALLS ROUTINE WOUT 5 TIMES WITH ASCII CHARACTERS
;         WOUT CAN BE CONSOLE OUTPUT, ETC.
;
BTOD    PUSH    AF
        PUSH    BC
        PUSH    DE
        PUSH    HL
        LD      IY,P10TAB        ; PT TO TALE
        LD      B,5
LAB1    XOR     A
        LD      D,(IY+1)
        LD      E,(IY+0)
;
LAB2    OR      A
        SBC     HL,DE
        JR      C,LAB3
        INC     A
        JR      LAB2
;
LAB3    ADD     HL,DE
        ADD     A,30H
        CALL    WOUT
        INC     IY
        INC     IY
        DJNZ    LAB1
        POP     HL
        POP     DE
        POP     BC
        POP     AF
        RET
;
P10TAB  .WORD   10000
        .WORD   1000
        .WORD   100
        .WORD   10
        .WORD   1
```

[Floating Point Arithmetic]. Floating point arithmetic is similar to what is called scientific notation in high school chemistry and physics. The basic concept behind scientific notation is that every number can be expressed as a power of ten. Thus if we use the ASCII symbol "^" (which prints on some teletypes as an up arrow) to indicate "to the power of," the number twenty is:

$$2 \times 10\text{^}1, \text{ that is, } 2 \times 10 = 20$$

and 200 is:

$$2 \times 10\text{^}2, \text{ that is, } 2 \times 100 = 200$$

and 2000 is:

                    2 x 10^3, that is, 2 x 1000 = 2000

The number 234 is 2.34 x 10^2, which is equivalent to 0.234 x 10^3.

[The IEEE Floating-Point Standard].   The IEEE has before it a proposed
standard for floating point numbers. The base reference for this standard as
of this writing is "Proposed Standard for Binary Floating-Point Arithmetic"
(Draft 8.0 of IEEE Task P754). Note that the terminology of this proposed
standard differs in several respects from common usage; for example, the
"main" part of the number, often called the mantissa, is called the
significand.

A floating point number is made up of three parts:

        1) a sign, which tells whether the number is positive or negative;
        2) the significand, being the "meat" of the number;
    and 3) the exponent, which gives the power of two (or ten) to which
              the significand must be raised.

The exponents can be positive or negative; this allows floating point numbers
to range, say, from 10^125 (very big) to 10^-125 (very small). However, for
purposes of computer storage, exponents are usually "biased" by adding a fixed
binary amount. In single precision binary floating point, the biased exponent
equals the unbiased exponent plus 127. This allows the exponent to be stored
as a "positive" number.

The significand in binary floating point has two components: a number to the
"left" of the binary decimal point (notice the contradiction of that term),
which, in a normalized number is always "1", and a fraction to the right of
the binary decimal point:

                    1.10101011001101010101000

The storage requirements for such numbers are: 1 bit for the sign (+ is 0, -
is 1); 8 bits for the exponent; and 24 bits for the significand. Note,
however, that if numbers are always normalized, the leading "1" of the
significand can be assumed.   Thus a 24-bit significant can be packed tightly
into four 8-bit bytes:

                    byte 3   byte 2   byte 1   byte 0
                   |SEEEEEEE|ESSSSSSS|SSSSSSSS|SSSSSSSS|
        bit number: 31   23   0

24 binary digits gives slightly better than 7 significant decimal digits of
precision. This is roughly the precision of the DEC PDP-11 or IBM 370 short
"real" number formats in FORTRAN.

[Floating Point Chips]. Several specialized chips, notably the Advanced Micro
Devices (AMD) 9511 and the Intel 8087, perform floating point operations at
high speed. California Computer Systems makes a floating point board using
the AMD 9511 for the Apple II; the Intel chip can be plugged into the IBM PC.

[The AMD 9511]. Floating point processors are typically programmed using a
stack and perform their operations between elements of their stack. The AMD

9511 has an internal stack that is a total of 16 bytes in size. Since the format of numbers can vary in the 9511, it is up to the programmer to keep track of whether the stack is divided into 16-bit integers, 32-bit integers, or 32-bit floating point numbers. The floating point format of the 9511 looks like:

```
SM SE E5 E4 E3 E2 E2 E0 M23 M22 ... M00
31 30 29 28 27 26 25 24  23  22  ...  00
```

The top of the 9511's internal stack is referred to as TOS; the next operand of the stack is called NOS. Thus the stack can be pictured as:

```
TOS --->   B8  B7  B6  B5
NOS --->   B4  B3  B2  B1
           --  --  --  --
           --  --  --  --
```

To use the 9511, data bytes must be pushed into its stack in the order shown. An alternative arrangement is as eight 2-byte operands:

```
TOS ---->      B4 B3
NOS ---->      B2 B1
               -- --
               -- --
               -- --
               -- --
               -- --
               -- --
```

Once the stack has been loaded up, the following commands can be used. These treat the stack as 16-bit integers:

```
SADD    add TOS to NOS; result in NOS; pop stack
SSUB    subtract TOS from NOS; result in NOS; pop stack
SMUL    multiply NOS by TOS; lower 16 bits in NOS; pop
SMUU    multiply NOS by TOS; upper 16 bits in NOS; pop
SDIV    divide NOS by TOS; result in NOS; pop
```

These treat the stack as two 32-bit integers but are otherwise the same:

```
DDAD    add TOS to NOS; result to NOS; pop
DSUB    subtract TOS from NOS; result to NOS; pop
DMUL    multiply NOS by TOS; lower 32 in NOS; pop
DMUU    multiply NOS by TOS; upper 32 in NOS; pop
DDIV    divide NOS by TOS; result in NOS; pop
```

These treat the stack as 32-bit floating point numbers:

```
FADD    add TOS to NOS; result to NOS; pop
FSUB    subtract TOS from NOS; result to NOS; pop
FMUL    multiply NOS by TOS; result to NOS; pop
FDIV    divide NOS by TOS; result to NOS; pop
```

The following are called derived functions; they use the lower part of the stack as scratch space, and leave only the TOS valid when finished:

```
SQRT      square root of TOS
SIN       sine of TOS
COS       cos of TOS
TAN       tangent of TOS
ASIN      inverse sine of TOS
ACOS      inverse cosine of TOS
ATAN      arctangent of TOS
LOG       common log of TOS
LN        natural log of TOS
EXP       e to the power of TOS
PWR       NOS to the power of TOS; result in NOS; pop
```

A number of data conversion commands are also available:

```
NOP       no operation
FIXS      convert TOS from FP to SP
FIXD      convert TOS from FP to DP
FLTS      convert TOS from SP to FP
FLTD      convert TOS from DP to FP
CHSS      change sign of SP operand to TOS
CHSD      change sign of DP operand to TOS
CHSF      change sign of FP operand to TOS
PTOS      push SP operand on TOS to NOS
PTOD      push DP operand on TOS to NOS
PTOF      push FP operand on TOS to NOS
POPS      pop SP operand from TOS; NOS becomes TOS
POPD      pop DP operand from TOS; NOS becomes TOS
POPF      pop FP operand from TOS; NOS becomes TOS
XCHS      exchange SP operands TOS and NOS
XCHD      exchange DP operands TOS and NOS
XCHF      exchange FP operands TOS and NOS
PUPI      push FP constant PI (3.1459...) to TOS; TOS to NOS
```

Several companies have produced software to take advantage of the AMD 9511 board for the Apple II. Applied Analytics sells a version of FORTH, called microSPEED, that uses the CCS AMD 9511 board (a functional copy of which Applied Analytics now makes on its own). The Computer Station (St. Louis, MO) sells a Pascal unit that patches AMD 9511 routines into the Apple TRANSCEND unit.

[The Intel 8087]. The Intel 8087 Numeric Data Processor, like the AMD 9511, is a specialized chip that is its own processor. The 8087 can operate currently with the Intel 8086 or 8088 processors, thereby offering parallel capability.

The 8087, like the AMD 9511, has stack operations on 32-bit floating point numbers. The following are the arithmetic operations of the 8087:

```
FADD      add real
FADDP     add real and pop
FIADD     integer add
FSUB      subtract real
FSUBP     subtract real and pop
FISUB     integer subtract
FSUBR     subtract real reversed
```

```
FSUBRP   subtract real reversed and pop
FISUBR   subtract integer reversed

FMUL     multiply real
FMULP    multiply real and pop
FIMUL    integer multiply

FDIV     divide real
FDIVP    divide real and pop
FIDIV    integer divide
FDIVR    divide real reversed
FDIVRP   divide real reversed and pop
FIDIVR   integer divide reversed

FSQRT    square root
FSCALE   scale
FPREM    partial remainder
FRNDINT  round to integer
FXTRACT  extract exponent and significand
FABS     absolute value
FCHS     change sign

TPTAN    partial tangent
TPATAN   partial arctangent
F2XM1    2^x-1
FYL2X    Y*log2 of x
FYL2XP1  Y*log2 of (X+1)
```

The 8087 also has instructions for loading common floating point constants:

```
FLDZ     load 0.0
FLD1     load +1.0
FLDPI    load pi
FLDL2T   load log 2 of 10
FLDL2E   load log 2 of e
FLDLG2   load log 10 of 2
FLDLN2   load log e of 2
```

The 8087 can perform floating point operations about 100 times faster than a 8086 performing the same operations with software.

[The 8087 for the IBM PC].   In mid-1982, several outfits announced the availability of 8087 chips and software for the IBM PC. South Coast Data Systems, of Costa Mesa, CA, announced a matched set of chips (a new 8088 processor along with the 8087 chip) for $450. Intel claims matched chips are required to prevent problems with synchronization. The 8087 alone costs $225 in quantity 1 from Intel in mid-1982. Microware (PO Box 79, Kingston, MA 02364, 617-746-7341) offers a $50 software package and instructions for installing a 8087 on the PC.

Artificial Intelligence

Artificial Intelligence (AI) is suddenly back in fashion. A research area of much interest in the 1960s, AI perhaps promised too much too soon and fell into disregard in the 1970s, with work continuing at only a few dedicated universities. Since 1980, however, AI is back in. Venture capitalists seem willing to pour millions into a field where, as in genetic engineering, tangible commercial products are possibly years away.

In the 1950s, AI developed as a field where big, clumsy computers were trained to do things like humans not because anyone thought they could do them better but primarily to try to understand the similarities and differences between the way computers do things and the way people do. In a sense, then, AI was always more theoretical and practical. The projects that tried to be practical - in particular, efforts at fully automatic machine translation from Russian to English - failed badly because computer scientists underestimated just how smart people are.

In the 1970s, some people pronounced AI to be impossible, a dead field. By the end of the decade, however, the reports of AI's death began to look premature. AI has always required mainframe computer power. The development of the micromainframe, more than anything else, has given AI research a new lease on life. In fact, rather than being a kind of sideshow of the computer industry (walking, talking, chess-playing computers), AI techniques are indicated as being fundamental in the next generation of computers, the so-called "5G" machines.

[Post von Neumannn computers]. Since the late 1940s, the basic principles of computer design have stayed static, resting on what is called the von Neumann architecture:

* a single computer that is processor, communications device, and memory;

* a linear organization of memory cells;

* a one-level address space of memory cells;

* simple operations on simple operands;

* sequential, centralized control of computation;

* restricted input/output capacity.

Although rapid improvements in chip technology have made possible von Neumann machines that are smaller, faster, and cheaper than before, a nagging question for many has been whether VLSI might eventually make the von Neumann architecture entirely obsolete. In 1979, the Japanese ministry of economic planning, MITI, launched a study of future computing, and 2 years later it produced a plan to develop, by the 1990s, so-called "fifth generation" computers (5G machines).

The Japanese project, which began in April 1982, has as its goals the development of machines that can process natural languages; that can handle uncoded and nonnumerical data like images, speech, graphics, and documents; that can learn and infer on the basis of expert knowledge; and that are highly interactive with their human masters.

To accomplish these tasks, a new architecture of non-von Neumann "data flow" machines is required. A data flow machine operates in parallel in a network, with objects passed from one processor node in the network to another. With VLSI techniques, multiple processors and large-scale memories need not cost a great deal of money. Rather than have their CPU power measured in operations per second (a measurement that itself assumes a centralized von Neumann machine), the Japanese prefer to measure performance in logical inferences per second, or LIPS, about the equivalent of 100-1000 conventional instructions.

["ELIZA"]. One of the most interesting experiments in artificial intelligence was the ELIZA program developed by Joseph Weizenbaum at MIT between 1964 and 1966. Weizenbaum has since written an important book in artificial intelligence, Computer Power and Human Reason, published in 1976 by W.H. Freeman & Company, San Francisco.

ELIZA imitated a Rogerian therapist, meaning that it simply "turned around" statements received from the patient. A sample dialogue with Eliza:

User:	Men are all alike.
ELIZA:	In what way?
User:	They're always bugging us about something or other.
ELIZA:	Can you think of a specific example?
User:	Well, my boyfriend made me come here.
ELIZA:	Your boyfriend made you come here.
User:	He says I'm depressed much of the time.
ELIZA:	I'm sorry to hear you are depressed.
User:	It's true. I am unhappy.

There is a story, unconfirmed, that an unwitting user of a MIT time-sharing computer got ELIZA on the line and thought that the program was a person giving him a hard time - in which case, it would be an example of a computer passing the Turing test.

Several points need to be made about ELIZA. First, it is a relatively simple verbal game, whose rules become obvious fairly quickly. ELIZA's success may say more in the negative about psychotherapy than in the positive about computers. Second, much progress in the parsing of natural language has been made since the time ELIZA was written, meaning that programs more sophisticated than ELIZA are certainly possible. In general, these programs, to pass beyond the point of being merely syntactic games, require computer models of a real universe to give them semantic understanding.

[Expert Systems]. Expert systems have been one of the first commercially successful products of AI research. An expert computer is like a human expert and, in fact, is usually created by carefully tracking the reasoning and knowledge needed by a real, live, human expert. In that way, computer expert systems are nothing more than computer codifications of what human experts know. The difference between a human expert and a computer expert is that the computer expert doesn't forget and, more importantly, may possess the knowledge of several human experts.

"Prospector", an expert system developed at SRI, asks a number of complex questions about a region's geology, with the questions becoming more focused by Prospector's ability to eliminate unpromising branches, just as a computer chess program searches ahead only on promising "trees". In 1981, Prospector correctly predicted the presence of molybdenum deposits in an area of Washington state. Other expert programs imitate medical specialists, including "Mycin", which diagnoses infectious diseases, and "Puff", which diagnoses lung problems. Doctors for computers are also in existence: "Dart", an IBM program, diagnoses sick computers and suggests repairs.

[Natural Language]. Computers have a great deal of difficulty with the ambiguities of natural language. In the early 1960s, it was thought that knowledge of language syntax and grammar would be adequate for computers to understand language. Now it is generally held that for a computer to be able to resolve ambiguities in natural language, it also needs to know "semantics", that is, to have an internal model of a world.

In general, this had meant that computers can understand natural language only in well-ordered, highly structured universes. In a block program at MIT, the locations of blocks in a room are stored inside the computer as a geometric model. Using its knowledge of the room, the computer can answer such sentences as "Where is the square block?" The LADDER system developed at SRI for the US Navy answers questions like, "What submarines are in the Mediterranean?" The LADDER program uses the InterLISP spelling corrector, a necessity for natural language programs that are to be used by imperfect humans.

[AI Firms]. Starting about 1980, AI research began coming out of the academic closet. Although they are not as sensational an offering as genetic engineering, AI firms have been very successful in attracting venture capital financing, despite the fact that commercial AI products are in most cases years away. These firms include:

   Artificial Intelligence Corp., of Waltham, MA (AI Inc.) is one
      of the first AI firms. It was founded by Larry Harris, a
      former Dartmouth professor. AI has venture capital from TA
      Associates of Boston and sells its "Intellect" package, an
      English language frontend for database managers, at
      $50,000-70,000 apiece.

   Cognitive Systems Inc. is the Yale to AI's Harvard. Founded by
      Roger Schank, Cognitive Systems is specializing in natural
      language software.

   Computer Thought, Inc. was founded in September 1981 by two
      former Texas Instruments scientists; Computer Thought is
      concentrating in CAI.

IntelliGenetics, Inc. is a Palo Alto firm started in 1980. IntelliGenetics is a venture capital fundraiser's dream; it sells AI expert programs in the area of genesplicing.

LISP Machines, Inc., of Culver City, CA, is a computer company that sells exactly that - computers specialized to run LISP, the favored language of AI research. A model introduced in mid-1982 carries a $55,000 price tag. Since the company's founding in 1980, 11 have been sold.

Machine Intelligence Corp. is a spin-off of SRI founded in 1979 by Charles Rosen. MIC has taken some of SRI's robot vision work to industry in commercial assembly line products. MIC had annual sales in 1981 of $3 million.

Symbolics, Inc. also sells computers designed especially for AI work, with approximately 60 machines shipped in 1982. Symbolics intends to sell expert systems.

Teknowledge, Inc. is a Palo Alto firm now primarily a consulting firm. Teknowledge will market its own expert systems in 1983.

Start-up, venture-capital funded firms are not, of course, the only ones doing interesting work in AI. Most academic work in AI takes place at MIT, Carnegie-Mellon, and Stanford, funded in the main by DARPA, the Defense Advanced Research Projects Agency, which does not require immediate payoff on its sponsored research. Recently, however, several computer firms, including Digital, Hewlett-Packard, and Schlumberger (Fairchild Instruments), have established AI laboratories, all with the idea of generating commercial products in the relatively near future.

ASCII

Computers store textual information as numbers. To most computers, the letter "A" is the number 65. The letter "B" is 66, and capital "C" is 67. This looks like the kind of code that might be used by children and is precisely that, a code. Far from being secret, however, the codes used by computers are highly publicized in an effort to allow programs and data to be exchanged between machines.

For all but large IBM computers, the standard code of information is the ASCII code, which stands for the American Standard Code for Information Interchange, and is pronounced "ass-key". The ASCII code assigns a number between 0 and 127 to the letters of the Roman alphabet, both upper- and lower-case, and to a set of special symbols.

There are, then, a total of 128 ASCII codes, meaning that any ASCII code can be represented by 7 binary bits. The codes from 32 to 127 decimal (96 in all) are called the "printable" ASCII codes. All the printable codes (except DEL, 127, which stands for delete), when transmitted to a CRT or printer, will produce a visible character. Thus a "65" sent to a printer will print an "A", and so on. On most computers the CHR function in BASIC will show the characters printed in ASCII set:

```
PRINT CHR$(65)     action: computer prints "A"
PRINT CHR$(66)             computer prints "B"
PRINT CHR$(33)             computer prints "!"
PRINT CHR$(109)            computer prints "m"
PRINT CHR$(125)            computer prints "{"
PRINT CHR$(32)             computer prints " "
```

Note that printing a "space", code 32, counts as a character, even though nothing is actually typed on paper or displayed on the screen. The following BASIC program will display a computer's character set:

```
10 FOR I = 32 TO 126
20 PRINT CHR$(I)
30 NEXT I
```

Many computers (for example, the Apple II) don't display lower-case letters and some of the "special" math symbols in the ASCII set.

The ASCII codes between 0 and 31 decimal are called control codes, because they usually cause various control functions to happen when sent to a device like a printer or CRT. Code 7, or BEL, will cause a "beep" to sound on most terminals and printers (PRINT CHR$(7) will work from BASIC). ASCII code 13, carriage return (CR) is among the most frequently used control codes. It is usually sent to a video display or printer in combination with a line feed (LF), ASCII 10, at the end of each printed or displayed line. The following table gives the 32 ASCII control codes and their official names. For all but the most common codes like CR, LF, and FF, however, what each code does when sent to a printer or terminal device varies from one manufacturer to another:

```
0  NUL - Null.  Used as a "filler", often
                while waiting for a carriage
                to return on slow printing
                devices.  Ignored and causes
                no printing or display.
1  SOH - Start of Heading.  Used as the
                first character of a heading
                in an information transmission.
2  STX - Start of Text. Used both to terminate
                a heading and to signal the start
                of the text.
3  EXT - End of Text.  Signals the end
                of text in a transmission, often
                used to ask a device to send an
                ACK when its buffer is clear.
4  EOT - End Of Transmission.  On time-sharing
                systems, an EOT sent by
                a terminal usually logs it off.
5  ENQ - Enquiry.  Used by a host computer to ask
                a terminal or remote station for
                identification.
```

```
 6  ACK - Acknowledge.  Used by a remote station
                to say "yes" to the host.
 7  BEL - Bell.  Sounds a bell on Teletype-style
                terminals; issues a 880-Hz, 1-second
                tone on video displays.
 8  BS  - Backspace.  Moves cursor back one space on
                video displays, without erasing the
                character there.
 9  HT  - Horizontal tab.  Sets print position
                to a preset tab position.
10  LF  - Line Feed.  Similar to "index"
                on an electric typewriter; moves
                print position down one line. Does
                not return carriage to left margin.
11  VT  - Vertical Tab.  Usually moves a
                printed page form to the next
                already-set vertical tab stop.
12  FF  - Form Feed.  Advances the paper on a
                printer to the next page.  Sometimes
                clears the screen on video terminals
                and leaves the cursor in the upper
                left-hand corner.
13  CR  - Carriage Return.  Moves the print head or
                cursor to the left margin.  Does not
                move it down a line.  Usually used in
                a pair with LF.
14  SO  - Shift Out.  Used, especially with foreign
                language and graphic character sets, to
                "shift out" of the standard ASCII set
                into an alternately defined character
                set.
15  SI  - Shift In. Used when in an alternate set to
                return to the standard ASCII set.
16  DLE - Data Link Escape.  Shift into a
                different set of control codes
                during communications.
17  DC1 - Device Control 1.  A "wild card"
                code otherwise unassigned.
18  DC2 - Device Control 2.  Similar to DC1.
19  DC3 - Device Control 3.  Similar to DC1.
20  DC4 - Device Control 4.  Similar to DC1.
21  NAK - Negative Acknowledge.  Used to say "no"
                to a host computer.  Opposite of ACK.
22  SYN - Synchronous Idle.  Used as a "pad" character
                in certain types of synchronous serial
                transmission.
23  ETB - End of Transmission Block.  Signals end of a
                block sent by host.
24  CAN - Cancel.  Disregard last line of data and return
                to mutually agreed restart point.
25  EM  - End of Medium.  The last character on this
                medium.  Analogous to an "end of file" mark.
26  SUB - Substitute.  Sometimes used as a fill character
                in fixed-length fields; also used to indicate
```

27   ESC - Escape. Often used to break a transmission or to
                     introduce special sequences of control characters.

28   FS   - File Separator. Introduced into ASCII to allow files
                     to be sorted and separated by a character lower
                     than "space" in the collating sequence.

29   GS   - Group Separator. Similar to FS.

30   RS   - Record Separator. Similar to FS.

31   US   - Unit Separator. Lowest order of the
                     four separators, not counting SP.

These 32 control codes are followed by the 96 printable ASCII codes. The following table gives the full 96-character ASCII set and the decimal codes for each character:

The ASCII Character Set

32	space	80	P
33	!	81	Q
34	"	82	R
35	#	83	S
36	$	84	T
37	%	85	U
38	&	86	V
39	'	90	W
40	(	88	X
41	)	89	Y
42	*	90	Z
43	+	91	[
44	,	92	\
45	-	93	]
46	.	94	^
47	/	95	
48	0	96	``
49	1	97	a
50	2	98	b
51	3	99	c
52	4	100	d
53	5	101	e
54	6	102	f
55	7	103	g
56	8	104	h
57	9	105	i
58	:	106	j
59	;	107	k
60	<	108	l
61	=	109	m
62	>	110	n
63	?	111	o
64	@	112	p
65	A	113	q
66	B	114	r
67	C	115	s
68	D	116	t

69	E	117	u
70	F	118	v
71	G	119	w
72	H	120	x
73	I	121	y
74	J	122	z
75	K	123	{
76	L	124	|
77	M	125	}
78	N	126	~
79	O	127	DEL

[International ASCII].   In the standard ASCII set, twelve codes vary with national usage. These twelve are:

Code 35 (#) is one of the two codes reserved for currency symbols.   In the U.K., West Germany, and France, this code is used for the script "L" sign for pounds sterling (British money).   In other countries, the hash mark "#" is printed, but interpreted as kilograms of weight, not pounds of weight, as in the US.   The US is the only country where # ever means "number", as in "#2"; most countries use "No. 2" for this.

Position 36, "$", is the second of the two currency codes. It is usually left as a dollar sign or the international currency sign, the scarab, which looks like a circle with four spikes coming out of it.

Codes 64 (@), 91 ([), 92 (\), and 93 ([) are called the primary national usage codes, and their assignment varies from country to country. The Scandinavian countries use them to complete their alphabets, which have 29 to 30 letters each.   In Japan, the yen symbol, which looks like a crossed Y, occupies the place of the back slash (\).

Codes 123 ({), 124 (|), and 125 (}) are called the secondary national usage positions and are filled with the lower-case codes corresponding to positions 91, 92, and 93.   In Spain, code 92 is a capital N with tilde (~); 124 is a small "n" with tilde.

Codes 94 (^), 96 (`), and 126 (~) are reserved for diacritical marks, which are common in all languages except English.   Code 94 is a circumflex, an accent mark used in French over vowels.   It is not an "up arrow", although many US companies, starting some time ago with Teletype, print it as such. Code 96 is an accent grave in France, or a lower-case accented letter in other countries.   Code 126, the tilde, is a flat overbar in some countries, including Japan, where as the macron it is an important mark in Romanized spellings of Japanese words.

[US Exceptions].   US equipment manufacturers have played fast and loose with the official ASCII characters.   This can cause confusion to those venturing into international waters for the first time.   For example, in the late 1960s, as BASIC became more popular on time-sharing systems, Teletype replaced the circumflex with an "up arrow".   This gave BASIC a single convenient symbol for exponentiation, e.g., "5^2 = 25".

Also note that ASCII does not have a true single quote (').   Rather it has two

accent marks, accent grave (`,96), and accent acute (',39), and double quotes
("). Most American equipment prints the accent acute as a straight up and
down single quote mark. Officially, it should slant - and actually looks
quite stylish as a quote when it does.

[Extending ASCII]. At present, ASCII is a 7-bit code. Since computers use
8-bit bytes, the left-most or high-order bit is either ignored or used as a
parity bit. As equipment and transmission methods improve in reliability,
parity checking has become less common and less necessary. There are various
plans to turn ASCII into an 8-bit code, with 128 more symbols, which would be
graphic symbols and APL-like math symbols. Many printer and microcomputers
already use codes 128-255 decimal for graphic characters.

There is, however, already a mechanism built into ASCII that allows its use
with extended sets of symbols. A computer respecting ASCII conventions can
use nearly all the alphabets of the world. Extension of ASCII is done in two
stages: designation and invocation. Designation tells the terminal device
which set alternative 128-symbol set will be used as the alternate set,
without actually switching in to it. Invocation of the alternate set can then
be done during actual transmission more efficiently.

A character set is designated by the sequence ESC C1 C2, where ESC is the
escape code, 27. C1 tells the terminal device about the C2 code following:

> ! - C2 designates "home" character set
> " - C2 designates alternate control set
> (- C2 designates "home" graphics set
>) - C2 designates alternate graphics set

A number of potential C2 sets have been assigned international codes:

> (- ISO 646 control code set
> A - Scandinavian newspaper control set
> C - IPTC control set
> (- International reference version
> A - UK character set
> B - US character set
> C - NATS characters (Finland, Sweden)
> D - NATS additional set (Finland, Sweden)
> E - NATS characters (Denmark, Norway)
> F - NATS additional set (Denmark, Norway)
> G - Swedish character set
> H - Swedish set for names
> I - JIS Katakana
> J - Japanese Industrial standard Roman
> Y - Italian
> Z - Spanish
> [- Greek
> K - German
> R - French
> U - Latin-Greek
> X - Greek biblographic

Once designated, the alternate set is "invoked" by the shift out and shift in characters. Thus, if Japanese Katakana has been designated, a SO means that the codes that follow are to be treated as Japanese, until a SI code "shifts in" to the home set. The North American Teletext Protocol also makes use of shifting between alternate character and control sets.

Assembly Language

Assembly language programming is one of the most difficult - and one of the most rewarding - things that can be done with a computer. Programming a computer in assembly language is like driving a car with a stick shift. Although it may be easier to drive a car with an automatic transmission - just like it is easier to program a computer in a higher level language - it is less fun. Assembly language gives a programmer perfect control over the computer by a kind of direct connection to its engine, the microprocessor.

That said, assembly language can prove difficult to learn. Like Latin or Greek, it is best learned young. Assembly language errors can be the most frustrating of all: instead of returning an obscure message number that can at least be looked up in a book, the computer simply dies. Assembly language programming takes time and patience - but can be worth it. When finally debugged, a microcomputer can run an assembly language program day in and day out for years, providing the user with a rock-steady feeling of reliability rare in the computer world.

[Learning Assembly Language]. The first step in assembly language programming is to forget about the convenient data structures of BASIC, FORTRAN, and so on. In general, in assembly language programming you are lucky to have integers - everything else must be built up from scratch. These integers, whether 8-bit or 16-bit, will spend much of their time in the registers of the microprocessor in question. On a sheet of paper, the would-be assembly language programmer should start with a diagram of the registers of the microprocessor. The 6502, used in the Apple, Atari, and early Commodore models, has the following registers:

```
A (accumulator)   _ _ _ _ _ _ _ _
X                 _ _ _ _ _ _ _ _
Y                 _ _ _ _ _ _ _ _
P (flag reg)      _ _ _ _ _ _ _ _
PCH               _ _ _ _ _ _ _ _
PCL               _ _ _ _ _ _ _ _
```

Each of the "_" in each of these 8-bit registers is either a 0 or 1. The state of the microprocessor then, is relatively simple. If necessary, any instruction can be exactly simulated by hand to get its result. Consider the 6502 instruction INX, increment X. This function adds one to the X register. If the X register looks like this before the instruction:

```
X              0 1 0 1 1 0 0 0
```

it   will,   without   fail,   look   like   this   afterwards:

Many microprocessor instructions move bytes between the registers and memory. On 8-bit microprocessors, a total of 16 bits is used to specify an absolute address, which ranges from 0 to 65,535 decimal (or 0000 to FFFF hexadecimal). The instruction:

```
          LDA    3
```

takes the 8 bits in memory location 3 and puts them in the A register. The instruction:

```
          STA    4
```

copies the 8 bits in the A register to memory location 4. If these 2 instructions were executed in this order, the contents of memory location 4, at the end, would be identical to those of location 3.

[Addressing Modes]. All microprocessors can compute memory addresses in more sophisticated ways. Indexing a memory address adds the value of a register to an absolute address to come up with the final result. Thus the instruction:

```
          STA    4,X
```

stores the 8 bits in the A-reg into the memory location given by adding 4 and the current value of X. If the X register holds 0, it is the same as the instruction above. But if X contains 1, it stores the value of A into memory location 5; if X contains 2, into memory location 6; and so on. Indexed addressing is often used to implement the arrays of BASIC and FORTRAN.

Another type of addressing, indirect addressing, is used on most machines. In indirect addressing, the address first computed by the microprocessor is not the final destination for the data but merely "points" the microprocessor to another location. Indirect addressing can send the computer anywhere for its data and is a very flexible method of locating data. Finally, indirect and indexing methods can be combined on many microprocessors - yielding even more flexible access.

[Arithmetic and logical operations]. Microprocessor operations usually take place between one register and another, or between a register and memory. Memory-to-memory operations are far less common. Thus, to add two numbers on the 6502, the following instructions must be used:

```
          CLC                     ; CLEAR CARRY
          LDA    NUMBER1
          ADC    NUMBER2
          STA    ANSWER
```

The "clear carry" operation is used because the 6502 always adds in the carry flag (a 1-bit number either 1 or 0) with the result. The carry flag is needed in 16-bit addition on the 6502. Consider adding two 16-bit numbers, N1 and N2, where each number is subdivided into two 8-bit bytes, LOW and HIGH:

```
          CLC
```

```
            LDA     N1LOW
            ADC     N2LOW
            STA     ANSLOW
            LDA     N1HIGH
            ADC     N2HIGH
            STA     ANSHIGH
```

Here the carry flag was "kept around" in case there was a carry out of the low byte addition into the high.

[Branching]. On any microprocessor, a number of individual bits can be tested inside a "flag" register. These flags tell if the result of an instruction was positive, zero, negative, or perhaps overflowed. On the 6502, the P, or flag register, looks like:

7	6	5	4	3	2	1	0
negative	overflow	unused	break	decimal	interrupt	zero	carry
N	V	-	B	D	I	Z	C

A "1" indicates that a condition is true. Thus a "1" in bit 2 of the P register tells that an interrupt has occurred. A "0" in bit 0 tells that there was a carry on the last operation. The CLC operation above always sets this bit to "0".

Bit 1, "Z", of the flag register tells if the result of an operation was zero. A "compare" operation on most microprocessors is like a subtraction of a number from the accumulator but does not actually change the contents of the accumulator; it only sets the flags "as if" a subtraction has been done. To test if two ASCII characters are equal, for example, the following code might be used:

```
            LDA     CHAR1
            CMP     CHAR2
            BEQ     EQUAL
```

The BEQ instruction is like a GOTO that tells the processor to "branch" on the condition of equality, that is, a zero result (Z flag = true = 1). Branch instructions are called jumps on the 8080 and Z-80 microprocessors.

[The Stack]. Stacks are such an important part of assembly language programming on microprocessors that it is impossible to believe that most big computers for years never had them. The stack is a special storage area in RAM memory. On the 6502, the stack uses the second 256 bytes of memory, and grows downs from location 1FF. Since memory on the 6502 is divided into 256-byte units called "pages", the stack is said to reside in page 2. On most other processors the stack can be anywhere in RAM, a feature important in running multiple users on the same machine.

The location of the stack is determined by a stack pointer (SP), which is a register that can be loaded and saved like any other. There are two fundamental operations done with the stack: PUSH and POP. These, like the stack itself, take their name from the operation of a pop-up stack of plates in a diner or restaurant. There, the plates sit on a spring in a circular rack. Newly washed plates are put on top of the stack, pushing the old ones down by their weight. When plates are needed by the waitresses, they are taken off the top, popping the older ones up. A stack is a LIFO affair - last in, 1st out.

On the computer, PUSHing to a stack has the following effect: the contents of the register are transferred to the RAM memory address pointed to by the stack register, and the stack pointer is decremented by one. Such a stack is said to grow down, since it occupies successively lower memory locations. If the stack grows into other needed RAM space, the stack is said to have overflowed, usually a fatal condition.

Note that the logic of the stack requires that the number of PUSHes equal the number of POPs, and that they must balance in reverse order to keep everything straight. Consider the following code used at the beginning of a subroutine in Z-80 assembler:

```
ENTRY   NOP                 ; the entry point
        PUSH    AF          ; save A and Flags
        PUSH    BC
        PUSH    DE
        PUSH    HL
```

This code saves the contents of the registers and the start of the subroutine and allows it to alter them at will. Upon exit of the subroutine, the registers should be restored to their original state, with the following code:

```
        POP     HL          ; restore reg
        POP     DE
        POP     BC
        POP     AF
        RET
```

If subroutines use the stack carefully, they can be made recursive, meaning they can call themselves. Recursion is a powerful programming technique that can be used to produce mathematically elegant solutions to many problems, especially in sorting and list processing.

In recursion the current state of work on a problem is put on hold (by pushing all the relevant data onto the stack) until the problem is solved at a lower level, at which time the computer works backwards up the stack to the main level. Use of the stack to save the state of a computer is very useful in multiprogramming and generally occurs during interrupts.

[Future of Assembly Language]. In general, microprocessors are developing more and more complex sets of assembly language instructions. The 6502, the simplest 8-bit microprocessor, has about 60 instructions. The newer 16-bit microprocessors, like the Intel 8086, Motorola MC68000, and Zilog Z8000, have several hundred each. There is some doubt whether or not programmers - outside a few engineers at the manufacturers - will continue to generate assembly language code for such increasingly complex microprocessors.

The Intel 432, a 32-bit microprocessor, is clearly not intended to be directly programmed by users in assembly language. (Intel does not even publish the assembly language instruction set.) The trend to use "C" as a language for writing operating systems and other near-assembly language code is part of this same movement to substitute hardware processor speed for labor time.

Astronomy and Astrology

At first glance, it may seem unusual to lump together a scientific field like astronomy with an unscientific one like astrology. However, many calculations in the two fields are the same. Both are concerned with the location of the stars and planets at various times, both in an absolute sense and in relation to various spots on earth.

[The Positions of Stars and Planets]. The motions of the planets were first described by Kepler in the early part of the 17th century. Later in that century Newton developed an iterative method that greatly eased the solving of Kepler's equations. Matrix algebra, developed in the 19th century, further simplified their solution.

In general, the following parameters are variable inputs to astrological or astronomy programs:

> date and time (Julian date + decimal fraction of day)
> viewer's latitude (degrees north or south of equator)
> viewer's longitude (degrees east of prime meridian)

In the case of an astrological program, the date and time are often the date and time of birth, and the latitude and longitude the site of birth.

Various base table information is also required to calculate the positions of the stars and planets. In general, the following is required:

> for stars, the right ascension and declination
> for planets, the elements of the elliptical orbits

Other solar satellites, like comets, require orbital elements. Earth satellites, including the moon and artificial satellites, also have orbital elements. The best sources for this table information is the Yale Catalog of Bright Stars and the American Ephemeris and Nautical Almanac.

[Planets]. In the case of planets, the task is usually divided into (1) the calculation of the locations of the planets at the specified time, and (2) calculation of their positions relative to earth.

Planets travel in elliptical orbits, where a focus of the ellipse is always the sun. The major axis of the ellipse is a line drawn the long way through the focus; the minor axis is perpendicular to the major, drawn through the sun. The first part of a solution usually makes computations in the plane of this ellipse.

However, the orbits of the planets are titled with regard to the sun, and the earth's orbit around it. Thus, while the calculation in the plane of the ellipse is two-dimensional, a three-dimensional calculation is needed. The reference point is a line in space drawn between the sun and a point opposite earth at the vernal equinox. This is clearly a line in the plane of the earth's orbit and serves to orient the planet's orbit relative to that of the earth. The second coordinate points north out of the earth's plane (but not directly out of the north pole, since the earth tilts -23.45 degrees on its axis). The final dimension points perpendicular to these two so as to form a "right-hand" coordinate system with the center at the sun.

The following elements describe a planet's orbit:

* INCLINATION is the angle between the plane of the
  planet's ellipse and the plane of the earth's ellipse, called
  the plane of the ecliptic.

* the ASCENDING NODE is the point where the planet's orbit passes
  through the earth's plane from south to north.

* RHO is an angle measured in the plane of the ecliptic, from the
  line between the sun and vernal equinox, to the ascending
  node. W is measured in the plane of the planet's orbit in a
  line from the sun and the ascending node, to the major axis on
  the side of the perihelion (side closest to the sun). These
  two angles can be combined as PERIANGLE.

* the PERIOD is the time required by a planet to make one orbit.

* ECCENTRICITY describes the degree of flatness of an elliptical
  orbit.

With the table of elements and date, a planet's position in a heliocentric system can be found. (The equations and other elements needed are described in Marion's Classical Dynamics of Particles and Systems.)

What follows next for a planet viewing program is a series of coordinate transformations. The following coordinate systems are typically used, in this order: (1) a two-dimensional system with origin at the sun in the plane of the planet's orbit; (2) a heliocentric cartesian system; (3) a geocentric (Earth-centered) ecliptic system, whose axes are parallel to those of the heliocentric system; (4) a geocentric equatorial system (the standard in astronomy), where the x-axis points to the vernal equinox, the y-axis to the north pole, and the z-axis points at a spot on the equator at the right ascension of the winter solstice. This system is derived from (3) by a rotation around the x-axis of 23.45 degrees, the tilt of the earth; and (5) an egocentric (viewer centered) system where the x-axis points south, the y-axis points to the zenith (a spot directly above the viewer), and the z-axis points west.

[Satellite Tracking]. Artificial satellites are just that: man-made versions of moons and planets. The computations required to locate artificial moons are similar to those used in classical astronomy but require special base tables input. Fortunately, the fact that much of the US space effort has been paid for by public funds means that this information is in the public domain.

An organization called SAT TRAK International (c/o Computerland of Colorado Springs, 4543 Templeton Gap Rd., Colorado Springs, CO 80909) sells a set of programs that allow space satellites to be tracked by personal computers. With the proper inputs, the STI programs can calculate look angles for low flying visible satellites, like SEASAT-A or SALUT-6. The programs can also calculate elevation, azimuth, and range information for amateur radio operators who want to use OSCAR 8, the ham relay satellite.

[Orbital Elements]. The orbit of a satellite around the earth can be fully described by a set of six parameters called orbital elements, sometimes called classical elements or the element set of a satellite. These parameters are primarily a set of angles (measured in degrees for the STI programs, not radians) that fix the satellite's orbit in relation to the equator of the earth and to other fixed points in space. The six classical elements are:

Inclination. The inclination of a satellite is the angle, measured counter-clockwise, between the orbital plane of the satellite and the earth's equatorial plane. A recent inclination for the Soviet space station SALUT 6 was 51.628 degrees.

Argument of Perigee. The perigee of a satellite is the point in its orbit where it comes closest to earth. The argument of perigree is the angle between the intersection of the orbital and equatorial planes, and the perigee, which of couse is in the orbital plane. The angle is measured in degrees in the direction of the motion of the satellite. A recent value for SALUT 6 was 333.5086 degrees.

Mean Anomaly. The opposite of the perigee is the apogee, which is the point at which the satellite is farthest from earth. Between the apogee and perigee is a mean position. The mean anomaly is an angle, defined as the angle between the perigee and the mean position. The mean anomaly is measured in the direction of motion of the satellite in the orbital plane. SALUT 6's mean anomaly recently was 26.3498 degrees.

Eccentricity. Satellite orbits are egg-shaped, not circular. Eccentricity is a measure of how much an orbit deviates from a perfect circle (or flattens). SALUT 6's eccentricity is 0.001214.

Right Ascension of Node. The right ascension is an angle measured in the equatorial plane of the earth, between the vernal equinox and the point at which the satellite's orbit crosses the equatorial plane from south to north. Right ascension is measured eastward in the equatorial plane. SALUT 6's right ascension was recently 20.3738 degrees.

Mean Motion. Mean motion is the number of revolutions a satellite makes per day. SALUT 6 recently averaged 15.76871515 revolutions per day.

With these six classical elements, a satellite's orbit can, in theory, be predicated forever. However, in reality, satellites experience some drag from the earth's atomsphere. Drag causes satellite orbits to decay. Decay can be observed and determined empirically, by radar, but can also be predicted. Thus orbital parameters must also be fixed by time.

[Epoch and Decay]. In space talk, an epoch is a specific date and time used as a reference point in discussions of a satellite's orbit. NASA defines it as the YEAR (last two digits only, e.g., "82"), ORDINAL DATE (the number between 1 and 366, allowing for leap year, of the day within a year), and FRACTION (a decimal fraction of a day, so that noon is 0.5, etc.). Several other measures help define the history of a satellite: revolutions at epoch is the number of times the satellite has gone round the earth since it was launched. The period decay rate tells how fast the satellite is slowing down. In technical terms, the period decay rate is the first derivative of the satellite's mean motion and is measured in revolutions per day squared. The decay rate, with proper computations, tells approximately how much life the satellite has left, before it slows to the point at which it falls.

[Getting Satellite Information]. The US National Aeronautics and Space Administration (NASA) publishes, as a public service, regular reports on all satellites in the sky. NASA's "Satellite Situation Report" is an inventory of space junk, listing orbiting items by satellite number (an ascending sequence by launch, now well over 10000) and by national designation, a code based on year and date of launch. This code has the form YY-DDDA, where YY is the year of launch, DDD is the ordinal date in the year, and A is the national code. A copy of this report can be obtained, free, by writing the National Space Science Data Center, Code 202, National Aeronautics and Space Administration, Goddard Space Flight Center, Greenbelt, MD 20771, USA.

When the code numbers of a specific have been determined from the "Satellite Situation Report", its orbital parameters can be obtained from a more frequent publication, the "NASA Prediction Bulletin". A free subscription or copy of the bulletin, usually mailed twice a week, can be obtained by writing to the Operations Center Branch, Code 512, Mission Operations Division, Goddard Space Flight Center, Greenbelt, MD 20771, USA. Care should be taken not to abuse this free service of the US government. Individuals should preferably request information on a small number of satellites, perhaps two or three, that they seriously intend to track.

[SAT TRAK International]. SAT TRAK's programs fall into two categories: those used to maintain a data base on 10 to 50 satellites, and those for computing orbital information from that data base. The data base manager keeps the following information: satellite number, epoch year, epoch day, fraction of day, period of decay, element set number, inclination, right ascension, eccentricity, argument of perigee, mean anomaly, mean motion, and epoch of revolution. Normally, these parameters are obtained for input from NASA publications, although SAT TRAK has a program that allows empirically observed data to be input.

SAT TRAK's analysis program includes POSN, which is given a time period as input, and produces a table of the satellite's latitude, longitude, and altitude. TRAK, a similar program, outputs this information in graphic form on a world map. LOOK calculates look angles for satellites. LOOK requires the latitude, longitude, and altitude of the observer and uses these to calculate when satellites are visible from the observer's location.

Normally, a satellite must be more than 20 degrees above the horizon to be visible, although LOOK allows any minimum elevation to be set (useful for tracking OSCAR, the ham radio satellite, whose signal can be picked up at -5 or -10 degrees of elevation, that is, when it is technically below the visual horizon). A further refinement of LOOK is a calculation of when a satellite is in the earth's shadow; and a calculation of when the satellite is in sun and the observer in shadow, the optimum situation for seeing satellites.

[Astrology]. "Natal" (birthdate) astrological programs are similar to star-mapping programs in that they take a date, time, longitud,e and latitude and calculate the location of the planets at that time.

Where astrological calculations differ from astronomical ones is in the system used to describe the whereabouts of the planets. Astrology divides the 360 degrees of sky into 12 equal houses of 30 degrees each. These divisions are purely symbolic: although they have the same names as actual constellations like Aquarius, Capricorn, and so on, the position of a planet in an astrological house has nothing to do with its location in the starfield of the night sky.

Consequently, although the preliminary calculations for astrology are the same - adjustment of the date and time of birth for daylight time, and so on - this date and time, once calculated, is looked up in an astrological ephemeris. Since these usually give the position of the planets at noon, logarithms are used to interpolate the table. The end result is given in degrees (<30) of a particular astrological house - for example:

                4 degrees 3 minutes Pisces
                17 degrees 54 minutes Taurus

[Microcomputer Astrology Software]. Astrological calculations are difficult to make by hand, and still more difficult to program. One specialized software house, Matrix Software (315 Marion Ave., Big Rapids, MI 49307, 616-796-2483) has a large catalog of astrology software for a variety of computers, including the Apple II, Commodore's VIC-20, Radio Shack Model III, and so on. The Matrix catalog is highly recommended.

Atari

Atari is one of the fastest growing companies in American history. Unlike Apple and a number of other personal computer makers who have flirted with the high-profit business market, Atari has always been firmly committed to the under $1000 home computer - even when all the experts denied that consumers would ever want them. Now, helped by its reputation in both the arcade and home video game field, Atari is enjoying strong consumer sales of its personal computers and has holding its own with rivals Commodore and TI.

[The Company]. Atari was founded in the early 1970s by Noland Bushnell, who invented "Pong," the first arcade video game. Since 1976, Atari has been owned by Warner Communications, a conglomerate that grew out of the old Warner Brothers movie studio.

Atari currently has three divisions: an arcade game unit; the home video game unit; and the personal computer division. Warner does not break out figures for its various subsidiaries, which include the movie company, Marvel Comics, a publishing house, and a news distribution operation; but Atari is believed to be the fastest growing company of its size in US history. According to one estimate, Atari doubled its revenues from 1981 to 1982, from $1 billion to $2 billion.

On December 13, 1982, Atari announced its "1200" home computer, a 64K 6502 machine in a sleek case. The 1200, which should be widely available by mid-1983, is designed to replace both the Atari 400 and 800. In unit sales, Atari's 400 and 800 computers lag behind the less expensive Sinclair ZX-81 and Commodore VIC-20, and in 1982 were passed by the TI 99/4A. The Atari 400 currently lists at $350 and can be found for as little as $270. Atari will have a "600" model, positioned between the 400 and 800 by the end of 1982. In dollar terms, in the consumer computer class, Atari ranks just behind Commodore.

[The Atari Computers]. Atari introduced its "400" and "800" computers in May 1979 at the 4th West Coast Computer Faire. Atari's computers threw much of the industry for a loop. At that time, the prevailing wisdom was that computers had to be sold to small business - in 1979 Commodore changed the name of its "PET" to Commodore Business Machine or CBM. Atari, going against the trend, introduced mchines that were clearly aimed at the home market. Atari's machines were also sneered at by low-budget software developers, since they used ROM packs for programs.

In retrospect, it can be seen that what the designers of the Atari 400/800 did was take the design principles established - but not quite carried through - by the Apple II, and perfect them. The genius of the Apple II was that it was designed with video games in mind: the game paddle ports are, in a peculiar way, its most significant innovation. But the designers of the Apple II missed the mark on who it was who would be playing games; from the point of view of "ergonomics," the Apple II is a computer for adults.

Atari, in improving on the Apple, accepted without question the need for game paddles but strengthened the connectors and moved them to the sides of the computer where children could use them (Bell & Howell, in its modifications to the Apple II, also did this). The Apple II has always suffered from its reliance on floppy disk-based software, both because (1) disks are hard for children to handle, and (2) they can be copied and kill off software development. Atari, in a move that was questioned in 1979, used ROM cartridges for software and put an interlock on the cartridge door, which, in turning off the computer when opened, protects it from electrical abuse.

[Components]. Both of the Atari computers are widely discounted at volume stereo stores and at mass merchandisers like K-Mart. Hence, the "street price" for the Atari varies widely from the official list price. Here, however, are mid-1982 prices for standard Atari 400 and 800 components:

SYSTEM	MANUFACTURER	DESCRIPTION/IDENTIFICATION	LIST	DISCOUNT
Atari		Disk - Crush Crumble Chomp		22.99
Atari		Disk - Invasion Orion		24.95

Atari	Atari	400 Computer 16K	349.00	275.00
Atari	Atari	400 Computer 32K	539.00	
Atari	Atari	400 Computer 48K	639.00	
Atari	Atari	410 Program Recorder	99.95	79.95
Atari	Atari	800 Computer 16K	899.00	666.00
Atari	Atari	800 Computer 32K	909.00	747.00
Atari	Atari	800 Computer 48K	1009.00	777.00
Atari	Atari	810 Disk Drive	599.95	444.00
Atari	Atari	820 Printer (40 col.)	299.95	259.95
Atari	Atari	822 Printer (thermal)	299.00	269.95
Atari	Atari	825 Printer (80 col.)	799.00	595.00
Atari	Atari	830 Modem (=Novation CAT)	199.95	159.00
Atari	Atari	850 Interface	219.95	159.00
Atari	Atari	Acc - Joysticks	20.95	18.00
Atari	Atari	Acc - Paddles	20.50	18.00
Atari	Atari	Cart - 3D Tic Tac Toe	34.95	
Atari	Atari	Cart - Asteriods	25.00	
Atari	Atari	Cart - Centipede		35.00
Atari	Atari	Cart - Computer Chess	34.95	
Atari	Atari	Cart - Missle Command	34.95	
Atari	Atari	Cart - Music Composer	39.95	
Atari	Atari	Cart - Pac Man		35.00
Atari	Atari	Cart - Space Invaders	34.95	
Atari	Atari	Cart - Star Raiders	44.95	
Atari	Atari	Cart - Super Breakout	34.95	
Atari	Atari	Cart - Telelink Module 850	24.95	
Atari	Atari	Cart - Video Easel	34.95	
Atari	Atari	Cart - Word Processor	112.50	
Atari	Atari	Consumer Pilot	59.95	
Atari	Atari	Disk - Dow Jones Investor		99.00
Atari	Atari	Educational Pilot	97.50	
Atari	Atari	Kit - "Communicator"	449.85	349.95
Atari	Atari	Kit - "Entertainer"	116.75	81.95
Atari	Atari	Kit - "Programmer"	79.95	59.95
Atari	Automated	Disk - Temple of Apshai		29.00
Atari	Axlon	Ramdisk	549.00	
Atari	Bit 3	610 80 col card	349.00	
Atari	Bit 3	Acc - 32K RAM expansion	179.00	
Atari	Bit-3	K-Razy Shootout	40.00	
Atari	Broderbund	Disk - Apple Panic	29.95	22.99
Atari	Budgco	Disk - Raster Blaster		23.00
Atari	Cavalier	Disk - Bug Attack		23.00
Atari	Datasoft	Acc - Le Stick Joystick		29.00
Atari	Datasoft	Disk - Text Wizard		75.00
Atari	Infocom	Disk - Deadline		37.00
Atari	Infocom	Disk - Zork I		29.00
Atari	On-Line	Disk - Asteroid		20.00
Atari	On-Line	Disk - Caverns of Mars		31.00
Atari	VisiCorp	Disk - VisiCalc	225.00	189.00

[Atari's Kits]. Atari would be happy to know exactly what consumers want from a home computer, but no one really does. In an effort to "seed" add-on spending for cartridges and cassettes, Atari has taken to offering various groupings of peripherals. At the moment, these kits include: the Atari

Entertainer Kit ($109.95 - includes "Star Raiders" and "Missile Command" plus joysticks); the Atari Communicator Kit ($399.95 - includes 850 Interface, Telelink cartridge, 830 Modem); Atari Educator Kit (includes 410 Program Recorder, "States & Capitols" cassette); Atari Programmer Kit ($69.95 - includes BASIC cartridge, reference manual, and self-teaching guide).

[Add-On Hardware]. The number of vendors offering add-on hardware for the Atari is not nearly as large as for the Apple II. On the other hand, the Atari computer has a more complete design and needs less. Memory can be added to the Atari 400 as follows. The 400 comes standard with 8K of RAM - not very much - and 10K of ROM, for the operating system. The BASIC language cartridge adds 8K of ROM. The 400 can be expanded at an Atari service center to a maximum of 16K of RAM using Atari-approved parts. One outside vendor, Intec Peripherals Corporation (3389 North Del Rosa Avenue, San Bernardino, CA 92404, 714-864-5269) makes a $299 board that will expand the 400 to 48K, using eight 64K RAM chips. It requires four jumpers; its installation may void the Atari warranty.

The Atari 800 can be expanded by the user up to 48K of RAM. A "full" 800 system would have a full 64K of memory, 48K of RAM, and 16K of ROM, the latter in the cartridge. Intec Peripherals, mentioned above, makes a 32K expansion board for the Atari 800 that sells for $150. Axlon (170 N. Wolfe Rd., Sunnyvale, CA 94086, 408-730-0216) makes a 128K RAM expansion board - also using 64K RAM chips - that gives the Atari 800 up to 128K of bank-switched RAM. Further, with a patch to the Atari DOS, the Axlon "Ramdisk" can be used as a pseudo-disk, which is of course about 20 times faster than an actual floppy.

[The Telelink Module]. The Telelink module is an Atari cartridge designed to allow easy communications. Telelink turns the Atari into a "dumb" terminal; it does not provide for capturing data on disk (in fact, the disk drives must be off for Telelink to work). To use Telelink, set the switches on the Atari 830 modem to ORIG (originate) and FULL (full duplex). Dial the telephone. When you hear the carrier tone, place it in the cups. The following control codes have special significance to Telelink:

          control-0: word wraparound, 40 columns
          control-8: use 80 columns for printout
          control-9: automatic (sends XOFF, dumps to printer
                        when buffer full) or manual mode

To indicate to Tymnet that XON/XOFF is to be used, type a control-R before anything else at the sign-in.

[Third Party Software]. Third-party software has developed more slowly for the Atari than for the Apple II. Atari computers, especially the 400, were designed to run game and education programs from ROM packs and don't have or need floppy disks. However, an increasing number of Atari 800s have disks, leading to a third-party software industry with floppies as a distribution medium.

["FileManager 800"]. Synapse Software (820 Coventry Road, Kensington, CA 94707) is among the more successful Atari software houses, with $2 million in sales in 1982. Synapse produces a number of games for the Atari on disk and cassette tape: "Dodge Racer", "Protector", "Slime", "Chicken", and "Nautilus". FileManager 800 is a $99.95 database manager similar to PFS for the Apple II. FileManager organizes data into files made up of records made up of fields. Fields can have up to 100 characters, with records made up of up to 20 fields. About 500 short records can fit on a disk. All information is kept in ASCII. The disk program is protected from copying by a hardware "key" that fits into joystick port #1 on the Atari.

K-Byte (Gaylord, MI), a subsidiary of Koltonbar Engineering, which makes automation equipment, has developed more in the line of system software for the Atari, including an operating system, K-DOS, for the Atari 800 ($89.95). USS Enterprises (San Jose, CA), run by Vincent Cate, sells a hardware interface box that allows an Atari to use an existing CP/M system in place of a floppy disk or cassette. Cate's product, called the CP/M/Atari Connection, sells for $147.

[Micro-Painter]. "Micro-Painter", by DataSoft, Inc. (19519 Business Drive, Northridge, CA 91343) is a $34.95 paint system for the Atari 800. The system stores pictures on a floppy disk, allowing them to to loaded or saved from memory. The movements of a simulated paintbrush are controlled by the Atari joystick; with the brush in position, the interior of an outlined area can be colored by hitting the joystick game button. A "rubber band" technique can be used to draw lines. The software disk comes with nine pre-drawn pictures ready to be colored in by children.

[Monkey Wrench]. "Monkey Wrench", by Eastern House Software (3239 Linda Drive, Winston-Salem, NC 27106) is a convenient cartridge of programming aids for Atari BASIC. The cartridge plugs into the right-hand slot on the console and is meant to be run with Atari's BASIC cartridge in the right. Monkey Wrench will not work on the Atari 400. The cartridge has on it a line renumbering feature (necessary for any serious BASIC programming) a RAM memory test, a machine language monitor, and decimal to hex (and back again) conversion routines. Commands are entered with a ">", single letter code, and parameters, if any. To renumber a BASIC program from line 10 by 10:

>R 10 10

As a bare board, the Monkey Wrench can be plugged in backwards and should be installed with care.

[ANTIC Magazine]. The largest circulation magazine for Atari computer owners is named after the system's video display chip (ANTIC Publishing, 297 Missouri Street, San Francisco, CA 94107). The magazine comes out every 2 months and costs $15 for a 1-year subscription, $27 for 2 years.

B

Bar Code

Bar code is a unique form of data entry that is enjoying slow, expanding growth as its benefits become better known. In the US, most items sold in grocery stores now carry the UPC or Universal Product Code, the familiar if puzzling markings that look like:

If you can read this, you can get a good job. Actually, bar code can be read by humans. The outermost thin lines in the UPC are a type of punctuation: they tell the bar code reader (usually a wand or a laser device) where the outer limits of the bar code are. The thin line third from the right is a parity check. The thick line and thin line in from the right, and the initial centered 0, tell the computer that it is reading a grocery item. The five digits printed next identify manufactruer: this number is printed in clear text below the code and is separated from the next group of five digits by two more thin punctuation lines in the code center.

UPC is an ambitious project to standardize coding among all popular food products, but obviously will be plagued by local brands and uncooperative firms. The product number is identified by five more numbers, again with the digits printed in clear text beneath. UPC allows additional digits to be printed off to the left; these codes are called UPC+2 or UPC+5, etc.

[Bar Code Applications]. As a data entry method, bar code is competitive with Optical Character Recognition (OCR), which it closely resembles, and other interactive techniques, such as touch screens and light pens. Bar code's advantage over OCR is its higher accuracy, although its advantage over any type of menu selection device (touch screen or light pen) is its information range, or bandwidth.

The main problem with bar codes is that they must first exist in order to be read. This makes them ideal for controlled inventory situations, like library book circulation, but more troublesome for open circulation.

[LOGMARS]. On September 1, 1981, in an ambitious move, the US Department of Defense announced its "LOGMARS" bar code standards for its suppliers. As planned, all vendors of goods to the US DOD will be required, by the mid-1980s, to label their goods with "3 of 9" bar codes, which will be scanned on receipt by the DoD. Specifically, Military standard 1189, dated 4 January 1982, requires (1) use of 3-of-9 code, with OCR style A alphanumeric clear text printed above or below the code, and (2) that the size and shape of the clear text for the bar code must conform to FIPS PUBS 32 (OCR-A). A typical example of 3-of-9 code:

← 3-OF-9 BAR CODE

A1P2C3D   ←———— OCR-A

The two pertinent LOGMARS standards (MIL STD 1189 and MIL STD 129H Change 3) can be obtained by writing to the Naval Publication and Forms Center (5801 Tabor Street, Philadelphia, PA 19120).

The LOGMARS testing program, carried out between 1979 and 1981, provides a virtual catalog of bar code applications. In one test, bar codes were applied to goods received at a wholesale warehouse; these tests showed that bar codes reduced the cost of processing receipts by 38%. In a shipping test, bar codes were used in picking and packing, resulting in a 9.5% improvement in processing time. In an inventory test, about 3000 storage locations were labeled with bar codes, and portable scanners were used to take inventory. These tests showed a 6% improvement in productivity.

[Other Applications]. Bar codes can also be used to (1) track work in progress, by scanning sub-assemblies at various stages of production; (2) control inventories by logging receipts and disbursements; (3) enter quality control reports; (4) track the effect of engineering changes on production; and (5) track customer orders, shipping, and receiving.

[Printed Bar Code Labels]. Bar code labels must be printed with special care to ensure that they can be read by bar code scanners. Light from random or unexpected sources can confuse a bar code scanner.

The material on which labels are printed is called the background substrate. In general, this should be white in color, have a matte finish, and produce diffuse reflectance of 70-80% in the near infared spectrum. The bars of the bar code itself are usually printed in black carbon ink (alcohol-based inks do not absorb enough light, giving low contrast). A good bar code ink should not exceed 24% reflectance in the near infared spectrum, and the reflectance should not vary more than 5% in the same character. The difference between the background substrate and ink reflectance is called contrast and should be 50-65%.

Various error conditions can result in printing bar codes. A "void" is a tiny pocket of no ink in a bar, caused by inadequate ink coverage. A "speck" is a

HP bar code wand as packaged for the Apple II by ABT

dot of ink on white paper where it shouldn't be. Overprinting with too much ink can widen bars (ink spread) beyond tolerances, wheras under printing can shrink them. The bars must be sharp along the long edges to maintain tolerances set in individual bar codes.

Several printing firms specialize in making bar code labels, often with adhesive backings and in special shapes. Computype (2285 West Country Road C, St Paul, MN 55113, 800-328-0852, 612-633-0633, TWX 910-563-3699 COMPUTYPE RVIL) is one, and Data Composition (1099 Essex, Richmond, CA 94801, 415-232-6200, 800-227-2121) is another.

Low quantities of bar code labels can be made on dot matrix or letter-quality printers, although the quality of these is not as good as preprinted labels. Several companies offer software for printing labels, including North American Technology, publishers of The Bar Code News, and Analog Technology Corporation (15859 East Edna Place, Irwindale, CA 91706, 213-960-4004), which makes a graphics attachment to the Texas Instruments 810 dot matrix printer.

[Bar Code Readers]. A bar code reader is made up of a light-sensing wand and various electronics. The wand has a LED light source and a sensor to pick up reflected light. Hewlett-Packard makes one widely used wand; Welch-Allyn makes another. These are then packaged, often with firmware for reading particular (or multiple) codes, by manufacturers into complete systems.

Electro-General Corporation (14960 Industrial Road, Minnetonka, MI 55343, 612-935-7704) makes a portable bar code reader, the "Datamyte 1000", that can read five different codes: Code 39, CODABAR, Plessey, 2-of-5 code, and 2-of-5 Interleaved. This device is designed to be used like a clipboard, with the bar code wand moved over the printed code like a pencil.

Bar code readers do not need human operators, however. Some sophisticated grocery store UPC readers use laser scanners. Datalogic Optic Electronics (2904 Southwood Drive, Westlake, OH 44145, 216-871-0604, Telex 241584) makes a moving laser beam scanner for scanning bar codes on cartons moving on conveyors at speeds up to 600 feet per minute. These devices cost about $5000 each.

Advanced Business Technology, Inc. (12333 Saratoga-Sunnyvale Rd., Saratoga, CA 95070, 408-446-2013) announced in late 1980 a "BarWand" bar code reader for the Apple II computer. (ABT also makes a 13-key numeric pad for the Apple II). The BarWand is a modified Hewlett-Packard HEDS 3000 reader that plugs into the game paddle connector of the Apple. ABT offers a software package for reading Universal Product Code (UPC). It also has a printer driver that prints bar code on inexpensive dot matrix printers, and it has a reader driver that understands this code. The ABT bar code reader with demo disk of UPC, LabelCode, and Paperbyte programs lists for $195. A ROM-based version of the software, which can read a number of different codes, is also available.

[More Information]. The best single source of information on bar code is "The Bar Code News", which is published every few months by North American Technology, Inc. (Strand Bldg., 174 Concord St., Suite 23, Peterborough, NH 03458, 603-924-6048). NATI, Inc., was started by, among others, Carl Helmers, founder of Byte magazine.

Bubble Memory

Bubble memory is a complex but promising storage technology that one day may be as important as the floppy disk or RAM. The concept of bubble memory was first described by Andrew Bobeck of Bell Labs in 1967.

At one level, the idea behind bubbles is simple. Rather than use a physically rotating device, with information magnetically coded on it, bubble memory, like transistors and semiconductor chips, is physically static but has moving magnetic domains or bubbles. The potential of bubble memory is that it can be mass-produced, like semiconductors, yet have most of the characteristics — nonvolatility, reasonable access time, low cost — of floppy disks.

Unfortunately, there remains a gap between the promise and the reality of the bubble. Floppy disks and disk drives have through large-scale production become near standard products for small computers. Mass production of 16K and 64K RAM chips has driven the cost of RAM memory down, making battery backed up RAM a potential competitor to the bubble, and superior to it in access time. Low ebb for the bubble was definitely 1981: in February of that year, Rockwell International abandoned its bubble memory project; in June, Texas Instruments announced the end of its bubble efforts; and in November, National Semiconductor became the third US company to get off the bubble bandwagon.

The bubble has made a slow comeback since. In the United States, ATT and IBM make bubbles for their own use, and Intel and Motorola make them for the general market. In Japan, Hitachi and Fujitsu seem to have mastered bubble fabrication. To reassure designers, Intel has taken the unusual step of publishing a schedule of progressively declining bubble memory prices extending to 1985. Bubbles have a large market in telephone equipment; Intel has signed a cross license agreement with Mitel, a Canadian semiconductor firm active in telecommunications. Motorola began sampling bubble components in 1982 for 1983 availability. In 1983, Intel will sample a 1-megabit bubble device.

There are other indications of the bubble's tenacity. The Grid Compass, a top of the line portable computer, was introduced in early 1982 using bubble memory, as was the BubCom, a Japanese microcomputer. A "semi-disk" floppy disk replacement board for the Apple II using bubble memory also appeared in 1982 (MPC Peripherals Corp., 9424 Chesapeake Drive, San Diego, CA 92123, 714-278-0630). All in all, the bubble seems not to have completely burst but rather to be rising to its natural place in the hierarchy of memory technologies.

[How Bubbles Work]. Bubble memory is made out of garnet, or more precisely G cubed - gadolinium gallium garnet. This thin sheet of garnet, properly conditioned, is placed between two permanent magnets. On the garnet sheet, magnetic domains or bubbles travel in loop patterns. In the Intel 1 Mbit bubble, there are 512 loops of 2048 locations. These bubbles are shifted, like treads on a tank, around the loops. The access time for any particular bit of information depends on where it is in the loop and the shift rate per bubble, typically 50 to 150 KHz. On the Intel bubble device, access time is about 20 ms, compared to several hundred ms for floppy disk access.

As with more sophisticated RAM memories, bubble manufacturers have had to allow spare loops to get adequate chip yields,. This, however, leads to difficult testing procedures for bubbles and is a source of control circuit complexity.

Compared to floppy disks, however, bubbles are very rugged, operating over relatively wide temperature ranges (although they are somewhat intolerant of heat over 70 degrees centigrade, too low for some military applications), and are unaffected by dirt and other environmental problems. Hitachi, which sells most of its bubbles to Nippon Telegraph and Telephone Public Corp., has done tests that show that the bubble memory devices in NTT switching systems will last 22 years.

Although slower than RAMs, bubbles are faster than floppies. In late 1979, Philips Data Systems in Holland demonstrated a prototype floppy disk replacement system that used eight 256K-bit Rockwell bubble memory chips to create a 256K-byte pseudo floppy. This pseudo disk had an average read access of under 6 ms, compared to 340 ms for a floppy. A disk I/O intensive benchmark program was executed on the bubble system in 20 seconds; it required 5 minutes to run with the floppy.

[Available Bubbles]. Both Intel and Fujitsu offer "plug-a-bubble" cartridges that are essentially floppy disk replacement devices. Intel offers a 1M-bit cartridge; Fujitsu offers a 64K-bit or 256K-bit bubble cassette. Intel, Fujitsu, and Hitachi sell board level bubble memory products, and Intel and Fujitsu sell chip sets for original design.

C

Calendar Calculations

Time calculations are constantly made by computers. However, the human system of counting time - 60 seconds in a minute, 60 minutes in an hour, 24 hours in a day - is not very well suited to their needs. Time conversions are the sort of work that computers are good at but that programmers don't enjoy teaching.

The unit second is the universal standard of time, and all other units - minutes, hours, days - can be defined in its terms. There are 60 seconds in a minute; 3600 seconds in an hour; 864,000 seconds in a day; and 604,800 seconds in a week.

[Calendar Dates]. The United States is one of the few countries in the world in which "month-day-year" is the standard order for giving dates. (In the US military, and in much of Europe, "day-month-year" is the convention.) In Japan, the "year" is often given as a count from the beginning of the Emperor's dynasty, currently a number around 60.

For the computer, none of these conventions is entirely suitable. In particular, it is difficult to compare dates if they are presented in either "month-day-year" or "day-month-year" order. To do this, the order must be reversed, working from the largest unit down to the smallest:

YEAR - MONTH - DAY - HOUR - MINUTE - SECOND

If numbers are kept in this form, a computer can tell by subtraction that New Year's Day 1984 (19840101) is earlier than that for 1985 (19850101). Note also that if year, month, and date are to be separated, the convention for doing so is to use hyphens, i.e., 1984-10-01, not slashes (84/10/01) or periods (84.10.01).

Subtracting two calendar dates in the "YYMMDD" format tells only if one date is earlier than, less than, or equal to another. It does not tell the number of days between two dates. To get the exact number of days between two calendar dates, we must calculate the Julian date for each, then subtract.

In astronomy and other fields, it is important to have a reference number for

every day. The most commonly used system is the Julian date. The Julian date
in effect takes "day zero" as Nov 25, -4713 and counts foward, a day at a
time, from there. The Julian date for January 1, 1983, is 2,445,336 and that
for January 1, 1984, is 2,445,701.

A number of computer algorithms exist for converting the calendar date
(YYYY-MM-DD) into the Julian date (JJJJJJJ). Microcomputer users should be
warned that the current Julian date is seven digits long. Not all
microcomputers can make the integer calculations to develop it with full
precision. Further, some published algorithms use rounding and truncation
conventions unique to FORTRAN, and they may need reprogramming to work in
BASIC. The following Julian date algorithm, written in UCSD Pascal, works
with data type long integer:

```
PROGRAM TESTJULIAN;

TYPE LONG= INTEGER[12];

VAR      MONTH,DAY,YEAR:INTEGER;
         ANSWER:LONG;

procedure JULIAN (var ANSWER:long; MONTH,DAY,YEAR:integer);

{this procedure is called with the integer month, day, and year
 and returns a long integer (the first parameter) as the Julian date}

var      LONGMONTH,LONGDAY,LONGYEAR:LONG;
         R,J:LONG; {intermediate variables}
begin

   {convert month, day, and year to type LONG}

   LONGMONTH:=MONTH;LONGDAY:=DAY;LONGYEAR:=YEAR;

   {now compute according to the algorithm}

   R:=(12*(LONGYEAR+4800))+LONGMONTH-3;
   J:=(2*(R-((R DIV 12)*12)) + 7 + (365*R) ) DIV 12;
   J:=J+LONGDAY+(R DIV 48) - 32083;
   J:=J+(R DIV 4800)-(R DIV 1200)+38;
   ANSWER:=J

end;

procedure REVERSEJULIAN(JULIAN_DATE:LONG; var MONTH,DAY,YEAR:integer);

{this procedure is called with a long integer and changes the month,
  day, and year named to equal the calendar equivalent date}

VAR L,N,T1,T2,T3:LONG;
    LONGYEAR,LONGMONTH,LONGDAY:LONG;

BEGIN
  L:=JULIAN_DATE;
```

```
        L:=L+68569;
        T1:=L DIV 146097; N:=4*T1;
        T1:=146097*N; T2:=T1+3; T3:=T2 DIV 4; L:=L-T3;
        T1:=L+1; T2:=4000*T1;
        LONGYEAR:=T2 DIV 1461001;
        T1 := 1461*LONGYEAR;
        T2:=T1 DIV 4; T3:=L-T2;L:=T3+31;
        T1:=80*L; LONGMONTH:=T1 DIV 2447;
        T1:=2447*LONGMONTH;
        T2:=T1 DIV 80;
        LONGDAY:=L-T2;
        L:=LONGMONTH DIV 11;
        LONGMONTH :=LONGMONTH+2-(12*L);
        T1:=N-49; T2:=100*T1; LONGYEAR:=T2+LONGYEAR+L;

        {pass back 3-part answer}

        MONTH:=TRUNC(LONGMONTH);
        DAY:=TRUNC(LONGDAY);
        YEAR:=TRUNC(LONGYEAR)

  END;

  begin {of test program}

  writeln('This is a Pascal version of the Julian date test.');
  writeln('Enter the calendar date in form MM DD YY <return>');
  writeln('Enter a date of 00 00 00 to end the program');

  while day<>0 do
          begin
            writeln;
            write('Enter MM DD YY:');
            readln(MONTH,DAY,YEAR);
            if DAY<>0 then
              begin
                JULIAN(ANSWER,MONTH,DAY,YEAR);
                writeln('The julian day of this date is ',ANSWER);
                REVERSEJULIAN(ANSWER,MONTH,DAY,YEAR);
                writeln('Reversing as a check yields ',MONTH,'/',DAY,'/',YEAR);
              end
          end;
  writeln('That''s All Folks....');
  end.
```

Note that to be historically accurate, this last step applies only if the
result of Step 3 is > 2299171, the Julian date of October 15, 1582, when the
current calendar went into effect.

[Test Values]. The Julian date of 1-1-1979 is 2443875. The Julian date of
1-1-2000 is 2451545. The Julian date for January 1, 1900, is 2415021. (This
last number is often kept on hand as a constant to be subtracted from the true
Julian date to produce an easier number to work with).

-89-

The following algorithm, published by H. F. Fliegel and T. C. Van Flandern in the Communications of the ACM (Vol. 1, No. 10, Oct. 1968, p. 657), is an example of a FORTRAN-based algorithm with hidden traps for BASIC programmers.

In FORTRAN, integers are "truncated" (cut off) after division, so that 3.5/2 = 1 and -4.5/2 = -2. At first glance, it seems possible to simulate FORTRAN integer truncation with the INT function in BASIC, which returns in integer when called with a fraction, e.g., INT(3.5/2) = 1. This works fine with positive numbers. However, the INT function in BASIC rounds negative numbers down along the number line, not up. In BASIC, INT(-3.5 / 2) = -2, not -1.

In addition to needing many digits of decimal accuracy, a number of date and calendar algorithms make explicit assumptions about rounding. The following Julian date algorithm is highly dependent on integer division of negative numbers. To use it in BASIC, a substitute for the INT function must be defined:

DEF FNI(X)=SGN(X)*INT((ABS(X))

This will produce FORTRAN-like truncation of negative numbers.

[Ordinal Dates]. In general, the Julian date is awkward to use in day-to-day business computations. At seven decimal digits, it is very long (even the Smithsonian, which intends to be around forever, reduces it to six digits, by subtracting 2000001, to create its own "Smithsonian Day"). The calculations involved are tedious, even for a computer. Since business records on a file often fall within the same calendar year, an easier number to use is the so-called ordinal date, which is simply the number of the day within the year. New Year's Day has an ordinal date of 1; December 31 has an ordinal date of 365 in most years and 366 in leap years.

Using the leap year function above, a fairly simple formula exists for finding the ordinal date X based on the calendar date MM,DD,YYYY. The reverse algorithm is more difficult and is implemented here by brute force:

```
program test_ordinal;
var      month,day,year: integer;
         oday: integer;

function leap(year:integer): integer;
{leap returns a 1 if a leap year, and 0 if not}
var      a,b,c: integer;
begin
  a:= (year - (year div 4)  *4    +3) div 4;
  b:= (year - (year div 100)*100 +99) div 100;
  c:= (year - (year div 400)*400+399) div 400;
  leap:= 1-a+b-c
end;

function ordinal(month,day,year: integer): integer;
var      longmonth,longday,longyear,longresult: integer[14];
begin
  longmonth:=month;
```

```
      longday:=day;
      longyear:=year;
      longresult := (3055 * (longmonth + 2) div 100)
               - ((longmonth+10) div 13 )*2
               - 91
               + leap(year)*((longmonth+10) div 13)
               + longday;
      ordinal:=trunc(longresult);
end;

procedure reverse_ordinal(odate,year: integer; var month,day:integer);
{alters months and day}
{requires leap function}
function firstday(month:integer): integer;
var      first:integer;
begin
  case month of
    1: first:=1;
    2: first:=32;
    3: first:=60;
    4: first:=91;
    5: first:=121;
    6: first:=152;
    7: first:=182;
    8: first:=213;
    9: first:=244;
    10:first:=274;
    11:first:=305;
    12:first:=335
  end;
  if ((month>2) and (leap(year)=1)) then first:=first+1;
  firstday:=first
end;

begin {of procedure reverse_ordinal}
   if ((odate<1) or (odate>366)) then exit(reverse_ordinal);
   month:=(odate+33) div 30;
   if month>12 then month:=12;
   while firstday(month)>odate do month:=month-1;
   day := odate - firstday(month) + 1;
end;

begin (* of main program *)

   year:=1979;
   for oday:=1 to 365 do
     begin
       reverse_ordinal(oday,year,month,day);
       writeln(oday:4,year:5,'   = ',month:3,day:3,year:5);
       writeln(month:3,day:3,year:5,' = ',ordinal(month,day,year));
     end;

end.
```

[Time of Day]. There are six standard formats for representing the time of
day. These are:

                    (1)   HH
                    (2)   HH.hhhh
                    (3)   HHMM   or HH:MM
                    (4)   HHMM.mmmm   or HH:MM.mmmm
                    (5)   HHMMSS   or HH:MM:SS
                    (6)   HHMMSS.ssss   or HH:MM:SS.ssss

In formats (2), (4), and (6), hours, minutes, or seconds are expressed as
decimal fractions respectively. In the standard, a 24-hour clock is assumed
unless the time is followed by an "A" or "P". On a 24-hour clock, note that
midnight is always 0, never 24. The American military sometimes uses 24 for
midnight, but then there is the right way, the wrong way, and the Army way.

[Time Zones]. Given time is either universal (Greenwich Mean Time) or local.
In 12-hour forms, universal time is specified by following the time with
"GMT", e.g.,

          05:45:34P GMT

In 24-hour forms, the universal form is called "zero time" (or "Zulu" time)
and specified by following the time by a capital "Z" with no space:

          17:45:34Z

Local time is specified by giving a time zone after the time, or by giving a
plus or minus Time Differential Factor (TDF), which directly follows the time:

          174534-0600 or 05:45:34P CST

Time zones have the following TFD equivalents in the USA:

          Zone   Standard   Daylight

          Atlantic   -0400 AST   -0300 ADT
          Eastern   -0500 EST   -0400 EDT
          Central   -0600 CST   -0500 CST
          Mountain   -0700 MST   -0600 MDT
          Pacific   -0800 PST   -0700 PDT
          Yukon   -0900 YST   -0800 YDT
          Alaska-Hawaii   -1000 HST   -0900 HDT
          Bering   -1100 BST   -1000 BDT

Commodore

Commodore Business Machines, Inc. (The Meadows, 487 Devon Park Rd., Wayne, PA 19087, 215-687-9750) is a subsidiary of Commodore International Ltd., (traded on the NYSE as CBU). The parent company also owns MOS Technology, developer of the 6502 microprocessor used in some competing computers, like the Apple II and Atari 400 and 800.

Commodore, unlike other companies in the personal computer field, has closely followed the fortunes of its founder, Jack Tramiel. Tramiel started the company in 1958 in the Bronx, NY, where he was working as a typewriter repairman. In 1960, the company moved to Toronto, Canada, finally ending its wanderings by incorporating offshore as Commodore International, Ltd., in Nassau, The Bahamas.

In the 1970s, Commodore was a participant in the calculator boom. To its credit, the company managed to survive the mid-1970s bloodbath that left only Texas Instruments, Hewlett-Packard, and the Japanese still in the business. Looking for new products, Commodore acquired MOS Technology, developer of the 6502 microprocessor, in November 1976. MOS Technology had been started by Chuck Peddle and a crew that had developed the 6800 microprocessor at Motorola.

In 1975, however, MOS Technology had been seriously weakened by expensive litigation with Motorola (the two firms later settled, with no admission of guilt on either side). Commodore made MOS an offer it couldn't afford to refuse. It also picked up Frontier Manufacturing at the same time, giving Commodore everything needed for microcomputer manufacturing (it almost got Steve Wozniak, Steven Jobs, and the Apple II, but that is another story).

In January, 1977 Commodore introduced the PET, which appeared in stores late that year. The name PET had something to do with the idea of home computers as pets and with the Pet Rock, a fad at the time, and officially stood for Personal Electronic Transactor. The PET was considered big news and, like the Apple II, generated great interest at the March 1977 West Coast Computer Faire. Commodore was one of the first companies to use MicroSoft BASIC, an important first step in establishing Gates's version as a standard.

[From PET to VIC]. In 1980, Commodore confounded the market by changing, or apparently changing, the name of the PET to the CBM, or Commodore Business Machine. The CBM had full keyboards and 80 columns in upper- and lower-case, but this concentration on high end-products proved to be a mistake. For several years, Commodore seemed to disappear from the US market. Although Tandy and Commodore shared most of the personal computer market in 1979, Apple pulled up even with Commodore in 1980 and passed it in sales in 1981.

Commodore, enjoying strong sales in Europe and Japan, appeared not to care about the US market, where it suffered from bad press and bad relations with dealers. However, the company had some tricks up its sleeves. Commodore

Commodore VIC-20 system

introduced the VIC-20 very quietly in late 1980 and introduced with it a new style in its computer operations.

With the VIC-20, Commodore did what it originally wanted to do with the PET - produce a computer that could be sold with a minimum of support from almost any retail outlet, including discount stores like K-Mart. (Commodore's first big distribution deal in the US was with the Mr. Calculator chain.)

Commodore has moved rapidly to have the VIC-20 stocked in stereo, camera, and department stores. The beauty of the device is that it was the first personal computer to be sold over the counter like a video game - it has the capabilities, if a buyer can make use them, of a full computer. Commodore's ad campaign for the device - "why buy a video game, when you can have a computer" - drove home the point.

At the CES show in June 1982, Commodore introduced 13 game cartridges, including three - "Gorf", "Omega Race", and "Wizard of Wor" - licensed from Bally (Midway) arcade machines. Other cartridges introduced included "Space Vulture", "Raid on Fort Knox", and "Pinball Spectacular". "Moles Attack" and "The Sky is Falling" are children's cartridges. Commodore also introduced five adventure games licensed from Scott Adams, "Adventureland Adventure", "Pirate Cove Adventure", "Mission Impossible Adventure", "The Count Adventure" and "Voodoo Castle Adventure." These can be played and stored on tape for continued play.

Commodore has an expanding line of peripherals for the VIC-20, including a 170K-byte single-sided, single-density disk drive (the VIC 1540, $595). This drive is compatible with the CBM 4040 and 2031 drives on larger Commodore computers. Commodore has a low-cost dot matrix printer that can do snapshots of the VIC-20 graphics screen. This device is called the 1515. A "Datasette" recorder for storing and reading programs is another VIC option.

Commodore MAX machine

Commodore has out an "Introduction to BASIC" manual that comes with two cassette tapes with programs. For assembly language programming, there is a "Super Expander Cartridge" and a "VICMON" monitor cartridge. Another Commodore program, apparently distributed on tape, allows custom character sets to be created.

[The Commodore "Max"]. The big news with Commodore since mid-1981 has been the VIC-20. However, in early 1982 the company announced a welter of other devices, some of them seemingly competing with each other. Commodore announced in Spring 1982 for Fall 1982 availability the Commodore Max (sometimes called the "Ultimax").

In late 1982 the The Max was apprarently cancelled, or at least delayed. When and if The Max appears (The Computer Cookbook expects Valley Girl Moon Zappa to take the place of William "Star Trek" Shatner in promoting this device), it will be, even more than the VIC-20, a combined computer and home video game. The Max has an announced retail price of $179.95, which makes it competitive with both video games - the Atari VCS, for example, is currently priced at $149.95 - and with computers, including Commodore's own VIC-20, currently about $249.

The Max uses a new 6510 microprocessor developed by Commodore's subsidiary, MOS Technology, which designed the 6502 microprocessor used in Apple and Atari computers, as well as Commodore's earlier "PET" series.

Another Commodore-designed chip, the 6581, is a three-voice music synthesizer, each voice having a nine-octave range. The 6581 has programmable envelope generators for each voice (attack, sustain, release, decay), filters, and resonance.

[The Commodore 64]. Shortly after announcing The Max, Commodore announced in 1982 the Commodore 64, a $595.00 computer with 64K of RAM. The Commodore 64 might be considered competition with Apple's Super II, or as a bridge between Commodore's VIC-20 and its larger machines. The 64 can run VIC-20 software, including games, and can also use CBM and PET peripherals with the addition of an IEEE-488 expansion cartridge. The 64 has a PET emulation mode, allowing it to run most PET software, and a Z-80 cartridge to run CP/M! The primary processor on the 64 is the new MOS Technology 6510.

[THE BX256]. Commodore first unveiled its 16-bit computer, the "BX256", to a luncheon of security analysts in New York in May 1982 and to the public at the National Computer Conference (NCC) in Houston in June 1982. The machine became available in September 1982.

The BX256 has two processors, a 6509 (a MOS Technology product, not to be confused with the Motorola 6809), and an Intel 8088. As its name implies, the machine comes with 256K of RAM. The 8088 is designed to give the machine CP/M86 - one might read this as "IBM PC" - compatibility. Like the IBM PC, the new Commodore machine has a detachable keyboard and built-in dual disk drives. A Z-80 CPU board is also planned. Suggested retail price is $2,995.

E

Electronic Mail

Electronic mail systems have three basic components: (1) a text editor, by which messages can be prepared; (2) a communications network or system, by which they are transmitted; (3) and some type of data base management operation, by which messages can be recalled by category or sender. To date, most electronic mail systems have gone in for simple implementations of these functions.   The text editors on most electronic mail systems are crude compared to specialized word processing software; the communications systems are generally simple 300-baud ASCII, all caps; and the data base managers are far from the most powerful or sophisticated in existence.

In some sense, of course, electronic mail doesn't need much in any of these areas to work, which is why an increasing number of local computer clubs and special interest groups are able to implement them on spare microcomputers and a dedicated telephone line. This points out the one real thing that an electronic mail system must have to be successful, which is a sociological, not technological, criterion, namely, a reason to get together and talk to each other. In short, electronic networks must be built on social networks.

Within a corporation or a community there must be highly motivated users who will take the time, trouble, and expense to talk via terminal rather than via phone, note, or any of the traditional alternatives. It is not accidental, for example, that local community bulletin board systems (CBBS), which differ from electronic mail systems only by the degree to which messages are publicly available, thrive among (1) owners of the same type of computer; (2) ham radio operators and other serious hobbyists, (3) and other special interest groups. A number of Gay Rights groups, for example, have highly successful bulletin board and message systems, the best-known being perhaps "Kinky Komputer" in San Francisco's Castro District. The point is motivation, not money.

[Packages Vs Services]. Vendors in the electronic mail business sell either a package or a service. A package is a software package, written for a particular computer or set of computers, that allows a customer, typically a large corporation, to set up its own in-house electronic mail system. The best-known and most successful electronic mail software package is COMET, by Computer Corporation of America (Cambridge, MA, 617-491-3670), which runs on

DEC and IBM computers, and has 21 installations worldwide, including Manufacturer's Hanover Trust, several U.S. Army installations, Sanyo Electric, the U.S. Department of Agriculture, and Citibank' London offices. "InfoMail," by Bolt, Bernek, and Newman (Cambridge, MA, 617-491-1850) is another recent electronic mail software package.

COMET, however, is also a service. This means that customers, corporate or not, can arrange with CCA to dial up CCA's computer in Cambridge, MA, and leave messages for other users with similar terminals. Most electronic mail operations are, in fact, services, with the software only sometimes offered as a package. GTE's Telemail is a service, with the software not available inside the USA; "Quickcom" (General Electric Infomation Services / Rockville, MD, 301-340-4000), GE's electronic mail operation, is strictly a service, as is the "InfoPlex" service of CompuServe.

With a service operation, the critical question is whether the mail service produces continuous monthly billings on either per-transaction or connect-time basis. Note that since in many large timesharing systems any terminal can function as a mailbox, comparisons based on mailboxes or number of potential users are deceptive. Actual billings, which are a function of usage, are a far better measure of penetration of an electronic mail system.

[Dialcom]. Dialcom's Electronic Mail service runs on Prime computers and is, in fact, the same software package on The Source.

After signing on, a user sits at the system level, indicated by the greater than (">") prompt. The command to enter the mail system is simply:

        >MAIL   - enter MAIL system

Of the other system commands, five offer time-shared word processing. These are:

        >ED   - start new file to edit
        >ED filename   - edit existing file
        >RUNOFF   - text formatting program
        >SPELL   - spelling checking system
        >JU.   - text justification program

Two other commands are really conveniences, one being the familiar DATANEWS, the other a scheduling system for executives called TICKLER:

        >UPI   - enter UPI Datanews system
        >TICKLER   - enter Exec Scheduling system

The balance of the system commands are for file and account management:

        >OFF   - sign off computer
        >WHO   - who belongs to this ID
        >PASSWD   - change ID password
        >L   - list files for this ID
        >F   - short list files this ID
        >RENAME f1 f2   - change name of file 1
        >DEL filename   - delete the file

[Options within "MAIL"]. Once inside the MAIL program, there are relatively few modes of operation: READ, SEND, or SCAN.

The SCANning program is a type of data base manager designed to extract messages in some categories but not in others. Limited keyword searching, either of message titles or text, is possible. SCAN commands include:

```
>SCAN SCAN        - scan all mailboxes
>SCAN UNREAD      - scan all unread items
>SCAN EXPRESS     - scan express items
>SCAN OUT         - scan outgoing messages
>SCAN FILE        - scan a holding file of msgs.
>SCAN HELD        - scan held mail
```

Messages identified in the above routines can be further specified by the from command, FR (from a given name).

[Telemail]. GTE'S Telemail was designed to provide additional usage of the GTE Telenet communications network. GTE (GTE Telenet Communications Corp., 8330 Old Courthouse Rd., Vienna, VA 22180, 703-827-9200) backed into the electronic mail business in 1979 in a slightly strange way when corporate GTE, which of course makes everything from telephones to light bulbs, leased the COMET system from Computer Corporation of America, COMET's developer. COMET was intended strictly for in-house use at GTE and not as a public offering on Telenet. However, COMET proved so successful in its "Beta test" at GTE that the company first announced plans to lease it for Telenet and then decided to write its own electronic mail software. COMET was then slowly phased out at GTE, replaced by the subsidiary's Telemail offering. Within the bowels of GTE, however, there are apparently still a few COMET users who either haven't heard or have ignored the changeover to the domestic brand.

The Telemail program runs on twin Tandem computers located at Telenet's headquarters in Vienna, VA. It can be accessed worldwide through Telenet, and much of GTE's tariff is based on connect charges ($13.25/hr prime time, $3/hr off-hours). Telemail is relatively easy to use, and offers the following familiar commands:

```
SCAN        - messages in the mailbox
READ        - display contents of a msg.
COMPOSE     - compose a message
SEND        - sends the message
ANSWER      - response to another msg.
HELP        - gives user options
CHECK       - read a bulletin board
```

The line editor for Telemail is line-oriented, somewhat like a BASIC interpreter editor. A MODIFY command must be used to edit inside lines.

["InfoPlex"]. "InfoPlex" is the electronic mail service of CompuServe, Inc. (Columbus, OH, 617-457-8600). It is actually offered through a subsidiary, Plexus Corporation, but the distinction seems minimal. As with most electronic mail services, InfoPlex's customers are primarily large, dispersed coporations, which want the service for in-house use, and specialized companies which desire use of the overseas facilities offered by connection through Tymnet and Telenet. Representative InfoPlex customers are NCR and Owens-Corning Glass. As with CompuServe's general service, an ASCII, RS232-compatible terminal is all that is required for an InfoPlex mailbox.

A slightly modified version of InfoPlex is offered on CompuServe's Micronet personal computer network as EMAIL. EMAIL differs from other electronic mail systems in being menu driven. The primary menu in the EMAIL system, for example, reads:

ELECTRONIC MAIL

1 READ MAIL
2 SEND MAIL
3 UNDELIVERED MAIL INFORMATION
4 FILE MAIL

0 USER INFORMATION

Subsequent menus take the user through creating a message, identifying the number of the recipient, and so forth. The basic advantage of the menu-driven over a prompted system is in the menu system's ease of use for inexperienced users. The disadvantage of the menu system is its slow speed and the redundancy felt by experienced users.

An interesting variant (because it is somewhat better designed) of the EMAIL system is provided in CompuServe's "Feedback" option for news stories and so forth. Here, because the name and number of the recipient is known, message creation is easier and simpler for the user.

[Mailgrams]. Microcomputer owners with telephone modems can send Mailgram messages if the owner has a Mailgram account with Western Union (Western Union Electronic Mail, Inc., Products and Service Coordination, PO Box 185, McLean, VA 22101, 703-821-5800).

Mailgrams are used by many businesses to dun overdue accounts and to inform customers of price changes. Using a microcomputer with a telephone modem to send Mailgrams eliminates the need to obtain a Mailgram terminal from Western Union, makes it easier to prepare messages and address lists off line, and reduces the time and number of errors involved in manual forwarding of Mailgrams to Western Union.

[Mailgram Accounts]. Mailgrams are handled by a relatively new division of Western Union, Western Union Electronic Mail, Inc. (WUEMI), located in McLean, VA. (Western Union's TWX and Telex services work out of the Western Union Telegraph headquarters in Upper Saddle River, NJ.)

Mailgram accounts can be set up for any business that has a number of Mailgrams to send per month and a reasonable credit rating. For microcomputer owners, Western Union Electronic Mail has a special $75 minimum monthly charge. At $2 per average Mailgram, this works out to a minimum of 40 Mailgrams per month in volume to justify opening an account. (Otherwise, of course, Mailgrams can be sent by the usual public method and billed to a telephone number, etc.)

Once a Mailgram account has been established, WEUMI provides a subscriber with a toll-free (800) number for calling the WEUMI computer and a six-digit answerback, which is essentially an account number. (Historically, the answerback derives from Telex and TWX machines, which at one time mechanically and later electronically "answered back" automatically with this number when called.) The answerback is much the same as a password on a timesharing system and is needed to log successfully onto the system.

[Sending Mailgrams]. The following is the procedure for sending Mailgram messages. In essence, the computer software must emulate a Mailgram terminal and send the appropriate codes, especially the answerback, to the WEUMI computer, which is physically located in McLean. To look like a Mailgram terminal, the microcomputer modem should operate in half-duplex at 300 baud (110 permissible) with even parity and one stop bit. Note that half-duplex operation meaans that WEUMI's computer, unlike a timesharing computer, will not "echo" received codes.

[How It Works]. A message or series of Mailgram messages, and possible listing of addresses, are assumed to have been prepared and stored in a string array in memory or on floppy disk. The following recipe gives the procedure for transmitting the Mailgram(s) once they are ready:

STEP 1. Establish a telephone connection with the Mailgram computer by the toll-free number supplied by WEUMI. If using an acoustic coupler, make the connection when the high-pitch screech comes onto the phone. The modem should operate at 300 baud, even parity, half-duplex, one stop bit. 110-baud modems also can be used; in their case, parity does not matter.

STEP 2. WEUMI's computer will send an ASCII "ENQ" (with even parity, 132 decimal) to prompt your terminal to identify itself. When the ENQ is received, your computer should respond with the six ASCII digits of your answerback code. These should not be followed by a CR.

STEP 3. WEUMI's computer will acknowledge a valid answerback with a SI code (control O).

STEP 4. To start your message, you must send ASCII character DC1.

STEP 5. Line 1 of each message to a U.S. address must read:

*ZIP 97404

where "*ZIP" is in upper-case and the five-digit zip code follows. Messages to Canada should have the Canadian postal code after the ZIP:

*ZIP R3P 2N8

Canadian postal codes have two groups of three letters and digits separated by a space. Mailgrams to overseas locations should start

*ZIP INTL

After this *ZIP indicator, subsequent lines of the address can follow on the same line separated by a back slash (\) or on new lines, e.g.,

*ZIP 38102 \ JOE SMOE \ 1313 BLUEVIEW TER
MEMPHIS, TN 38102

A carriage return and (optional) line feed end each line.

STEP 6. The end of the address section and the start of the text section is marked by a line beginning:

*VTX

(if a "canned" messaged stored on WEUMI's computer is being invoked, this line can be

*STX nnnnn

where nnnnn is the five-digit ID number assigned by WEUMI to this stored message.)

STEP 7. The text follows here and should be made up of upper-case ASCII characters. Carriage returns (CR) and line feeds (LF) are the only ASCII control codes that may be mixed in the text. Up to 15,000 characters can be sent in a single message.

STEP 8. The end of the text is marked by sending on the following line:

*END (CR)

If another message is to be sent, go to Step 5 and send another *ZIP, etc. Otherwise, send a EXT (decimal 3, Control C) code, which marks the end of transmission.

STEP 9. At this point, WEUMI's computer will analyze the message and, if it accepts it, respond with the following:

ACCEPTED [CR] [LF]
nnnnnnnnn

where nnnnnnnnn is a nine-digit "acceptance number" for the Mailgram that will also be used for billing.

F

Finance

Computers have a number of important uses in financial modeling. Although much attention has been paid to VisiCalc and other spreadsheet programs, there are still many other money-related calculations at which computers excel.

[Interest]. Interest is a fee paid for the use of money. People who make loans or have savings accounts usually receive interest; people who own houses, take out loans, or use credit cards often pay it. The amount of interest paid is a function of four things: (1) the amount of money borrowed, or the principal; (2) the interest rate, usually given as a percent of the money borrowed per a unit of time; (3) the length of time the money is borrowed; and (4) the way in which interest is calculated, either simple or compound.

The formula for simple interest is just that:

    simple interest = principal * interest rate * time

Unfortunately, simple interest is not very interesting to people who make loans in the real world. Nearly all loans and savings use compound interest. Compound interest means that interest is earned not only on the principal but also on the interest earned in every compounding period. Many institutions compound interest daily, but some do it quarterly or monthly. The calculation of compound interest involves repeated calculations, one for each compounding period. On a computer, these calculations are usually done in a "loop", with one repetition for each compounding period.

[Continuous Compounding]. Some sophisticated calculations require continuous compounding. In theory, a graph of an account getting compound interest (no matter how frequently compounded) interest shows a "staircase" effect, with a jump discontinuity after each compounding period. Continuous compounding tries to create a smooth upward curve, using the following formulas:

    present value = future value * (e^(-RATE*N))
    future value = present value * (e^(RATE*N))

where "e" is Euler's constant, 2.718281829; "^" means "to the power of"; and RATE is the interest rate per period over the N periods.

[Nominal and Effective Rates]. Nominal interest rates are usually round figures, given for a period of time like a year, and qualified by the period of compounding, e.g., 6% annual interest compounded monthly. From a nominal interest rate it is often wise (and in the US, often required by law) to compute effective rate, that is, the rate actually paid. Thus for 6% annual interest compounded monthly, the effective annual rate is 6.17%.

[Loan Schedules]. Although they have an imposing name, amortization schedules are simple tables that show how much of a loan has been paid off at any given period. They are often desired by consumers or needed by savings and loan banks. Loan schedules are easily computed by microcomputers. Amortization schedules are useful in determining (1) how much interest has been paid on a loan, often needed at the end of the year for tax purposes, and (2) the remaining unpaid principal, needed to make accurate calculations of equity.

Consider the following auto loan: after a down payment, $4,000 was borrowed at 18.75% for 2 years (24 months). In any given month, how much of the car does the borrower own? In the first few months, most of the monthly payment in fact goes to cover interest. During the first year, the borrower's equity in the car is not as high as he probably imagines:

MO	PAYMENT	PRINCIPAL	INTEREST	BALANCE
1	201.14	138.64	62.50	3861.36
2	201.14	140.81	60.33	3720.55
3	201.14	143.01	58.13	3577.55
4	201.14	145.24	55.90	3432.31
5	201.14	147.51	53.63	3284.80
6	201.14	149.82	51.32	3134.98
7	201.14	152.16	48.98	2982.83
8	201.14	154.53	46.61	2828.29
9	201.14	156.95	44.19	2671.34
10	201.14	159.40	41.74	2511.94
11	201.14	161.89	39.25	2350.05
12	201.14	164.42	36.72	2185.63
13	201.14	166.99	34.15	2018.64
14	201.14	169.60	31.54	1849.04
15	201.14	172.25	28.89	1676.80
16	201.14	174.94	26.20	1501.86
17	201.14	177.67	23.47	1324.18
18	201.14	180.45	20.69	1143.73
19	201.14	183.27	17.87	960.46
20	201.14	186.13	15.01	774.33
21	201.14	189.04	12.10	585.29
22	201.14	191.99	9.15	393.30
23	201.14	194.99	6.15	198.30
24	201.40	198.30	3.10	0.00
TOTAL INTEREST			827.62	

This table was produced by the following Pascal program:

```
program amortization_schedule;
```

```
      var     last_months_interest, remaining_balance, monthly_payment,
              rate, amount_applied_to_principal, total_interest : real;
              month : integer;
              P: text;
  begin
    rewrite(P,'PRINTER:');
    writeln(P,'MO      PAYMENT   PRINCIPAL     INTEREST      BALANCE');
    month:=0;
    total_interest := 0;
    remaining_balance := 4000.00;
    monthly_payment := 201.14;
    rate := 0.1875;
    while remaining_balance>0 do
      begin
        month:=month+1;
        last_months_interest := remaining_balance * (rate/12);
        total_interest := total_interest + last_months_interest;
        if remaining_balance<monthly_payment then
            begin
              amount_appled_to_principal := remaining_balance;
              monthly_payment := remaining_balance + last_months_interest;
            end
          else
          amount_applied_to_principal:=monthly_payment-last_months_interest;
        remaining_balance := remaining_balance - amount_applied_to_principal;
        writeln(P, month:2, monthly_payment: 12:2,
                amount_applied_to_principal: 12:2, last_months_interest: 12:2,
                remaining_balance : 12:2)
      end;
    writeln(P,'TOTAL INTEREST             ',total_interest:12:2);
  end.
```

[Annuities]. Although the word once referred to a fixed payment per year, an annuity is now defined as a series of equal payments made at any regular interval. Many types of loans, including home mortgages, auto loans, and personal loans, can be described as annuities, in that they involve fixed payments, often per month. Four key variables fully describe an annuity:

R - the interest rate per payment period;
PV - the principal or original loan amount;
PMT - the fixed payment per period;
N - the number of periods.

Note that R is expressed as a decimal fraction, e.g., 0.0023. In the table above, which uses monthly payments, the annual rate, 18.75%, must first be divided by 12 to get the monthly rate, or 1.5625%, then divided by 100, to get it out of percentage form to a number by which we can multiply, 0.015625.

If three of the four variables that describe an annuity are known, the fourth can be calculated. If the rate of interest, principal, and number of payment periods is known, the amount of each payment can be computed by the following formula:

$$\text{let } K = (1 + R1) \hat{} N$$
$$PMT = PV * R * K / (K - 1)$$

The amount of the fixed payment in period I that is being applied to principal is:

$$APPLIED = (PMT - PV * R) * (1 + R) \hat{} (I - 1)$$

The "paid off" principal in period I is:

$$PAIDOFF = ((1 + R) \hat{} I - 1) / (K - 1) * PV$$

The amount of interest paid in a given period is PMT - APPLIED, and the total interest paid at any point is I * PMT - PAIDOFF. Note that these expressions must be very carefully evaluated in BASIC's order of precedence: exponents (^) first, multiplication and division next, addition and subtraction last.

Floppy Disks

Floppy disks have become standard equipment on small computer systems. Although some home computers, like the Atari 400, TI 99/4A, and Commodore VIC-20, can function on ROM cartridges or use cassette recorders, a random-access magnetic storage medium — like the floppy — is required to do serious work on a computer.

Floppy disks have three attributes that no other single device can provide: random access; low cost, and removability. To consider these each in turn:

Random Access. Floppy disks, which look like magnetic phonograph records, offer the same advantage in access speed that a record offers over a prerecorded tape. To find a particular song on a cassette tape, one must search all along the tape. If the song is at the end, and the tape is at its beginning, the tape must be run through in fast forward; if the song is at the beginning and the tape at the end, it must be rewound. On a phonograph, the needle can be moved directly to the start of the song. This ability to move anywhere on the medium quickly is called random access, in contrast to sequential access, where items (like songs) must always be accessed in the same sequence.

Although a floppy disk is magnetic, like tape, it has a recording head that moves over the disk like a phonograph needle (actually there is a slight difference: the "tracks" on a floppy are concentric, like rings on a tree, whereas the grooves on a phonograph record spiral inward).

Low Cost. Floppy disk drives can be added to most microcomputer systems for about $600 and often for as little as $400. The floppy disks themselves are also extremely cheap. Minifloppy

(5-1/4-inch diameter) disks retail for $5 each and can be
bought at discount or in quantity for as little as $2.50 each.
With these disks typically holding 200 kilobytes of
information, the cost per bit stored is generally lower than
on any other medium.

Removability. Although some expensive hard disk systems have
disk packs that can be carefully removed from the disk drive,
only floppies allow the creation of a large library of
information. Floppies are second in cost only to digital
magnetic tape as an archival storage medium (other archival
media, like video discs and microfilm, are not reusable, and
thus are more expensive except when mass-produced) and are
much more convenient to create.

[Floppy Terminology]. In the computer industry, the term "floppy disk" is
used several ways. (It is also spelled several ways, including "disc",
"diskette", and so on. The Computer Cookbook strongly believes that "disk" is
correct.) As used by personal computer users, a floppy is the disk itself - a
circle of plastic either 5-1/4 or 8 inches in diameter, coated with a ferric
oxide similar to that on a recording tape, and packaged in a protective square
paper envelope that prevents fingerprints and dirt from damaging the disk
surface.

In the jargon of computer professionals, "floppies" are not the medium, but
the drive - the mechanical device that reads and writes information on these
disks. Manufacturers of floppies, like Shugart, Tandon, and so on, make
hardware. The people that make the disks - 3M, Memorex, BASF - are called
media manufacturers and usually make recording tape and other audio and video
products.

Floppy disks and drives now come in three sizes: full sized, or 8 inches in
diameter; "mini", or 5-1/4 inches in diameter; and "micro", a new size
introduced in 1980, which is as yet unstandardized, and is roughly 3-1/2
inches in diameter.

Floppy disk drives can write on either one side of a disk or, with more
expensive drives, on both sides. These types of disks are called single-sided
and double-sided, respectively.

Finally, there are two types of recording techniques used: "single density"
and "double density". Double-density recording techniques pack twice as much
information into the same space as single-density techniques, at somewhat
higher cost and lower reliability. Drives that are both double-sided and
double-density are often called quad drives - adding to the confusion.

[Inside a floppy]. If we dissect a floppy disk, we find the following:

* A plastic substrate or base, usually of Mylar, although
non-duPont polyethylene products are also used. This flat
platter is 0.003 inches thick, and for a full-sized floppy,
7.88 inches in diameter, with a 1.5-inch hole in the middle.
These disks are stamped out by cookie-cutters from large,
continuous plastic sheets and have a grain that runs in the

direction in which the sheet was rolled (this grain causes read/write problems in advanced applications). The thickness of the disk prevents "talk through" on double-sided disks.

* A ferric oxide coating whose particles actually record the magnetic information. This coating is 125-microinches thick and is placed on both sides of the disk. In recent years, lubricants have been added to coatings to reduce wear on the drive read/write head, which comes in direct contact with it. The thickness of the coating on the floppy disk limits the linear bit density at which information can be recorded. A thinner coating of, for example, 75 microinches, comparable to coatings on high-performance audio tape, would allow more information to be packed on a disk, but disks with thinner coatings would wear out quickly. Alternatively, ferric oxides with what is called higher coercivity, such as chrome or cobalt-doped iron oxides, could be used to increase bit density, but these would wear out the drive read/write head.

* A poly-vinyl-chloride (PVC) jacket that protects the disk from fingers, coffee, and other hazards of the environment. This jacket has a number of notches cut in it: a center circle for the hub of the disk; two long slits, one on each side, that allow the drive's read/write head to reach the disk surface; a write-protect notch used to prevent the drive from writing on protected disks (on mini floppies, disks with tabs out can be written; the opposite is true for full-sized floppies); an index hole, used by the drive to mark the disk's rotation; and two half-moon semicircles on one edge that allow the floppy to flex without puckering. Inside the jacket, and barely visible, is a quilted liner that wipes the disk clean continuously as it turns.

Information is written on a floppy in concentric tracks, which are arranged like the rings of a tree. The number of tracks placed per inch along the radius is called the track density of the drive. Increases in track density have been the major source of increased storage capacity on floppies in recent years. Standard full-size floppy disks have 77 tracks, numbered from 00, the outermost track, to 76, closest to the center of the disk. The tracks are evenly spaced, 48 per inch, and take up only 1.6 inches of the total 4-inch radius of the disk. Track 76, the innermost track, is 2.03 inches from the center of the disk; track 00, the outermost track, is 3.62 inches from center.

Every track on a floppy is a circle. Along its arc, each track is divided into sectors. On full-sized floppies, there are usually 26 sectors per track; on mini-floppies, there are either 10 or 16. Each sector contains a certain number of bytes of information, usually either 128, 256, or sometimes 512. Note that the same fixed amount of information is stored on the inner tracks and the outer, even though the inner tracks have a considerably smaller circumference than the outer. Pulse crowding on inner tracks puts another limit on how close to the center of a disk information can be recorded; pulses tend to flatten and gap on outer tracks. This source of error is complicated by the fact that in typical operating environments, heat expands

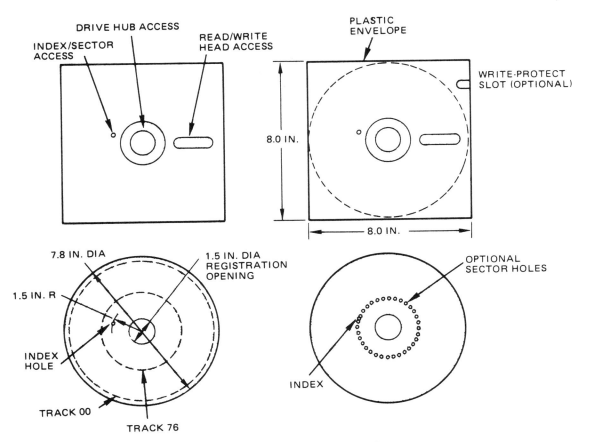

Anatomy of a Floppy Disk

the mylar disk, and cold makes it contract, leading to tracking errors. Expansion and contraction is also uneven, with the disk moving more along its grain than across it.

[Hard- and Soft-Sector Disks]. All floppy disks have an index hole punched in the plastic of the disk. Within the floppy disk drive, a small LED shines a light beam at the point on the floppy where the index hole should be. As the floppy rotates, this light beam, coupled with a photocell at the receiving end, sends an index pulse as the hole cuts across the beam. The index pulse is used as a reference mark to tell the disk controller where the disk is.

On soft-sector disks, such as those used on the Apple II, a distinctive bit pattern called a preamble and postamble is coded to mark off sectors. Soft-sector disks don't need index holes; the Apple, for example, can use any type of 5-1/4-inch disk in its drives. Unfortunately, soft-sectoring adds overhead bytes, reduces the storage capacity of the disk, and can also be less reliable than hard-sectoring. Soft-sectoring was introduced by IBM and is the usual technique for dividing full-sized floppies into sectors.

For mini-floppies, however, as well as for some specialized full-sized floppies, hard-sector formats are used. In hard-sectoring, a ring of holes punched around the center of the disk (either 10, 16, or 32, depending on manufacturer) send pulses at the start of each sector. Hard-sectoring allows simpler controller design and more efficient use of the recording surface of the disk. However, each manufacturer of a hard-sector disk tends to use a unique format. Where interchange of floppy data is required, IBM's single-sided, full-sized, soft-sector format - the 3740 format - is the only de facto industry standard.

[History of the Floppy]. Magnetic recording on a disk surface is an old idea. Al Shugart, later a founder of Shugart Associates, claims he proposed the floppy disk to IBM in 1960, only to have the idea turned down. Nevertheless, in the late 1960s, IBM developed a dedicated floppy - ironically, to load program code into a hard-disk device.

Several independent firms attempted to develop floppy products, but, as in the early days of aviation, progress was slow. One design, by a now-bankrupt Massachusetts firm, featured a disk that stood still and a recording head that spun. (Within the trade, this device is still called the "Polish floppy".) In Italy, Olivetti Corporation, the typewriter manufacturer, recorded on disks in an inward spiral similar to a phonograph groove, thereby giving up random access, a vital feature of the disks.

Finally, in the early 1970s, IBM sponsored a competition among several research teams to design a replacement to its infamous card punches. The final choice was between a floppy disk device and a magnetic cassette device. IBM chose the floppy.

IBM's 3740 data entry station put its stamp of approval on the floppy. The 3740 format is still the de facto interchange medium within the industry. IBM had as many as 500,000 keypunches in the field at the time it announced that the floppy disk device would replace them. Naturally, more than a few companies wanted a piece of this replacement market.

IBM's design for the 3740 was very conservative. At the time, IBM believed that floppies would be used to "batch" entry data. The full-sized floppy was designed to hold the same amount of information that 3,000 punch cards would hold - the maximum of what a single keypunch operator could do in a day. The 3740 format has 128 bytes per sector, 26 sectors per track, and 77 tracks per disk, a total of 256,256 bytes per disk.

[3740 Format]. The 3740 format is highly specific. Each sector has a preamble and a postamble, whose unique bit pattern tells the disk controller where in its spin the disk is.

The point of reference for the disk controller (the controller circuits are sometimes located inside the floppy drive case, sometimes inside the computer) is the index hole. When the index hole goes by, the controller looks on a track for 40 bytes of hexadecimal FF, 6 bytes of 00, a 1-byte index address mark, and 26 bytes of FF. After that, each of the 26 sectors on the disk have the following format:

6	00	}
1	ID ADDRESS MARK	}
1	TRACK NUMBER	}

```
1          00                          } ID FIELD
1          SECTOR NUMBER               }
1          00                          }
2          CRC                         }

11         FF                          } GAP

6          00                          }
1          DATA ADDRESS MARK           }
128        DATA BYTES                  } DATA FIELD
2          CRC                         }
27         FF                          }
```

After 26 complete sectors like this, the remainer of the track is filled with approximately 247 bytes of FF.

Beyond this physical structure, however, 3740 and 3741 disks have a particular formatting. Track 00 on the disk is the index track. Sectors 1-6 on the index track are reserved for IBM. Sector 7 contains the volume label for the disk. Sectors 8-26 contain one data set label for each set of data on the disk, up to 16 total. Data occupies tracks 1-75 and must be blocked into 128-byte records. Tracks 76 and 77 are reserved. See IBM publications GA21-9131-4 or GA21-9183 for exact format details.

[Double Density Disks]. By the mid-1970s, a number of uses beyond data entry were being found for the floppy. These new uses strained the capacity of the single-sided, single-density floppy. Two solutions came to mind: double the density, and use both sides of the disk. In 1976, IBM announced a double-sided disk, the 3601, although a number of independent firms led the way with double-density recording. (IBM finally announced a double-density Diskette II in late 1978.) These innovations made it possible to store well over a megabyte (1 million bytes) of information on a single disk.

Single-density floppies use one of the most reliable recording formats for magnetic media, the FM or double-frequency code. The FM code pairs every information bit (either a 1 or 0) with a clock bit. This produces a simple recording scheme with excellent timing margins (e.g., tolerance to too fast or too slow drives) and good immunity from media-induced distortions. On the other hand, FM wastes half the capacity of the disk, since it uses two pulses or flux transitions to represent one bit of data.

The rule for decoding FM encoding is simple: a clock pulse marks every cell boundary. If a flux transition occurs at the center of the cell, the data bit is a 1. If no flux transition occurs, the data bit is a 0.

As floppy drives improved in manufacturing quality, and as disk media improved, it became an increasingly attractive option to use the clock bit to carry information. This was not without some risk, since the clock bit could not longer be counted on to provide a simple, steady tick. Two coding schemes, MFM and M2FM, were developed to turn, in essence, both clock and data bit into data bits. MFM uses the following convention, different for the former clock and information bits: a flux transition occurs at the boundary between cells having successive "0" information bits (this is the rule for

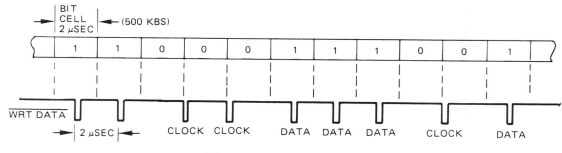

DOUBLE-DENSITY ENCODING (MFM)

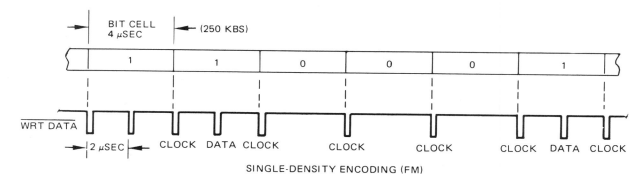

SINGLE-DENSITY ENCODING (FM)

Two Data Encoding Schemes for Floppies

clock bits); a flux transition occurs at the center of a cell if the information bit is 1; if no transition occurs, the information bit is a 0 (data bit rule). For example:

The limiting factor in recording on floppy disks is the number of flux transitions that can be squeezed together on the innermost tracks. MFM, by using the clock bit, packs twice as much data into the same space. M2FM offers an improvement in reliability over MFM in that it reduces the number of flux transitions required, with only a slightly more complex algorithm. In M2FM, a transition occurs at the boundary of two cells if no clock bit was written at the previous boundry, and the boundary is between successive data bits 0s (this is the clock bit rule); and a transition occurs in the middle of a cell if the cell contains an information bit "1" (data bit rule).

[Capacity Wars]. In the late 1970s and early 1980s, a constant stream of improvements were made both to full-size floppies and particularly to mini-floppies that allowed sharp increases in data capacity, although sometimes with reliability problems. In March 1980, Commodore unveiled a 5-1/4-inch floppy, the CBM 8050, with over 1 megabyte of storage. The drive has 100 tracks per inch and is double-sided, with an OEM price of $1,695.

Most of these improvements came by increasing the track density (number of tracks per inch along the diameter of the disk), the total number of tracks (by using more of the area of the disk), or the packing density. Micropolis developed 100 track/inch technology for mini-floppies in 1976. Micropolis double-sided 100 track drives have a 1.170-Mbyte capacity using group code recording (GCR) and a 0.960-Mbyte capacity using MFM. Double-headed drives began shipping in quantity in 1980 after delays due to media wear problems in the prototypes. (Special alignment disks for high track density disks are available from Dymek of Santa Clara, CA.)

Shugart introduced its own 96-track/inch drives in late 1980. The Shugart SA410 is a single-sided drive; the SA460 is double-sided. Further, the drives can read 48-track/inch disks written by Shugart's older models, the SA400 and SA450. The drives use a helical cam v-groove lead screw to position heads and have a track to track average access time of 160 msec. Micro Peripherals, Inc. makes a 96-track/inch drive, which it has modified to work at 100 tracks/inch for use in Durango Systems computers. Tandon Magnetics TM-100, introduced in 1980, has 80 tracks on two sides, each with 5,877-bits/inch recording density. Tandon's drives are used in North Star, IBM, and other computers A complete list of models:

TM-100-1	40 tracks X 1 side	(250K capacity)
TM-100-2	40 tracks X 2 sides	(500K capacity)
TM-100-3	80 tracks X 1 sides	(500K capacity)
TM-100-4	80 tracks X 2 sides	(1M capacity)

[The Micro-Floppy]. For consumers, the price of mini-floppy disk drives has stubbornly hovered above the $500 mark. Although CPU and RAM memory prices have fallen sharply in recent years, the high prices of electromechanical devices like floppies and printers have been a major problem in efforts to reduce the cost of personal computers to consumer price levels. Further, mini-floppy disk drives, although smaller than full-sized drives, are heavy and not easily portable.

For some time, then, the industry has seen the need for an even smaller floppy disk drive - a "micro-floppy". In 1980, Sony introduced one for its Series 35 word processor. The Sony micro-floppy is 3-1/2 inches in diameter and stores 437 kbytes of data on one side. In 1982, Sony introduced a lightweight personal computer using micro-floppies, and, in a move that may have guaranteed the success of the small disk, Hewlett-Packard signed a $30 million OEM agreement to buy the disks from Sony for its own systems. Jonos, Ltd., maker of another portable computer, has a smaller OEM agreement with Sony.

Although the Sony 3-1/2-inch format has an edge on the market, in 1982 there were two other micro-floppy formats, a 3-inch diskette from Matsushita Electric that is also supported by Hitachi, Ltd., and Hitachi Maxell, Ltd.; and a 3.8-inch disk from Canon. In early 1982, a number of US manufacturers, including Shugart Associates, Tandon Magnetics, Dysan, Tabor, and Verbatim, formed a committee to set a standard for micro-floppy disks. Micro-floppies are likely to use rigid cartridges to house the spinning magnetic media rather than the paper envelopes of conventional disks.

FORTH

Forth is an extendable stack language originally developed by Charles Moore at the National Radio Astronomy Laboratory in New Mexico. Although Moore's company, Forth, Inc., based in Mahattan Beach, CA, has registered "Forth" as its trademark, there are a number of implementations of "Forth-type" languages - especially for the Apple and 6502 - for sale by companies other than Forth, Inc.

(Note that "BASIC" is also a registered trademark, of the Trustees of Dartmouth College, where it was developed in the 1960s, and that "Ada" is a trademark of the US Department of Defense, which one must assume has the ability to enforce its claim!)

The following discussion uses the syntax conventions of an implementation of Forth by Applied Analytics Incorporated (8910 Brookridge Dr., Upper Marlboro, MD 20772), which sells a product called "microSPEED". "microSPEED" consists of two items: (1) an arithmetic processor board for the Apple II (the first 100 or so buyers of microSPEED received a board manufactured by California Computer Products; later, Applied Analytics began making its own, functionally identical board), and (2) a two-disk software package containing an implementation of the Forth language with special verbs designed to take advantage of the hardware.

Talking about Forth is similar to talking about religion: it is best to let prejudices be known early. Although Forth is an excellent tool for increasing the productivity of individual programmers, Forth programs tend to be highly individual - unreadable by others. Forth is not necessarily a good choice of language for large-scale programming projects where code must be shared among several programmers. For these applications, The Computer Cookbook believes that structured languages like Pascal, Ada, or C are preferable.

Forth operates on VERBS or NUMBERS. The beauty of Forth is that it not only gives the programmer access to the system-defined verbs - comparable to commands in BASIC - but it also allows him or her to define new verbs. Consider a Forth system, like Microspeed's, that has the verbs HOME and TEXT. A new verb, DOWNHOME, could be defined by the following command:

```
# : DOWNHOME HOME TEXT ;
```

Forth keeps a list of valid verbs in its dictionary. To see what primitives are defined in any given Forth implementation, the command VERBS usually provides a list of those defined in the system.

[The Stack]. Stacks, as many programmers know, are important in nearly all computers, although BASIC programmers may never be aware of them. One of the major differences between Forth and other higher-level languages (there are those who would dispute that Forth is a high-level language at all, but rather maintain that Forth is a macro language instead) is that it not only allows, but requires, manipulation of a stack.

The best way to keep track of a stack is with pencil and paper - a process that in assembly language programming used to be called "hand simulation". A stack has a top and a bottom. The top of the stack is always active. Consider the following stack of numbers:

234 4532 32 325 2

Here, the top of the stack is on the right, and the bottom of the stack is on the left. "Adding the two numbers on the top of the stack" means adding 325 and 2 - the result being 327. The command "add the two numbers on the top of the stack, and place the result on the top of the stack" results in this:

234 4532 32 327

Taking numbers off the top of the stack is called popping them off the top. Putting new values onto the stack is called pushing them. In operations like addition, the real description of the operation is, "pop the two top numbers off the top of the stack, add them together, and push the result onto the stack." Note that this operation decrements (decreases by one) the size of the stack.

In stack operations, it is vital to keep track of the net change to the stack - is it decremented or incremented? (Pushing something puts an item on the stack and is sometimes said to increment the stack pointer; popping something takes one item off the stack and is sometimes said to decrement the stack pointer).

In dealing with Forth verbs, it is important to keep a table of their effect on the stack. The standard verb "." prints the number on top of the stack and decrements the stack by one. A table of its effect might look like:

verb	before	after	action
.	a -	--	print top of stack using base

[Stack Manipulation Primitives]. Arithmetic operations in Forth must generally be specified in Reverse Polish Notation, also called "postfix" notation. In postfix, the operation of adding "a" and "b" is expressed "ab+". (In "prefix," or simple Polish Notation, it is "+ab"; our usual way of writing it, "a+b", is technically called "infix".) The trouble with Reverse Polish Notation, as those who have used Hewlett-Packard calculators know, is getting the order of things right. Forth comes with a number of convenient stack-switching operations defined. These include:

verb	before	after	action
DUP	a -	a a -	duplicate top entry of stack
ROT	a b c	b c a	rotate top three entries

```
SWAP    a b -    b a -    swap top two entries
DROP    a -      - -      drop the top entry
OVER    a b -    a b a    copy the second entry over top
ABORT   x y      - - -    clears stack
```

[Constants]. Most Apple implementations of Forth use integers between -32768 and +32767, as does Apple Integer BASIC. (The number range, equal to 2 to the 15th power, is a result of using one bit out of 16 as a sign bit; the difference of one is due to the fact that the 6502 uses two's complement arithmetic, where a negative number is represented by its logical complement plus 1).

Most implementations of Forth allow use of multiple radi, that is, number bases. In MicroSPEED Forth, the verb DEC sets the system to work in base 10, until changed by a subsequent verb, such as HEX (set to base 16). The verb BASE? responds (places on the top of the stack) with the current number base in decimal.

[Arithmetic Operations]. Forth has the following arithmetic operations: +, -, *, /, which operate with the top two items on the stack. Thus if a and b are on the stack, the operator "/" divides a by b and places the result, c on the stack where a was. The net result is to decrement the stack by one. A useful verb "/MOD" operates like division but pushes the remainder on the stack, then the quotient, for no net change in the stack pointer.

[Variables and Memory]. So far, Forth is just a stack-oriented calculator. The verb "!" stores the value of the top of the stack in the memory location given by the next-to-top value. Both are removed from the stack, meaning a net loss of two. The verb "@" fetches a number from the memory location given by the top of the stack; there is no net change in the stack count.

Constants can be given names in Forth by using the verb CONSTANT. The format is:

                   <fixed value> CONSTANT <name>

Simple integer variables can be likewise declared and initialized by:

                   <initial value> VARIABLE <variablename>

However, use of the verb <variablename> puts the variable's address, not its value, on the stack. The "@" command must then be used to get the value. Thus, the two lines of Forth:

                   28 VARIABLE DAYSINFEB
                   DAYSINFEB @ .

prints out "28", the verb for printing being a period, ".".

Defining arrays in Forth is more tricky. A verb "," will pop the stack and put the number into the dictionary as an "amendment" to the last definition. The code:

                   15 VARIABLE XARRAY

```
111 , 222 , 333 ,
```

creates, in effect, an array with four integer values, 15, 111, 222, and 333.

[Logical Operators and Program Control]. Forth defines the following logical operators: =, <=, >=, <, >, and <> (not equal to). Like the arithmetic operators, they take two items, a and b, from the stack and push a result (0 if false, 1 if true) onto the stack.

Once a logical value is on top of the stack, it can be used to control the flow of a program. This is done by including, in verb definitions, IF ELSE THEN constructs. The code between the IF and the ELSE is executed if the top of the stack is true; otherwise, the code between the ELSE and the THEN is executed. The code that follows in the THEN is always executed.

A BEGIN...END structure in Forth also uses the stack; if, on encountering the verb END, the number on the top of the stack is not 1, the code starting with BEGIN is repeated. A "DO LOOP" structure is defined as follows: two constants are pushed on the stack; the DO verb removes them and places the index counter and limit in a special place; the LOOP verb increments the index counter and compares it with the limit. Inside a loop, the index has a special name, I. Note that this structure does not allow convenient nesting. Up to three levels of index pointers ("I", "J", and "K") can be accessed in the microSPEED implementation.

[Microcomputer FORTHs]. Forth is available on almost every microcomputer made — if one looks hard enough for the small company or individual programmer selling it. A good place to start in Forth research is Mountain View Press, Inc. (PO Box 4656 Mountain View, CA 94040, 415-981-4103) which specializes in Forth books and software.

A major "brand" of Forth is that defined by the Forth Interest Group (PO Box 1105, San Carlos, CA 94070). FIG is in some competition with the more commercial Forth language vendors, but it serves as a standards body for smaller companies. The best Apple II Forth, FIG-inspired, is from Cap'n Software (PO Box 575, San Francisco, CA 94101, 415-540-0202), John Draper's ("Easy Writer") company. An OSI FIG Forth is available from Software Consultants (7053 Rose Trail, Memphis, TN 38134, 901-377-3503). "Forth 79", another FIG Forth, is sold by Micromotion (12077 Wilshire Blvd., Suite 506, Los Angeles, CA 90025, 213-821-4340).

Forth has tended to be a 6502 and Apple language, although a Z-80 Forth is available both from FIG and Laboratory Microsystems (4147 Beethoven St., Los Angeles, CA 90066). Several things calling themselves Forth, with unknown pedigree, are "OmniForth", from Interactive Computer Systems, Inc. (6403 DiMarco Rd., Tampa, FL 33614), and "First", from First is Fast (6829 Waterman, St Louis, MO 63130). "mmsFORTH" from Miller Microcomputer Services (61 Lake Shore Rd., Natick, MA 01760, 617-653-6136) is a professional-looking Forth. However, one should write for details or invest in the manual before buying these minor FORTHs, even though they may be excellent.

G

Computer Games

Today, an equal number of people know that (a) George Washington, in the US, is called "the father of his country", and (b) "Pong" was the father of all video games. "Pong", however, is like the anthropoid monkeys with names like "Lucy" and "Sam" - no one is exactly sure how we got from there.

After "Space Invaders" there are far fewer doubts about actual paternity of individual games. "Space Invaders" was invented in 1977 by Taito, Ltd., a little Japanese company who up to that time had been outfitting Pachinko parlors. Pachinko parlors, for those who have never been to one, look very much like the slot saloons in Atlantic City or Vegas and are filled with equally mesmerizing machines. Pachinko has an important place in Japanese society, namely because playing pachkinko is about the only place you can be alone on that island.

Since World War II, or the Pacific War, as they call it, the Japanese have been understandably nervous about intrusions into their airspace, but their pacifist constitution and good manners require that they transpose these fears into serious worries about alien creatures attacking earth. "Space Invaders" was a perfect incarnation of Japanese xenophobia and Japanese electronics.

"Space Invaders" has many of the attributes that we look for in a classic, be it a motor vehicle from Detroit or a stage play from Moliere. "Space Invaders" has clarity, simplicity, and rationality. Like soldiers in the Napoleonic Age, the invaders march toward the defender in rows, only to be mowed down by a horizontally mobile, machine-age cannon. In military terms, "Space Invaders" makes it to the era of trench mouth and trench warfare.

Personal computer games can be divided into large "families", or, to borrow a term from literary studies, genres. Arcade games derive from the shooting gallery. There are targets, and there is a shooter. Various subspecies of games develop when the target(s) move in novel ways ("Galaxian" versus "Space Invaders") or when the shooter moves ("Asteroids").

A second major family of games is the "point of view" (POV) game, in which the computer user, at his or her console at home, is put into a dangerous or otherwise difficult but realistic situation. The classic example of this family is the "flight simulation" program, which simulates flying an airplane, often quite well. "3-D Grand Prix" is a similar concept with auto racing, as are some variants of "Lunar Lander", in which one views the onrushing moon surface. Mattel sells a downhill skiing simulation that would also qualify, as would presumably a parachute-jump simulation, etc.

These games, which rely heavily on graphics to produce a realistic effect, must be distinguished from what are commonly called "simulations" in the educational software field. Simulations, of which the Huntington II package is the classic example, take complex relationships (food and population, etc.) and use the computer's computational ability in a series of "rounds" to attempt to illustrate multivariate cause-and-effect relationships. They are often numerical and not graphic at all. Sports simulations, which rely heavily on percentages and statistics, are a major subgroup of this type.

Computer versions of board games are yet another category. Good for shut-ins, unattended children, etc., in these games the computer takes the place of a 2nd (or more) player. The key here is that the computer is simulating a human. The mechanical blackjack dealer is one end of this scale; at the anthropromorphic end is "Monty Plays Monopoly" (Personal Software). In general, war games and strategy games (Avalon-Hill, Strategic Simulations) fall into this genre. Often, these games are packaged like board games.

Adventure games might be called "interactive literature"; they are original to the personal computer. Adventure is an unfolding story that depends on previous action by the "reader". Adventure games can take months to play. Most Adventure games use folk-tale conventions. Perhaps predictably, a new twist to the Adventure game appeared in mid-1980 when a number of cheesecake ads in the computer magazines announced "Interlude", which, doubtless with some exaggeration, was subtitled "The Ultimate Experience".

Interlude is a version of "Adventure" where, instead of running into such PG items as dragons and fairy kings, the encounter was with an equally fantastic member of the opposite sex, viz., Interlude #42, "A surprise on the way home from dinner". A few special Interludes were kept "hidden" on the disk, to be revealed only when a prelimary "interview" with the computer (that is, an intelligent, or at least spiteful, menu selection program) decided the user was ready.

Adventure games have the interesting property of communicating in "near English". As microprocessor power increases and becomes more sophisticated, mainframe-like software will run on micros with sufficient response time, and adventures should become yet more intelligent.

[Educational Games]. Although the distinction between entertainment games and educational games is hard to draw, there are clear subtypes of educational games. The computer is a patient holder of "flash cards" for memory drill; cards flashed can be either textual (vocabulary drill) or graphic ("Flags of the World" on the 1st National KidDisc; "Airplane Identification", a microcomputer program). A star-gazing program for learning the constellations of the night sky is another example.

Speech synthesizers open up a much larger category, especially for pre-literate children. Conceptually, what is restricted to printed text output in nearly all game categories can be replaced by spoken text by simply considering the speech synthesizer to be a "talking printer"; this extends the age range of these games downward. Aural versions of other games are possible. "Simon", the hand-held electronic game, is an aural memory drill. There are a number of highly interesting games possible with synthesizers for the learning disabled or physically handicapped, as well as foreign language drills of all types.

[The I Ching]. The I Ching or Book of Changes is one of 5 Confucian Classics that dates to the 12th century BC. It is wise to consult the I Ching before making important decisions and to improve your outlook on life.

Using a computer to generate the hexagrams of the I Ching is an interesting exercise in simulation and in how far it should go.

A hexagram is made up of 6 horizontal lines, which are either broken "yin" lines or solid "yang" lines. Naturally, 6 lines with 2 possibilities each yields 2**6 or 64 different hexagrams. A typical hexagram, T-HAI, "Peace", looks like:

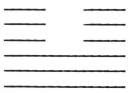

Each line of the hexagram is generated in the same way, starting with the lowest of the 6 horizontal lines. In the classic method, 50 yarrow stalks are used to determine the lines as follows:

    Step 1: Set aside 1 stick from the bundle of 50. Discard it.

    Step 2: Divide the bundle roughly in half. Call the left hand
        bunch L, and the right-hand bunch R.

    Step 3: Take 1 stick from R and move it to a 1st "active pile",
        A1.

    Step 4: Take 4 sticks away from L. Repeat until 4 sticks or
        less remain. Put these in the active pile, A1.

    Step 5: Take 4 sticks away from R. Repeat until 4 sticks or less
        remain. Put this in the active pile, A.

    Step 6: Take all sticks not in the active pile(s) and recombine
        them. Using these sticks, repeat steps 2 to 5 to create 2
        more active piles, A2 and A3.

    Step 7: If Steps 1-6 were followed correctly, the first active
        pile, A1, will have 9 or 5 sticks, A2 will have 8 or 4 sticks,
        and A3 will have 8 or 4 sticks.

Step 8: Map the stick count to a numerical value. If A1=9, it
    maps to 2. If A1=5, it maps to 3. A2 and A3 map to 2 if they
    equal 8, and to 3 if they equal 4.

Step 9: Total the mapped values. A total of 5 generates an old
    yang line: ---O---. A total of 9 generates an old yin line:
    ---X---. A total of 7 generates a young yang line: -------.
    A total of 8 generates a young yin line. --- ---.

Step 10: Repeat for each of the six lines of the hexagram.

The old and young lines are sometimes called static and moving lines.
Moving and static lines add twists to hexagram interpretation.

Several points should be noted. First, yin and yang are not, apparently,
evenly distributed. There is more yang in the world than yin. In tests, yang
turns up about 56% of the time, and yin turns up the rest. Although yang is
the "male" principle, and yin the female, this pecentage split between the
sexes is contrary to the way it is in nature.

Simulating a split bundle poses an interesting computer problem, namely,
generating "about half" randomly. What is wanted is a normal distribution:
unfortunately, most computer systems generate random numbers smoothly between
the interval 0 to 1.

Once the computer has generated the hexagram, the text of the I Ching must be
consulted to interpret it. The best translation is by Richard Wilhelm and is
published by Princeton University Press, although paperback translations are
available. Some hexagrams:

```
____  KH-YEN      __ __  KH-WAN      __ __  KHUN          ____   MANG
____  (Yang)      __ __  (Yin)       ____   (Growing      __ __  (Youthful
                                            Pains)                Ignorance)
____              __ __         __ __              __ __
____              __ __         __ __              ____
____              __ __         __ __              ____
____              __ __         ____              __ __
```

["Startrek"]. Although computers can play arcade-style video games, their
true capabilities are better exercised on complicated simulations and
adventure games that require the use of floppy disks or local storage.

Versions of the computer game "Startrek" - based, of course, on the TV series,
which is both copyrighted and trademarked - have floated around timesharing
computers since the early 1970s. Here are the rules for one version:

STARTREK

DESCRIPTION

"... TO BOLDLY GO WHERE NO MAN HAS GONE BEFORE". Welcome captain, It
is your mission to destroy the Klingon stronghold in the galaxy. You
must captain the Enterprise to the completion of your mission before
time runs out and it is too late. You may be hindered by sabotage.
You may be destroyed by Romulin probes. You could run into a star, or

even leave the space time continuum!

INSTRUCTIONS

To Execute: PLAY STARTREK
Start by typing a number from 1 to 9 indicating the difficulty level
you want (9 is the hardest). When the computer prints 'COMMAND-'
your command should be typed, followed by a 'RETURN'.

   Available commands are:

Command   Function
-------   --------
M (Move)   Indicates that you want to rev up the engines in
           order to move the enterprise. You will be asked:

              'ENTER COURSE'

           Respond by typing a number from 1 to 9 according
           to the direction you want as this chart indicates:

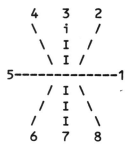

           Fractional numbers, like 2.7, can be used as desired.
           Next, type the distance you want to travel, if your
           warp engines are damaged you can't go above 0.2. A
           distance of one is sufficient to move you the distance
           equal to the length of one quadrant.

(Short-   This command gives the Short-Range Sensor Scan. It
Range   includes information on what is in your immediate
Sensor   vicinity. The symbols used are as follows:
Scan)
              # Planet   +++ Klingon   <E> Enterprise
              * Star   >!< Star Base

           By docking with a Starbase you will replenish your
           energies and supplies.

L   This command displays the Long-Range Sensor Scan. It
(Long-   shows what is in your current, and in surrounding quadrants
Range   in the form of a three-digit number. The first digit is
Sensor   the number of Klingons in the quadrant, second is the
Scan)   number of starbases, and third is the number of stars.

           For Example:

```
                    2 - Klingons        0 - Klingons
                    1 - Star Base       0 - Star Bases
                    7 - Stars           3 - Stars
```

P   Fire Phasars. The computer will lock onto the target
(Fire   and then ask for the amount of energy you want to expend.
Phasars)   The higher the number, the better your chances of destroying
             the target, but the less energy you'll have afterward.

T   Fire Photon torpedos on a course. The course for the
(Fire   torpedo is directional, like the course you need to
Photon   maneuver the enterprise. See the diagram for course
Torpedo)   numbers.

E   Allocate how much energy, of that which you have remaining,
(Shield   is to be put into supporting the shields. Each time you
Energy   receive a hit, energy is depleted from the shields; the
Control)   closer the shot is fired, the stronger the shot and the more
             energy is depleted. If the energy in the shields ever drops
             to zero and you sustain a hit, you will be destroyed.

D   Report the current functional of the main ship equipment.
(Damage   The 'State of Repair' code indicates the condition
Report)   of the equipment; the lower the number, the better
             the equipment is. 0 indicates fully functional.

C   Computer facilities
(Computer)   The computer supports the following services:
             Command   Function
                R   Display the cumulative Galactic record
                S   Display current status report
                T   Display photon torpedo attack data for
                        any Klingons in the current quadrant
                C   Initiate navigational subsystem for
                        interquadrant travel

N   Prints the chart of what numbers to type for a desired
(Chart)   course. See command 'M'.

R   Radio the nearest command post for emergency reserve
(Reserve   power. This option may be used only once through the
Power)   course of a single game.

A   Abort the mission.
(Abort)

H   Give a short list of commands including a brief description
(Help)   of what they do.

You may stop the game at any time by depressing the 'BREAK' key,
or by typing the 'A' command when your command is requested.

SAMPLE OUTPUT
------ ------
>PLAY STARTREK

 ENTER A NUMBER FROM 1 TO 9 FOR HOW DIFFICULT OF GAME
 YOU WANT TO PLAY (1 IS THE EASIEST TO PLAY)

ENTER DIFFICULTY FACTOR -3

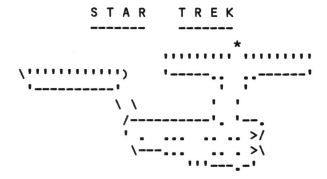

S T A R   T R E K

 THE USS ENTERPRISE IS ON PATROL IN THE ARCTURUS
 SECTOR OF THE GALAXY NEAR GAMMA TRIKELLION - 1
 YOUR MISSION IS TO DESTROY THE DEADLY KLINGON MENACE.
 YOU MUST DESTROY 16 KLINGON BATTLE CRUISERS IN 27
 STARDATES. THERE ARE 3 STARBASES IN THE GALAXY.

COMMAND -Scatinf

```
 -  -  -  -  -  -  -  -
 -    *        *        -  RATING           0.
 -      <E>         *   -  STARDATE      2000
 -               *      -  CONDITION    GREEN
 -                   *  -  QUADRANT       4,1
 -                      -  SECTOR         2,3
 -                      -  ENERGY     3745.000
 -                      -  TORPEDOES       14
 -    *        *     *  -  SHIELDS      0.000
 -                      -
 -  -  -  -  -  -  -  -
```

COMMAND -L

 L.R. SCAN FOR QUADRANT 4,1

 !   ! 108 ! 1 !

 !   ! 8 ! 6 !

 !   ! 5 ! 103 !

COMMAND -M
ENTER COURSE (0-9) -3

```
ENTER WARP FACTOR (0-8) -.8
 COMBAT AREA         CONDITION RED!!!
 COMPUTER PUT SHIELDS TO 200 UNITS


    -  -  -  -  -  -  -  -
  -    *              *    -  RATING           0.
  -                        -  STARDATE         2001
  -    *                   -  CONDITION        RED!!!
  -      <E>               -  QUADRANT         3,1
  -        *               -  SECTOR           4,3
  -          *      *      -  ENERGY           3544.000
  -            +++ *        -  TORPEDOES            14
  -      *                 -  SHIELDS          200.000
    -  -  -  -  -  -  -  -


COMMAND -M
ENTER COURSE (0-9) -1
ENTER WARP FACTOR (0-8) -.3
 ********** PHASOR HIT ON THE NUMBER 5 SHIELD **********
    187.352 UNIT HIT ON THE ENTERPRISE FROM SECTOR 7,5
     12.648 UNITS LEFT FOR SHIELDS
 DAMAGE CONTROL REPORT
    DAMAGE CONTROL DAMAGED


    -  -  -  -  -  -  -  -
  -    *              *    -  RATING           0.
  -                        -  STARDATE         2001
  -    *                   -  CONDITION        RED!!!
  -          <E>           -  QUADRANT         3,1
  -      *           +++ -  SECTOR           4,5
  -        *      *        -  ENERGY           3543.000
  -               *        -  TORPEDOES            14
  -      *                 -  SHIELDS           12.648
    -  -  -  -  -  -  -  -


COMMAND -E
 SHIELD CONTROL IS INOPERATIVE

COMMAND -C
COMPUTER ACTIVE AND AWAITING COMMAND -T
 DIRECTION =    8.6667
 DISTANCE  =    3.0000

COMMAND -T
ENTER TORPEDO COURSE (1-9) -8.6667
 L.R. SENSORS   REPAIRED
 TORPEDO TRACK
        4.333  6.000
        4.667  7.000
        5.000  8.000


{The game continues in this fashion}
```

GPIB

Long before it became a computer company, Hewlett-Packard was a maker of quality scientific and laboratory instruments. In 1972, in an effort to standardize the way in which laboratory instruments were wired together, HP designed the General Purpose Instrument Bus (GPIB), also called the "Hewlett-Packard Instrument Bus". In 1975, after active lobbying by HP, this bus became IEEE standard 488-1975. In the late 1970s, the IEEE-488 bus was designed into a number of microcomputers, including the Commodore PET. As one of the few standards in a highly unstandardized world, IEEE-488 still holds a solid place, especially in European and Japanese designs.

Unlike local area networks or even RS-232-C connections, the GPIB was designed to work over a limited area, about the size of a scientific lab. The GPIB can string together up to 15 devices, including the controlling computer. The maximum distance between each device is 5 meters; the total length of the wiring is a maximum of 20 meters. GPIB connectors have 24 pins; instruments attaching to a GPIB net almost always have female connectors. The general pinout of a GPIB connector is:

DIO1	1	13	DIO5
DIO2	2	14	DIO6
DIO3	3	15	DIO7
DIO4	4	16	DIO8
EOI	5	17	REN
DAV	6	18	GRN (DAV)
NRFD	7	19	GRN (NRFD)
NDAC	8	20	GRN (NDAC)
IFC	9	21	GRN (IFC)
SRQ	10	22	GRN (SRQ)
ATN	11	23	GRN (ATN)
SHIELD	12	24	GRN (LOGIC)

The physically larger side of the connector is to the left, which is commonly the top side.

Of the 16 active lines, 8 are data lines, 5 are bus management lines, and 3 are handshaking lines. The data lines are DIO1 to 8, with DIO8 the most significant bit. The GPIB is thus a byte-parallel bus.

The GPIB is somewhat like a telephone party line: there are Talkers and Listners. It is important for everybody not to talk at once. A Master or Controller, who might be thought of as an electronic moderator, decides when Talkers can talk. Some devices are Talk only (TON); typically these babble away and are sometimes difficult to shut up. Other devices are listen only (LON).

[The Controller]. When the Controller comes on, it usually asserts IFC, or interface clear (line 8). This resets the network. The Controller then has available to it two types of commands, Uniline commands, which use one of 5 special bus management lines, and Multiline messages, which use the data lines.

The IFC command, the first of the 5 Uniline commands, resets the bus. The ATN (Attention) line is the next most important. When ATN is true, the byte on the DIO lines is a command. If ATN is not true, it is data. EOI (End of Message) should be on the last of a string of data bytes but in practice is not always used by instruments, many of which send an ASCII CR/LF when done. SRQ (Service Request) allows an instrument to request attention but is infrequently used. REN (remote enable) allows the Controller to remotely take an instrument "off line" so that it is controlled by its front panel switches.

[Handshaking]. The GPIB works on the buddy system: everybody waits for the slowest reader. When a device is not ready for data, it asserts NRFD - not ready for data. This holds up everybody until it is ready for data. When it is, the Talker on the bus can send a byte of information. The Talker then asserts (makes true) DAV - data valid. The Listeners then read the data byte and set NRFD true until they digest it, at which time they make Not Ready for Data false. When all have read the byte, the Talker makes DAV false and then does the whole thing over again.

Talking and Listening is controlled by a device's address. Most IEEE-488 devices have a 5-position dip switch that allows an address from 0 to 31 to be selected. A device becomes a Talker if it receives from the Controller a command byte (where ATN is asserted) whose value is 32 plus the device address. Likewise, a device becomes a Listener if it receives a command byte of 32 plus its address. Device address 31 is reserved. Several commands affect all devices: 95, "untalk", tells everybody to pipe down, and 63, "unlisten", tells them all to cover their ears.

[The HP 59309A Digital Clock]. The Hewlett-Packard 59309A Digital Clock is a typical device that might be attached to a GPIB. When the clock is addressed to talk, it will send a month, day (of month), hour, minute, and seconds message in the following format:

?MMDDHHMMSS cr lf

The question mark is present only if the clock has not been set since it was last powered up; otherwise, a space is sent. When the clock is told to listen, it obeys the following commands: P (stop); T (start); R (reset); S (increment seconds); M (increment minutes); H (increment hours); D (increment days); C (note time, send it when addressed). A variable length string of these is needed to set the clock.

[Negative True Logic]. To avoid confusion, nothing has been said about what it means, electrically, for a Listener or Talker to assert a line as "true". The GPIB differs from some common microcomputer buses in that it uses a better bus logic, called negative true logic. In negative true logic, a grounded line is true (logic 1), although the quiet state of the system is +5 volts (logic 0). This not only helps in the party line aspect of the bus - grounded by one, grounded by all - but is more natural than, say, S-100 bus logic in that lines will often "drift" high. With negative true logic, this drift is not a problem, but it is for positive true, where an upward drift produces, in effect, a "false positive". The problem plagued the S-100 bus in its early days and led to a thriving industry in active termination equipment.

Graphics

Computer graphics is an area of booming interest within computing. Once a sleepy subgroup in the ACM, the Association for Computing Machinery's Special Interest Group on Graphics (SIGGRAF) conference, held each July or August, has become a convention as large as many trade shows.

"Graphics" has become surrounded by some mysticism, as perhaps is appropriate to a field that is half technology, half art form. Computer graphics means drawing pictures on display screens. With most micro and minicomputer systems, these pictures are made up of tiny dots or picture elements - "pixels". Graphics is nothing more than the manipulation of pixels. Some might say that that's enough.

Since computer-drawn pictures are relatively crude in their resolution, they look a lot like cartoons. When computer-drawn cartoons are put together and flashed at a rate approaching 24 frames per second (movie projector speed) or 30 frames per second (television speed), they can, through the well-known phenomenon of persistence of vision, appear to move. Computer animation is a field that has grown out of computer graphics and rests on it as a base.

[Raster Scan and Vector Devices]. Graphics in microcomputer systems nearly always involves raster scan, as opposed to vector, display devices. Raster scan devices are low-cost - as cheap as a television set for the basic raster scan display. A raster is an electron beam that sweeps rapidly from the upper left corner of screen across it in a horizontal line, then returns rapidly to the left-hand side, slightly lower down, and "paints" another horizontal line.

This process is repeated, on an American or Japanese television set, 525 times per television frame; 30 frames are projected per second. Of the 525 lines, only about 484 are actually visible on the screen of the set. Thus if one holds a magnifying glass to a television set, one could count each and every line.

A television is an analog device because the brightness - that is, the white level - along each horizontal scan line varies continuously with the voltage of the video signal. With computer-generated displays, the horizontal scan line is also broken up into discrete dots, often 160, 280, or 640. The number of vertical lines times the number of individual horizontal dots is called the resolution of the graphic display. Thus the resolution of the Apple II is 192 vertical by 280 horizontal. That of the IBM Personal Computer, in black and white mode, is 240 vertical by 640 horizontal. Only a few Japanese computers offer the next step up in vertical resolution, which is 480 or so lines.

In the mainframe and minicomputer world, other specialized vector devices are used to display graphics. Vector displays take two X and Y coordinate values, and draw a line between them. Vector displays are fast and draw sharper lines. Most vector displays start at about 1024 resolution and go up to 4096 resolution. A good place to see a vector display (such as Atari "Asteroids") is at a video game arcade.

In August, 1982, a home video game system, Vectrex, was introduced with a dedicated vector beam monitor. Although black and white vector monitors are not too expensive, color vector beam monitors, such as the Quadrascans used in some video games (Atari "Tempest"), are. In general, raster technology is taking over the low and the middle ground in graphics, whereas vector displays are safely entrenched for higher-priced systems.

[Graphics Standards]. A major issue of 1982 was the implementation of graphics standards. Three companies - Digital Equipment Corporation (DEC), Tektronix, and Intel - agreed to support the North American Presentation Level Protocol (PLP). This standard is being considered by ANSI Committee X3L2, "Character sets and coding". Another ANSI technical committee to watch is X3I3, "Computer Programming Graphics Languages".

Some have pointed out that a graphics standard of sorts, the so-called "Core Standard", has been in existence since 1976. The Core Standard was a product of the Graphics Standards Planning Committee of SIGGRAPH and was officially released in 1979. Since then, Hewlett-Packard, Aydin Controls, and Tektronix have implemented versions of the Core system.

The SIGGRAPH Core describes the workings of a generalized graphics display device. Like a "Turtlegraphics" system, there is at all times a current drawing point or current position. In the standard, the drawing point is expressed not in absolute screen coordinates (e.g., points 0-279 horizontal, as on the Apple II screen) but in world coordinates - that is, "real" values, like 1 mile or 2 meters. It is the responsibility of the system to map these world coordinates to the screen.

Primitives are defined as simple instructions. "Move" primitives change current position of the drawing point, without marking on the screen. "Line" primitives draw visible lines from the current position to another world coordinate point, which then becomes the current position. "Polygon" primitives are sets of 3 or more points that define closed areas; "polyline" primitives draw 1 or more lines.

Text and special symbols are an integral part of any graphics system. In the Core system, "marker" primitives can be used to put a symbol at the current position. There are 5 standard markers ("+", "X", and the like) and some specialized ones, such as oil wells and dollar signs.

"Color" is a command that defines the drawing color of non-text primitives. "Intensity" defines relative brightness of lines; "Line style" defines their style (solid, dashed, dotted, and so on). "Line width" defines the relative width of lines, polylines, and polygon edges; "polygon edge style" defines what should be done on the border of a polygon - that is, whether to draw it or not. "Polygon interior style" defines interior of a polygon as empty, filled, or patterned - in the last case, a cross-hatched or similar pattern.

It is desirable for a graphics system to be able to write text easily, and even to be able to write it vertically or upside down. The Core standard contains the following text primitives: string precision (length in characters); character spacing, the move before each character; character path, which is the direction (up, down, left, right) of the string; character font, e.g., italic or simplex Roman; character justification, both horizontal and vertical alignment; character size, the height and width of individual characters; the so-called character gap, or spacing between characters in a string; and the character base, which is the orientation of the baseline in world coordinate system.

[Segments].   Segments, in the Core system, are collections of primitives. There are both temporary segments and retained segments: temporary segments are like macros, retained segments like subroutines.

[Modeling Transformations].   In many graphics applications, the object of the game is to take a numerical description of the world - a "model" - and have the computer produce a drawing of it, like a blueprint or sketch. Changing the position of an object in the model, or changing the viewer's location, produces what is called a transformation.

The classical transformations are (1) "translation", the shifting of something along one axis, be it X, Y, or Z; (2) "scaling", which is an enlargement or reduction along a dimension; and (3) rotation, which is turning around an axis. Translation, scaling, and rotation, even in 3 dimensions, can always be described by a 4 x 4 transformation matrix. Objects in the Core system are always transformed in their own coordinate space before they are mapped onto the virtual display space.

A second type of transformation, called viewing transformations, map 2-D or 3-D regions of the world coordinate system (as measured in meters, inches, etc.) into the unit cube. The unit cube has its origin at (0,0,0) and its far point at (1,1,1). In 2-D work, the viewing transformations define a rectangular window in the X,Y plane. In 3-D work, the viewing transformation defines the position, orientation, line of sight, and lens configuration of a "camera" in the 3-D world coordinate space. The viewfinder of this virtual camera is the window. Objects visible in the viewfinder are mapped onto the virtual coordinate system viewport. Orthographic, perspective, and oblique projection can be defined, and 3-D clipping planes may be generated to produce cutaway views of 3-D objects.

Finally, the Core standard defines some of the input devices useful in a graphics system. "Buttons" return an integer value equal to the number of the fire button pushed; "locators" return virtual coordinate pairs; "valuators" return floating-point values in the range (0.0<=VALUE<=1.0); "keyboards" return strings of characters; "stroke" devices return streams of virtual coordinate pairs (for digitizing); and "pick" devices return the name of a visible segment on a display device.

[Dithering]. Dithering is a technique used to create an illusion of added colors, by using blocks of pixels. Consider a 2-color monitor. By using 4 pixels in a 2 X 2 square, 5 shades can be created:

O O   X O   X O   X X   X X

Dithering is useful where resolution is cheap, but colors are not - as on color printers. With the 3 primary colors (yellow, magenta, cyan), the dithering scheme above can produce 5^3 or 125 color shades.

[3-D Graphics]. With proper software, microcomputers can generate impressive line drawings on their 2-D video screens that create the illusion of depth. An impressive software package on the market today is SubLogic's airflight simulation, in which the user feels like he or she is landing a small plane on a runway (SubLogic, Box V, Savoy, IL 61874; Apple version, A2-FS1, $25, add $10 disk; Radio Shack version, T80-FS1, $25, cassette only).

Three-dimensional graphics is a new world to many. It is surprising how our minds and feet operate unconsciously in a 3-D world, yet our brains are stuck on flat 2-D paper. Using fast 3-D graphics on a video screen is like peering through the looking glass into reality. We might speculate that in the future, with computer assistance, we will move around n-dimensional concept spaces with as much ease as we have now in 2- and 3-D spaces.

Three-dimensional graphics employs the following major concepts:

* Three-Axis System. Beyond the x,y axis system familiar from plane geometry, 3-D graphics uses a third or z-axis to determine a point in space. Thus the origin point in a 3-D system is (0,0,0), and a point 10 units back from us is (0,0,10).

* World Size. In microcomputer 3-D, it is necessary to think of the world as a cube of space defined by the maximum allowable values on the 3 axes. Thus a system where the maximum values are 100 miles in each direction would be working with a 100 x 100 x 100 mile world.

* The Eye. Within the world of a 3-D system, the user's viewpoint can change. The (x,y,z) coordinates of the user form what is called the location of the eye. Frequently, an object remains stationary in 3-D space, but the location of the eye changes. A typical 3-D maneuver is the orbit, in which the viewer's eye circles an object and views in from every angle (of a given plane).

* Viewer's Pyramid. Because we see in perspective, the location of the eye in 3-D creates a pyramid, the tip of which is at the eye location, and which grows bigger and bigger at the base as it goes away from the eye. When we make a 2-D representation of a 3-D scene, we typically slice the pyramid at some distance from the eye. We can see only those lines inside the boundaries of the pyramid at that point.

* Field of View. The steepness of the sides of this pyramid determines how much we can see and how close we see the objects. A flat pyramid coming out from the user's eye is like a wide-angle lens - we see everything up close. A

narrow, steep pyramid is like a telephoto lens - we see
everything far back.

* Aspect Ratio. The base of the pyramid need not be square and
can even be conical. The ratio of the width of the image to
the height is called its aspect ratio. We are most familiar
with the aspect ratios of motion picture film and television
images.

* Viewing Direction. From any one spot, we can, of course, look
in many different directions. Three variables, familiar in
flying, determine the direction in which the eye is looking:
its heading (rotation around the y axis, like a compass
heading on a map); its pitch (angle up or down relative to the
x,y plane); and its bank (roll around the lateral axis created
by the heading and pitch angles.) Banking rotates the object
viewed; pitching moves the object up or down; and changing
heading moves the object left or right.

[True 3-D]. True 3-D requires that each eye receive a different image. What
most companies called "3-D" graphics are, of course, really 2-D projections of
3-D objects. Some clever tricks used to heighten the illusion of depth in 2-D
representations of 3-D scenes include "depth queuing", in which the intensity
of distant objects diminishes, and shading, which makes objects look as if
they have a light source.

However, microcomputer devices have recently become involved with true 3-D. In
1981, Genisco introduced a display with a vibrating mirror, which becomes
alternately concave and convex. This device, which must be worn with hood,
produces true 3-D.

Lenses of lead lanthanum zirconate titante (PLTZ) provide the most interesting
form of true 3-D. PLTZ glasses can run off a belt-mounted power supply and
controller. A pulsed voltage causes each lens in the glasses to alternate
from clear to opaque; the change takes only 1 ms. The computer, synced to
the glasses, alternates left and right frames at a rate of 30 Hz per eye,
creating the impression of continuous 3-D TV.

H

Handhelds

Handheld microcomputers are direct descendants of the small language translators introduced as novelty items in 1978. These devices, which look very much like pocket calculators, store a fixed number of words useful to travelers and have a one-line liquid crystal display and an alphabetic keyboard on which entries can be typed. In theory, upon encountering an unfamiliar word in a foreign country, the electronic tourist punches a few keys and is rewarded with a display of the needed word in his native tongue.

In short, language translators were simple dictionaries packed into a gadget. As such, they provided a minor advance in the field of machine translation of languages (heavily researched, largely unsuccessfully, on mainframe computers in the late 1950s and early 1960s) and a major source of amusement at the expense of the world's affluent tourists. By late 1979, three language translators were on the market: (1) the Lexicon LK 3000, designed and built by a Miami, FL-based firm of the same name; (2) the Friends/Amis translator, designed by the San Francisco-based firm of that name and sold under the Craig label in the United States, and under a variety of labels abroad; and (3) the Texas Instruments language translator, which employed a voice synthesizer adapted from TI's highly successful Speak & Spell children's toy.

Estimates for the market for these devices fluctuated with the fund-raising efforts of the companies involved. (Lexicon, prior to a public offering of stock, estimated 250,000 of its machines would be sold in 1979, later fine-tuning that figure to 50,000.) Approximately 400,000 of the machines were sold in 1979 and approximately the same number in 1980, this leveling off due to saturation of the market and passing of the fad.

[Lexicon]. Two of the language translator firms, Lexicon and Friends/Amis, started as small ventures and rapidly acquired outside investment. Lexicon was founded in 1976 by Anastasios Kyriakides, a former loan officer at a Miami bank, and went public in 1978, raising $500,000. However, by late 1979, the company was out of cash, and in May, 1979, Kyriakides was forced out.

Kyriakides' successor, Michael Levy, the engineer who did much of the design work on the Lexicon translator, turned to Nixdorf Computer AG, the West German computer manufacturer, to bail the company out. On September 1, 1979, Nixdorf took over manufacturing and marketing of the machine, since renamed the Nixdorf LK 3000, and Lexicon has become a contract software and hardware development supplier to Nixdorf.

Under Nixdorf's tutoring, Lexicon developed a number of additional "modules" for the language translator, which Nixdorf has been marketing since January 1980 as the LK-3000 personal computer. Nixdorf now sells these components through its US office, Nixdorf Personal Computer Systems, Inc., at 168 Middlesex Turnpike, Burlington, MA 01803. Nixdorf also sells a modem, which looks very much like the Novation CAT, as the LK-4040. This modem and the RS-232 module turn the Nixdorf LK-3000 into a remote terminal.

Lexicon, while continuing to do development work for Nixdorf, has a number of products of its own, including a low-cost ($175) Bell 103-compatible modem, the LEX-11. Lexicon announced a light-weight, 40-column printing terminal in March 1981, and a $995 handheld terminal competitive with the IXO in May 1982. Lexicon does business at 8355 Executive Center Drive, Miami, FL 33166, 305-592-4404.

[Friends/Amis]. Lexicon's rival in the language translator business, Friends/Amis, has had a comparable history. Founded in 1977 by Ron Gordon, an experienced consultant in international electronics assembly and marketing, Friends/Amis spent some $700,000 on initial research and development before the prototype translator was ready in December 1978. In May 1979, Gordon signed an agreement for manufacturing of the translator with Matsushita Electric. In the US, the device was distributed by Craig as the M100, and assembled in Asia under a variety of arrangements. Like Lexicon, Friends/Amis is now primarily involved in contract research, and for Matsushita it has developed the HHC, sometimes called "The Link", sold in this country under the Panasonic and Quasar brand names. In late 1982, in an otherwise routine business transaction, Friends/Amis was sold to Matsushita, provoking a flurry of interest when the US Central Intelligence Agency interviewed some of the parties involved.

[Texas Instruments]. Although it has no handheld computer as of this writing, Texas Instruments bought out a language translator of its own in late 1979. Unlike Lexicon and Friends/Amis, who apparently both saw the translator as a step toward a handheld computer system, TI sees the language translator as a single product. With its hard-won dominance in the calculator market, however, as well as its language translator, TI is a natural candidate to eventually develop a handheld computer. TI typically is late to bring out products, loses money on them for some time, then slowly gains market share as its competitors crumble. This marketing stragety worked in calculators, where TI eventually took over much of the market, but has thus far failed in personal computers, where TI trails well behind Tandy, Apple, Commodore, and others. Presumably, if the handheld market develops major volume, TI will gain the same kind of advantages it has in the calculator market.

[Applications]. Unlike current personal computer configurations, which are almost as varied as the number of personal computer owners, handhelds will fall into two major modes of use: as stand-alone personal computer systems, and as remote, easy-to-carry terminals. Handhelds can, of course, function as noncommunicating, stand-alone personal computers. In this kind of configuration, a device like the Panasonic computer would require a RAM module to provide it extra memory, a cassette interface for storage, a miniprinter, and the video module and RF modulator for display on a home television set.

Except on the basis of cost, a unit of this sort does not at present have much appeal compared to comparable personal computers like the Apple or TRS-80. In general, specialized, dedicated software will be required to give handhelds, because of their portability, an edge over the stationary home computers. Here the use of handhelds will be much like that of today's programmable calculators, except that their programs will be far more versatile and easier to develop. Nevertheless, handhelds should be able to generate software many times more powerful than the programmables because their faster CPU speed and ability to use higher-level languages. Unlike the current personal computer market, however, software for handhelds, being far more demanding than that written in BASIC for personal computers, and because of the mastering costs of putting software on ROM, is likely to come from professional "module" development houses. A cottage industry of software providers, as has existed in the personal computer field for several years, is much less likely to develop for handhelds.

[On-Line]. Of the handhelds now on the market, all but the Sharp device are configured to act as remote terminals. The Nixdorf handheld has an RS-232 interface "module" that implements the basic signals of that communications standard (TX data, RX data, Ready to Send, Data Set Ready, and Data Terminal Ready). This module can be connected to a 300-baud, Bell 103-compatible modem (Nixdorf sells the Novation CAT modem under the name LK-4040), allowing the Nixdorf to communicate one line at a time with a mainframe computer. The RS-232 module with modem adds $385 to the $140 price of the LK-3000, providing a portable pocket terminal for a total of $525.

From its announcements, Panasonic clearly intends to feature the "briefcase terminal". In some respects, this device is not so different from the portable terminals sold by vendors like TI, with the exception of its ability to record and format data off-line, then communicate in an intelligent manner on-line. In the first two years, briefcase handhelds will undoubtedly show up in large custom systems requiring field queries and/or order entry. Clearly, a tool allowing a salesperson to check inventory and enter a complete order before the customer's eyes will have great appeal to marketing firms serving scattered geographic areas. Note that the savings here is not only in communications but also in data entry, and that one of the significant benefits will be customer satisfaction. In fact, should they be inexpensive enough, regular customers may simply be "given" their own handhelds for checking their shipments, accounts, and status.

A typical "briefcase configuration" of the Pasonic device might consist of: (1) the handheld computer; (2) a cassette interface for recording data for transmission and during on-line sessions; (3) a "miniprinter"; and (4) an acoustic coupler/telephone modem. Other additions to this system would be Panasonic's video ram, which, with an RF modulator, allows use of a home television set as a display screen.

In the longer view, widespread acceptance of handhelds will lead to a specialization of functions, where large files are kept remotely and small ones are kept within the handheld's memory, which, unlike current personal computer memory, is always on (owing to the batteries). The Grid Compass uses a similar system in a $8,000 portable computer. In this way, timesharing companies will be providing a utility service for large numbers of users, a sort of information parking garage where files are temporarily left and then retrieved by their owners. This trend will encourage high-volume, low-cost timesharing, possibly local in nature.

If the development of handhelds is an inevitable stage in the cost reductions accompanying electronics manufacturing, handhelds also present the possible tilting point between the profitable, high-priced computer industry and the condition IBM analysts refer to as "profitless prosperity" - everybody has a computer and benefits by using it, and no one firm makes any money providing them. The situation is very similar to the calculator market, where only a few firms were able to survive the crunch created by intensive competition and low margins.

As a mass market item, the handheld will be primarily a product of chip technology. For these reasons, the Japanese manufacturers, who have long ago mastered large-scale chip manufacturing (e.g., digital watch and calculator chips, 16K-bit RAMs), have the most to gain from the success of these devices, and not a great deal to lose. The Japanese are committed to making smaller and more intricate consumer electronics products, and the handheld, rather than being a computer, is in the tradition of the Sony Walkman or the various minicassette products. (Indeed, a dictation cassette attachment to the handheld - making it an all-round businessperson's tool - is planned.)

This shift - from making computers, which, despite the success of Apple and Tandy, is not yet in the consumer electronic realm - to the mass manufacture of a computer-like consumer product will be fundamental in the history of the computer industry. The "home" computer phenomenon - in some ways a pop or media phenomenon rather than a real one - was a first unsuccessful attempt to crack the consumer electronic barrier. Handhelds and the Japanese will now make another try.

Although the language translators may accurately be dismissed as another "pop" electronic product, the technology employed in them paved the way for the handheld microcomputer. The following handhelds have been introduced or will be introduced shortly:

[Sharp]. A handheld computer manufactured in Japan by Sharp has the honor of being the first hand-held computer to go on sale in the US, under Radio Shack's label. Developed out of Sharp's $150 language translator, the IQ3100, the Radio Shack/Sharp device, priced at $249, has a 24-character display. It is relatively primitive technically, using a 4-bit CMOS chip as central processor. The Sharp device is perhaps accurately called "a calculator that speaks BASIC" or, more precisely, Tiny BASIC, a restricted subset of the language. Nevertheless, Radio Shack, with its usual bravado, is called the Sharp machine "pocket TRS-80", thereby associating the device with Tandy's computers, not its calculators. Additional features of the Sharp device include an audio cassette interface for storing programs. Sharp exhibited a speech synthesizer module at a trade show in Atlanta in late 1979 but apparently has not put it into production.

[Nixdorf]. As outlined above, Nixdorf has adopted the Lexicon translator and turned it into a personal computer/remote terminal. The LK-3000 has additional memory "modules" (ROM programs, and some scratchpad RAM) that allow it to be used as an electronic notebook and an electronic file. Nixdorf also has: an RS232-C interface for the LK-3000, allowing it to be used with a modem for communications over telephone lines; a 20-milliamp loop interface (Teletype equivalent), allowing replacement of older Teletype equipment and communicating gear; and a parallel interface for computer breadboarding.

In general, the Nixdorf device seems limited to being a remote terminal and will not have the "compute power" required to be the nucleus of a stand-alone personal computer system. The Nixdorf device uses an 8-bit NMOS processing chip located in each individual cartridge.

[Panasonic]. Panasonic (US office: One Panasonic Way, Secaucus, NJ 07094, 201-348-7657), introduced what it is calling its RL-H1000 handheld computer (HHC) at the Summer Consumer Electronics Show in Chicago in June 1980.

Panasonic's HHC was developed by the San Francisco firm of Friends/Amis and financed by Matsushita Electric of Osaka, Japan. (Matsushita, one of Japan's largest electronic firms, sells its products in the US under the Panasonic, Quasar, and JVC brand names.) The same device, with minor alterations, will be sold in the US under Matsushita's English trade name Quasar (Matsushita also uses the US trade name National).

The technical problems involved with making both the translators and handheld microcomputers include: (1) power supply problems created by the need to run relatively large amounts of memory, both RAM and ROM, off a battery supply; (2) the general shrinkage of the keyboard and display unit - that is, the problem of packing, without undue compromises, the general features of a conventional computer's typewriter-style keyboard and 24-line by 80-character screen display into a pocket device; and (3) data compression problems, created by the need to squeeze large amounts of information into limited memory.

The Panasonic device uses a 6502 microprocessor, the same microprocessor in the Apple II and Commodore PET computers. The device uses special circuitry that "powers down" the microprocessor and memory when not in use, thereby cutting power consumption and making it possible to run the device on (rechargeable) batteries.

The Panasonic keyboard has 65 keys, arranged in 5 rows of approximately 13 keys each. Overlays, placed on top of the keyboard, redefine the keys for use with specific programs. The one-line LCD display presents 30 letters at a time; these being either upper or lower case ASCII (the standard computer character set); graphic symbols definable in an 8 x 8 dot matrix; and foreign letters. The display has a "10-speed" rate control that prevents information from flashing by too fast to be read.

Although many personal computer users will scorn handhelds as lacking items like full keyboards, "real" displays, and other seeming necessities of computing, from a more objective view the computer market is merely making a somewhat overdue adjustment to the persistent economic realities of electronics manufacturing.

Whereas most consumers perceive the cost of electronic items as steadily falling, manufacturers know that only certain components follow the "log curve" of decreasing cost. In particular, memory chips (RAM and ROM) and successful central processor chips (e.g., Zilog's Z-80) follow a declining curve where their unit cost approaches the materials cost, since the primary expense of producing the chip is in the fixed, initial research and development. With "best-selling" chips (only!), this cost is amortized over so many units that its per chip basis is barely noticeable. (In fact, to fairly gauge the profitability of a chip manufacturer, one should probably sum across the entire product line, just as a publisher's earnings should not be measured by one best-seller but must add in all the "dogs" as well.)

Outside the area of chips, however, most of the cost elements of personal computers are actually going up, despite higher volume levels. Raw materials, including oil-based products, climb just as the do in the rest of the economy, and labor costs also increase. Thus labor-intensive items, like printers, keyboards, and other items, stubbornly resist price reductions, and in fact increase in cost.

The handheld systems are essentially making an end run around these problems by giving the consumer a computer without these expensive attachments. The handheld very naturally focuses on those items - CPU's on a chip, RAM and ROM memory, and LCD displays - that lend themselves to mass production. Thus the computer of only a few years hence may have no floppy disks at all but rather a large amount of RAM, a modem and serial interface on a chip, and a low-cost calculator keyboard and display. Data storage, now done locally, could be on network mainframes instead of on expensive and relatively crude local devices like floppy or hard disks. Some purists might contend that such a device is a terminal, not a computer, but such objections will be academic. Low-cost items (like floppy disks) have always struggled for acceptance in the computer world in their technological youth but then enjoy a maturity where the nasty things once said about them are all forgotten.

Hard Disks

Hard disk drives became popular items on business microcomputer systems in 1980. They remain a bit too costly for personal and home systems but have come way down in price. At the West Coast Computer Faire in March 1982, a 5-1/4-inch mini-Winnie (Winchester technology) disk was on sale for $995.

Winchester disks, unlike older disk technologies, have sealed, air-tight environments to keep out dust and cigarette smoke particles, which are actually big enough to jam between the read/write head of the disk and the rapidly rotating disk surface. Winchesters also have "landing pads" for the disk heads on the disk surface and typically have servo tracks on one platter surface. The platters of a Winchester, since they are sealed tight, cannot be removed like those of traditional, disk pack type units.

This type of technology was originally developed at IBM, where for a time the product number for the disk pack was thought to be 3030; hence the nickname

"Winchester", as in the 30-30 gauge rifle used in the Old West.
Although there are a number of vendors of hard disks for microcomputers,
Corvus Systems (2029 O'Toole Ave., San Jose, CA 95131, 408-946-770) was one of
the first and sets the pace with its line of disk and network products.

The Corvus 11AP Disk System gives users of the Apple some 9.6 megabytes - the
equivalent of 82 floppy disks. This amount of storage makes the Apple capable
of maintaining large mailing lists, and business inventories.

The Corvus drive for the Apple consists of: (1) an IMI 7710 8-inch Winchester
drive; (2) a "personality card" that plugs into one of the free slots inside
the Apple; and (3) a power supply for the drive. The power supply uses a
standard AC wall outlet and runs a DC cable to the drive. The drive and the
computer are connected by a ribbon cable that runs from the drive to a
"personality board" inside the Apple. (Corvus apparently uses this term
because the board inside the Apple is not, technically speaking, a disk
controller. The disk controller on the Corvus 11A, as on all of the Corvus
models, is packaged inside the IMI drive.)

With this hardware, Corvus supplies software for the disk on a standard Apple
floppy. The Corvus system is designed to be added to an Apple system that has
a floppy disk, not to replace every floppy in a system.

[Interface with Apple DOS]. To the Apple DOS, the Corvus disk, by virtue of
the firmware on the "personality" card, looks like 82 separate floppy disks.
Each of these floppies is called a "volume" in the Apple Disk Operating
System, so that an Apple with the Corvus disk would be said to have a
"library" of 82 volumes. (Note that it would take 82 floppy disks to
completely back up the Corvus system, copying each of the 82 volumes from the
Corvus disk to an individual floppy.)

Any of the 82 volumes on the Corvus disk can be reached by specifying the
volume in the Apple DOS command. Thus to list all the files on volume 21 of
the Corvus system, the command:

CATALOG V21

would be used. Likewise, the DOS command:

INIT NAME,V3

will initialize volume 3 on the Corvus disk and create on it one file, NAME.
A special Corvus command, CATALOG V99, produces a directory of all volumes on
the Corvus disk, listing the name of the first file in the volume if it is an
"A" or "I" type file. A volume will not be listed in the directory (1) if the
volume is not initialized, or (2) if the first file is a "T" or "B" type file.

With the Corvus system, individual files can be LOCKED and UNLOCKED by the
Apple DOS in the usual way. Corvus has adopted a convention that if the first
file in a volume is LOCKED, the entire volume is write-protected - that is,
the files in that volume can be read but not written over. The write
protection can be removed from a volume by the first file, e.g.,

POKE 1272+S,1
UNLOCK FILENAME

where S is the slot number in the Apple occupied by the Corvus controller card.

Apple's DOS is not set up to have files open on more than one "volume" at a time. Consequently, it is necessary to force the DOS to switch volumes before reading and writing by POKEing the correct volume number into Apple memory location 1144+S (where S again is the slot number of the Corvus board) before the read and write. Two files on different volumes used in this way must have different names.

The Corvus disk has a special 48K byte area on the disk reserved for a "bootstrap" load memory image. Once placed on the disk, this 48K image can be swapped into the Apple's memory (1) by the Apple auto- start PROM, if this Apple II option is installed and if the slot occupied by the Corvus disk is higher than the number of the slot occupied by the Apple system's floppy disk controller, or (2) manually by the usual:

<control P><slot number>

from the Apple Monitor or by:

PR#<slot number><control-P><return>

command from Apple Integer BASIC. Turnkey operation coupled with the auto start PROM is extremely useful in setting up "turn on and go" systems for inexperienced computer users.

Corvus supplies a number of utility programs on the floppy disk supplied with its system. These are:

COPY2, which copies a volume from one part of the system to another. COPY2 asks for slot number, drive number, and volume number of both source and destination volumes. COPY2 ignores write protection. Notice that this utility can be used to save volumes from the Corvus disk onto floppy disks if these have been initialized by the DOS "INIT" command or the FLOPPY PREP program below.

FLOPPY PREP, like the DOS "INIT" commands, initializes a floppy so it can be written on.

VOLUME INIT, which initializes a volume and "hides" it from the Corvus directory. It cannot be accidentally used on a write-protected volume.

FILE FINDER, which searches the 82 volumes on the Corvus disk for a particular file name. If the file is found, it reports the volume number and asks for instructions. Typing "N" on the keyboard will terminate the program. Typing "RETURN" will send it off looking for further occurrences of the file name.

[Other Vendors]. IMI shipped the 1st 8-inch disk in January 1979. Corvus Systems, which showed its prototype drive for the Apple II at the May 1979 West Coast Computer Faire was one of its first customers.

Competing companies, however, were quick to follow. Shugart introduced an 8-inch SA1000 Winchester series in September 1979. The SA1000 uses 1 platter and has 5.3-Mbytes of storage; the SA1002 uses 2 platters for 10.7-Mbytes of storage. In early 1980, Shugart introduced a 58-Mbyte 14-inch Winchester, the SA4100. The SA4100 uses the same interface as the 14.4-Mbyte SA4004 and 29-Mbyte SA4008 and fits into the same rack space, being only 5-1/4-inch high. Interestingly, although there are many vendors of drives, there are relatively few vendors of hard disk platters or media: Athana (Torrance, CA), BASF Systems, Control Data, Dysan, IBM, 3M, Memorex, and Nashua.

Other companies besides Corvus now package drives for the Apple, TRS-80, and IBM computers. Lobo has used the IMI 7710 drive to create hard disk products for the Radio Shack, Apple, and S-100 computers. Each of these systems has 10-Mbytes of storage.

[The Mini-Winnies]. Al Shugart's company, Seagate Technology, introduced the first 5-1/4-inch hard disk, quickly dubbed the "mini-Winnie", in late 1980. (Even smaller drives that started sampling in 1982 are being called "dink Chesters".) The 5-1/4-inch Winchester drives are often electrically and physically identical to mini-floppies and flesh out the following hierarchy: 5-1/4-inch (usually 5 Mbytes); 8 inch (about 10 Mbytes); and 14 inch (about 20 Mbytes).

Home Computers

In 1982, the popular media once again discovered home computers. The cover of Newsweek magazine (February 22, 1982) features Whistler's mother at something looking like the NEC computer and the legend, "Home Is Where The Computer Is". Money magazine, in its March 1982 issue, featured an elaborate spread on everything from how to buy a personal computer to how to invest in personal computer stock.

To read these stories, the era of home computers is upon us: soon everyone will need or want a home computer, and, further, they will will cost little more than calculators or digital watches do today.

As usual, there is a strong element of exaggeration and oversimplification in these television and newspaper accounts. The era of the home computer is in truth already here. But these are the early days of this epoch, and it is too soon to know what form computers will take - or how they will fit into the home 5 years from now. Reasonable projections can be made about what computers will look like two or three years from now, since these products are already on the drawing board.

But those who know computers best are the least likely to speculate about what path computers "must" take. The technological development of computers has a logic all its own. The short, 25-year history has been full of twists, turns, and reversals - such as the popularity of floppy disks, or the development of microcomputers themselves - that have often fooled the all-too-human experts.

[Microcomputers]. Some things can be said with accuracy about what has happened to computers in the recent past. Small computers called microcomputers first appeared in 1975. Like many computer terms, the term "microcomputer" can be misleading. In the best definition, a microcomputer is a computer that has the circuits of its central processing unit or CPU placed on a single integrated circuit or chip called a microprocessor. In short: a microcomputer is one that uses a microprocessor.

There is no mystery about whether a computer's CPU is a microprocessor: if in doubt, open up the case and take a look. The 6502 used on the Apple II is a long chip mounted horizontally in the center of the Apple's base or "motherboard". The Z-80 microprocessor used in the Radio Shack TRS-80 takes a little more digging - it is inside the keyboard - but is easy to spot if the unit is opened.

However, despite the reduced physical size of these chips, there is nothing small or inadequate about a microcomputer. The current generation of microcomputers compares in computing power to the room-size vacuum-tube computers of the late 1950s and early 1960s, which were considered pretty hot stuff in their time. The next generation of 16-bit microcomputers, which will come to market in the early 1980s, will be equivalent or equal in power to the "minicomputers" of the late 1960s and 1970s. By the late 1980s and early 1990s, all computers, including the largest, most expensive IBM "mainframes" will in fact be microcomputers, in the sense that their "brains" or CPUs will be blocks of silicon and not the maze of wiring they are today.

[Home Computers]. What, then, of the "home" computer? The Computer Cookbook is concerned with small computers that fall into several criss-crossing categories. In the past, say around 1977, much of the ballyhoo over the home computer revolution was in fact about new, low-cost small business computers. There is nothing wrong with being excited about small business computers - in fact, it is intriguing that nimble small businesses with the nerve to take some risks can out-computerize and become more efficient than the slower-moving, dinosaur bureaucracies - but the the terms should be kept straight. A small business microcomputer system can easily cost in the $10-20,000 range. This may be cheap compared to IBM's old business computers and well worth the price, but it hardly makes this kind of computer a consumer item.

At the other end of the scale, a type of computer, of which the Apple II is a perfect example, developed out of home video games. (It is no surprise that companies like Mattel and Atari, once toy and video game manufacturers, have become personal computer companies.) These computers and are akin to (and compete for disposable income against) other consumer electronic items like VCRs and color TVs.

In thinking about computers, it is highly important to remember that they are general-purpose devices and are rarely "dedicated" to a single task. As with a car, or as a better example, a light truck, a computer can be used for fun or for work. This fact drives crazy those who need clear-cut categories, such as the IRS. The line between what is "personal" and what is "business" is often hard to draw. The Computer Cookbook is familiar with a number of people who play games on computers at work and who work on computers at home.

Consider a writer who replaces his typewriter with a word processor. Is this a personal or a business computer? The IRS would consider the money spent on it a business expense only if the writer's income from writing itself was large enough to justify the expense; otherwise, the IRS would consider his writing, and probably his computer, part of a personal hobby.

Or consider a man who owns a small business, buys a computer, takes it home, and begins playing computer games and doing simple programming. Is this computer a piece of office equipment - or an adult educational toy? Such dichotomies confound the modern-day taxperson but need not concern us here. The Computer Cookbook takes a simplistic position: it feels there is nothing wrong with adults having toys, educational or not!

[How to Shop for a Computer]. Kick its tires? Drive it around the block? Although you might easily spend as much on a home computer as a used car, the field is far too new for there to be any tried and true methods of shopping for one.

The Computer Cookbook offers the following 6 rules for first-time computer buyers:

RULE 1. Think about where are you going to put it. Is it mostly for the kids? If so, you'll probably want to put it in the living room and attach it to the TV. Are you really buying the system for yourself? If so, it will probably go in the den or study.

RULE 2: Limit your desires. Most people come up with mile-long "wish lists" when asked what they want their computers to do. Be reasonable - or be prepared to pay. For one example - the Apple II computer was never designed for word processing. You can do it on the Apple, but the extra hardware and software required will cost you at least $1,000. Make a list of all the functions you want the computer to perform; then prune it sharply.

RULE 3: Look and learn. Shopping for a computer takes a much bigger investment in time and effort than shopping for other items. It's as if you were shopping for a car and had to learn to drive at the same time. Take a class. Visit your friends who already have computers.

RULE 4: Buy from a store. This may sound like silly advice, but any serious shopper for a computer will quickly notice that attractive discounts can be had from various mail-order companies in places like Arizona. Don't be tempted - unless you're an expert. Computers, except those that are practically video games, require support. A patient local retailer willing to teach you about your computer can be a godsend. Don't expect his services to be free: you pay for this "handholding" in the retail price. Look for a good store close to where you live or work - wherever it will be easiest to spend time.

RULE 5: Buy software. An amazing number of people will spend any amount of money on computer hardware but don't think at all about buying computer software - programs - to make them work. Hardware without software is junk: a computer can't do anything without a program. In the "big" computer industry, the rule of thumb now is that software costs match or exceed hardware costs. This isn't true for microcomputers, where "packaged" software is much more common. But if you want to do word processing on your computer, be prepared to buy a word processing program. There's of course nothing wrong with doing programming yourself, especially if you enjoy it - just consider the true cost in terms of your time. When corporate managers face this "make or buy" decision, they almost always opt to buy.

RULE 6: Put in some time. Buying a computer isn't like buying a stereo or VCR - you don't have to learn to watch TV. The computer is like a mental Exer-cycle: if you don't work out on it, it won't do you any good. Don't be afraid of the computer. You usually can't damage it, and the only thing it can wound is your pride. Consider the computer the ultimate in patient teachers. It won't hold it against you if you make mistakes. You can't learn to fly an airplane, play the accordian, or dance the tango without disicipline and practice. Learning to play the computer like an instrument will also take time - but once you make it sing, it will be worth it.

[Origins of the Microcomputer Industry]. Nothing is wrong with confusion in small doses, and the microcomputer market is confusing. However, the market can be clarified slightly by looking at the recent history of the microcomputer industry. The industry did not actually grow out of any one other industry in a linear way, but really grew together, like a broken bone healing, from at least three different directions. This is especially clear if we look at the markets in which microcomputer makers were previously involved:

Video Games. One of the most frequently heard questions about "home" computers is "What can you do with it?" One of the most frequently heard answers, usually offered with an apologetic tone, is "play games". One strong line of development in the microcomputer industry has been out of the video or home television game market. Atari, originally famous for its arcade game, "Pong", and later for its home TV games, now has a low-cost home computer that, like the Apple computer, uses a home color television set for its video display. Mattel, the toymaker, also has a home computer that plugs into the TV and can be programmed in BASIC.

Pocket Calculators. In many ways, small computers, especially small desk-top computers, are "super" calculators. Commodore, now known for its PET (recently rechristened Commodore Business Machine, or CBM) computer, was an important calculator company in the early 1970s, as of course Texas

Instruments, who has a new "home" computer, was and still is. "Programmable calculators", popular in the late 1970s, were in fact primitive computers, with limited input and output and simple, machine-language programs. Hewlett-Packard, known for its advanced calculators, has made the logical step of introducing a personal computer made by its Corvalis, OR calculator division.

Big Computers. Pocket calculators and video games are usually considered as part of the consumer electronics market. However, most of the growth in the microcomputer market has come downward out of the traditional market for expensive computers, word processors, and the like. Microcomputers make it possible for many natural candidates for data processing - including small businesses, professionals, and industrial users, among others - to have their own computers. Some years ago a small law firm would never have considered a computerized word processing system: now the small firm without one is at a competitive disadvantage. The same holds true in other industries.

[Microcomputer Systems]. The word "system" has been much abused of late: we now buy "shaving systems" instead of razors, "wall systems" instead of shelves, and are told in 1984-ish terms by AT&T that "The System is The Solution".

However, computers must be thought of as systems - which simply means that a computer is really not one device but rather a set of different devices connected together. This is significant because the performance of a computer system is usually held down by its weakest link. A good analogy can be made between small computer systems and stereo systems. Most stereo systems now attach a number of different devices to the central receiver.

Input can come to a stereo system from one of several different sources: the FM tuner, the record turntable, or a cassette deck. If the FM tuner is on but not being taped, music flows through the stereo system but is lost. Tapes and disks provide a means of "storing" music. A cassette deck or reel-to-reel tape recorder provides an erasable, re-usable form of storage for the system. An LP record also stores music, but it is not erasable or re-usable.

Output from a stereo system is the audible music, whether played through speakers or headphones. A reasonable stereo system balances components in quality, or it is a never-ending process of upgrading where the quality of one piece is raised to match the others. A good turntable does no one any good if it is played through tinny speakers; likewise, the best speakers in the world will simply amplify the grumbles and groans of a shoddy turntable.

[Building A Computer System]. The same general considerations hold with computer systems, but the wide choice of input, output, and storage devices makes possible a far more complex range of systems. Most small computer systems, however, have at least the following elements: (1) a keyboard, similar to a typewriter keyboard, which allows information to be typed into the system; (2) a central processor unit (CPU) and memory, which together allow manipulation and limited storage of this information; and (3) a video display, either a video monitor or television set, or a video terminal that allows processed information - the "answers" - to be displayed in a form humans can read.

Not considering the CPU, then, which ties everything in a computer system together, all computer equipment falls into three categories: input, output, and storage. Many individual products, like video terminals, which have both keyboards (for input) and display screens (for output), combine two or more functions, but with some thought their features can be logically divided into the basic three.

The problem of putting together a cost-effective computer system is that of matching the performance of the input, output, and storage components. In computer jargon, the problem is that of maximizeing the "throughput" of the system at a given price range. "Throughput" is a measure of efficiency that takes into account both input and output.

For systems put together on a low budget, this comes down to oiling the squeaky wheel first. Every computer system - even the biggest - will have a point where the shoe pinches: if the CPU is fast, the disks will be too slow; if the disks are fast, the printer is too slow. Although well-matched systems can be achieved, the process sometimes never ends. A typical acquisition pattern for a male personal computer "junkie" who does his or her own programming might run as follows:

A computer like the Apple II, with a cassette recorder and a limited amount (32K) of memory ($1200);

Extra RAM memory - that is, a chip set that plugs in and gives 48K, allowing longer-running BASIC programs ($70);

A floppy disk, because the cassette is too slow and too frustrating to use, and because many good games and programs are distributed on floppies ($650);

A thermal printer, allowing output from the computer to be saved on paper ("hardcopy") ($750);

A 2nd floppy disk, allowing sorting and additional storage of programs and data ($450);

A telephone modem to access services like Dow Jones, CompuServe, or the Source ($395);

Major system software, like Pascal or CP/M, for serious program development and to make available other programs in these languages ($500);

Various input-output gadgets like a graphics tablet ($700), speech synthesizer ($300), light pen ($40), and music synthesizer, mainly to play with;

A hard disk, for greater storage capacity and faster response ($5350);

A 2nd computer, for which the cycle starts all over again.

Note that the original $1000 investment now exceeds $10,000 worth of hardware alone - without considering the value of the programming going into the system, or legal fees for a divorce, which probably occurred just after the total amount climbed above $5,000, and the vacation was cancelled.

[Take It All Off]. Under terms of the Economic Recovery Act of 1981 (signed in August of that year), a small business or self-employed professional can deduct as an expense up to $5000 of the cost of a computer bought in 1982, and larger amounts in years to come. For many PCs, including IBMs, which sells for about $4000, the entire machine can be written off the same year as purchased.

[ACRS Depreciation]. Persons who bought computers in 1981 or earlier need not despair. The tax laws provide a better investment tax credit for computer equipment purchased in 1981 and simplify depreciation calculations. Whereas the IRS had remained unnervingly silent on the subject before, it has now decreed that computer systems have a 5-year useful life. Systems bought for research and development have a 3-year useful life. For items with a 5-year life, 15% of the cost of the system can be taken as an expense in the 1st year; 22% of the cost of the system will be deductible as an expense during the 2nd year; and 21% is deductible during each of its last 3 years.

[Investment Tax Credit]. Under the new law, this means that 10% of the cost of a computer system can be subtracted as an investment credit from taxes owned. Unused credits can still be carried forward. Note that systems bought in or after 1982 and fully expensed do not also generate the tax credit.

[Research and Development]. Computers bought for research and development can be written off in 3 years. However, there is a trade-off in that a smaller investment tax credit (6%) is allowed. Current tax law provides an additional credit of 1/4 the increase in R&D spending over a 1980 baseyear.

I

The IBM PC

IBM put an end to several years of rumors by announcing its personal computer August 12, 1981, at a press conference at the IBM offices in New York City. No subject, except perhaps the Japanese "invasion" of the personal computer market, had generated more mindless conjecture and paranoid fantasy in the personal computer industry than of IBM's "home" computer. Microcomputer users by nature seem to believe that big is bad: IBM, a company with world-wide annual revenues exceeding $10 billion, is big; therefore, IBM is bad, and its entry into the personal computer market is evil.

In truth, the days when a computer company could be started in a garage have been gone for some time. Apple Computer Company is now a very large company that went public in 1980 and at times now seems more interested in holding up the price of its stock than pushing down the cost of its machines. Tandy, a company with $1 billion per year in sales, and Atari, owned by Warner Communications, are hardly small or ill-capitalized concerns.

[The Giant Learns Some Lessons]. IBM's personal computer, far from showing that the computer giant slow and slothful in responding in micros, is suprisingly well thought out and is technically much more interesting than Xerox's 820 system announced a few months before. To summarize:

- The IBM personal computer uses the Intel 8088 microprocessor chip, a processor with 16-bit internal operation but 8-bit wide data path to the outside world. IBM's choice of the 8088 (also used in the IBM Displaywriter) seems to secure the place of 16-bit processors in the evolution of microcomputers. Previously, there had been much talk of microprocessors, like baldness, skipping a generation - that is, of micros moving directly from 8-bit processors (Z-80s and 6502s) to 32-bit processors like the Intel 432. IBM's use of a 16-bit processor means there will be a slower, more gradual evolution to the wider-bit-path machines.

- IBM has given its blessing to a plethora of non-IBM suppliers of software (and, apparently, hardware) for its new personal computer. This marks a philosophical change for IBM, whose rough handling of manufacturers of so-called "plug compatible" (PCM) equipment in the mainframe market has been subject to repeated lawsuits that accuse IBM of monopolistic and predatory practices. "IBM will provide information for the existing cottage industry to design boards," or so quotes Byte magazine, in its October 1981 issue, of Don Estridge, Director of Entry Systems Business for IBM. "We're open to any software proposals." The IBM personal computer is also, to this author's knowledge, IBM's first product that uses "minifloppy" disk drives, a product introduced by Shugart Associates, not IBM.

[Summary of the PC]. IBM's PC is representative of a type of desktop computer that can do: basic business computing, including running such programs as VisiCalc; word processing; and high-resolution graphics. The Apple /// can do all these things but is a slower computer; the TRS-80 Model II is limited in its graphics. The most important thing about the PC, however, is that IBM's corporate weight, and its enlightened attitude, has guaranteed a vigorous third party market for hardware and software. The Apple II thrived on this kind of market; the IBM PC seems destined to take its place as the focus of development efforts.

[The Components]. IBM's system has three major parts: a detachable keyboard, which connects to the central or "System Unit" as IBM calls it, through a curled, telephone-like cord; the System Unit itself, which has (1) space for two 5-1/4-inch floppy disk drives to be mounted horizontally in front, and (2) 5 slots in back for expansion boards and other connectors; and a detachable monitor (the one IBM sells is made by Sanyo) that can sit on top of the System Unit or be moved around.

The IBM handles memory as follows: the unit comes standard with a great deal of ROM, 40K, given over to Microsoft BASIC. The System Unit comes standard with 16K of RAM on the motherboard, with space on the motherboard for an additional 48K. This memory is sold by IBM as "Memory Expansion Kits" (1501001); it is unclear now but likely that some cheap chips will do. Beyond 64K, additional memory can be placed on one of two types of RAM expansion cards: a 32K card (1501011), and a 64K card (1501012). If three of the 64K cards are used in addition to the 64K installed on the motherboard, the system tops out at 256K RAM.

IBM's monitor, unlike, say, Apple's, does not attach directly to the computer but attaches instead to a card in one of the five expansion slots. (Thus, as originally configured for "standard" operation, at IBM's quoted $1565, the system can't be used! Then again, this is also true of the Apple II.) Actually, there is a choice of two cards: the Monochrome Display Card (IBM part no. 1504900), and the Color/Graphics Monitor Adapter (1504910).

The monochrome card is basically for text processing: it puts 25 rows by 80 characters on the screen in upper and lower case, with underlined, blinking, high intensity, reverse image, and nondisplayed character attributes. To conserve card slots, this card also connects to a printer, which is an Epsom MX-80 with an IBM label on it. Thus a basic word processing system can be set up with only one additional card, and of course the monitor, printer, and word

The IBM Personal Computer

processing software - IBM is using "EasyWriter" from Information Unlimited Software (IUS). The monochrome card usually goes in slot 2.

The Color/Graphics Monitor Adapter is an interesting product with its high resolution and the fact that it provides either separate RBG outputs or NTSC composite video. The card has three modes: a text mode with 16 colors; a medium-resolution color graphics mode (320 dots horizontal, 200 dots vertical, 4 colors possible); and a high-resolution black-and-white graphics mode (640 dots horizontal, 200 vertical). Unfortunately, it does not appear that the color card can be used at the same time as the monochrome card, and thus a separate card (1505200) must be used to connect a printer to a color system.

[Disk Drives]. IBM also handles disk drives through a controller card, called the Diskette Drive Adapter (1503780). This device will run up to two drives, which are part number (1503800). Each drive holds some 160,000 bytes, roughly the same as, say, a North Star double density disk. The disks use one side with 40 tracks per side not 35. Apparently multiple controllers can be used allowing 2, 4 or 6 drives per computer. A hard disk can be expected soon and will apparently plug directly into the back of the System Unit.

[Communications]. The IBM personal computer, like IBM's other computers, apparently does not speak ASCII well without an adapter. For communications, IBM provides a card that is basically a programmable serial interface and seems also to do some code conversions. It can be set from 50 to 9600 baud, 5 to 8 bits of data, and so on. More important is the fact that IBM has software turning the personal computer into a remote terminal (e.g., 3270) for its Series/1 and other larger computers.

[Other Goodies]. IBM, still learning lessons from Apple, has made available a "game paddle adapter" (1501300), although the fact that using the paddles requires an additional expensive card may spoil some of the fun. IBM is not selling actual game paddles - this may lack dignity - but apparently Apple or Atari paddles can be used. Of equal interest is the fact that the color card comes standard with a light pen port, allowing (with proper software, of course) sophisticated graphics applications.

[Software]. IBM's choice of software for its new personal computer is as radical as its choice of hardware. The IBM will support three different operating systems: MS-DOS, supplied by Microsoft and at 1st designed for use with BASIC and unique to the new computer; CP/M-86, by Digital Research, Inc.; and UCSD P-system, best thought of as both a programming language and an operating system.

IBM's disk operating system started as "86-DOS" at Seattle Computer Products, (which markets a fast, 8-MHz 8086 S-100 bus computer), which then sold the project to Microsoft Consumer Products. Microsoft also developed the BASIC used on the IBM computer and contributed substantially to the decisions made by IBM about hardware.

CP/M-86 is Digital Research's version of CP/M for the 8086 processor. Announced at the introduction of the machine in mid-1981, CP/M-86 was not really available for the PC until April 1982. By that time, Microsoft's MS-DOS had become strongly entrenched as a PC operating system, and the two OSs were in fierce competition.

[MS-DOS versus CP/M-86]. IBM introduced CP/M-86 for its PC on April 5, 1982. It comes on a single 5-1/4-inch disk, with a manual in IBM's familiar slipcases. At $240, CP/M-86 is $200 more expensive than MS-DOS. One of the raging questions of 1982 was: MS-DOS or CP/M-86?

The question can be analyzed as follows: MS-DOS is more user-friendly than CP/M-86 and is a better choice for inexperienced or novice users. CP/M-86 has better development tools - namely, the assembler - than MS-DOS and is a better choice for serious programmers who need to work in assembly language. Concurrent CP/M, which allows several programs to run at once on one CPU, is a definite upcoming attraction of CP/M-86.

   User-Friendliness. Microsoft has the advantage over CP/M-86 in
      being easier for use by nonprogrammers and computer novices.
      CP/M-86 has better help messages, however.

   Error Recovery. MS-DOS is far more crash proof than CP/M-86.
      All versions of CP/M have had terrible, indecipherable error
      messages. If a disk is taken out of a drive, for example,
      CP/M-86 simply dies or shuts down, with a complete loss of the
      file in memory. MS-DOS allows recovery from such errors.
      MS-DOS also allows programs to trap disk errors at run time,
      but CP/M-86 does not.

   Booting. Both CP/M-86 and MS-DOS restart by pressing
      CTRL-ALT-DEL. When CP/M boots, it tells that it is reading
      the disk drives ("READING 1...2...3...4") and then displays
      what hardware it thinks is on the system. MS-DOS will only
      add bootstrap information to a disk when it is created - that

is, formatted. However, MS-DOS allows programmers to create turnkey disks that automatically start into a program when the computer is turned on or reset. Turnkey operation is valuable for applications programs written for novice computer users who do not need or want to memorize how to run a program from CP/M.

System Resources. Other than the disk drives, CP/M-86 generally makes better use of PC system resources, including memory beyond 64K.

Disk Use. A CP/M master disk must have the CP/M system on it and afterward has 141K of free space. MS-DOS has about the same. MS-DOS is faster in disk operation, because it uses large buffers and keeps file information in memory, whereas CP/M-86 uses smaller buffers, and keeps disk information on the disks themselves. File copies take about twice as long in CP/M-86 as MS-DOS.

Serial Printer. MS-DOS has a problem in that the asynchronous serial port cannot be used easily for a printer (the IBM is set up to use a parallel printer, the Epson; serial printers include daisy wheel devices like Qume, Diablo, and so forth). CP/M-86 has two special commands, PROTOCOL, which allows selection of either XON/XOFF or ETX/ACK protocols for serial devices, and SPEED, which allows selection of baud rates, stop bits, and so on. At the West Coast Computer Faire in March 1982, Microsoft president Bill Gates claimed that his company would produce a fix of MS-DOS to allow support of serial printers.

Memory Management. Only CP/M-86 can take real advantage of large amounts of memory on the PC. Although MS-DOS has some features that allow it to use more than 64K, these are poorly documented at present. CP/M-86 has a dynamic memory allocation table that allows it to use noncontiguous blocks of memory. With the PC's ability to handle up to 512K of memory, and with memory prices falling rapidly, certain memory intensive applications will be better done in CP/M-86.

Development Considerations. For assembly language work, CP/M-86 is better than MS-DOS, having a better assembler and debugger. In higher-level language work, MS-DOS may have a slight advantage.

Assembler. MS-DOS has a linker but no 8086 assembler. CP/M-86 has an assembler, but without such desirable features as macros.

Languages. Higher-level languages run on top of an operating system. MS-DOS will run the Microsoft languages, BASIC, BASCOM, FORTRAN, COBOL, and Pascal. A "C" compiler running MS-DOS has been written by Lattice, Inc. (PO Box 648, Hoffman Estates, IL 60195) and has been distributed by Lifeboat

Associates since May 1982. From independent vendors, CP/M-86 has various languages available for it, including "C" (from BDS).

[Concurrent CP/M]. At the West Coast Computer Faire in March 1982, Digital Research previewed Concurrent CP/M-86. Concurrent CP/M-86 allows a single user to run several programs to run simultaneously on the PC, using virtual terminals. Concurrency should allow heavy, efficient use of a PC, although it may be unnecessary to casual users of the machine.

Digital Research uses MP/M as its network operating system. Since the company will probably implement CP/M on the Motorola MC68000, future configurations might be able to mix all types of microcomputer machines, from Z80s to 8080s to MC68000s, with some ability to transport programs at the source code level.

[MS-DOS 2.0]. On March 10, 1982, Microsoft outlined plans for version 2.0 of MS-DOS. MS-DOS 2.0 will be even more user-friendly, provided menu selection of filenames, utility programs, and so on. It will also have an extensive help function. MS-DOS 2.0 will also heavily standardize screen display, using the ANSI standard escape sequences, and graphics display, using AT&T's Presentation Level Protocol (PLP). This should make applications programs developed on the PC under MS-DOS 2.0 extremely generic and portable to other systems. MS-DOS 2.0 will also have a print spooler, allowing files to be printed while other work is in progress.

Microsoft is moving toward implementing Xenix, its version of UNIX, on networks of PCs, although as of this writing it has not decided between Ethernet protocol, or US Department of Defense IP/TCP network protocol.

[Applications Software]. The existence of CP/M on the PC gives it immediate access to a large amount of business software already developed for other, mostly S-100 bus, machines. IBM has, however, made some choices of its own among applications software, licensing "EasyWriter," (originally developed, somewhat ironically, in FORTH as a word processor for the Apple II) as its word processor; Peachtree software for small business accounting; and, of course, the ubiquitous VisiCalc. IBM had only a nominal computer game — "Adventure," crediting Microsoft, not Scott Adams, as its originator - in its original announcement but promised more to come.

[Pascal]. One interesting software offering of IBM with its new system is a Pascal compiler. The Pascal compiler runs under IBM DOS (not CP/M) and produces native code for the 8088, not "P code". This compiled code should be very fast in execution speed. IBM has also contracted with Softech Microsystems, of San Diego, to produce a version of "standard" UCSD Pascal for the computer. UCSD Pascal for the PC was introduced in the spring of 1982.

[User Software]. Yet another lesson learned by IBM concerns the value of user-written software. In olden days IBM was well-known for wanting it all: sell the hardware, write the software, and all at a price. The personal computer market, as IBM has wisely realized, can't wait for a group of overbooked systems engineers to get around to writing a new version of "Space Invaders". It's far better to let this programming be done by actual users, who, The Computer Cookbook might add, are a sight closer to knowing what they want anyway.

With the announcement of the personal computer hardware, IBM simultaneously announced that it was setting up a "Personal Computer Software Publishing Department." This department will accept programs from individuals and companies and market them on a royalty basis under the IBM imprimatur. More information and submission information packets can be obtained by writing IBM Personal Computer Software Submissions, Dept 765, Armonk, NY 10504.

[Prognosis]. Prospects for the PC are excellent. There are some price adjustments that will need to take place, either on the initiative of IBM or outside vendors (the floppy disk drives, for example, are expensive and should come down to the $5-600 range), but these adjustments will occur. Personal computers are made or broken by the amount of software available for them. IBM has solved that problem in the short-term by adopting CP/M and will solve it in the long term by its name and staying power in the market. The Computer Cookbook expects to see the relative amount of CP/M software used relative to IBM DOS-based software and Pascal software drop over the life of the machine.

SYSTEM	MANUFACTURER	DESCRIPTION/IDENTIFICATION	LIST	DISCOUNT
IBM	AMDEK	Color Monitor II-A	999.00	
IBM	AST	Serial card, 2S (CC-132)	275.00	
IBM	AST	Serial card, 1S (CC-032)	145.00	
IBM	AST	Memory board, 64K	445.00	
IBM	AST	Memory board, 128K	620.00	
IBM	AST	Memory board, 192K	795.00	
IBM	AST	Memory board, 256K	970.00	
IBM	AST	Sync serial board, 2S (CC-232)	295.00	
IBM	AST	Multi card, M, 1P, 1S		
IBM	Apparat	Floppy drives, 2S 40track	630.00	
IBM	Apparat	Multi card 1P,1S,CLK	279.00	
IBM	Apparat	Floppy drives, 1S, 40 track	450.00	
IBM	Apparat	Memory, motherboard 48K	75.00	
IBM	Apparat	Memory board, 64K	425.00	
IBM	Apparat	Memory board, 128K	525.00	
IBM	Apparat	Memory board, 192K	625.00	
IBM	Apparat	Memory board, 256K	725.00	
IBM	Apparat	Prom blaster (25XX,27XX)	149.00	
IBM	Apparat	Clock card	129.00	
IBM	Apparat	Prototype card	29.95	
IBM	Apparat	Printer card, 64K buffer	399.00	
IBM	Chrislin	Memory board, 256K		
IBM	DATAMAC	Memory Board		
IBM	DG Elect	Memory board, 64-256K		
IBM	Datamac	Hard disk		
IBM	Davong	Memory board, 64K	325.00	
IBM	Davong	Memory board, 192K	750.00	
IBM	Davong	Memory board, 256K	950.00	
IBM	Davong	Hard disk, 5",5MB,DSI-501	1995.00	
IBM	FutureSoft	Program Generator	259.00	
IBM	IBM	Floppy, 2S, 320K	650.00	
IBM	IBM	Computer, 16K (5150001)	1265.00	
IBM	IBM	Computer, 48K (5150013)	2235.00	
IBM	IBM	Monitor, B/W (5151001)	345.00	
IBM	IBM	Printer, Epson MX-80 (5152001)	755.00	

IBM	IBM	Word Processing card (1504900)	335.00
IBM	IBM	Color Graphics card (1504910)	300.00
IBM	IBM	Printer adapter (1505200)	150.00
IBM	IBM	Motherboard memory, 16K	90.00
IBM	IBM	Memory board,32K (1501011)	325.00
IBM	IBM	Memory board, 64K (1501012)	540.00
IBM	IBM	Floppy disk cont. (1503780)	220.00
IBM	IBM	Floppy disk drive (1503800)	570.00
IBM	IBM	Serial card (1502074)	150.00
IBM	IBM	Game paddle card (1501300)	55.00
IBM	IBM	Printer stand (1525614)	55.00
IBM	IBM	Printer cable (1525612)	55.00
IBM	IBM	Diagnostics Package (6025077)	155.00
IBM	IDETIK	Image Processor, Light Pen	3450.00
IBM	Intermedia	Memory board, 64-256K	750.00
IBM	Lab Micro	FORTH	
IBM	Macrolink	Memory board, 64K	490.00
IBM	Macrolink	Memory board, 128K	699.00
IBM	Macrolink	Memory board, 192K	899.00
IBM	Macrolink	Memory board, 256K	1099.00
IBM	Maynard	Floppy cont card	165.00
IBM	Maynard	Floppy cont card + 1P	249.00
IBM	Maynard	Floppy cont card + 1S	249.00
IBM	Maynard	Floppy drives, 1	450.00
IBM	Maynard	Floppy drives, external, 2	700.00
IBM	MemTech	512K RAM, "Maxi-RAM"	1295.00
IBM	Microsoft	MS-DOS 1.1 (6/81)	
IBM	Microsoft	BASIC compiler (6/82)	
IBM	Microsoft	Pascal compiler (3/82)	
IBM	Microsoft	FORTRAN compiler (12/81)	
IBM	Microsoft	COBOL compiler (5/82)	
IBM	Microsoft	BASIC interpreter (8/81)	
IBM	Microsoft	256K RAM, DOS, "RAMDrive"	1095.00
IBM	Network	UCSD P-system	
IBM	Peachtree	Inventory Control	425.00
IBM	Peachtree	Accounts Receivable	425.00
IBM	PerSysTech	Persyst Spectrum	1215.00
IBM	PerSysTech	I/O, 2S 1P, Flex-Comm	300.00
IBM	Quadram	256K RAM, "Quadboard"	995.00
IBM	Quantum	QUNIX op system	
IBM	Santa Clara	Hard disk	
IBM	Seattle	Memory Board 64-256K	
IBM	Sigma	Memory board, 64K	395.00
IBM	Sigma	Memory board, 128K	560.00
IBM	Sigma	Memory board, 192K	725.00
IBM	Sigma	Memory board, 256K	895.00
IBM	TG	Joystick	64.95
IBM	Tall Tree	Cache memory board	1500.00
IBM	VisiCorp	VisiCalc	180.00
IBM	XEDEX	Baby Blue 64K + Z80 + CP/M	600.00
IBM	XEDEX	Baby Blue bundled w/W*, MM	980.00

Interrupts

Interrupts are a feature of a microprocessor or computer system that allow peripheral devices, such as printers, card readers, video terminals, or timers, to operate independently of the CPU but to break in and interrupt it when they need service.

Interrupts are important to implement when: (1) the CPU's time is very valuable, as it is on mainframe computer systems; (2) external devices attached to the computer are slow, or signal at unpredictable times; (3) the devices require small amounts of constant attention and would monopolize CPU time without an interrupt scheme.

Some classic cases.where interrupts are desirable are: (1) a computer with a real-time clock that has to be updated; without interrupts, the computer would spend all day watching the clock - an expensive way to tell time; (2) printer spooling, as in a word processing system with a slow letter quality printer; here it might be worthwhile to move a finished page to a buffer and feed it to the printer by an interrupt routine, thereby freeing the computer and the typist or operator to move on to the editing or writing of a new page, without waiting for the last page to come out; and (3) a computer controlling an industrial process, which has sensors that generate interrupts only if some unusual condition occurs, such as a power failure or overheating.

However, these advantages of the interrupt scheme must be balanced against the considerable overhead (both in hardware and, more importantly, in software) involved in implementing the interrupt scheme. In the microcomputer world, the CPU's time is not always critical: it usually has nothing better to do than sit around and wait for the next character to be typed. Interrupt-driven operating systems are hard to implement, difficult to debug, and not always worth the extra cost.

In most microcomputer systems, interrupts usually come from one of three sources: (1) internal timers and clocks; (2) I/0 devices; and (sometimes) (3) front panel switches. To take a typical example, on the Digital Systems computer - a singleboard micro using a Z-80 CPU and running CP/M as its operating system - interrupts can come from the following sources:

> a 1202 Hz clock;
> a 60 Hz clock;
> a front panel switch;
> any of four UARTs (serial ports),
>   indicating either that a character
>   is available or that a transmit
>   buffer is empty;
> from the disk controller, indicating
>   that a DMA transfer between disk and
>   memory is complete.

Likewise, on the Cromemco single-card computer (an S-100 board popular for machine control) interrupts can come from the following sources:

(1) timer 1 timeout
(2) timer 2 timeout
(3) INT (external request)
(4) timer 3 timeout
(5) UART receiver data available
(6) UART transmitter buffer empty
(7) timer 4 timeout
(8) timer 5 timeout
and NMI (S-100 pin 12)

[Priorities]. A human being faced with interruptions has a number of choices. Consider a man working at home in his study when the phone rings. If he is very busy he may decide not to answer it - that is, to ignore the interruption; he may even unplug the phone from the wall. Next, his child pounds at the door and wants to show him a drawing. This time, the man decides to allow the interruptions, since it will only take a short time to tell the child that the picture is beautiful and to now please leave daddy alone. Then, however, the man's wife comes in, announcing that she will leave him if he fails to come to dinner. This interruption, the man may decide, overrides all others, and he takes off to take care of it.

A CPU is in a position similar to that of this busy man. In general, the CPU can make an across-the-board decision to either enable (allow) or disable (not allow) interrupts from external devices. (The default condition for most computers on start-up is that interrupts are disabled; this allows the CPU to get on its feet before being hit with external requests.)

Furthermore, most computer systems are set up so that the computer can enable interrupts generally but mask out those that are low priority or with which it doesn't want to deal. In a critical timing loop, for example, the CPU may need to mask out all but one interrupt from the timer; then, when the timing operation is complete, it will go back and service those that have piled up during the loop.

Interrupts are usually assigned different priorities, so that a choice can be made if 2 occur at the same time. Simple priorities can be established in hardware by a device like the Intel 8214 Priority Interrupt Control Unit, which is designed to feed interrupts to the 8080 or Z-80 CPU in an orderly fashion. Notice that software can, however, completely control interrupt priorities by masking; a low-priority interrupt, if all others are masked out, will of course become the highest-priority interrupt until the others are enabled.

The highest-priority interrupt is often for something like a power failure, where either a switch to batteries or an orderly shutdown can be completed before the electricity runs dry (for a computer, of course, the few seconds before the power completely goes can be a long, long time). An interrupt that the CPU cannot under any circumstances ignore is called a "nonmaskable interrupt" (NMI) and is usually implemented with separate logic from the maskable interrupts. NMI is pin 12 on the S-100 bus; a signal on this pin will always override program execution.

[Interrupts on Microcomputers]. Most microcomputer systems can allow a small number of interrupts (usually 8), although nearly all computers can be configured to accept many more, limited only by the CPU speed of the processor in question. Multiple interrupts tied to a single hardware interrupt line (as is always the case, for example, on the Apple) requires the computer's interrupt-handling software to determine the exact source of an interrupt by looking at various status bits, or polling. The Z-80 is somewhat exceptional here, allowing up to 128 interrupts in its maskable interrupt mode 2. Usually, however, the Z-80 is limited to 8 interrupts (Mode 0) to maintain 8080 compatibility.

In all cases, an interrupt coming in from an external device causes the CPU to finish the instruction it is working on, save its current location (PC counter) on the stack, and jump to a fixed location in memory. The exact technique by which this happens varies from microprocessor to microprocessor, but the effect is almost always the same.

[The 8080]. On the Intel 8080 microprocessor (and on many Z-80 systems for reasons of downward compatibility with the 8080), external devices place a restart instruction on the data bus and force the CPU to execute it. Restart (RST) is a single-byte instruction that is really a subroutine call (CALL) to 1 of 8 fixed locations in low memory. These locations in page 0 (1st 256K) start at 0 and are 8 bytes apart:

0	0000H	(0 decimal)
1	0008H	(8 decimal)
2	0010H	(16 decimal)
3	0018H	(24 decimal)
4	0020H	(32 decimal)
5	0028H	(40 decimal)
6	0030H	(48 decimal)
7	0038H	(56 decimal)
NMI	0066H	

Interrupt service routines for each of the nine possible interrupts should start at these locations. Since the interrupt service routine rarely fits into eight bytes, these locations usually contain JMP instructions, or vectors, to real interrupt routines, which can be located anywhere in memory.

[Intel 8085]. The Intel 8085, a spruced-up version of the 8080, has four additional inputs that RST to the following locations:

TRAP	24H
RST5.5	2CH
RST6.5	34H
RST7.5	3CH

To trigger these restarts, an external device need not put the RST instruction on the bus, but merely apply a signal to the input pin of the same name. This simplifies things for the external device.

[The Z-80]. To maintain 8080 compatibility, the Z-80 microprocessor has as its default mode (Mode 0) the same type of interrupt set-up above. However, the Z-80 has two more special interrupt modes. These modes are established by the Z-80 IM instruction and can, of course, be changed by the CPU at any time, although most often the mode stays set once the system is initialized.

Mode 1 is designed for simple systems where the cost of having an external device place a RST on the data bus is prohibitive. In this mode, a signal on the INT line will cause a RST to location 38H, just as a signal on NMI will cause a RST to location 66H. It is then up to software to determine exactly where the interrupt came from and what to do about it.

Mode 2 is designed for large-scale systems, with up to 128 interrupts possible from external devices. The Z-80 maintains a special I register, which can be loaded and unloaded into the accumulator (A register). In Z-80 interrupt mode 2, the eight bits in the I register are used as the base of a table in memory. When an interrupt comes in from an external device, it supplies an 8-bit value that is combined with the I register to come up with an address in the table, e.g., IIIIIIIIDDDDDDDD. The two bytes at this location are then fetched by the Z-80 and stuffed into the program counter - in effect, an indirect subroutine call.

[The 6502]. The 6502 has a fairly simple interrupt structure, with two lines on the processor, IRQ and NMI, for maskable and nonmaskable interrupts respectively. A signal on IRQ always causes the processor to fetch the contents of memory location FFFE and FFFF (the top two bytes in memory) and transfer to that location. A signal on NMI will cause a similar transfer to the address given at location FFFA-FFFB.

[Interrupt Service Routines]. To the programmer, interrupts are best thought of as involuntary subroutine calls. If interrupts are allowed, no assumptions should be made about where they will occur. In the worst case, an interrupt can occur between a test instruction and a branch, as in this sample code in Intel 8080 assembly language:

```
        ....
        CPI  32     ; TEST ACCUMULATOR
>>>> INTERRUPT HERE <<<
        JZ   SPACE  ; JUMP IF SPACE
        ....
```

Here, for example, an 8080 or Z-80 microprocessor will have compared the A register to see if it contains 32 (a space), but the program will have been interrupted before it can act on the results of the comparison.

This points out the first principle of programming interrupts: interrupt servicing routines should be invisible to the main program, which means in general that the interrupt routine should save or leave undisturbed the CPU environment. In the example above, the first thing the interrupt routine should do is save the Program Status Word (PSW), and then restore it just before returning to the main program. If the interrupt service routine does this correctly, the main program will have been interrupted without knowing a thing has happened, i.e.:

```
INTER  PUSH PSW ; PUSH PSW TO STACK
       PUSH B   ; SAVE B REGISTER
```

```
                PUSH C    ; SAVE C REGISTER
                PUSH D
                PUSH E
                PUSH H
                PUSH L
                EI        ; REENABLE INTERRUPTS
                ........  ; service this interrupt
                POP L
                POP H
                POP E
                POP D
                POP C
                POP B
                POP  PSW  ; RESTORE PSW
                RETI      ; RETURN TO MAIN PROGRAM
```

Note that the enable interrupt instruction comes just after the registers have been saved on the stack. On most microprocessors, when an interrupt is taken, other interrupts are automatically disabled. This protects the interrupt routines from other interrupts coming in on top of it and disturbing critical operations like saving PSWs and registers. However, once all registers are saved, and given an assurance that all interrupt routines are invisible to the interrupted program, there is no reason not to allow other interrupts to break into the interrupt service routine itself. This situation is identical to that of nested or recursive subroutines. As long as the stack does not overflow, it is a perfectly workable procedure.

In general, however, interrupt routines should be kept short. This is especially important if they can occur at bad times (e.g., during disk I/O) where they may throw off critical timing operations (if they can, they should be disabled before calling a disk routine). The Zilog Z-80 has several special instructions and an entire extra set of registers specially provided to facilitate fast interrupt servicing. The Z-80 has exchange instructions that switch the primary set of registers with an identical second set built into the CPU. Since this operation does not require the CPU to access the main memory, as does pushing the registers onto a stack, these instructions make possible one level of fast interrupt service. On the Z-80 the above code would look like:

```
        INTER   EX        ; SAVE A REG AND FLAG REG
                EXX       ; EXCHANGE OTHER REGISTERS
                .......   ; service the interrupt
                EXX       ; BRING BACK 1st SET
                EX        ; BRING BACK A & F REGS
                EI        ; REENABLE INTERRUPTS
                RETI      ; RETURN TO MAIN PROGRAM
```

Notice, however, that this routine cannot enable interrupts until it is done, since switching the register sets again will destroy the original (main program) set.

[Selective Enabling and Disabling]. The microprocessor instructions that enable and disable interrupts do so on an across-the-board basis, primarily to protect the CPU from unwanted interruptions. On nearly all systems, however, interrupts can be selectively enabled or disabled, usually by sending the proper bit pattern to one of the output ports. Furthermore, most systems have an input port that can be read to determine which interrupt has signaled. This duplication allows an interrupt routine to handle more than one interrupt and in fact makes it possible to implement an interrupt-like system without actually using interrupts at all, by polling.

J

Japanese Computers

The Japanese are the preeminent manufacturers of consumer electronic goods in the world. A very large percentage of the world's television sets are made in Japan (or in Korea or Taiwan under Japanese license) as are nearly all its VCRs. With such a track record, it is not surprising that the Japanese are mastering microcomputer manufacturing.

Since 1979, the Japanese have captured much of the US market in two products where high-quality but low-cost manufacturing is important: printers and floppy disk drives. The Epson printers, made by a company that is part of the Seiko watch group, is itself a jewel of a device and has won a large chunk of the US personal printer market from companies like IDG, maker of the Paper Tiger, and Centronics. The Paper Tiger was a fine printer but relatively expensive ($1000 plus) and unreliable. Centronics had an early lead in the printer market but never cut costs for personal computer customers.

[NEC]. Nippon Electric Corporation (NEC Information Systems, 5 Militia Drive, Lexington, MA 02173, 617-862-3120) makes 4 computer models sold in Japan: the low-cost PC-6000; a middle-range PC-8000 system; a still more elaborate PC-8800; and a small business computer, the N5200. The PC-8000 is the 1st Japanese computer to have achieved a respectable sales level in the US (although for some reason its sales figures seem exaggerated by the US business press). NEC is building a factory to produce computer products in Massachusetts.

[The NEC PC-6000]. The NEC PC-6000 system is a low-cost computer comparable to the Atari 800, Commodore VIC-20, or Tandy Color Computer. The PC-6000 was introduced in Japan in late 1981 but has yet to show up in the US in significant numbers. The PC-6000 uses NEC's version of the Z-80, has 16K bytes of ROM with BASIC, and 16-48K bytes of RAM. A keyboard unit, the PC-6000 has small square keys (which can take overlays) and a slot on the right-hand side for connection of ROM packs with programs. It can use Atari joysticks and has an RS-232-C and a parallel (Centronics) port on the back of the unit. NEC also has a graphics tablet for the unit (it connects to the joystick ports) and a cassette data recorder.

[The PC-8000]. The NEC PC-8000 was introduced in 1980. The NEC PC-8000 uses
NEC's version of the Zilog Z-80 (the uPD-780C-1) as its processor and runs a
version of Microsoft BASIC called N-BASIC. The PC-8001 is the basic keyboard
unit, which houses the CPU and 32K of RAM. An expansion unit, the PC-8012A,
can hold an additional 32K of RAM, 2K of PROM, and 7 expansion slots.   A
floppy disk drive unit, the PC-8031, plugs into 1 of the expansion slots but
can also plug directly into the keyboard unit alone through the PC-8033 disk
interface unit. Four disks can be added by daisy chaining an additional 2
drive unit, the PC-8032, to a PC-8031.

In the US, Renaissance Technology Corporation (3347 Vincent Rd., Pleasant
Hill, CA 94523, 415-930-7707) supports the PC-8000 with a variey of hardware
products, including The Wedge, which functions like the PC-8012 expansion unit
but fits inside the case of the keyboard unit. The Wedge adds 32K to the
PC-8000 and can optionally add 32K more, for a total of 96K, and also supports
the floppy disks. Ren Tec has a number of NEC-compatible items.

[Oki]. Oki Electric (US computer distributor: BMC Computer Corporation, 860
East Walnut Street, Carson, CA 90746, 213-323-2600; US corporate address:
Okidata Corporation, 111 Faither Drive, Mt Laurel, NJ 08054, 609-235-2600, TWX
710-897-0792) makes 2 computers as of mid-1982, the BMC if800 Model 20, and
the BMC if800 Model 30. The Model 20 was introduced in Tokyo in June 1980,
and has an interesting design in which the monitor and 2 horizontally mounted
mini-floppy drives are packaged above the keyboard unit on legs. The
clearance (about 3 inches) provided by the legs is used for an 80 column
hardcopy printer, giving the lower, keyboard unit the look of a printing
terminal. To the right of the printer is a microcassette unit, mounted above
a right-hand-side numeric keypad.

The Oki 20 uses mini-floppy disk drives that have 280K capacity. The Model
30, by contrast, uses 2 slim line drives mounted vertically next to the
monitor. The Model 30's printer is slightly more sophisticated, with a
tractor feed. Either model can use a 10-megabyte hard disk from Oki.

The Oki models are reminiscent of the Tandy TRS-80 Models 3 and 2; the less
expensive model has mini-floppy disks, the more expensive has full-size. Each
model has a RS-232-C interface built in and also has connectors for RGB as
well as monochrome video. A clock with battery backup is also provided along
with a speaker and a music language. Optional interface cards provide a
parallel port; an IEEE-488 interface; analog and digital converters; and
additional RS-232-C ports.

[Hatachi]. The Hatachi MB-6890 is third level of evolution of Hatachi's
"Basic Master" series. The machine uses a Motorola 6809, which is a cross
between an 8- and 16-bit processor. The system can have 64K of memory, with
about 32K available to the user, plus additional memory to control the color
mode of the video display. The MB-6890 is a good graphics machine: 640H by
200V graphics are standard, and a light pen interface (but not the pen) is
standard equipment. In Australia, the Basic Master is sold as "The Peach".

[Sharp]. Sharp makes a very stylish looking personal computer, which it calls
the MZ-2000 in Japan. This unit has a high-resolution green screen monitor on
top of a keyboard with numeric pad and 10 function keys. To the right of the
screen is a vertically mounted cassette unit. The unit uses a Z-80A

microprocessor running at 4 MHz, has 64K of RAM standard, and uses Sharp's own MZ-80 BASIC and FDOS operating system. The MZ-2000 might be compared to the North Star Advantage.

Sharp makes a number of products sold in the US under other names. The company makes floppy disk drives and other peripherals for Commodore and makes the Radio Shack Handheld computer. Sharp's version of the handheld came on the US market in 1982 and features a 4-color printer/plotter for about $200! The Sharp handheld is called the PC-1500, and the printer and cassette interface unit is the CE-150. The CE-150 also has an AC adaptor, allowing the computer to be run from wall current and recharge the batteries.

[Panafacom]. Panafacom is a 50-50 joint venture of Fujitsu and Matsushita Electric. Fujitsu is best known as a semiconductor manufacturer and mainframe computer maker. Matsushita is a large manufacturer something like General Electric and makes audio and video equipment sold in the US under the "Panasonic" and "Quasar" brand names. The C-15 is marketed by both companies. It uses a special Fujitsu microprocessor, the MN1601.

[Panasonic]. In addition to its handheld computer, sometimes called The Link, introduced in mid-1980, in 1982 Panasonic (US office: 1 Panasonic Way, Secaucus, NJ 07094) started marketing in Australia an IBM PC-compatible computer called the JB 3000. There is an interesting story behind the JB 3000: apparently, it was designed by Matsushita to official IBM specs, as part of a competition to see who would create the PC. IBM's Boca Raton group won, but Matsushita has started to salvage its work with a plug-compatible PC or "PC-PC". In 1982, Panasonic also introduced a dot matrix printer, the KX-P1160, similar to the Epson MX-80.

[Teac]. Teac, a manufacturing company, makes the PS-80, a domestic Japanese version of Tandy's TRS-80.

[Casio]. Casio, well known in the US for its popular piano keyboard handheld music synthesizers, introduced a personal computer, the FX-9000P, at the Consumer Electronics Show in Las Vegas in January 1982. The Casio machine uses a Z-80 processor running at 2.7 MHz, and it partitions memory into 4K CMOS RAM packs. CMOS technology has low power requirements: the Casio packs, priced at $189 for 4K, back up their memory for 3 years. These removable packs are really an alternative to floppies or bubble memory. The basic system comes with 12K of ROM for the operating system and BASIC (Casio's own), 4K of video RAM, and a single 4K CMOS pack. Casio's BASIC has special trig and hyperbolic functions as well as graphic commands.

[Canon]. The Canon CX-1 is a business machine without graphics that sits in a complete desktop unit. The unit includes a green screen monitor with dual intensity and 2 mini-floppy disk drives with 320K bytes on each disk. The unit has rear jacks for a light pen, 2 extra disk drives, up to 3 RS-232-C ports, and up to 3 Centronics-compatible parallel ports. The CX-1 uses a 6809 processor and runs its own operating system MCX, a FORTRAN-inspired version of BASIC with CALL (subroutine) statements, and some other features.

[Bubcom80]. The Bubcom (the Japanese like to concatenate English words, even if the result sounds funny; Login, sister publication to ASCII magazine, is subtitled "Magazine for Personal Compunication", which means Computers and

Communications) is the product of an offshoot of Fujitsu called Systems Formulate Corporation. Bubcom's major attraction is that it uses a Fujitsu bubble memory unit as a standard feature.

The Bubcom is a Z-80 based machine with 64K of RAM standard. The machine loads BASIC into RAM from its bubble memory rather than keeping BASIC permanently in ROM, thereby leaving free about 12K of address space for non-BASIC (e.g., assembly language) programs. This is also an extended BASIC with a "MENU" command. An optional high-resolution memory board gives the machine 640H by 200V resolution; with the extra memory, the resolution is 160H by 100V. The monitor (Bubcom sells a special RGB color monitor for about $1400 US; it has a contoured front to fit with the machine) fits to the top of the keyboard unit. To the side, a slimline, full-sized, double-sided, double-density floppy disk unit can be housed; it holds 1.2 Mbytes on a single disk. Blank bubble cartridges cost $175 each but run faster than floppies; conceptually, to the operating system, the bubble memories are disks 1 and 2.

SYSTEM	MANUFACTURER	DESCRIPTION/IDENTIFICATION	LIST	DISCOUNT
Casio	Casio	FX-9000P 16K dynamic RAM pack	129.00	US
Casio	Casio	FX-9000P CMOS 4K RAM packs	189.00	US
Casio	Casio	FX-9000P Computer	1199.00	US
Casio	Casio	FX-9000P OP-1 clock/printer IF	379.00	US
Casio	Casio	FX-9000P OP-2 disk IF, RS232,DOS		
MBC-1000	Sanyo	Z80 computer system		
MBC-2000	Sanyo	Z80 computer system		
MBC-3000	Sanyo	Z80 computer system		
NEC	NEC	PC8001A CPU/Keyboard unit, 32K	995.00	
NEC	NEC	PC8011 Expansion Unit, Rs232/IEEE		
NEC	NEC	PC8012A I/O Expansion unit	649.00	
NEC	NEC	PC8021 Dot matrix printer		
NEC	NEC	PC8022 40 char thermal printer		
NEC	NEC	PC8023A 100 cps dot matrix ptr	695.00	
NEC	NEC	PC8031 Dual Mini Disks (1st unit)		
NEC	NEC	PC8031A Dual disk unit	995.00	
NEC	NEC	PC8032 Dual Mini Disks (2nd unit)		
NEC	NEC	PC8033 I/O Port for 8031		
NEC	NEC	PC8041 12" Green Monitor	210.00	
NEC	NEC	PC8043 12" RGB Monitor	995.00	
NEC	NEc	PC8044 RF modulator		
NEC	Ren Tec	Hard Disk (Konan) IF		
NEC	Ren Tec	RS-232-C card		
NEC	Ren Tec	Speech Synthesizer		
NEC	Ren Tec	The Wedge, 32K RAM, Music, Joy	595.00	US
Printer	NEC	Spinwriter 3500Q		
Printer	NEC	Spinwriter 7700Q		
Sharp	Sharp	PC-3100 Hobby Computer		
Sharp	Sharp	PC-3200 Personal Computer		
Toshiba	Toshiba	T100 64K Z80	1000.00	US
Toshiba	Toshiba	T-200/4 560K Disk	2995.00	2097.00
Toshiba	Toshiba	Printer P-1240 TEC 40 Daisy	1995.00	1496.00
Toshiba	Toshiba	T-25014 2MB Disk System	4495.00	3147.00
Toshiba	MicroPro	Wordstar for T-200	495.00	

L

LISP

LISP is a programming language that is often difficult for even experienced programmers to understand. LISP's difficulty lies not so much in the syntax of the language but in its data structures - lists. As with APL, LISP is worth the effort required to understand it. LISP was created in the late 1950s at MIT by a team led by John McCarthy, whose paper "Recursive Functions of Symbolic Expressions and Their Computation by Machine", published in the Communications of the ACM for April 1960, marks LISP's public announcement. LISP is the favored language of artificial intelligence research and has the mathematical elegance of few other computer languages.

[Lists]. A simple linear list looks something like this on a computer:

```
[A] ------> [B] -----> [C]
```

This can be interpreted as: start with A, follow the arrow to B, then to C. A, B, and C are called elements of the list. The arrows are called pointers. A is called the head of the list, and C is the tail. Usually lists have a terminator to let the computer know it has come to the end of the list; this terminator is called NIL.

When elements of a list can have two or more pointers, the data structures produced are called trees. The head of the list called the root, and the elements are called nodes. A tree might look like:

```
        [A]   - root
        / \
      [B]   [C]
      /     / \
    [D]   [J] [E]
```

This type of tree, where there are no more than 2 items coming from each element, is called a binary tree. Binary trees are useful in sorting and searching.

[LISP Syntax]. LISP is a functional, not an algebraic, language. LISP turns the computer into a giant calculator, on which a single function - however complex - is evaluated. Typing the expression:

TIMES((DIFFERENCE 28 6) (SUM 3 7))

on a LISP computer would cause the machine to think for a while, then print 220. Note that simple addition, 3 plus 7, is done by a function, SUM, whereas in an algebraic language, it would be written "X+Y". LISP has two subtraction operations: DIFFERENCE, which subtracts one number from another, and MINUS, which is unary (1 operand) minus, e.g., (MINUS X). Although it is awkard to use functional notation for simple arithmetic, the beauty of LISP is that everything in the language can (and must) be expressed as a function.

LISP functions are called S-expressions (for Symbolic expressions). The elements of an S-expression, like A, C, or PLUS, are called atoms. The only other thing in an S-expression is a dot, which combines two S-expressions, and parentheses - lots of them. Parentheses must balance in a meaningful way:

(PLUS 4 2)) (PLUS (PLUS 5 6)

is not a proper S-expression. The way to tell if an expression is well formed is to set a counter to zero at the left of the expression and add 1 for every right parenthesis encountered, and subtract 1 for every left parenthesis. The expression is well formed if the counter never becomes negative and is 0 at the end.

LISP starts to differ very much from conventional language by the fact that it can manipulate symbols as well as numbers. The function (SETQ X 5) acts like an assignment statement, giving X the value 5. But the function (SET X Y) can "equate" X and Y for part of the operation of a program. Every atom in LISP has a value. Numbers (literals) are atoms whose values are themselves, but the value of an atom also can be another atom with a symbolic name. An atom looks like:

[name of the atom] [value of the atom] {other properties}

A list in LISP is a list of pairs:

[pointer to atom | pointer to sublist] [pointer to next pair]

[[P-System LISP]. A LISP interpreter that runs under the UCSD P-system, including Apple Pascal, is available from PCD Systems, Inc. (PO Box 143, Penn Yan, NY 14527, 315-536-7428) for $225. The manual alone is $30.

[TLC-LISP]. A microcomputer implementation of LISP is available from The LISP Company, Box 487, Redwood Estates, CA 95044. TLC-LISP, as it is called, implements most of the features of MACLISP, the "standard" LISP that came out of MIT's Artificial Intelligence Project MAC, but lacks an interactive editor. TLC-LISP will run on a 48K CP/M or CDOS system and can read and write CP/M files. The implementation allows only 10K for programs on a 48K machine. Documentation is adequate but requires previous knowledge of LISP. The package price is $250, the manual alone $20.

Local Networks

Within the next three to five years, local networks of small computers and word processors will make serious inroads into the market now enjoyed by minicomputers, and into the yet-to-be-determined market for the office of the future. Local networks are based on a simple fact but on complicated technology. The simple fact is that a number of small computers, tied together, can perform computing and word processing tasks more efficiently than a single large computer. Furthermore, these small computers can share and make economical expensive computer resources, like hard disks and letter quality printers.

The complicated technology is the network. Within the last year, all of Xerox, DEC, Intel, and Datapoint, along with smaller, microcomputer-oriented companies like Corvus and Nestar, have announced plans for a local area network. Such networks, each company hopes, will be a vital part of the office of the future. Local networks of small computers offer two major advantages over minicomputers: resource sharing, and incremental implementation.

It is well established that parts that can be placed on chips, such as CPUs and memories, are falling steadily in price, and that electromechanical devices, such as printers and disk drives, cannot be reduced in cost nearly as rapidly. By resource sharing - that is, by putting multiple CPU-memory units on a single device - expensive electromechanical devices can be used by more than one computer, thereby reducing significantly their cost per user.

Resource sharing, and therefore networking, is a practice driven by the fundamental dynamics of the semiconductor and small computer industry. A further type of economy makes networks even more attractive: namely, the entire network need not be implemented at one time but can be added to gradually, as needed.

For all these reasons, local networks of personal and small computers will begin, once network technology is fully worked out, to impact on sales of small minicomputers. In addition, networks will open a path upward, from the stand-alone office word processing station to more complicated systems, including those with gateways to national networks, and to mainframe processors. The commonly discussed era of linked computers will be at hand - but not involving ties to national databases like The Source or CompuServe. Linkage, like so many other things, will begin at home - or at least in the local office.

[The Technologies]. At present, three major technologies are competing to be the local area network architecture of the future. These are: (1) baseband coaxial cable systems, most notably Xerox's Ethernet system and Datapoint's ARC local area network; (2) twisted-wire pair systems, such as Crovus's OminNet, which have cost advantages over coaxial cable systems; and (3) broadband or wideband coaxial systems, which are at the moment favored by AT&T

(ACS system), to some extent by IBM (at least by its partial subsidiary Satellite Business Systems) and the IEEE standards committee. Wideband systems carry much more data than baseband or twisted-wire pair systems but technically are not as well developed. Finally, there are also digital PBX systems, which, although unable to transfer data at the rates of the above systems, have the advantage of using low-cost or already installed telephone lines.

[Collision Avoidance]. No matter how implemented in hardware - whether with twisted-wire pairs or with coaxial cable - major software and protocol problems remain to be solved. The major problem to be solved in local networks is the contention problem - the problem of having more than one device on the line at the same time. Local area networks can be thought of as party lines for computers, word processors, and other devices. This means, however, that they must be designed to prevent interference from disrupting the operation of the line.

Contention-based networks allow any device to have access to the network. When more than one device gets on the network at a time, transmissions are said to collide. The result is bad transmissions, like conversations talked over on a party line. If a conversation is talked over, it fails various tests and must be re-transmitted. Distance increases the probability that messages will collide. In general, this makes voice communications (other than intercom-type paging) impractical on contention-based networks. Consequently, contention-based networks, like Xerox's Ethernet, will always need to be co-wired with PBX or telephone systems.

Xerox's much-publicized Ethernet was the first and will be the most important of microcomputer local networks. The politics of Ethernet are as intriguing as the network itself. In 1974, Xerox suffered a massive humiliation in the mainframe computer business when it wrote off Xerox Data Systems. XDS, which Xerox had acquired in the late 1960s as SDS, a pioneer developer of what are now called mini-mainframes, had been widely touted as Xerox's attempt to compete head-on with IBM. The result was an unqualified loss for Xerox that not only sent XDS down the drain but somehow hamstrung its development efforts in other areas as well. In the late 1970s, when companies like Wang in the word processing market were doubling sales in every year, Xerox's Office Products Division sold antiquated (e.g., mag card), expensive electric typewriters and a word processor that no one could afford.

Xerox, of course, makes its money from copiers, and the Office Products Division in 1980 accounted for only $300 million of $8.2 billion total sales. In early 1978, using its corporate cash, Xerox acquired Shugart Associates, an aggressive and highly successful manufacturer of floppy disk drives. In short order, Donald Massaro, president of Shugart at the time of the acquisition, was co-opted into the Xerox corporate hierarchy as head of the OPD.

Ethernet, announced in December 1979, was really the opening salvo of Xerox's revitalization of OPD. Although Ethernet worked with Xerox's 860 communicating typewriters, the announcement of Ethernet was more importantly a promise of things to come. Having lost once to IBM, Xerox was committed to getting back into the fray, but this time turning it into a tag-team match.

In so far as Ethernet barely existed outside the laboratory, Xerox was playing the IBM game: establish a de-facto standard, then make people come to you. (Not coincidentally, Donald Massaro's former company, Shugart Associates, is, with its 5-1/4-inch mini-floppy disc drive, the only non-IBM computer company in recent memory to establish a de-facto hardware standard.)

In May 1980, enlisting all the help it could get in the fight against IBM, Xerox lined up two more heavy hitters on its side, Digital Equipment Corp., the minicomputer manufacturer, and Intel, the semiconductor maker. Both committed themselves to Ethernet and, more to the point, committed themselves to establishing Ethernet as the de-facto local network standard.

Since the initial Ethernet announcement, Xerox has made one major announcement after another in the office products field - all devices that can communicate over Ethernet, including:

> (1) The Star (May 1981), Xerox's entry into the high-end of the automated workplace, is primarily noteworthy for its high-density graphics display and its user-friendly features, which allow filing, for example, to be accomplished by merely pointing at an ideogram (small picture) of a file cabinet;

> (2) The 820 Personal Computer (June 1981) is essentially a competitor to the more expensive personal computers and runs CP/M, a microcomputer industry-standard operating system that immediately makes available for it a large, pre-existing library of business, accounting, and word processing programs;

> and (3) Saber (September 1981) is Xerox's attempt to break IBM's hold on the typewriter market.

Both Olivetti and Qyx, the Exxon affiliate, have introduced smart typewriters in the last year. Xerox, however, seems to have taken one major step beyond these designs and has made it possible to interface its typewriter easily to a computer - word processing network. In this sense, Xerox is willing to let its typewriter be used as a peripheral device, possibly for someone else's computer or word processor, rather than insist on selling a stand-alone, incompatible unit. (Xerox also owns Diablo systems, which makes a highly successful line of letter quality computer printers.)

The complete picture for Xerox, however, is not quite so rosy. There are still technical problems to be worked out with Ethernet, the spine along which Xerox hopes to hang its office of the future. In particular:

> (1) Ethernet is a contention-based multiple access scheme, which means in short that the various devices hung on the network fight for its control. This has two important consequences: first, that Ethernet cannot be used for voice communication (as can Datapoint's ARC local network, and WANGnet) and thus must be co-wired with PBX or telephone wire; and second, that the distances involved with Ethernet are relatively short. Attempts to lengthen Ethernet distances, or chain multiple Esternets together, will result in the use of active repeaters, which will essentially defeat Ethernet's passive design (i.e., the network is passive, and any device can be

taken off it without affecting any other) and compromise its reliability.

(2) In the original announcement, many of Ethernet's technical problems were in effect kicked upstairs, to be solved later with other layers of software and hardware, with results yet to come. Here Xerox is gambling heavily on the expertise of Intel (and, to a lesser extent, American Micro Devices) to solve its problems with silicon, and of DEC to solve them with software. The problems are presumably solvable - but aren't solved yet. These problems are being more realistically addressed by a standards committee of the IEEE, which for over a year has complained about what it perceives as an attempted railroading by the Xerox-DEC-Intel consortium, and which feels that Ethernet, although perhaps ultimately compatible with a full local network standard, is only a piece and not the whole pie.

(3) Finally, it must be pointed out that by its well-timed announcement of Ethernet, Xerox has managed to become a force in an office products market in which it has (yet) no market share. Xerox has done a wonderful job of selling the public on Ethernet - but has yet to sell the products. Companies like Wang, Datapoint, and IBM are already in the market and selling, whereas Xerox is talking. Both Wang and Datapoint have announced non-Ethernet local networks, and IBM's big shoe has yet to drop. When it does, Xerox will have a limited amount of time to make Ethernet less etherial and more real.

[Datapoint-Tandy ARCnet]. One of the important unresolved issues about local networks is whether or not they replace conventional office wiring for telephones. Datapoint, the San Antonio, TX-based maker of office automation and telephone switching equipment, has opted for a hybrid approach that combines high-speed local coaxial cable network, called by Datapoint the ARC system, with a digital PBX system, which is used not only for voice but for low-speed data. Datapoint calls this system the Information Switching Exchange or ISX. One feature of this system is its ability to interleave data communication with voice communication on WATS calls, thereby maximizing usage of this type of flat-rate line.

[WangNet]. Wang Laboratories, Inc., the Lowell, MA-based manufacturer of word processing equipment, has made little secret of its intention to develop a broadband local networking scheme that will accommodate both voice and data. Voice communications on the wideband cable network will be digitized. Wang, unlike some other manufacturers, is relatively eager to supply gateways to non-Wang equipment and has already announced software that makes its VS computers, and ultimately entire office clusters of Wang products, compatible with IBM's Systems Network Architecture (SNA).

[Nestar]. Nestar Systems, Inc. (430 Sherman Ave., Palo Alto, CA 94306) began as a company primarily involved in the educational market but later increased its involvement in business and distributed office data processing. Nestar, founded in October 1978, was originally involved in educational sales of Commodore's PET computer (it still sells a Programmer's Toolkit ROM for the

PET) but later shifted its emphasis to the Apple computer as domestic sales of Commodore dropped relative to those of Apple.

The Nestar ClusterBus is a 26-wire ribbon cable that connects peripheral Apple II computers in a star-like pattern to a central Apple. This Apple must be dedicated to the network: its only job is to serve up files from the disk system to other computers in the network asking for them. Attached to the file server is a large capacity disk system, which is the mass storage device for all the computers on the network.

Nestar's first system, the CLO-2001, used dual 8-inch floppy disks, with total storage capacity of 1.26 Mbytes; it later added an optional 14 Winchester hard disk system, the CLO-2002, which increases the storage capacity by 16.5 Mbytes) Other computers are then attached to the central controller by ribbon cables, usually 2 or 5 meters in length. These computers must have a special ClusterBus communications card installed in the slot usually reserved for the Apple II's floppy disk controller.

Printers, modems, and other devices must be added to this network by attachment to Apples other than the system controller. Files for printing must be transferred first to the central controller Apple and then must be accepted by the correct peripheral Apple for printing.

For schools, the Nestar system has a number of advantages: in particular, young students need not handle the floppy disks, and teachers can control a wired classroom from their own machines. Like all network-type systems, schools, once past the intial $6000 investment in the Nestar system, can add work stations as needed at a relatively low ($400, plus the price of the Apple) incremental price.

With its educational systems, Nestar can generally rely on a teacher (or students) to possess enough computer programming and hardware hacking skills to manage the installation. Within the last year, Nestar has devoted increasing attention to business and professional office applications of its network. Nestar's biggest problem in business and professional applications to date has been a lack of software designed to make the system easier for relatively inexperienced business users. It remains to be seen how successfully Nestar can penetrate this potentially lucrative market, particularly in light of competition from larger, better-known companies like Xerox, Wang, and Datapoint.

[Corvus]. Unlike Nestar, which began with the idea of creating a classroom network, Corvus Systems, Inc. (2029 O'Toole Ave., San Jose, CA 95131) was started as a hard disk company and added its Constellation product later as an enhancement for its disk system.

Corvus was founded in May, 1979 and introduced that same year its first product, an 8-inch, 10-Mbyte Winchester disk drive. The Corvus disk, although now available for a wide variety of microcomputers, has always basically been an Apple add-on product and owes much of its success to the deficiencies (slow speed, low storage capacity) of Apple's soft-sector floppy disk design. Recently, Corvus has broadened its product line to include a 20-Mbyte and a 5-Mbyte drives, as well as a MC68000-based computer, the Concept. All of the disk drives can work with Corvus's Constellation and OmniNet network systems.

To increase the appeal of its relatively expensive ($5300 list) disk, Corvus introduced in 1980 the Constellation, a device that allows up to 8 computers to communicate with its hard disk. The Corvus disk controller is, in fact, a Z-80 microprocessor with 16K of its own RAM (the controller boots off reserved tracks on the disk upon start-up). Corvus sells the Constellation with a considerable amount of system software, the most recent version of which allows implementation of pipelines between computers and spooling of data for later output to slow devices like printers.

Unlike the Nestar system, the Constellation does not require a dedicated computer, relying instead on the intelligence of the Z-80 disk controller. Each computer in a Constellation network is wired with an interface card to the Constellation, which in turn is wired to the hard disk. Corvus had sold somewhat over 2500 of its hard disks by 1981, and about 1000 of these have been equipped with the Constellation. Although much of Corvus' appeal is to the educational market, a number of software houses have introduced distributed processing office systems using the Constellation. Although both companies are guarded about sales figures, shipments of the Corvus Constellation appear to be greater than that of Nestar system.

In April 1981, Corvus introduced OmniNet, a product that evolved from the Constellation. With the Constellation, computers must be wired together with a thick ribbon cable limited to 100 feet in length. Corvus sells this cable at $3 per foot, meaning that a 100-foot link to the hard disk can cost $300. To reduce these costs, Corvus's OmniNet uses twisted wire-pair (the RS-422 standard), similar to telephone wire. Individual computers are connected to OmniNet through $500 interface cards called "transporters". These transporters are built around a Motorola 6801 microprocessor, and operate at a rate of 1 million bits per second. Data transfers do not interfer with software running in the individual computers of the network. OmniNet will, in theory, run without the Corvus disk system but is not economical without some type of resource sharing, most obviously the Corvus disk, and less obviously a printer or communications system.

M

Memory

We can best visualize computer memory as a series of boxes similar to those at the post office. Each box has a number: this is called the "address" of the box. The box also has inside it another number - its contents.

[Bits and Bytes]. The decimal number system, familiar to almost everyone in the modern world, uses ten different symbols to represent numbers: "0", "1", "2", "3", "4", "5", "6", "7", "8", and "9". All numbers are made up of combinations of these ten symbols. Computer circuits work much better if the range of symbols is more limited: indeed, if it is limited to just two numbers, "0" and "1". Every number that can be represented in decimal can also be represented in binary; it just takes more digits to write it out. Thus:

$$
\begin{array}{rcl}
0 & = & 0 \\
1\ 0 & = & 2 \\
1\ 0\ 1 & = & 5 \\
1\ 0\ 1\ 0\ 1\ 1 & = & 43
\end{array}
$$

Computer circuits use binary because an electrical circuit is usually either on (1) or off (0). Such a circuit can represent one binary digit, or bit, of information. At times, as in true/false situations, a single bit of information is all that is needed. A friend agrees to leave the porch light on if he goes out and turn it off if he comes in. The light circuit is carrying one bit of information:

light on	=	friend out
light off	=	friend in

A single bit can be used to represent whether a person is married or not. But what if we need to know whether a person is unmarried, married, separated, or divorced? Now we need 2 bits to encode these 4 possibilities:

BIT PATTERN	INFORMATION
0 0	unmarried

```
0 1          married
1 0          divorced
1 1          separated
```

With three bits we can encode 8 combinations; with 4 bits, we can encode 16 different combinations. In general, with n different bits, 2^n power combinations can be represented.

All microcomputers work with combinations of 8 bits, called "bytes". (At first, the term "byte" was a bit of a joke, but now nobody seems to notice. Four bits are often called a "nibble."). Because a byte has eight bits, it can range in value from 0 to 255 and has 256 different bit patterns:

```
0 0 0 0 0 0 0 0  =  0
0 0 0 0 0 0 0 1  =  1
          ...
1 1 1 1 1 1 1 0  =  254
1 1 1 1 1 1 1 1  =  255
```

Some microcomputers can work with 2 bytes at once, or a 16 bit-word. In general, a word is the smallest "natural" unit that the computer can take out of its memory and put back at once. On mainframe computers, words can be very large: on the CDC 6400 series, for example, words are 60-bits long. On most mainframes and on a few new microprocessor chips, words are 32-bits long.

[Looking at Memory]. From most versions of BASIC, it is possible to look directly at a microcomputer's memory and to examine its contents. In Microsoft BASIC, these commands are PEEK and POKE. The following commands will print numbers between 0 and 255 that are the contents of these memory locations:

```
PRINT PEEK(0)
PRINT PEEK(17645)
PRINT PEEK(17646)
PRINT PEEK(65000)
```

The PEEK command can allow us to map out every location in memory:

LOCATION	VALUE
0	13
1	200
65354	255

The POKE command can be used to change these values. POKEing should be used with care; since the program running the computer is also in memory, a misplaced POKE can change it.

[Memory Maps]. To form memory addresses, eight-bit microprocessors use 2 bytes. This means that valid addresses can range from 0 to 65,535. A computer with 16K is using only 16,384 of 65,535 possible locations. (Note that a "K" is only approximately 1000 - it is actually 1024. And 64K is really 65,535).

A chart that shows where a computer has memory and what is usually in that memory is called a "memory map". Memory is usually thought of in spatial terms. Memory locations near address 0 are called low memory, and those with larger addresses are called high memory. In all computers, various sections of memory will be reserved for special purposes. This need not affect most users, but it is of concern to assembly language programmers.

[RAM and ROM]. "ROM" stands for Read Only Memory. ROM can be looked at but not changed, even accidentally; if the PEEK location is used to look at a section of ROM, it will always give the same result. ROM can and in fact usually does contain program code. Because code burned into ROM is solid, it is called "firmware", a pun on "software". "RAM" stands for Random Access Memory. Actually, all memory allows random access; RAM really means that the memory can be written on. Thus a POKE to a RAM memory location, followed by a PEEK, will show the number just poked. (PEEKs of nonexistent memory locations - valid addresses where no memory is actually installed - usually show all 1's or 255).

Two types of memory similar to ROM are used in program development. EPROM stands for Eraseable Programmable Read Only Memory. EPROMs can be erased and reused by exposing them to ultraviolet light. PROM stands for Programmable Read Only Memory; it is a ROM that can be created on a special device called a PROM burner. True ROMs are stamped out in bulk during the semiconductor manufacturing process and thus require high volume to justify. PROMs can be made a few at a time as needed during the development stages of a project.

[The Speed of RAM Chips]. RAM chips operate at certain speeds. In general, 400 ns chips are the slowest that can be used in Z-80 systems running at 4 Mhz; 250 and even faster chips are now available. If in doubt about the speed of a chip, check its part number. Usually chips faster than 300 ns have a "-2", "-3", or "-4" following the base number. 300 ns chips have either no number following the part number or a "-C" (AMD), "-5" (Fairchild), or "-30" (Motorola).

Microprocessors

The microprocessor is the prime cause of the revolution in computing prices that occurred in the 1970s. The micro revolution is far from over; it continues at full speed in the 1980s, and shows every sign of continuing into the 1990s. By the mid-1990s, all but a few very specialized computers will be microcomputers. These computers will have nothing small about them, however, except their physical size. In computing power, they will be equivalent to today's mainframes. In manufacturing cost, they may be comparable to today's video games.

[The CPU]. Microprocessors provide new wine in small bottles. Since the mid-1950s, every computer has had a central processing unit, or CPU. The CPU typically pulled information out of the computer's memory, altered it, and put it back. Large computers like the IBM 7094 had instructions like "load accumulator", "store accumulator", and so on. On these machines, the accumulator was wide - the CDC 6400 series, for example, has a 60-bit word - and made out of wires, transistors, and the like.

The first microprocessor took existing computer architecture and implemented it in silicon. At first, there were serious limitations as to what microprocessors could do. The 1st microprocessor, Intel 4004, which was introduced in 1971, had only a 4-bit accumulator. Although adequate for calculators and adding machines, it was not a terribly interesting part around which to build a computer. Ironically, this first microprocessor was commissioned by a Japanese company for a desktop calculator.

[8-Bit Microprocessors]. 8-bit microprocessors were introduced in the early 1970s. Intel's 8008 is the granddaddy of 8-bit microprocessors, having been introduced in 1972. It was originally built as a CRT controller for Datapoint. The 8008 was quickly followed by Intel's 8080. This device is the father of such diverse branches of the microprocessor family tree as the Zilog Z-80 and the 16-bit 8086. Intel and Zilog combined form this family:

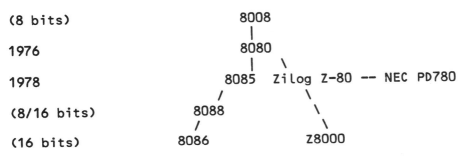

The other dominant family of microprocessors might be called the Motorola family. Motorola, originally known as the maker of car radios, designed the 6800 microprocessor a short while after the 8008 came to the market. From that time on, however, the history of the two families has diverged:

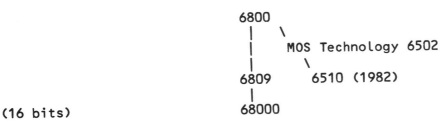

[The Chip Wars]. Chips operate in an economic world that is much like that of paperback books or record albums: in short, semiconductors obey the economic laws of fashion. What matters most is that a chip set a trend and become a "best seller" fast. If it does, more and more designers begin to use it, and more and more software is developed for it. This additional work - all out of the hands of the semiconductor manufacturer - snowballs for successful chips. If this secondary design effort fails to appear, no expense on the part of the manufacturer can revive it.

The comparison of chips with high fashion items is not trivial. As with designer clothes and paperback novels, the major expense of production is not in the material cost (silicon, coming from sand, is hardly expensive; there is about 50 cents of sand in a chip) but in the initial design cost. If sales take off, this one-time cost is amortized over an increasing and possibly very large number of units. If prices are maintained, this makes high profits for the manufacturer; if not, it makes lower prices for consumers, a condition some manufacturers call "profitless prosperity".

What drives chip prices down is, of course, competition. Semiconductor companies often compete with companies selling exact imitations of chips they spent millions designing. Although a chip's schematic can be copyrighted and various other legal steps taken to theoretically protect a design, in practice chips can and are "reverse engineered" as soon as they come out. Most semiconductor manufacturers will officially license a new chip to another manufacturer, called a "second source".

Unauthorized second sources also exist, however, and usually sell popular chips at slightly less than the original manufacturer's price. Advanced Micro Devices, Jerry Sander's firm, during the early 1970s made a business of being a second source, sometimes authorized, sometimes not. (Later ADM developed its own proprietary designs.) A key event in the history of the microcomputer was the announcement of an unauthorized version of the Intel 8080, the 9080, in 1975. At a time when Intel was selling the chip for $70 each in minimum quantities of 100, ADM offered to sell the 9080 for $35 in quantity one. Intel promptly dropped its price to meet this competition, and the microcomputer was born.

Price cutting, however is only one aspect of the chip wars: headhunting is another. The families of microprocessors are related by more than just a vague resemblance: many chips, as it were, have the same father, if different mother firms. The transistor was at Bell Labs in the late 1940s, an achievement for which William Schockley (later infamous for his unfortunate racist theories), Robert Noyce, and Gordon Moore received the Nobel Prize. Schockley spun off a private firm called Shockley Research Laboratories, in NJ, later Fairchild Electronics in CA's Silicon Valley, one of the early successful integrated circuit companies.

In 1968, two key executives of Fairchild - Robert Noyce and Gordon Moore - left that company and formed Intel - "Integrated Electronics". Intel, today, is a major company and a leader of the semiconductor industry. But in 1975, after Intel's successful 8080 had been designed, 3 employees of Intel left to form Zilog: Frederico Faggin, Ralph Ungermann, and chip designer Matushi Shima. Zilog - at one time working out of offices above a suburban shopping center - received start-up money from Exxon, which still owns the firm. Zilog's first and most successful product to date, the Z-80, was the "second-generation" 8080 and skimmed a lot of cream off Intel's market.

The 6502 family has some skeletons in its family tree as well. In 1974, Motorola designed the 6800 microprocessor, when Chuck Peddle and several others left the company to start MOS Technology. They quickly designed a very similar chip, the 6502, which they introduced in 1975 at the Wescon show. The part was simple, cheap, and immediately popular with personal computer designers like Steve Woznick and Steven Jobs, then at work on the Apple I in their garage. However, as the 6502 took off, Motorola sued. The suit was settled out of court, but it left MOS soweakened that its founders sold out to Commodore International in 1976. Commodore, then making calculators, brought out the PET computer the next year.

[8-Bit CPUs Compared]. While most of the excitement in the microcomputer world is now over 16- and-32 bit processors, there are still significant differences among the 8-bit devices. Zilog's Z-80 emerged from the design wars of the late 1970s as the champion in the 8-bit field. The MOS Technology 6502, used in the Apple][, Apple ///, Atari, and others, runs number two. Intel's 8085 runs a bad third. Motorola's 6800 has a limited market in older "SS-50" bus computers (Smoke Signal Broadcasting, GIMIX, SWTPC), and its newer 6809 has a small slice of the hybrid 8/16 bit-market. Each processor has its adherents, and taking sides can be dangerous.

However, microprocessors can be compared on speed, instruction sets, and several other variables. Speed is the most obvious comparison. Each microprocessor has a basic cycle or clock time. This clock is a signal fed into the chip from an external crystal that establishes the fundamental speed of the chip's operations. Chip speeds are measured in how many million cycles they have per second - that is, in megahertz (1 Hz is 1 cycle per second; mega means million). The Apple II's 6502 runs at 1.023 Mhertz, which seems like an odd speed, but it fits well into color video generation. Late-model Z-80 computers run at 4 MHz, which newer 16-bit Motorola 68000 and Intel 8086 chips can run at up to 8 MHz.

For chips with comparable instruction sets, increasing the clock speed makes the computer faster. Thus, when the 4-MHz Z-80 became available in 1977, it ran programs twice as fast as the Intel 8080, which ran at 2 MHz. Comparing unrelated microprocessors is more difficult. The 6502 runs slower than the Z-80, but has a somewhat more efficient instruction set. Comparisons between microprocessors require the use of benchmarks, where the same higher-level operations, like adding, multiplying, etc., are repeated many times. In general, the speed rating of current microprocessors is:

Motorola 68000 (8 MHz)
Intel 8086 (8 MHz)
Intel 8088 (5 MHz)
Zilog Z-80 ("B"-6 MHz; "A"-4 MHz)
Motorola 6809 (usually 2 MHz)
MOS 6502 (usually 1 MHz)

Unfortunately, faster versions of the microprocessors are sometimes hard to obtain and often are more expensive than slower versions. Naturally, faster processors require faster memory and other system components, which increases cost as well.

Instruction sets vary widely among processors. The key differences can be spotted usually by looking at instructions specifically designed to support higher-level data types, like floating point numbers, long integers, and strings. Thus the Z-80 has several "string like" instructions that the 8080 does not have; the 8088 has integer multiply and divide instructions for both 8- and 16-bit data, which the Z-80 does not have. However, good sense must prevail in looking at instruction sets: in fact, most fancy instructions are used infrequently. The critical test is how fast one processor is over another on a set of statistically representative instructions from actual programs.

[The 16-Bit Race]. IBM's August 1981 introduction of its PC using the Intel

8088 microprocessor put an official seal of approval on 16-bit systems - even though in many benchmark tests the IBM PC proved slower than 4-MHz Z-80s. In 1982, everyone talked about 16-bit microprocessors, and a few people did something about it. In particular, in 1982 the contenders in the 16-bit race narrowed to two: the Intel 8086 (and its relation, the 8088) and the Motorola 68000.

In 1982, Intel's 8086 seemed to have a guaranteed future thanks to IBM's use of its relation, the 8088, in its PC announced in August 1981. (Ironically, IBM designers were in love with the 68000 in mid-1982, and rumored to be planning a dual MC68000-system for mid-1983 introduction.) Following IBM's lead, a wave of Japanese and European "PC compatible" systems using the 8088 and 8086 were also announced in 1982. Other interesting 8086/8088 systems included those by Godbout (Oakland, CA); Seattle Computer (an 8-MHz 8086 S-100 bus system); TecMar (8086); and Discovery.

However, the news of 1982 was the success of Motorola's powerful 68000. Several important 68000 computers were announced at the West Coast Computer Faire in March 1982, including the Sage II, a 8-MHz Pascal machine and the Fortune 32:16, a business machine with substantial venture capital backing. Corvus Systems, known for its hard disks and networking, announced the Corvus Concept in May 1982. A dozen or so other 68000-based computers were in the works, including "Lisa", Apple's step beyond the Apple ///, for 1983 introduction. A semicomplete list of announced or anticipated 68000 systems: WICAT; Fortune 32:16; Vector Graphic; Apple (Lisa); Dual Systems/Control (Berkeley, CA); MicroDaSys (Los Angeles, CA); Charles River Data Systems; Chromatics (Tucker, GA); and Lexidata (Billerica, MA).

By contrast, only a few companies had Z8000 machines. Two of these, Onyx (San Leandro, CA) and Intersystems (NY) bet early and perhaps lost. The Z8000 has been more popular in Europe, however, where Olivetti announced a microcomputer using it in early 1982.

[The Minicomputer Makers]. Actually, 16-bit microprocessors have been around for some years. Not surprisingly, the first companies interested in making 16-bit microprocessors were the minicomputer companies, all of whom had 16-bit machines on sale in the early 1970s. Digital Equipment (DEC), the leading minicomputer company, commissioned Western Digital to make the LSI-11 then - in a move that nearly wrecked Western Digital - began in-house fabrication of the chip in 1976. Data General's MicroNova chip, which executes similar but not identical instructions as DG's Nova computers, has been available since 1977. In-house, Hewlett-Packard has has a variety of 16-bit designs for an equal amount of time.

Unfortunately, the makers of minicomputers had the wrong attitude about their 16-bit products, viewing 16-bit processors as a way to trim production costs in their traditional operations, not as new devices. None of the minicomputer makers really wanted to encourage outside companies to design with their chips, for fear they would produce a minicomputer competitive with and perhaps superior to their own.

It took the semiconductors companies, whose main interest was in pushing parts, to popularize 16-bit processors. Intel introduced its 8086 in mid-1978; the early introduction of that chip has been a major factor in its success. The 8088, which has identical 16-bit registers to the 8086 but which fetches data from memory a single 8-bit byte at a time, was announced in 1979. The 8088 is used in the IBM Personal Computer. Zilog began limited sampling of its 16-bit microprocessor, the Z8000, in March 1979, after many delays, and officially announced the chip in April of that year. Zilog's Memory Management Unit (MMU) for the chip was not available until 1980, however. Motorola's 68000 was last on the market, with sampling beginning in October 1979.

[Second Sources for 16-Bit Chips]. The Z8000 is 2nd sourced by Advanced Micro Devices. Motorola's US second source for the chip is Rockwell International, which makes it at its Anaheim and Newport Beach, CA, facilities. In Europe, Thompson-CSF makes the 68000, in Japan, Hitachi is the second source. Motorola has a Microsystems Group facility in Mesa, AZ, that produces support products for the 68000.

Modems

"Modem" is one of those ugly words with which we are stuck. The only good thing about it is that it is a concatenation of two equally awful words – modulator and demodulator – so perhaps we're better off with one than two.

Modems are a computer's way of communicating with the external world through the telephone lines. When computers are in close proximity to each other (within about 500 feet), they can be directly linked, or hardwired, often using a simple serial RS-232-C connection and 4 wires. So-called local networks, many of which use coaxial cable, allow computers to be linked within office buildings and sometimes up to distances of a mile.

But over very long distances, it is logical for computers to talk to each other the same way people do – by telephone. The problem here is that the phone system has been built over the years for people, not machines, which have a hard time using the phone.

The average caller rarely notices it, but the telephone company plays some extraordinary tricks with his or her voice on long distance transmissions. The phone company, for example, actually turns off the speaker's line between words, to suppress echoes on calls over 100 miles. It also mixes one call with hundreds of others for transmission by microwave relay. A long distance call in the US may easily go through 10 different switching centers, starting with a Class 5 End Office, working up to a Class 1 Regional Center, and moving to another regional center, and then working its way down again to a local Class 5 End Office.

For years, the phone company has designed its system to provide a low-cost service with acceptable audio quality. The system wasn't designed for computers, and the massive amounts of capital invested in it makes it for all practical purposes, impossible to change. Computers are stuck with the system they find.

[Modulation]. To send data over the phone, computers whistle. In short, they whistle back and forth at preset frequencies in the audible range. The human ear can hear frequencies from about 10 Hz (cycles per second) to 16 KHz. As is well known, voices on the phone lack the richness of real voices: the telephone line can carry frequencies between only 300 Hz and 4 KHz. Higher-quality voice transmission, needed for radio and television transmission, can be obtained by using special equipment on conditioned lines.

The attraction of using the ordinary phone network, however, is that its service is available almost anywhere. To use it, then, computers must live with the limits of its equipment. Transmission rates on switched lines generally can go no higher than 4800 bits per second. Faster transmission rates require expensive, private-line arrangements that avoid voice grade switching centers by connecting directly to central telephone system nodes.

Transmission of information with a modem requires two steps: the conversion of computer data to serial, one-bit-at-a-time form, followed by the modulation ("whistling") of the bits across the telephone line. In a similar way, reception of information by a modem requires decoding the whistle ("demodulation") followed by assembly of the serial bit stream into a

[Word Length and Parity]. Consider what is required to send the letter "A" from one computer to another. In the memory of the first computer, the ASCII code for the letter A looks like this:

0 1 0 0 0 0 0 0 1

This data byte is usually accessed all 8 bits at once. The first step in transmitting it is to serialize it - that is, send it out one bit at a time. Most computers use integrated circuits called UARTs to serialize data, UART standing for Universal Asynchronous Receiver Transmitter. Most UART chips contain control registers that determine: (1) the baud rate at which to send or expect bits; (2) the number of stop bits to add to characters on their way out; and (3) what to do about parity - either nothing, or add even, or add odd.

In asynchronous transmission, each (data-parity) byte is framed by a start bit, and one or two stop bits. Devices operating at 110 baud (e.g., older Teletypes) usually work with two stop bits, higher-speed devices get by with one. Stop bits are rarely the cause of transmission problems; improper word length parity setting usually is. In the US, eight bits no parity is the most common setting, followed by seven bits even parity. Note that a total of 10 bits, and possibly as many as 12, are required to transmit a single 8-bit byte: 1 start bit, 8 data bits, and 1 stop bit. This is why, in serial communication, 300 baud, or bits per second, is equal to 30 characters per second. 110 baud, Teletype speed, is 10 characters per second.

When a computer has a serial port, getting data to the UART is generally no more complicated than using a PRINT statement from BASIC. Once sent to the UART, what happens next to the data depends on the settings of the UART control registers (sometimes these are initialized from software, and sometimes by switches). The length of the transmitted character length can be either 5, 6, 7, or 8 bits. For most communications, 7 or 8 bits are normal.

5 bits are used in some older Baudot codes and tickertapes. ASCII takes 7 bits to transmit, and it typically does as 7 bits with even or odd parity, or 8 bits with no parity. Odd parity means that a bit will be generated after the transmitted byte that makes the bit count come out as an odd number of 1's; even parity means that it will come out as an even number of 1's.

Modulators are dumb - they take whatever 1's or 0's come over the RS-232 line, and they send out one set of frequencies for 1, and another set for 0. Note that the particular technique of modulation, per se, is independent of the baud rate. A 300-baud modem modulates at whatever rate the data comes to it; it will work well sending and receiving at 300 baud. In fact, Bell 103 modems will usually work at 600 baud and of course can be used at 110 baud. Modulation and demodulation should be thought of as audio tone processing, not digital logic.

[Originate and Answer Mode]. When modulated tones are received by computer B, they are demodulated by its modem. Computer A, the sending computer, is said to be in the originate mode. Computer B - the one called by the other - is said to be in the answer mode. Originate and answer are a sort of computer version of role playing. Which computer places the call is in fact insignificant; the only thing of importance is that one device is in the originate mode, and the other in the answer mode. Note also that being in the originate mode is independent of the direction in which data is flowing; one computer may call another and receive data from it passively for hours and still be in the originate mode.

In answer mode, a Bell 103 modem demodulates a 1270-Hz signal on the phone line into a data bit 1, and a 1070-Hz signal into a 0. These data bits are taken in one at a time and assembled into a parallel byte by the receiving computer's UART. In the originate mode, the computer listens for data coming at 2225 Hz (1) and at 2025 Hz (0). Four frequencies, then, are involved:

> 1070 Hz - 0 in originate mode
> 1270 Hz - 1 in originate mode
> 2025 Hz - 0 in answer mode
> 2225 Hz - 1 in answer mode

These 4 frequencies were carefully chosen to avoid interfering with each other. This allows Bell 103 conversations to be full-duplex - meaning both computers can talk at the same time. (If both computers can talk, but only one at a time, the line is called half-duplex. Bell 202 modems are half duplex. A transmissionis strictly 1-way, as are broadcast or point-to-multipoint transmissions, is called simplex.)

On a full-duplex link, two types of items will be coming from the computer in answer mode: the echo of everything sent in by the computer in originate mode, and whatever information it generates. On most terminals, echoed characters - which have often made a round trip of thousands of miles - are the ones displayed on the screen. This practice lets the operator know exactly what the host computer has received, and sometimes creates a spongey sensation when typing as a result of transmission delay. If characters are displayed directly as they are typed on the keyboard, a local echo is said to be in effect. If typed characters duplicate LLIIKKEE TTHHIISS when logging onto a timesharing service, the terminal program is probably set for half-duplex and should be set for full-duplex.

[Control Characters]. In addition to the originate/answer protocol, certain control characters are often used to allow one computer to say, in effect: Slow down - you're going too fast! Often, a control-S tells the one computer to stop, and a control-Q tells it to resume. This is called (X-ON/X-OFF) protocol, a term deriving from the days of paper tape on Teletypes. Actual conventions used by timesharing services vary slightly. The following table gives those of The Source and CompuServe:

	SOURCE	COMPUSERVE
cntrl-A		suspends output at end of line
cntrl-H	backspace	backspace
cntrl-O		turn off output, but continue program as if on
cntrl-Q	resume output	resume after cntrl-A or Q
cntrl-P	simulates break	
cntrl-S	suspend output	suspend output

[Quick Modem Guide for Personal Computers]. Modems have become nearly standard equipment on personal computers. Most computers are set up to use modems through standard serial ports. The IBM PC generally uses the Asynch Communications card with an external modem, like the Hayes Smartmodem. Tandy sells several different 300-baud modems for its computers that can be used with other brands; in 1982, Tandy introduced a 1200-baud Bell 212 compatible modem. Internal board modems are available for the Apple II, Commodore PET, and S-100 bus computers.

[External Modems]. If a computer has a free RS-232-C port, then only a modulator/demodulator is needed to modulate and demodulate the serial bit stream coming in and going out of this port. An external modem connects to an RS-232-C port by a 25-line ribbon cable, usually male-male. A typical low-cost external modem is the Novation CAT. For some computers, modems are sold as plug-in boards that are really modems combined with RS-232 ports. The Micromodem by DC Hayes for the Apple II is such a product.

Apple Computer recommends and sells an external modem (a Novation) along with its 110/300-baud Communications Card. The most popular communications device for the Apple II, however, is the Hayes Micromodem, a single-card Bell 103 type modem that usually goes either into slot 2 or 3 of the Apple. There is a lot of software written for the Micromodem, including patches to the Dow Jones Portfolio Evaluator Program sold by Apple. Novation makes a 1-card Bell 103/202 modem for the Apple with many nice features like touchtone receiver, BSR control, and the like. An upgrade card turns this Apple-Cat II into a Bell 212 system, but users should be warned that the Apple is generally too slow to use 1200 baud efficiently. The Apple /// usually uses an external modem on its standard serial port.

[Commodore]. A modem for the Commodore PET is made by TNW Corporation (formerly The Net Works). The TNW488/103 uses two Listen and two Talk addresses on the IEEE 488-1975 bus connector on the back of the PET. TNW sells a Darcom D-101 Data Access Arrangement (DAA) connector for connecting the TNW488/103 to a standard telephone USOC-RJ11C jack.

[S-100 Bus Computers]. Modems for S-100 bus computers include those

Tandy 1200 Baud Modem

manufactured by Hayes (PO Box 9884, Atlanta, GA 30319, 404-455-7663) and Potomac Micro-Magic (First Lincolnia Bldg., Suite B1, 4810 Beauregard St., Alexandria, VA 22312, 703-750-3727). Both these modems are FCC-approved for direct connection to the phone system and allow automatic dialing. They attach to the telephone company's standard RJ11C modular jack. The Hayes modem sells for $379; the Potomac Micro-Magic MM-103 sells for $360.

[Dialing the Phone]. In the US, two types of dialing are used: rotary and Touch-Tone ("Touch-Tone", by the way, is a registered trademark of AT&T). Tone dialing is much faster than rotary but is also more difficult to implement. Rotary dialing, however, uses a convention dating from the 1890s, when the dial telephone was invented, and is relatively simple for a computer to do.

Two wires run between the telephone and the exchange. When the telephone is taken off the hook, the mechanism in the phone completes the simple circuit to the exchange. The exchange sends a dial tone. After a dial tone is established, for each digit in the telephone number, repeat these:

(1) Get the ASCII code of the digit to be dialed. Mask with 0F hexadecimal to get a binary count 0-9. If the count is 0, make it 10; to dial 0, the phone must be pulsed 10 times.

(2) For each number in the count, go on hook for 70 milliseconds, then go off hook for 30.

(3) When the count for a digit is up, wait at least 550 milliseconds before going to the next digit, if any.

(4) When the complete number has been dialed, of course, stay off the hook until the call is answered. If this is a computer timesharing service, it will pick up the phone and send an answer carrier. Presence of a carrier can usually be tested by a bit in a modem status word.

[1200-Baud Modems]. In 1982, a number of low-cost 1200-baud modems for personal computers were announced. Bell 212 modems use phase modulation, as opposed to the frequency-modulation technique of the Bell 100 series. Phase modulation is less susceptible to line noise than is frequency modulation but is more expensive to implement. In 1980, however, a number of LSI modem components - almost modems of a chip - came on the market, making low-cost 212 modems possible.

[UDS]. Universal Data Systems (5000 Bradford Drive, Huntsville, AL 35805) is an established maker of high-speed modems whose 212LP ("low price"), announced in early 1982, is its first personal computer product. The LP certainly is LP: $495, about $200 cheaper than the competition. The LP does not have auto dialing and must be used with a telephone. However, the LP takes its power off the phone line, eliminating ac adaptors and yet another cord. The LP can be used in either originate (most common) or answer mode.

[Novation]. Although Novation (18664 Oxnard St., Tarzana, CA 91356, 213-996-5060) had a 1200-baud Apple-Cat modem for the Apple available since mid-1981, this modem was only Bell 202 (half-duplex) compatible, not Bell 212, as needed to communicate at 1200 baud with most US timesharing services. Novation announced a $389 upgrade board for the Apple-Cat II in early 1982. Together, the 2-board set (sold together for $725) makes a complete 212 auto dial, auto answer modem. A fully loaded Novation 212 board set with BSR controller, firmware, and touch tone receiver option comes in at $974.

[Tandy]. Tandy, meanwhile, introduced its own 212 modem in June 1982, at $699 retail, with an optional auto dial accessory at $150. Tandy's part numbers are (76-1005) for the DC-1200 High-Speed Direct Connect Modem and (76-1009) for the auto dial accessory. If set for auto answer, the Tandy modem will pick up the phone when it rings and adjust automatically to either a 300 or 1200 incoming baud rate, making it useful for CBBS-type systems.

[Hayes]. Hayes Microcomputer Products, not to be left behind, introduced a 300/1200 baud modem in mid-1982. The Hayes 1200-baud modem is combatible with its 300 baud Smartmodem, features auto dial and auto answer, and will also automatically detect data rate. The Hayes 1200-baud modem lists at $699.

The Computer Cookbook's current modem price guide:

SYSTEM	MANUFACTURER	DESCRIPTION/IDENTIFICATION	LIST	DISCOUNT
Modem	Hayes	Smartmodem, 300 baud	279.00	189.00
Modem	Hayes	Smartmodem, 1200/300 baud	699.00	482.00
Modem	Hayes	Micromodem 100 (S-100 board)	399.00	270.00
Modem	Hayes	Micromodem II (Apple II board)	379.00	245.00
Modem	Novation	490190-4 CAT (acoustic)	189.00	
Modem	Novation	490268 D-CAT (direct connect)	199.00	
Modem	Novation	490401 AUTO-CAT (auto answer)	249.00	
Modem	Novation	490501 212 AUTO-CAT	695.00	
Modem	Novation	490402 Apple-CAT II	389.00	
Modem	Novation	490412 Apple-CAT 212 upgrade	389.00	
Modem	Novation	490502 212 Apple-CAT II system	725.00	
Modem	Novation	490403 Apple CAT II backplate	39.00	
Modem	Novation	490404 Apple CAT II handset	29.00	

Modem	Novation	490405	BSR Control	19.00
Modem	Novation	490406	Cassette Recorder Cable	5.00
Modem	Novation	490407	Touch Tone Receiver	99.00
Modem	Novation	490408	Ap-CAT II firmware chip	29.00
Modem	Novation	490409	Deaf Firmware	29.00
Modem	Novation	490410	Software Disk	29.00
Modem	Novation	490411	EIA Cable (RS-232)	19.00
Modem	Novation	490006	Condenser Mike WE500	14.95
Modem	Tandy	76-1005	1200 direct connect	699.00
Modem	Tandy	76-1009	Auto dial for 1005	149.95

Computer Music

Computer music is a growing field that has only started to tap the resources of microcomputers. As with word processing, which covers everything from simple typing to database management and newspaper production, computer music means different things to different people.

A first and most important distinction that must be made is whether or not the computer is actually performing music. A number of composers have no interest in computers as performing instruments and are interested in them strictly as compositional aids - much like a writer might use a word processor to write a novel but still have it typeset and printed in the usual way. Alternately, the computer can be used for "rough drafts" and then the final piece performed by orchestra.

The increasing popularity of low-cost "home" computers has led to software that turns them into electronic music boxes. New video games and low-cost computers coming on the market have standard programmable sound generators; Commodore's music chip introduced in 1982 has 3 voices in a 9 octave range. Software here is of 2 sorts: the playback program, and a library of sounds.

[Some Basic Music Terms]. Although performance is an art, sound is physics. To create music on computers, musical events must be translated into their basic physical features.

Music, by definition, is an organized collection of sound frequencies, or pitches. At one time, this definition would have included some language about music being a pleasing sequence of sound; but such judgments are subjective and definitely out of favor in all fields of modern art. Nevertheless, music is organized sound, as opposed to noise.

Individual musical notes are pitches of a certain frequency. Frequency always comes down to Hertz (Hz): a certain number of cycles per second (1 Hz = 1 cycle per second). There are any number of tuning systems that map notes to frequencies.

In the traditional scale, the octave is the fundamental unit of pitch. A note in one octave is exactly twice as high as a note in the octave lower. A piano has a range of about 8 octaves. Since the octaves are relative measurements, an anchor to the absolute world is needed. Over the years, A above middle C, also called A natural, has been defined as 440 Hz. The frequency of a note an octave below this note is 220 Hz, and an octave above is 880 Hz.

The relationship of notes within an octave is also subject to convention. Western music uses the so-called equally tempered scale. There are 12 notes in each octave; the frequency of one note can be computed by multiplying the previous note by the 12th root of 2, whose decimal value is 1.05946309435. Thus the note above A natural, B, has a frequency of 466.16 Hz. The 12 notes of the scale have the following traditional names:

```
                              C
                              C#
                              D
                              D#
                              E
                              F
                              F#
                              G
                              G#
                              A
                              A#
                              B
```

The # sign after a note is called a sharp. In general, a sharp can be thought of as "plus 1" note. A flat, represented in musical notation by a square with tails looking somewhat like a "b", can be thought of as "minus 1".

If an instrument or performer makes a sound that is off the ideal frequency, they are said to be sharp (too high) or flat (too low). Tuning errors are measured in "cents". A cent is 1/100th of a note. The following table gives an 8-octave range of values for the General Instruments AY-3-8910 Programmable Sound Generator chip (PSG), showing the ideal musical frequency, a divider value used to program the chip, the actual note frequency produced by the chip, and the tuning error in cents. Note that the chip is very much in tune in the lower octaves, and out of tune in the higher. Tuning errors of 2 and 3 cents are difficult for untrained humans to hear.

NOTE	FREQ	DIVI	ACTUAL	CENTS	NOTE	FREQ	DIVI	ACTUAL	CENTS
C 1	32.703	3421	32.698	0	C 5	523.249	214	522.713	-1
C#1	34.648	3228	34.653	0	C#5	554.368	202	553.765	-1
D 1	36.708	3047	36.712	0	D 5	587.328	190	588.740	4
D#1	38.891	2876	38.895	0	D#5	622.256	180	621.448	-1
E 1	41.203	2715	41.201	0	E 5	659.248	170	658.004	-2
F 1	43.654	2562	43.661	0	F 5	698.464	160	699.129	2
F#1	46.249	2419	46.243	0	F#5	739.984	151	740.799	2
G 1	48.999	2283	48.997	0	G 5	783.984	143	782.242	-3
G#1	51.913	2155	51.907	0	G#5	830.680	135	828.597	-3
A 1	55.000	2034	54.995	0	A 5	880.000	127	880.792	2
A#1	58.270	1920	58.261	0	A#5	832.320	134	834.781	5
B 1	61.735	1812	61.733	0	B 5	987.760	113	989.917	4
C 2	65.406	1710	65.416	0	C 6	1046.50	107	1045.43	-1
C#2	69.296	1614	69.306	0	C#6	1108.74	101	1107.53	-1

Note	Freq		Freq		Note	Freq		Freq	
D 2	73.416	1524	73.399	0	D 6	1174.66	95	1177.48	4
D#2	77.782	1438	77.789	0	D#6	1244.51	90	1242.90	-1
E 2	82.406	1357	82.432	1	E 6	1318.50	85	1316.01	-2
F 2	87.308	1281	87.323	0	F 6	1396.93	80	1398.26	2
F#2	92.498	1209	92.523	0	F#6	1479.97	76	1471.85	-9
G 2	97.998	1141	98.037	1	G 6	1567.97	71	1575.50	8
G#2	103.826	1077	103.863	1	G#6	1661.22	67	1669.56	9
A 2	110.000	1017	109.991	0	A 6	1760.00	64	1747.82	-11
A#2	116.540	960	116.521	0	A#6	1864.64	60	1864.34	0
B 2	123.470	906	123.466	0	B 6	1975.52	57	1962.47	-10
C 3	130.812	855	130.831	0	C 7	2092.99	53	2110.58	14
C#3	138.592	807	138.613	0	C#7	2217.47	50	2237.21	15
D 3	146.832	762	146.799	0	D 7	2349.31	48	2330.43	-13
D#3	155.564	719	155.578	0	D#7	2489.02	45	2485.79	-1
E 3	164.812	679	164.743	0	E 7	2636.99	42	2663.35	17
F 3	174.616	641	174.510	0	F 7	2793.86	40	2796.52	2
F#3	184.996	605	184.894	0	F#7	2959.94	38	2943.70	-9
G 3	195.996	571	195.903	0	G 7	3135.94	36	3107.24	-15
G#3	207.652	539	207.534	0	G#7	3322.43	34	3290.02	-16
A 3	220.000	508	220.198	2	A 7	3520.00	32	3495.64	-11
A#3	233.080	480	233.043	0	A#7	3729.28	30	3728.69	0
B 3	246.940	453	246.933	0	B 7	3951.04	28	3995.02	19
C 4	261.624	428	261.357	-1	C 8	4185.98	27	4142.99	-17
C#4	277.184	404	276.883	-1	C#8	4434.94	25	4474.42	15
D 4	293.664	381	293.597	0	D 8	4698.62	24	4660.86	-13
D#4	311.128	360	310.724	-1	D#8	4978.05	22	5084.57	37
E 4	329.624	339	329.972	2	E 8	5273.98	21	5326.70	17
F 4	349.232	320	349.564	2	F 8	5587.71	20	5593.03	2
F#4	369.992	302	370.399	2	F#8	5919.87	19	5887.40	-9
G 4	391.992	285	392.493	2	G 8	6271.87	18	6214.48	-15
G#4	415.304	269	415.839	2	G#8	6644.86	17	6580.04	-16
A 4	440.000	254	440.396	2	A 8	7040.00	16	6991.29	-11
A#4	466.160	240	466.086	0	A#8	7458.56	15	7457.37	0

[Timbre and Other Qualities]. Other terms found in music relating to pitch can also be given in physical terms. Vibrato is a small variation of pitch around a central note. Vibrato is typically a change of 3% or 4% of the frequency; a C2, whose frequency should be 2XX, might vary between 259.4 and 264.6 Hz. Violin vibrato has a frequency of about 6 oscillations per second. Music that is transposed has the frequencies of all notes moved up or down by a fixed number of semitones. Transposition has a scope equal to the duration of the piece.

Timbre is a difficult-to-define but key aspect of musical quality. Timbre is that quality of sound that allows two sounds of the same pitch and loudness to be distinguished. Most people can tell the diference between two instruments, even if they can tell the name of the instrument; each instrument has a different timbre.

What, exactly, makes one instrument sound different from another? As with research in artificial intelligence, the availability of computers has shown just how little is known about this question. Recent research indicates that timbre is a function of at least: (1) the spectral envelope, that is, harmonics generated by an instrument; the (2) attack, rise, duration, and decay of individual notes; (3) the prefix of the sound; and (4) microintonation, or small up and down frequency changes.

Most work in computer synthesis of sounds has focused on the contributions of harmonics, or, more properly, of parials, to a finished sound. Fourier analysis can be used to break down existing sounds into their components. Such analysis produces a chart of harmonics. The 2nd harmonic is twice the frequency of the fundamental; the 3rd harmonic is three times the fundamental; and so on.

However, classical analysis does not always hold. Percussion instruments, including the piano, generate inharmonic partials. Timbre varies at different frequencies: the clarinet in its upper register has a much different sound than in its lower. Timbre also varies with amplitude. When instruments are played louder, higher-frequency partials become audible - one reason loud music sounds brighter than soft.

When all is said and done, each harmonic or partial can be analysed as a separate note. Further, each harmonic has all of the characteristic of an individual note: attack, sustain, decay, release.

At best, computer synthesized music can only approximate tone colors. The following table of harmonics has been used for tone color:

	1	2	3	4	5	6	7	8
Trumpet	224	240	240	160	80	64	48	48
Oboe	64	128	240	128	240	32	16	16
Clarinet	224	0	80	0	240	0	48	80
Organ	240	64	0	128	0	0	0	32

A note's frequency can be modified by a sharp or a flat. A sharp raises the frequency one semitone; a flat lowers it one. Thus A# is the same as B natural. There are a variety of combinations:

#	Accidental Sharp
&	Accidental Flat
%	Accidental Natural
##	Double Sharp
&&	Double Flat
%#	Natural Sharp
%&	Natrual Flat

The length of notes is primarily determined by the score. Typical values for duration, in milliseconds, are:

    500   170   500   170   950   500   170   500   170   1950

The tempo of a piece can be thought of as a weighting that affects all time values. In performed music, a metronome can be used to set the tempo of a piece. Metronome settings can be related to absolute time values, as measured in seconds. For a metronome setting of 60, the following holds:

```
whole note        - 4 seconds
half notes        - 2 seconds
quarter note      - 1 second
eighth notes      - 500 milliseconds
```

A metronome setting of 80 sounds reasonably fast to the human ear. On most instruments, human performers can play no more than 13 or 14 notes per second. This limits notes to about 70 milliseconds.

The loudness with which music is played can be measured in decibels. Sections of music are marked by Italian words indicating a general loudness level: "fortissimo" means strong, or loud; "mezzo forte" means medium; and "pianissimo" means softly. A rough table for loudness is:

```
fff               100 db
f                  80 db
p                  60 db
ppp                40 db
```

For reference, the pain threshold of the human ear is 120 db. A low-flying jet plane produces this much noise. A truck starting its engine makes about 80 db of noise. A performer in an orchestra, with a violin on the left and a flute on the right, lives in an environment of 90 to 100 db of noise. A telephone making a dial tone and held closely to the ear makes about 80 db.

[Computer Sheet Music]. A number of systems - none compatible with the other - have been used to create computer files that contain musical information. In a sense, the problem here is similar to that of word processing: how to represent what appears on the printed page inside the computer. For Roman alphabets, computers have evolved a standard, limited set of codes - the ASCII symbols - that can more or less represent what is on a page (although special characters, graphic symbols, and typographical information remain a problem).

The symbol set of music, although finite, is richer than the ASCII set. Unlike text, however, sheet music is nonlinear: whereas one character follows the other in text, there are often several voices and tempo instructions changing simultaneously on a musical score. Thus although music is most naturally ordered by time, this ordering is more complicated than usual.

Only a few music publishers in the US have heavily automated their typesetting and composition: much of the work is still done by hand, mostly in Taiwan. Music publishers are one of the few groups working in computer music that have an economic interest in getting all the notes right. When a computer, however, is to play the music, a number of shortcuts can be (and usually are) taken.

[NOTRAN]. The classic example of a music programming language is NOTRAN, which stands for Note Translation, just as FORTRAN stands for Formula Translation. Voices in NOTRAN are identified by number. Thus a middle C quarter note for voice 3 would be defined:

                         3C4Q

The general syntax of a note statement is:

```
```

<voice identifier> <pitch> <duration> <articulation>

A <voice> is an instrument sound that is defined higher up in a NOTRAN program by control statements. The <pitch> of a note is given in the conventional way for computers, by a letter A-G followed by an octave number. (The middle range on a piano is 4, low is 1, high is 8.) If a pitch is to be sharp or flat, a # or @ follows.

The <duration> of a note is defined in relative terms; control statements set the clock rate (metronome speed), allowing whole sections to be speeded up or slowed down without reprogramming. The codes for notes are:

W	whole note
H	half note
Q	quarter note
E	8th note
S	16th note
T	32nd note

Duration can be modified by dotting. One dot adds 50% to a note's duration; 2 dots add 75%, and so on in progression. A triplet in music is a sequence of 3 notes that are played in the time of 2; a triplet indicator ("3") reduces the previously specified time by 2/3. The <articulation> of a note is either staccato or legato; a staccato note is given a sustain duration of zero and is specified in the note syntax by a final S.

Voices in NOTRAN are defined by giving various paramaters that specify the envelope and waveform of an instrument:

AD	attack duration in milliseconds
DD	decay duration in milliseconds
RD	release duration in milliseconds
SA	sustain amplitude in % of peak attack amplitude
VA	voice amplitude in % of DAC full range
AW	attack waveform
DW	decay waveform
SW	sustain waveform
RW	release waveform
Hn	harmonic number

Harmonics are specified inside the definitions of the waveform (W) parameters:

```
TRUMPET AD=90; DD=50; RD=250; SA=35; VA=15;
        AW=H1,50,50; H2,20,25; H4,30,60;
        DW=H1,100; H2,80; H3,20;
        SW=H2,75; H3,50;
        RW=H1
```

The 2 numbers used for harmonics specify the amplitude in percent and the phase of the harmonic in units of 2*PI/100. If no phase parameter is present, a random phase is generated.

O

Online Services

Online information services are a vital part of the computing environment: without them, life for computerists would be much more dull. Online transmission of information is like blood circulation: it constantly freshens a computer system in an intimate, connected sort of way.

[History of Online Services]. An online database is simply a large mainframe computer, usually with a great deal of disk storage, that can be accessed over telephone lines from remote locations. In a sense, this is nothing but timesharing - that is, the use of one powerful central computer by many users simultaneously. In timesharing, however, the emphasis has always been on improving the utilization of an expensive CPU. In online systems, the emphasis is not on the CPU, which indeed need not be all that powerful, but on the communications - the telephone lines.

Online services grew up with timesharing in the late 1960s and became a separate thing in the 1970s. Following this reasoning further, videotex, a phenomenon of the 1980s, can be considered a step beyond online systems, where the emphasis is almost exclusively on communications. Videotex systems use highly standardized mass market protocols and terminals; often the central computer is little more than a switching device.

These distinctions are, of course, a matter of degree. One key point is to look at the CPU: is it doing numerical calculations, e.g., running FORTRAN programs (timesharing, merging into numerical online databases); is it searching and manipulating text (a typical online service); or is it merely sending pages in answer to requests from users (videotex)?

[Online Databases]. A database must be considered a separate entity from the computer system on which it resides. A database might best be thought of as a large mass of information, usually text but sometimes made up of numbers and statistics. As of 1982, there were approximately 1200 online databases in the US, according to Cuadra Associates (1523 Sixth St., Suite 12, Santa Monica, CA 90401, 213-451-0644), which publishes a "Directory of Online Databases" on a subscription basis for $60 a year.

Typically, online databases are created by publishers and grow slowly over the years. The major problem with creating a database is the cost of entering the information and then of organizing it. Most creators of databases solve the data entry problem by capturing information as it flows through typesetting systems; the general idea is to capture the keystrokes used to generate the print edition and to feed those into the online base.

[Searching]. Organizing a large database so that information can be found in it is yet another problem. Over the years, various sorts of indexing techniques have been tried, none with any clear-cut superiority. In general, because amounts of information are so large, any system requiring humans to do abstracting and indexing is likely to be too expensive. As computers increased their speed and power, it has proved more economical to let the computer - guided by a person, of course - search the actual text of an article for words that occur in it.

This is called "free text" or "full text searching". The problem with free text searching is that the computer usually finds too much: a search of this book for the word "computer" would probably find it on every page. The problem is to narrow the number of hits. One way of doing this is with Boolean logic: the computer is told, in effect, to return all articles containing "computer" and "online" but not "videotex". Most online information services have some type of Boolean logic system.

However, the meter is always running while searching a database. Being able to search one effectively is a definite skill. Many reference librarians at large universities and in corporate research departments are full-time searchers; there are also services, like Information on Demand (POB 4536, Berkeley, CA 94704, 415-841-1145), that will, for a fee, take casual requests and search an agreed-upon list of databases. These services are called "retailers" in the trade. Retailers have primarily corporate clients.

[Connecting to Online Services]. The procedure for connecting to an online service can be highly intimidating to the computer novice: a long list of code numbers with instructions about "do this, but don't dare do that". However, the process is logical if broken down and understood step by step.

Connecting to an online service requires making a telephone call. It is possible to call some computers directly; The Source, for example, whose computers are physically located in McLean, VA, just outside Washington, DC, has direct connect numbers for the Washington area.

However, the large majority of connections to online services are made through one of the networks, Tymnet and Telenet being the most important. Tymnet and Telenet run an information highway. They have local numbers or "nodes" in most major US cities, and in many large cities abroad. Tymnet's and Telenet's customers are services like The Source; they may have 50 to 100 customers each, with much duplication. The Source, for example, is available over both Tymnet and Telenet; Dow Jones News Retrieval Service is available over only Tymnet; CompuServe has its own network covering about 50 US cities and is available over Tymnet and Telenet.

A would-be subscriber must 1st decide what number to call. In some cities, New York, there are multiple numbers for 300-baud access, several more numbers for Bell 212 1200 baud access, a number for Vadic 1200 modems, and even a Bell 202 number. This book has a reasonably current list of Tymnet, Telenet, and Uninet numbers. If in doubt, the numbers nearest you can be found by calling 800-336-0437 for Telenet (in VA and DC, 800-572-0408); 800-336-0149 for Tymnet (in VA 800-572-0368); and 800-821-5340 for Uninet (in MO 800-892-5915).

When a network number is called, a Tymnet or Telenet minicomputer answers and sends a carrier tone. This is a distinctive, high-pitched tone that quickly becomes very familiar to online service users. When successfully connected, the user's modem or microcomputer should indicate that a "carrier" is present. Some modems have red LED's to indicate carrier; some terminal programs put the word "CARRIER" on the screen.

The 2nd step is to let the network know to what kind of terminal it is talking. Network controllers are now relatively intelligent and can often determine the baud rate from the user's initial keystroke. Some networks, such as Tymnet, have a set of codes for various makes of terminals. The code for a standard, 300 baud terminal is "A".

The 3rd step, now that conversation can take place, is for the user to identify which of the network's customers he or she wants to talk with. Thus, if successfully connected to Telenet, one connects to The Source by giving the Telenet controller The Source's code, "C 30128" (the space is significant). After receiving this code, Telenet knows to connect the user to the right "host". Note that one can talk to 4 or 5 different services with a single local call to Telenet or Tymnet.

With the host on line, the 4th step is to provide it user identification, usually an account number. In addition to the account number, a password of some type is generally used. Account numbers have to do with billing and stay the same as long as subscription is in effect. Passwords are provided to prevent unauthorized access to a system and can be changed, if necessary, once inside the system. A typical (but invalid) account number on The Source is:

>ID TCA094 OPENSESME

Here, ">" is a prompt from The Source's Prime computer. "ID" is actually a system command for the Prime, telling it that the user is going to identify himself. "TCA094" is an account number; it is associated with a billing address, runs up so much time per month, and so on. "OPENSESME" is an arbitrary password; it can be changed by a Prime system command, PASSWORD.

At this point, one should be successfully inside the system. An announcement with recent news usually appears, followed by the master menu of the system. These vary from service to service and must be described separately.

[The Major Services]. Almost any online service is available to a personal computer owner who has a modem and terminal emulation software (Mead Data Central's "Lexis", a legal search system, and "Nexus", for news, require special terminals leased from Mead.) The Time and Newsweek of online services are The Source and CompuServe. Both were started in 1979 - The Source as an undercapitalized entrepreneurial venture, CompuServe as an off-hour subsidary of a business timesharing company.

Of the two, CompuServe now has the most subscribers. As of May 1, 1982, CompuServe claimed 24,721 users, with the most being in California (3756) and 2nd most in New York (1864) followed by Texas (1708), Ohio (1452). CompuServe is headquartered in Columbus, OH (5000 Arlington Center Blvd., 43220, 800-848-8990). In late 1980, the company was bought by H&R Block, the income tax preparation firm.

Since mid-1980, CompuServe has had a marketing arrangement with Tandy, and the easiest way to see it demonstrated is at a Radio Shack store. At that time, CompuServe picked a screen format 32 characters across and 16 lines down to maintain compatibility with the Radio Shack Videotex terminal introduced in fallof 1980. This breaks up the CompuServe information base into many tiny screens that seem to require endless paging to work through.

On the other hand, CompuServe has generally better content than The Source. In 1980 CompuServe signed an agreement with 11 major US newspapers, including the New York Times, the Los Angeles Times, and the Washington Post, all of whom agreed to put up electronic editions - in some cases, merely an existing wire service - as an experiment in electronic publishing. (The experiment ended July 1, 1982). CompuServe also has a number of good personal computing features, as well as a CB Radio simulation that allows a user to chat with anyone in the country, even over an X-rated channel!

The Source, however, remains the best known of the 2 services. Unlike CompuServe, which was started by a computer company (CompuServe has 2 giant facilities of DEC computers in Columbus, with a satellite link between them!), The Source was started with an eye to publishing and has grown into a sprawling magazine with many interesting bits. The Source, heavily in debt, was bought by Reader's Digest in September 1980, and has considerably improved its operations under that company's reign. Although Reader's Digest is located in upstate New York, The Source is in McLean, VA (1616 Anderson Rd., McLean, VA 22102, 800-336-3366; in VA 703-734-7500). It uses Prime computers, which are managed for it by Dialcom. A Source sample:

```
THE SOURCE MAIN MENU

1  NEWS AND REFERENCE RESOURCES
2  BUSINESS/FINANCIAL MARKETS
3  CATALOG SHOPPING
4  HOME AND LEISURE
5  EDUCATION AND CAREERS
6  MAIL AND COMMUNICATIONS
7  CREATING AND COMPUTING
8  SOURCE*PLUS

      1
      NEWS & REFERENCE RESOURCES

      1  NEWS AND SPORTS
      2  TRAVEL AND DINING
      3  GOVERNMENT AND POLITICS
      4  CONSUMER INFORMATION
      5  SCIENCE AND TECHNOLOGY
```

1
NEWS AND SPORTS

1   NY TIMES NEWS HEADLINES
2   NY TIMES BUSINESS HEADLINES
3   UPI NEWS SERVICE
4   THE EDITORIAL PAGE
5   UPI SPORTS

2
TRAVEL & DINING

1   DOMESTIC FLIGHTS
2   INTERNATIONAL FLIGHTS
3   TRAVEL TIPS & SPECIALS
4   TRAVEL RESERVATIONS
5   METRO RESTAURANT GUIDES
6   NATIONAL RESTAURANT GUIDE
7   WINE

3
GOVERNMENT AND POLITICS

1   PRESIDENT'S SCHEDULE (DAILY)
2   SENATE COMMITTEE
3   HOUSE COMMITTEE
4   POLITICAL COMMENTARY
5   LEGI-SLATE

4
CONSUMER INFORMATION

1   NYT CONSUMER DATABASE
2   CONSUMER CORNER COLUMNISTS
3   BUYING WINE
4   TOLL FREE NUMBERS
5   RESTAURANT GUIDES
6   HEALTH GUIDE

5
SCIENCE AND TECHNOLOGY

1   ELECTRICAL ENGINEERING
2   MECHANICAL ENGINEERING
3   SIMULATION
4   GEOGRAPHY
5   STATISTICS

2
BUSINESS/FINANCIAL MARKETS

1   FINANCIAL MARKETS
2   ANALYSIS & COMPUTATION
3   NEWS AND COMMENTARY

```
        4  PERSONAL FINANCE
        5  RESEARCH AND REFERENCE


                1
                FINANCIAL MARKETS

                1  NYSE CLOSING PRICES
                2  AMEX CLOSING PRICES
                3  UNISTOX
                4  MEDIA GENERAL STOCK ANALYSIS
                5  COMMODITY NEWS SERVICE


                2
                ANALYSIS & COMPUTATION

                1  RAYLUX
                2  MODEL1 FINANCIAL MODELING
                3  COMPUTATIONAL PROGRAMS
                4  MEDIA GENERAL STOCK ANALYSIS


                3
                NEWS AND COMMENTARY

                1  UPI BUSINESS NEWS
                2  RAYLUX FINANCIAL SERVICES
                3  DAILY INVESTOR COLUMN
                4  MANAGEMENT CONTENTS


                4
                PERSONAL FINANCE

                1  COMPUTING INTEREST
                2  AMORTIZATION OF LOANS
                3  ANNUITY PAYMENTS & ANALYSIS
                4  BOND ACCRUED INTEREST


                5
                RESEARCH AND REFERENCE

                1  INFORMATION ON DEMAND
                2  MANAGEMENT CONTENTS


3
CATALOG SHOPPING

1  DATA BUCKS
2  BARTER
3  BOOKS
4  RECORDS, TAPES, VIDEOTAPES
5  RADIO RECORDINGS
6  CLASSIFIED ADS
7  COMP-U-STAR

                1
```

4
HOME AND LEISURE

1 GAMES
2 ADVICE & HOROSCOPES
3 TRAVEL & DINING
4 ENTERTAINMENT
5 HOME FINANCE

5
EDUCATION & CAREERS

1 FOREIGN LANGUAGES
2 GEOGRAPHY
3 MATHEMATICS
4 FINANCIAL AID FOR COLLEGE
5 ELEMENTARY EDUCATION
6 CAREER NETWORK

6
MAIL AND COMMUNICATIONS

1 MAIL
2 CHAT
3 POST

[Dow Jones and Newsnet]. Whereas The Source and CompuServe have tried to be general interest online services, which something for everybody, 2 services have specialized in business information and news. Dow Jones, the Princeton, NJ-based publisher of the Wall Street Journal and Barron's, has for some years had its News Retrieval Service available online. The DJNS has the distinction of being one of the few online services that is actually profitable: both The Source and CompuServe probably cost their parent companies money.

Dow Jones had a laudable early interest in personal computers and in June 1978, announced the Dow Jones Portfolio Evaluator package in conjunction with Apple. Like VisiCalc, this software package has sold a lot of Apples. Dow Jones was less sensitive to the pocketbooks of its subscribers and created off-hour rates only in 1981. Dow Jones will provide a 1-day free password for those interested in trying out the system (Information Services, PO Box 300, Princeton, NJ 08540, 609-452-2000). A DJNS sample:

```
    //WSJ                        {this command gets the
        THE WALL STREET JOURNAL   Wall Street Journal service}
            HIGHLIGHTS ONLINE
            COPYRIGHT (C) 1982
        DOW JONES & COMPANY, INC.

        THIS DATA BASE ENABLES YOU
    TO VIEW ONLINE HEADLINES AND
    SUMMARIES OF MAJOR STORIES IN
```

```
        THE WALL STREET JOURNAL. FOR
        DETAILS ON THESE AND OTHER
            STORIES, PLEASE SEE
            TUESDAY'S JOURNAL.

     PRESS    FOR
       A   TUESDAY'S EDITION
       B   PREVIOUS EDITIONS


   A                              {look at Tuesday's edition}

     WSJ 1/12/82

            THE WALL STREET JOURNAL
            THE EDITION FOR TUESDAY
                JAN. 12, 1982

     PRESS      FOR

       1     FRONT PAGE
       2     EDITORIALS
       3     FRONT PAGE -- SECTION 2
       4     MARKET NEWS
       5     BACK PAGE


   1                              {look at the front page}

     WSJ 1/12/82  -1-   FRONT PAGE

     PRESS    FOR
     1  ACCENT IS ON GROWTH,
          AS TAX LAW CHANGES
          MANY INVESTORS' WAYS
     2  MANY WORKERS OPPOSE
          EMPLOYERS' PRESSURES
          TO GIVE TO CHARITIES
     3  WHAT'S NEWS--BUSINESS &
          FINANCE
     4  WHAT'S NEWS--WORLD-WIDE
     5  LABOR LETTER
     6  PEACE CORPS SHRINKS
          BUT REMAINS A FORCE,
          AT LEAST IN GHANA
              {etc.}
```

NewsNet (945 Haverford Rd., Bryn Mawr, PA 19010, 215-527-8030), owned by Independent Publications Incorporated, once the publisher of the Philadelphia Bulletin, started commercial operation April 1, 1982. NewsNet has focused on carrying business newsletters, particularly where their contents can be captured from typesetting systems and posted quickly. Updates to this book are available on NewsNet.

[NYTIS and Nexis]. Two service exist to search general publications like newspapers and magazines for recent articles on subjects. Although Dow Jones has the full text of the Wall Street Journal, Barron's, and the Dow Jones wire service, it does not have references to other papers. NYTIS, The New York Times Information Service (1719-A Route 10, Parsippany, NJ 07054, 201-539-5850) does have references by way of abstracts - but not full text - of a large list of publications, far beyond the New York Times alone. Full text on New York Times stories can be searched from June 1, 1980, onward. An example of the Times taken off The Source:

{ these "go to" items would be called "reefers"
in printed newspaper lingo}

(c) New York Times   Page NYT-1   {GO nn, where nn is
     THE NEW YORK TIMES   a page number, is a
     COPYRIGHT (C) 1981 BY   way of shortcutting
THE NEW YORK TIMES COMPANY   the menu pages, and
                                         going directly to
  *FOR NEWS KEY ENTER GO 11   the page desired.}

  *FOR ARTS & LEISURE GO 12   {note copyright notice
  ... LIVING & HOME GO 13   on every page}

  *FOR SUBSCRIPTIONS, BOOKS
   AND GIFTS GO 14

{this page is a more traditional menu}

     (c) New York Times   Page NYT-11

          THE NEW YORK TIMES

     1 NEWS OF THE DAY
     2 BUSINESS NEWS
     3 EDITORIALS/COMMENTARY/LETTERS
     4 NEWS ANALYSIS & BACKGROUND
     5 ARTS & LEISURE
     6 LIVING & HOME
     7 SCIENCE/TECHNOLOGY/MEDICINE
     8 SPORTS
     9 SUBSCRIPTIONS/BOOKS/GIFTS

     Last menu page. Key digit
     or M for previous menu.

          !1   {get the news of the day}

     (c) New York Times Page NYT-4602   {news menu}

     3 NYT NEWS SUMMARY/OCTOBER 16
     4 SENATE PANEL OPPOSES AWACS
     5 REAGAN TOUTS 3RD WORLD TRADE
     6 MIDEAST TENSIONS WORRY US
     7 POLES AGREE ON PRICE FREEZE
     8 CANETTI WINS NOBEL PRIZE
     9 US EASES BRAZIL ATOM BAN

O TAIWAN ARMS KEY US-CHINA TIES

Input a number or key
<ENTER> for more choices

!4   {get story #4 about AWACS}

(c) New York Times Page NYT-4680

NYT 10/16 15:35 EDT W2489
By CHARLES MOHR
    WASHINGTON -- The Senate
Foreign Relations Committee
voted 9 to 8 Thursday to
disapprove President Reagan's
plan to sell Airborne Warning
and Control System planes and
other air combat equipment to
Saudi Arabia.
    The margin of defeat for
Reagan was narrowed when Sen.
    {etc.}

NEXIS is Mead Data Central's 2nd product, a service similar to its LEXIS system for legal offices but aimed at news research. NEXIS contains primarily business news, including such publications as American Banker, Congressional Quarterly Almanac, the Kyodo News Service (Japan), and Jiji Economic News (Japan). Both the NYTIS and NEXIS are expensive; NEXIS has a training charge of up to $2250.

[Dialog and SDC]. Two major services exist for specialized scientific searching. Lockheed's "Dialog" service (3460 Hillview Ave., Palo Alto, CA 94304, 415-858-2700) is a sort of international smorgasbord of data, with over 50 substantial bases ranging from Excerpta Medica, an index to biomedical literature, to Pollution Abstracts and the Philosopher's Index. Lockheed uses IBM equipment. Search charges vary by database on Dialog, typically running $65/hour, with a monthly minimum for all use of $200.

SDC (System Development Corporation, 2500 Colorado Ave., Santa Monica, CA 90406) has a system similar to Lockheed's but slightly smaller in scope. Both Lockheed and SDC offer a Selective Dissemination of Information or "SDI" service. SDI is essentially a continuous search: keywords are entered once, and when databases are updated, a check is made, without the user needing to be online, if the keyboard is there. If it is, the user is notified; the exact method of notification, whether on next sign-on or by mail or whatever, varies.

[LEXIS]. Started in 1973 by Mead Data Central, a paper products company with some long-range ideas, LEXIS as of late 1980 was performing 32,000 searches a day of its full text base of legal decisions and was far out in front of 32 other electronic legal retrieval services. LEXIS, which attempts to record the full text of legal decisions, has over 25 billion characters of text online. LEXIS uses twin Amdahl 470 V7A computers. Their new site, opened in 1980, is in Miamisburg, OH; Mead Corporation, the parent company of Mead Data

Central and best known as a forest products firm, is located in Dayton. Mead Data Central has sales offices in many major cities in the US; th one in New York is at 200 Park Avenue (the Pan Am Building), NY, NY 10166, 212-853-8560. LEXIS uses dedicated 1200-baud terminals and requires training of its operators, typically research librarians at larger law firms. Mead is experimenting with a supplementary keypad (SKP), which would allow other terminals to be used and might open up the service to more casual users.

[CBBS-type Systems]. Anything a mainframe computer can do, a micro can do also - but maybe not as well. Since the late 1970s, homebrew online services have sprung up under the generic name of Community Bulletin Board Systems or CBBSs ("CBBS", however, is a registered trademark).

The prototype of these systems was perhaps the Community Memory System organized with a surplus SDS 940 in San Francisco in the early 1970s by a group that included, among many, this author and Lee Felsenstein, later designer of the Processor Technology SOL-20 and the Osborne I computers.

In the early 1980s, as the question of what to do with that old TRS-80 came up, a thousand CBBSs bloomed. A reasonable current list:

TYPE OF BBS & CITY	NUMBER
ABBS NEW JERSEY	(201) 891 - 7441
FOR 80 UNION NJ	(201) 688 - 7117
CBBS HALEDON NJ	(201) 790 - 6795
FOR 80 MONMOUTH NJ	(201) 528 - 6623
CBBS LIVINGSTON NJ	(201) 992 - 4847
ABBS DUNELLEN NJ	(201) 968 - 1074
CBBS PRINCETON NJ	(201) 874 - 6833
FOR 80 UNION NJ	(201) 688 - 7117
CBBS CRANFORD NJ	(201) 272 - 1874
CBBS BOUNDBROOK NJ	(201) 457 - 0893
ABBS ACG NJ	(201) 753 - 1225
CBBS SHREWSBURY NJ	(201) 747 - 6768
CBBS COMMUNIQUE NJ	(201) 992 - 4847
CP/M ISELIN NJ	(201) 283 - 2724
CBBS WASHINGTON DC	(202) 337 - 4694
CBBS DANBURY CT	(203) 744 - 4644
CBBS STANFORD CT	(203) 357 - 1570
CBBS BETHEL CT	(203) 743 - 9281
FOR80 MONTGOMERY AL	(205) 272 - 5069
ABBS SEATTLE WA	(206) 244 - 5438
SEACOMM-80	(206) 763 - 8879
CBBS SEATTLE	(206) 723 - 3282
ABBS SEATTLE WA	(206) 248 - 2600
ABBS SEATTLE WA	(206) 546 - 6239
FOR80 EVERETT WA	(206) 334 - 7394
CBBS SEATTLE WA	(206) 937 - 0444
CBBS REDMOND WA	(206) 883 - 0403
CBBS NEW YORK	(212) 787 - 5520
CBBS NEW YORK	(212) 997 - 2186
CBBS NEW YORK	(212) 933 - 9459
CBBS NEW YORK	(212) 245 - 4363

```
ABBS LOS ANGELES        (213) 276 - 4276
CBBS LOS ANGELES        (213) 291 - 9314
CBBS LOS ANGELES        (213) 954 - 8582
CBBS LOS ANGELES        (213) 465 - 1431
ABBS LOS ANGELES        (213) 340 - 0135
CBBS LOS ANGELES        (213) 826 - 0325
ABBS LOS ANGELES        (213) 459 - 6400
CBBS LOS ANGELES        (213) 881 - 6880
ABBS LOS ANGELES        (213) 921 - 2111
ABBS WOODLAND HILLS     (213) 346 - 1849
CP/M PASADENA CA        (213) 799 - 1632
ABBS LONG BEACH         (213) 424 - 3506
ABBS LOS ANGELES        (213) 349 - 5728
CBBS LOS ANGELES        (213) 709 - 5423
CBBS INGLEWOOD CA       (213) 673 - 2206
ABBS DALLAS  TX         (214) 361 - 1386
ABBS DALLAS  TX         (214) 327 - 3585
ABBS DALLAS  TX         (214) 369 - 0427
ABBS DALLAS  TX         (214) 530 - 0858
ABBS DALLAS  TX         (214) 634 - 2668
ABBS DALLAS  TX         (214) 661 - 2969
ABBS DALLAS  TX         (214) 824 - 7455
ABBS DALLAS  TX         (214) 931 - 3437
CBBS PHILADELPHIA       (215) 398 - 3937
ABBS AKRON  OH          (216) 745 - 7855
ABBS AKRON  OH          (216) 644 - 1965
CBBS AKRON  OHIO        (216) 724 - 1963
ABBS CLEVELAND          (216) 779 - 1338
ABBS AKRON  OH          (216) 867 - 7463
ABBS URBANA IL          (217) 334 - 1296
CBBS ILLINOIS           (217) 429 - 5505
CP/M BALTIMORE          (301) 337 - 8825
CP/M BALTIMORE          (301) 655 - 9439
ABBS ROCKVILLE          (301) 983 - 9317
CBBS ELLICOTT CITY      (301) 465 - 3176
CBBS SILVER SPRING      (301) 593 - 7033
CBBS GREENBELT MD       (301) 344 - 9156
ABBS COLUMBIA    MD     (301) 730 - 0922
CBBS BALTIMORE   MD     (301) 944 - 0399
FOR 80 DENVER           (303) 771 - 3826
ABBS DENVER CO          (303) 759 - 2625
FOR80 DENVER CO         (303) 399 - 8858
CBBS DENVER CO          (303) 320 - 6715
ABBS MIAMI FL           (305) 261 - 3639
FOR 80 FT LAUDERDALE    (305) 772 - 4444
FOR 80 ORLANDO          (305) 862 - 6917
ABBS MIAMI   FL         (305) 821 - 7401
CBBS DEERFIELD BCH      (305) 427 - 6300
CBBS FT LAUDERDALE      (305) 462 - 8677
ABBS FT LAUDERDALE      (305) 486 - 2983
ABBS WEST PALM BEACH    (305) 689 - 3234
ABBS GALESBURG IL       (309) 342 - 7178
ABBS PEORIA    IL       (309) 692 - 6502
CBBS ARLINGTON HTS      (312) 255 - 6489
```

```
CBBS LAKE FOREST IL    (312) 234 - 9257
ABBS ARLINGTON HGT     (312) 255 - 6489
ABBS CHICAGO           (312) 289 - 1198
ABBS NORTHBROOK        (312) 291 - 1619
ABBS PALATINE    IL    (312) 295 - 6926
ABBS CHICAGO           (312) 337 - 6631
CBBS CHICAGO           (312) 338 - 8827
CBBS PALATINE          (312) 359 - 9450
CBBS CHICAGO           (312) 384 - 4762
ABBS CHICAGO           (312) 392 - 4150
ABBS NAPERVILLE        (312) 420 - 7995
ABBS CHICAGO           (312) 475 - 4884
ABBS GLEN ELLYN        (312) 537 - 7063
ABBS CHICAGO           (312) 622 - 9609
CBBS CHICAGO           (312) 743 - 8176
CBBS CHICAGO           (312) 782 - 8180
CBBS AURORA            (312) 859 - 2622
ABBS ROSELLE           (312) 882 - 9237
ABBS OAK BROOK         (312) 941 - 9009
ABBS DOWNERS GROVE     (312) 964 - 7768
ABBS MORTON GROVE      (312) 967 - 0453
ABBS ROGERS PARK       (312) 973 - 2227
ABBS SOUTHFIELD MICH   (313) 357 - 1422
CP/M ROYAL OAK MICH    (313) 588 - 7054
CBBS DETROIT           (313) 288 - 0335
FOR80 PATOMIC MI       (313) 335 - 8456
FOR 80 MICHIGAN        (313) 465 - 9531
CBBS FRASER MI         (313) 294 - 8248
CP/M DEARBORN MI       (313) 846 - 6127
CBBS ST LOUIS          (314) 781 - 1308
CBBS ST LOUIS          (314) 227 - 8495
CBBS ST LOUIS          (314) 839 - 4307
CBBS ST LOUIS          (314) 394 - 7233
CBBS ST LOUIS          (314) 838 - 7784
FOR 80 WICHITA KS      (316) 682 - 2113
FOR80 SHREVEPORT       (318) 631 - 7107
ABBS IOWA CITY         (319) 353 - 6528
ABBS DUBUQUE           (319) 557 - 9618
ABBS LINCOLN NB        (402) 423 - 8086
CBBS ATLANTA           (404) 394 - 4220
CBBS ATLANTA           (404) 939 - 1520
ABBS AUGUSTA           (404) 793 - 1045
ABBS LAWTON OK         (405) 353 - 2554
ABBS SAN JOSE CA       (408) 296 - 5799
CBBS SANTA CLARA       (408) 296 - 5799
FOR 80 WISCONSIN       (414) 241 - 5406
CP/M MILWAUKEE WI      (414) 774 - 2683
ABBS LOS ALTOS CA      (415) 948 - 1474
CBBS PORTOLA CA        (415) 851 - 3453
FOR 80 SAN FRANCISCO   (415) 348 - 2139
ABBS LAFAYETTE CA      (415) 284 - 9524
CBBS BERKELEY CA       (415) 357 - 1130
CBBS MILL VALLEY       (415) 383 - 0473
CBBS LARKSPUR          (415) 461 - 7726
```

```
CBBS PALO ALTO            (415) 493 - 7691
ABBS LOS ALTOS           (415) 863 - 4703
CBBS MOUNTAIN VIEW       (415) 968 - 5140
ABBS TOLEDO OH           (419) 531 - 3845
CBBS TOLEDO OH           (419) 865 - 1594
ABBS BOWLING GREEN       (419) 352 - 4477
ABBS LOUISVILLE KY       (502) 426 - 2975
FOR 80 BREVERTON         (503) 646 - 5510
CBBS PORTLAND            (503) 224 - 6409
CBBS BATON ROUGE         (504) 273 - 3116
CBBS BATON ROUGE         (504) 926 - 0181
ABBS SPOKANE  WA         (509) 456 - 8900
ABBS SAN ANTONIO TX      (512) 737 - 0214
CBBS CORPUS CHRISTI      (512) 855 - 1512
ABBS DAYTON  OH          (513) 223 - 3637
CBBS CINCINNATI          (513) 244 - 2983
ABBS CINCINNATI          (513) 671 - 2753
CBBS HAMILTON            (513) 863 - 7681
ABBS DES MOINES          (515) 279 - 8863
ABBS AMES                (515) 294 - 8204
CBBS LONG ISLAND         (516) 939 - 9043
CBBS LONG ISLAND         (516) 588 - 5836
CBBS LONG ISLAND         (516) 334 - 3134
CP/M LONG ISLAND         (516) 698 - 8619
ABBS JACKSON MISS        (601) 362 - 8755
ABBS PHOENIX AR          (602) 955 - 1486
CBBS PHOENIX             (602) 957 - 4428
CBBS PHOENIX             (602) 996 - 9709
ABBS PHOENIX             (602) 866 - 0258
FOR80 NASHUA NH          (603) 882 - 5041
CP/M VANCOUVER BC        (604) 687 - 2640
CBBS ENDICOTT NY         (607) 754 - 5571
CP/M COMM SVC NY         (607) 797 - 6416
ABBS NEW JERSEY          (609) 228 - 1149
ABBS MARLTON NJ          (609) 983 - 5970
ABBS MINNEAPOLIS         (612) 929 - 8966
CBBS MINNEAPOLIS         (612) 929 - 669)
CBBS OTTAWA              (613) 725 - 2243
CBBS COLUMBUS OH         (614) 268 - 2227
CBBS NASHVILLE           (615) 254 - 9193
ABBS BOSTON              (617) 354 - 4682
FOR 80 BOSTON            (617) 963 - 8310
FOR 80 WELLESLEY MA      (617) 431 - 1699
CBBS CAMBRIDGE           (617) 864 - 3819
FOR 80 WESTFORD MA       (617) 692 - 3973
CP/M AMESBURY MA         (617) 388 - 5125
CBBS GRANITE CITY IL     (618) 877 - 8080
FOR 80 LAS VEGAS         (702) 873 - 9491
CBBS LAS VEGAS           (702) 454 - 3417
FOR80 LAS VEGAS          (702) 362 - 3609
CBBS ALEXANDRIA VA       (703) 620 - 4990
FOR 80 FAIRFAX VA        (703) 978 - 7561
CBBS WASHINGTON DC       (703) 620 - 4990
ABBS VACAVILLE CA        (707) 448 - 9055
```

```
ABBS FREEPORT TX        (713) 233 - 7943
ABBS HUNTINGTON BCH     (714) 963 - 7222
CBBS ORANGE CNTY        (714) 633 - 5240
ABBS ORANGE COUNTY      (714) 952 - 2110
ABBS SAN DIEGO          (714) 287 - 9379
ABBS SANTA FE SPNG      (714) 739 - 0711
CBBS ORANGE COUNTY      (714) 751 - 1422
ABBS LAGUNA NIGUEL      (714) 495 - 6458
CBBS FULLERTON          (714) 526 - 3687
ABBS ORANGE COUNTY      (714) 772 - 8868
CBBS SANTEE CA          (714) 449 - 5689
CBBS SAN DIEGO CA       (714) 582 - 9557
CBBS SAN DIEGO CA       (714) 295 - 8280
ABBS LOGAN UTAH         (801) 753 - 6800
ABBS COLUMBIA SC        (803) 772 - 1592
FOR 80 S CAROLINA       (803) 279 - 5392
FOR80 VIRGINIA BCH      (804) 340 - 5246
FOR80 CHESAPEAKE VA     (804) 543 - 7194
CBBS VIRGINIA BEACH     (804) 340 - 5246
FOR 80 VENTURA CA       (805) 484 - 9904
CP/M SIMI VALLEY CA     (805) 527 - 9321
ABBS AMARILLO TX        (806) 355 - 5610
CP/M BLOOMINGTON IN     (812) 334 - 2522
FOR 80 TAMPA FL         (813) 223 - 7688
CBBS LARGO FL           (813) 577 - 3095
FOR 80 KANSAS CITY      (816) 861 - 7040
CBBS KANSAS CITY        (816) 523 - 9121
FOR 80 KANSAS CITY      (816) 931 - 3135
FOR 80 KANSAS CITY      (816) 931 - 9316
FOR 80 WICHITA FLS      (817) 855 - 3916
FOR 80 MEMPHIS TN       (901) 362 - 2222
FOR 80 MEMPHIS TN       (901) 276 - 8196
ABBS FT WALTON BCH      (904) 243 - 1257
FOR 80 LEVENWORTH       (913) 651 - 3744
CBBS BEARSVILLE NY      (914) 679 - 6559
ABBS EL PASO  TX        (915) 533 - 6255
CBBS SACRAMENTO         (916) 393 - 4459
CBBS SACRAMENTO         (916) 483 - 8718
FOR 80 TULSA            (918) 224 - 5347
```

Some CBBSs operate for special interest groups: astronomy clubs, HAM radio operators, and so on. The Computer Cookbook's favorite is "Kinky Komputer" of San Francisco.

In the board rooms of large corporations, much to-do is made about the coming importance of "home shopping" by personal computer. The more forward-looking of these analysts see a day in the far-distant future when, from a terminal, one will be able to call and request any item one wants from the local butcher and baker.

Actually, some advanced forms of "home shopping" already exist - and we don't mean ordering books from The Source (The Computer Cookbook ordered the 2nd edition of Newman & Sproull, "Principles of Interactive Computer Graphics," via The Source, giving our name and Mastercharge number. The book took 6 weeks to arrive by mail. At the McGraw-Hill book store in New York, where it was only temporarily out of stock, the book took 3 days to come in. The bookstore has its own online ordering number. But perhaps for those in Kansas...).

The most important principle of computer neworks is this: if they are to be successful, computer networks MUST be built on existing social networks. We have many strong networks in this country: most people call or visit members of their families regularly, and traditional networks still thrive around work, school, and church.

New media make a difference where they connect special interest networks that had trouble connecting before. CB radio brought truckers, who have special interests (e.g., is there a cop up the road ahead - a "Smokey" in CB talk) in touch with each other. Years ago, ham radio did the same.

Computer bulletin boards and local telephone networks (not to be confused with local office networks, another subject entirely) will do the same. The most advanced work in local networking is currently being done by gay rights groups.

Homosexuals have the problem - like other people in our society but made worse by a repressive sexual climate - of finding each other and matching up mutual interests.   Heterosexuals also have this problem but have more social mechanisms to deal with it - ranging from the "meat rack" singles bar to Aunt Sally, who knows a nice girl for you.

As a result, various gay media, including newspapers such as "The Advocate" and so on, have for some years run active personal columns (as do "respectable" straight publications like the New York Review of Books). These personal columns have now been placed on-line on various "lambda" bulletin boards around the country. These systems essentially match bid and ask offers - the essence of a marketplace. They demonstrate some very interesting characteristics of "match-up" systems (preliminary anonymity, subsequent personalization) and are the most advanced of their kind.

The following sample session is with Kinky Komputer, which operates out of San Francisco, where The Computer Cookbook's a author lived for many years. A hetrosexual, this author strongly supports gay rights and admires the enterprise and technical expertise of the gay bulletin board groups.

{A Session With Kinky}. When a caller logs on to Kinky Komputer, he gets the following warning message:

        WARNING! YOU HAVE CALLED A GAY, SEXUALLY EXPLICIT
        B B S SYSTEM! IF THAT'S O.K. WITH YOU, HIT ANY KEY.

        * * * * * K N Y K M U E * * * * *
        ********** K I N K Y   K O M P U T E R **********

If a user hits the ? or asks for help, the following list of system commands is displayed:

        THE SYSTEM ACCEPTS THE FOLLOWING COMMANDS :

```
B : CHANGE BAUD RATE
C : SELECT UPPER CASE ONLY OR UPPER/LOWER CASE MODE
F : FIND A MESSAGE BY SUBJECT OR NAME
S : SUMMARIZE MESSAGES
R : RETRIEVE MESSAGES
E : ENTER YOUR MESSAGE INTO FILE
K : KILL AN OLD MESSAGE
M : SENDS MENU OF OTHER AVAILABLE PROGRAMS
H : HELP WITH SYSTEM
G : GOODBYE (HANG UP AND DISCONNECT)
Q : SHORT (SUBJECT ONLY) SUMMARY OF MESSAGES
? : SUMMARIZE COMMANDS

TO USE THE SYSTEM, SIMPLY TYPE THE LETTER OF YOUR CHOICE, AND HIT
RETURN. INSTRUCTIONS ARE PROVIDED AT EACH STEP. YOU MAY
"STACK" COMMANDS BY SEPARATING THE COMMANDS WITH A SEMICOLON.
FOR EXAMPLE, R;220 WILL RETRIEVE MESSAGE NUMBER 220. ALSO,
A NEGATIVE MESSAGE NUMBER WILL CAUSE MESSAGES TO BE SCANNED
FROM THE END OF THE FILE TOWARD THE BEGINNING.
```

The "Q" (quick scan) function produces a list of the titles of messages. The
idea here is to allow users to quickly locate the sort of thing they are
looking for. Here is a list from one session:

```
27 TRY ME!
28 # SERVICE
29 HI
30 ???--???
31 YOU FORGOT.....
32 A PLACE
33 HOUSEBOY
34 MEETINY OTHERS
35 LIPLOCK
36 FFA
41 BRIDGE, SEX, & ROCK N' ROLL
72 24 HOUR KINKY!
```

The "S" or "scan" command reviews the messages in more detail, listing not by
the subject or headline but by the author, date, and so on. Note that as in
"CB land," authors use "handles" or pseudonyms. (This is true on straight
services as well).

```
FUNCTION: S
 165 MESSAGES ON FILE.
STARTING MESSAGE NUMBER ? 111

# 111
TO   : TRUCK DRIVING STUDS
FROM : STEVE S
DATE : 06-19-81
SUBJECT: TRUCK DRIVING
```

The "R" function produces the actual message:

```
FUNCTION: R
165 MESSAGES ON FILE
MESSAGE # TO RETRIEVE ?
# 100
TO   : ALL
FROM : LEN
DATE : 06-12-81
SUBJECT: MEETING

I AM INTERESTED IN MEETING WITH OTHER CLOSET GAYS
FOR USUAL ACTIVITIES.  LOOKING FOR OUT-OF-TOWN GUEST ONLY.
PLEASE CALL IF YOU INTEND TO VISIT OUR NATION'S CAPITOL.
MY NUMBER IS 301 XXX XXXX.  PLEASE BE DISCRETE WHEN
CALLING ESPECALLY IF WIFE OR KIDS ANSWER.
P.S. THIS IS MY FIRST TIME ON THIS SYSTEM
```

A number of other gay bulletin boards exist across the country.

P

Parallel Ports

Two types of interfaces, parallel and serial, are used to connect devices to computers. Of these, parallel interfaces are the most efficient but unfortunately the least standardized and most intimidating.

The goal in communication between a computer and an external device is to move a byte of information in one direction or another. In a sense, then, all interfaces must either be parallel or serial. In a parallel interface, all eight bits move at the same time. Bits move one at a time over a serial interface.

[Parallel or Serial?]. The most obvious difference between a parallel and a serial interface follows from the number of information bits being transferred at once. A connection between two serial ports can have as few as two wires - one line for data, and the other for "ground." A parallel circuit, on the other hand, must have at least 8 wires - one for each data bit in the byte being transferred. In actuality, most parallel cables have between 10 and 20 wires; most serial cables have 4.

Over long distances, the cost of cable alone can make a serial interface the only way to connect various devices (although coaxial cable and twisted-wire pair "RS 422" cable is increasingly used for local office networks). Other technical considerations can also force the use of serial links between computers and remote devices. Computer data is sent over telephone lines by "modulating" the line at a given frequency for data equal to one, and at a different frequency for data equal to zero. At the receiving end, these tones are "demodulated" and the series of ones and zeros reconstructed. Nearly all modems, therefore, work with serial data streams.

[Lack of a Parallel Standard]. In the 1960s, with the expansion of remote "timesharing" of large computers, the connection between "data terminal equipment" (DTE) and modems or "data communications equipment" (DCE) became fully standardized with the issuance of the Electronic Industries Association (EIA) Recommended Standard RS-232-C. A copy of this classic standard, adopted in 1969, can be obtained for $6.90 from the Electronic Industries Association, Engineering Dept., 2001 Eye Street, N.W., Washington, DC 20006.

In the 1970s, a lot of microcomputer equipment was designed to work with existing timesharing-type terminals, and "serial ports" or serial interfaces became a standard item. Because there are now so many RS-232 devices, the cost of parallel and serial interfacing now reflects ecomonic as well as technical issues. Serial devices require more hardware to interface than do parallel devices; typically a "UART" (Universal Asynchronous Receiver Transmitter) takes a parallel data byte, which is how information comes off the computer's internal "bus", and serializes it - that is, sends it out one bit at a time, at the approriate baud rate. The large-scale manufacture of RS-232-C devices, however, has driven down UART prices and generally made this hardware cost gap between parallel and serial negligible.

Because of their universality and interchangeability, RS-232 devices keep a certain residual or resale value, since it is easier to integrate them into new or foreign systems. The trend of the past few years among microcomputer peripheral manufacturers is create RS-232-C products out of items that were once done in parallel or as bus-dependent cards - for example, the Hayes "Chronograph" RS-232 clock, or the Votrax "Type 'n' Talk" RS-232 speech synthesizer.

[The Advantages of Parallel Interfaces]. Despite such economic considerations, there are a number of situations where a parallel interface is the best or only choice. Parallel interfaces transfer data at considerably faster rates than do serial interfaces (their speed is discussed in terms of their "transfer rate", usually expressed in bytes per second, and can be compared to the baud rate of a serial interface by dividing the baud rate by 8 or 10, as appropriate). A parallel interface, for example, is almost the only type of interface possible between a computer and a hard disk controller. Likewise, if proper hardware handshaking can be worked out (see below), a parallel interface is the best type for computer-to-computer transfers.

Many buffered printers are also capable of receiving data at high speeds and then printing it at leisure. If the buffer does not fill - that is, if the total amount of printing required does not exceed, in a long period of time, the total printing possible by the machine - a parallel interface is the best possible way of transferring data, without undue waiting on the part of the computer.

In the world of printers, at least, there is a de-facto industry standard, "Centronics compatibility". Printers manufactured by Centronics Corporation (Hudson, NH) use a 7-bit ASCII code and a certain wiring convention that has been widely copied by other manufacturers ("Centronics", by the way, is a registered trademark of the company). Centronics compatibility has become somewhat less important in the last few years as newer printers add foreign language character sets, raster graphics, and other functions needing a full 8-bit connection.

[Making a Parallel Cable]. The Computer Cookbook has the following advice for anyone thinking of doing a parallel cable: avoid this task if humanly possible. If the manufacturer of a board or peripheral device sells a made-up cable that goes with their product, buy it. It may cost $45-50; consider that you're saving 3 or 4 hours of your own time.

If making a cable is unavoidable, The Computer Cookbook has this second piece of advice: do it on paper first. Because there are only two or three important lines, an RS-232 cable can sometimes be done by trial-and-error: if the data is not coming out on pin 2, you know it's coming out on pin 3. Not true with parallel cables: with 10 or 12 important pins, you have too many permutations and combinations for this approach.

First, map out the important control lines. The two most important lines are called the "strobe line" and the "acknowledge". An output operation on a parallel port - for example, from a computer to a printer - generally goes like this:

> (Step 1). The computer places voltage levels (plus for 1,
>   negative for 0) on the eight data lines. As yet, however,
>   they have not been read or sensed by the receiving device.

> (Step 2). Electrical signals require some time to settle - that
>   is, become stable. The computer waits 5 microseconds
>   (millionths of a second) for the data lines to set up and come
>   to their proper levels.

> (Step 3). When the data is stable, the computer "hits" the
>   printer with the "strobe". This strobe pulse tells the
>   printer that there is valid data on the data lines. The
>   strobe signal can be as brief as 1 microsecond,
>   although the length of time is not standardized, and 3
>   microseconds is a safer time length because it guarantees that
>   most devices will "feel" the strobe.
>
>   More important, however, is that the polarity of the strobe
>   signal can vary from one interface to another. The most
>   common is for the strobe line to be "high" (have positive
>   voltage) when at "rest" and then go negative to indicate
>   data. This is called a "negative going" strobe and is usually
>   written STROBE with a bar across it to indicate that it is
>   "negative true". In keeping with the convention for
>   discussing electrical signals in ASCII, The Computer Cookbook
>   uses the term STROBE* to indicate a negative-going signal.

> (Step 4). After the printer reads in the data lines, it sends an
>   acknowledge signal to the computer to indicate that it is
>   ready to receive a new character. The acknowledge line is
>   usually abbreviated ACK; it can also be negative true, in
>   which case The Computer Cookbook would write it ACK*.

The simplest program to write to a parallel port would do this: write a character; loop until the ACK signal is received; write another character. A more subtle program might initialize by writing a "dummy" character; then in the standard loop, test for ACK first before writing anything. This would free the computer for processing during the time that the printer was "digesting" the character.

Another difficulty is possible: what if there is no ACK? Some sophisticated parallel drivers have "timeouts" that let the computer loose from its loop if the acknowlege is delayed.

Most parallel interfaces have a number of lines other than ACK that feed status information back to the computer. It is better to think of these lines as forming a "control word" that can be read by the computer software. The most important control line is BUSY. On older, nonbuffered printers, BUSY is often held true during carriage returns and other times when the printer can't accept data. Testing BUSY is the preferable way of keeping the computer from overrunning the receiving device with data (not sending ACK is another).

A complete list of signals typically sent from a printer includes:

        BUSY - indicate buffer full or not ready for data
        PAPER EMPTY - a sensor in the printer shows no paper
        FAULT or ERROR - shows a general problem in printer
        SELECT - shows that the printer has been manually
                      taken "off line"
        POWER ON - usually just a constant voltage (+3 volts),
                      which indicates printer power on
        RIBBON OUT - some printers can sense this

An additional output signal (computer to printer) is sometimes called "prime". A pulse on this line initializes the printer for operation.

In making a parallel cable, the first thing to do is think. Slow down, get a pencil and paper, open a can of beer. On a piece of paper, write down the "pins" of computer side connector. Typically, these will be numbered 1 to 20 or 1 to 15. Answer these questions from the computer system's documentation: what pin is the strobe pulse going out on? Is it negative going or (possibly) positive going? For reference, note the duration of the strobe pulse; you may need this (if things don't work out) later.

Next question: on what line does the computer expect to see an ACK? Does it want a negative-going or a positive-going acknowledge?

Now find, in the printer or other parallel device's documentation, the pins on which it receives the strobe and sends acknowledge. Do polarities match? What about timing? Will the computer's strobe last long enough for the printer to see? Will the computer see the acknowledge?

With these two "handshaking" signals taken care of, the rest is easier. The data lines should be easy to identify; note, however, that some companies number the lines from "bit 1" and others from "bit 0". Count the lines: are there 7 or 8? If seven - possibly a Centronics-style interface - the most significant bit is not connected at the printer and may even be the strobe! Try to match up at least 7 lines in the proper order.

Now try to match up the "grounds". It is not a good idea to link the frame ground (the ground of the chassis, or AC ground) to signal ground (the zero voltage point of the line signals).

[Making the Cable]. This matching-up process should all take place on paper. Once the interface is understood, the cable can be actually wired. First, the proper end connectors are needed. The connector at the computer end will vary. Some computers use a DB-15. On other parallel interface cards, 20-pin connectors are popular.

At the printer end, nearly all machines use what is commonly called an "Amphenol" connector, which has 36 pins (Amphenol, of course, is a company that makes many types of connectors, just the company name is used to describe this popular one, just as "RCA" is used to describe a common video and stereo jack, and no one seems to confuse that with the owner of NBC television, etc.). This Amphenol connector is part no. #57-30360 or #157-32360; many other companies make equivalent 36-pin connectors.

For the cable, use a striped or colored ribbon cable. Having color codes is the only way to follow a number of confusing lines from one connector to the other. Spectra and Mohawk both make color-coded ribbon cables. It should have at least as many (12-16) conductors as needed; unused conductors can be trimmed at the ends. Stranded wire (7x30) is best, because it flexes better than unstranded, although it is harder to solder. The individual conductors should be 22 gauge (AWG).

Finally, since Amp-type connectors require close soldering, it is advisable to have little rubber hoods for each pin, to prevent shorting when the cable is flexed. If these are available, silicon filler can be squirted around the solder points of a completed and tested cable (only!).

[An Example]. Consider the construction of a cable between the North Star computer and a Centronics printer. Following the advice given above, the first step is to look at the interface specifications in the manuals. The Centronics interface looks like this:

CENTRONICS PARALLEL INTERFACE

PIN	SIGNAL NAME	COMMENTS
1	STROBE*	Negative-going
2	DATA1	High=1,Low=0
3	DATA2	
4	DATA3	
5	DATA4	
6	DATA5	
7	DATA6	
8	DATA7	
10	ACKNLG*	From printer to computer
11	BUSY	Printer can't receive data
12	PE	High=paper empty
13	SLCT	High=printer selected
14	0V	Zero-volt signal ground
15	OSCXT	A 100-KHz signal
16	0V	Another signal ground
17	CHASSIS GND	Frame ground
18	+5V	Source of +5 volts
31	INPUT PRIME*	Negative level clears printer
32	FAULT*	Printer fault condition
34	LINE COUNT PULSE	Goes true during every LF

Not all of these pins are implemented on every Centronics model. Looking at the North Star documentation, we see these pins available at the parallel output connector, a DB-15 (fifteen pins) on the motherboard of the computer. To keep things straight, the original North Star names are retained:

NORTH STAR PARALLEL PORT

1	BIT 8	MSB of output byte
2	BIT 6	of data byte
3	CHASSIS GROUND	
4	BIT 3	
5	BIT 1	
6	FLAG*	A strobe-like output
7	ACK*	
8	SPARE*	An additional output
9	BIT 7	
10	BIT 5	
11	BIT 4	
12	BIT 2	
13	SIGNAL GROUND	
14	SIGNAL GROUND	
15	SIGNAL GROUND	

Actually, we have skipped a step. The North Star, as with many computers and interface cards, has a jumper block that allows us to select either a negative-going or a positive-going strobe and acknowledge. ACK is no problem: the Centronics sends a negative-true acknowledge, so we want ACK*.

The STROBE, however, is a headache. Looking at the North Star documentation, we see that the only signal we have available "indicates execution by the processor of a data output instruction to the parallel output port (HIGH while valid data on bus)". This sounds like a strobe, and in fact is, but the problem is that it is positive-going (goes "HIGH"), not the negative-going strobe required by the Centronics.

Now we see one of the reasons for the popularity of the Centronics 7-bit interface: we can "fake" the strobe using data bit 8, the most significant bit. This requires some clever software, which keeps bit 8 always "high" (equal to 1), then hits it with a "low" (=zero) at character output time. The Z-80/8080 code to do this is:

```
ORI     80H     ; SET STROBE FALSE=1
OUT     0       ; OUTPUT THE CHARACTER
XRI     80H     ; INVERT BIT 8 TO ZERO
OUT     0       ; AND SEND "FOR REAL"
XRI     80H     ; SET STROBE FALSE AGAIN
OUT     0       ; AND PUT AT REST
```

Nearly all parallel output ports are "latched" - that is, the data, once placed there, stays there. Thus, after initialization, the strobe bit will always look like "high" (=1), except for the brief moment when the routine above "zaps" it with a zero.

Now we have solved the basic problem and can match up 7 data bits, ACK* and STROBE*. We have a lot of additional status data coming from the printer: busy, paper out, select, and so on. However, we know that the Centronics will not send an acknowledge if a character we sent it makes it go "busy" or out of service. Thus, for a simple interface, we can live with the ACK* line being the only line back to the computer. Now putting in the colors from our Mohawk ribbon cable, our final chart looks like:

NORTH STAR - CENTRONICS PARALLEL CABLE

NORTH STAR PIN	CABLE COLOR	SIGNAL NAME	CENTRONICS PIN
1	White/Red	BIT 8=STROBE*	1
2	White/Green	BIT 6	7
3	Black	CHASSIS GROUND	17
4	Pink	BIT 3	4
5	White/Black	BIT 1	2
6	not connected		
7	Brown	ACK*	10
8	not connected		
9	Yellow	BIT 7	8
10	Gray	BIT 5	6
11	White/Orange	BIT 4	5
12	Tan	BIT 2	3
13	Green	SIGNAL GROUND	19
14	not connected		
15	not connected		

The rest is soldering!

Plotters

Pen plotters are interesting output devices useful if you have a use for them and otherwise just fun to play with.

Pen plotters are just that: a pen, in a holder, that moves over a piece of paper on a flat bed (although one type of low-cost plotter puts the paper on a round drum instead). The pen can be moved in fine increments, often that of several hundredths of an inch or a millimeter: this degree of fineness is called the "resolution" of the plotter.

In 1982, most major plotter companies had multi-color plotters on the market. The low-cost versions of these used one plotting arm, and a rack with multiple pens. When the plotter wants a different color, it executes a canned program to put its old pen away and to get a new on. Hewlett-Packard makes an expensive plotter with multiple-pen arms that is of course much faster for color plotting than the single-arm versions.

Plotters compete with dot matrix printers, including the new color printers such as the IDS Prism. However, plotters still produce better quality lines than these and are better for blueprints and other work that must be reproduced photographically. Ink-jet printers and laser phototypesetters may

give pen plotters a run for their money in the future.
[Houston Instrument's HI PLOT]. The major manufacturer of low-cost plotters in the US is Houston Instruments (1 Houston Square, Austin, TX 78753, 512-837-2820), a division of Bausch & Lomb, the medical company. Until the appearance of the Watanabe plotter on US shores, HI was without competition in the personal computer plotter market.

HI makes a series of "Digital Micro Plotters". All use a Z-80 microprocessor internally and use a highly nonstandard RS-232 interface (more on this below) or a Centronics-type parallel interface. The "DMP-3" ($699) has an 8-1/2 x 11 inch (17.5 x 25.4 cm) plotting area and no manual controls; it must be driven by a computer. The "DMP-4" is similar but has buttons along the side that allow the pen to be moved incrementally by hand. The "DMP-6", like the -3, has no manual controls, but a larger, 10 x 15 inch (30 x 50.8 cm) plotting area. The "DMP-7", similarly, has both the manual controls and larger plotting area.

[Interfacing]. HI is to be taken to task for its nonstandard serial interface (The Computer Cookbook encounters moral difficulties in describing a nonstandard serial interface as "RS-232".) It does use a DB-25 connector, with the following pins:

```
            1 - Frame Ground
            2 - Serial Stream from Plotter
            3 - Serial Stream to Plotter
            4 - RTS - tied to CTS at plotter
            5 - CTS
            7 - Signal Ground
```

So far, so good. However, instead of putting a baud rate select switch on the plotter, HI does this trick:

```
            6 - jumpered to a baud rate pin below
            14- if tied to 6, sets 9600 baud
            15- if tied to 6, sets 4800 baud
            16- if tied to 6, sets 2400 baud
            17- if tied to 6, sets 1200 baud
            18- if tied to 6, sets  600 baud
            19- if tied to 6, sets  300 baud
```

If the serial interface is used, one of two different communications protocols can be used. Plotters, by nature, are very slow, and there is much danger of overrunning their input buffers (the DMP models have a 512-byte buffer).

The first protocol for the DMP is familiar from paper tape punches and teletypes - namely, the XON/XOFF protocol. When the plotter's buffer fills to 512 bytes, it sends a XOFF (13 hex, ASCII symbol DC3) to the computer, which is then supposed to stop. When the number of bytes in the buffer falls below 256, the plotter sends a XON (11 hex, 12 decimal, DC1), and the computer, if programmed properly, starts up again.

The second communications protocol is more block-oriented, and is used with either the serial or parallel interface. It is best thought of as a bastardized version of an ETX/ACK protocol, where ETX is programmable and ACK is always a carriage return. Thus, when the ETX character is removed from the buffer, the plotter sends the ACK (this protocol is used on most serial printers, such as the Diable and Qume). However, the DMP allows the ETX to be programmed and also to set a delay. This delay is the time from removal of the ETX from its buffer by the plotter to the time it sends the ACK and allows the computer time to "set up" to read the return line. The following command to the plotter initializes the code for the ETX and sets the response delay:

Inn,ddd,

where "I" is the command, nn are two hex digits (e.g., 0D) for the code sent by the computer, and ddd is the delay time 0-255.

HI calls the XON/XOFF protocol "Mode 1", and the ETX/ACK protocol "Mode 2". These are also selected by a jumper on the serial connector:

9 - if grounded (tied to 7), Mode 2 selected

[Plotter Commands]. Because it has an "intelligent" microprocessor, the DMP responds to simple ASCII commands:

H (home) - raises the pen and moves it to
        the lower left-hand corner

O (origin) - sets the origin (0,0) at the
        current pen position

D (down pen) - puts the pen on the paper

U (up pen) - lifts the pen up

A followed by xxxx,yyyy - set to absolute
        mode; move to absolute position
        X=xxxx, Y=yyyy

R followed by sxxxx,syyyy - set to relative
        move mode; move plus or minus xxxx
        or yyyy steps from current location

Ln - set line type from 0 (solid line) to 8
        (dash-dot-dot)

Srh sss_ - write character string, with
        rotation r (1=0 degrees, 2=90, 3=180
        (upside down writing), 3=270; height
        code h (1=.07 inches, 5=1.12 inches);
        and ASCII string 'sss...', terminated
        by an underscore ('_', hex 5F)

Mhn - plot a marker (triangle, box, cross, etc.)
        of height h and type n (n from 1 to 5)

T - run plotter through self-test pattern

@ - deselect plotter

;: - select plotter

[Interfacing to the Apple II]. The HI plotters can be interfaced to the Apple II using either the Apple Serial Card, the California Computer Systems (CCS) serial card 7710A, or the Apple Communications Card. For some reason, HI has been using the Apple Communications Card - designed to operate a modem at either 110 or 300 baud - and making extensive hardware modifications required to operate the card at 4800 baud. The Computer Cookbook recommends the CCS 7710A, described elsewhere in these pages, which has a baud rate select switch. HI says that the Communications Card works in ETX/ACK mode with a return delay of 0; the CCS serial card needs a delay of 15 (=15/100s of a second); and the Apple Serial card needs a delay setting of 20. Thus, to initialize the plotter using the CCS card, the following ASCII line should be "printed" to the plotter:

;; I OD 15

HI has available a canned BASIC program called "HIGRAPH-1", which is a menu-driven Applesoft program that does a line graph, a pie chart, and a bar chart to demonstrate the plotter's capabilities. HI also offers a BASIC program called APPLE/START, written by West Coast Consultants (1775 Lincoln Blvd., Tracy, CA 95376, 209-835-1780). West Coast, according to a HI newsletter, has more elaborate software packages for the DMP series available.

[The HI-PAD]. Houston Instrument's HI-PAD is a digitizing pad competitive with Apple's graphics tablet. It comes, at no extra charge, with a special Apple interface card DT-11-128. The cable required to connect the interface card to the HI-PAD is HI part #DT-11A. The HI-PAD card needs to be installed in slot 4 of the Apple to run HI's user-contributed graphics software.

Power Filters

Power line filters and other accessories for personal computers - as with some types of accident insurance - are not always necessary for technical reasons but desirable for their pyschological effect.

Line filters and other power-line devices protect computer equipment in varying degrees from the irregularities of residential and small-business power. In the earlier days of computing, when large mainframes needed carefully prepared sites with air conditioning, raised floors, and so on, power supplies were not an issue - just a part of the package.

Personal computers generally function quite well in an office environment and have no more need for controlled power or heat than a typewriter or TV. That said, however, there comes the "yes, but..." sort of considerations. The following two rules, if followed, can generally ensure happy computing:

Use a "Clean" Line. An electrical line running through a house or office will often have a number of appliances on it. When larger appliances such as refrigerators or air conditioners turn on and off, they send transitory voltage "spikes" through the line. These spikes are harmless to some computers but knock others - notably the TRS-80 model I - for loops. Know what appliances are on the same line with the computer. Avoid putting it on the same line with heavy-duty items such as refrigerators or troublesome electric blanket controls.

Buy a Low-Cost Line Filter. If you must put the computer on a noisy line, buy one of the less expensive line filters, such as the Radio Shack $49.95 26-1451. This device will not protect the computer against lightening or power failures, but can improve the day-to-day operation of the machine. Notice that if an electrically noisy device (e.g., Model 33 teletype) is part of the computer system, such a line filter may be the only solution if all of the computer equipment must run to the same outlet.

[Other Power Problems.] These precautions will generally result in better day-to-day operation of a small computer and are all that are necessary under normal circumstances. However, more extreme power line problems exist; these include transient surges, power failures, and brownouts:

Transients. Transients are brief, sharp fluctuations in line voltage, typically lasting less than one-half second. A lightening strike near a house or on a near-by pole can create a transient of 5600 volts; heavy equipment switching on a line (an oil burner in a basement) can produce perhaps 2500 volts. In lightening-prone areas, such as the Midwest, a "Blitzbug" or other device is a sensible investment. These devices are somewhat like fuses and simply "blow out" in the event of a sharp transient. The Blitzbug costs about $29.95.

Power Failures. Transients are almost imperceptible (to humans) changes in voltage, often to very high voltage, and should not be confused with power failures, which are a complete loss of voltage. Most computers, especially those with dynamic RAMs, will not tolerate a loss of power for over 15 milliseconds without "memory loss". Such amnesia may or may not be fatal to a program, depending on where it occurs. Large computer installations that need to continue running whether power is on or not use Uninterruptible Power Systems (UPS) to keep going in power failures or at least to allow an orderly shutdown of the plant without loss of vital data.

Brownouts, or Low Voltage. In general, American utility companies hold themselves to plus or minus 5% of 120/208-volt service. The American National Standards Institute (ANSI) lists 111/193 volts as minimum permissible service voltage on these lines. This is a -7.2 and -7.5 volt drop respectively. Although most electrical equipment is designed to keep running at -10% drops, it should be remembered that voltage may drop up to 3% or 4% from the service entrance of a building to the actual terminals of the equipment. Voltage regulators, which start in the $400 range, can provide constant voltage and compensate for brownouts.

["Apple Juice"]. In the last few years, several "micro-UPS" systems have appeared in the personal computer market, notably the "Apple Juice" power supply for that computer (from High Technology, Inc., 1611 Northwest 23rd St., Oklahoma City, OK 73104, 405-528-8012).

"Apple Juice" will keep the following Apple II configuration going 25 minutes (APS-2A) or 1 hour (APS-3):

> 48K Apple II or Apple II+
> Language Card
> Printer or Serial Card (card only!)
> Disk Controller Card

Since the printer is presumably down, along with the Apple's, the ability to run the serial card is somewhat academic. The important feature is that Apple Juice can run the disk long enough to save vital files from memory during a complete power failure, and it can keep the system running during brownouts. Note, however, that in a complete blackout the Apple's other peripherals (such as the monitor!) may not be running off the "juice", and the user will be typing blind.

For serious hardware hackers and programmers, the Apple Juice, when it cuts in, can be used to generate an interrupt or reset of the computer. This is done by wiring a line from the Apple Juice to the proper pin on a peripheral card in the Apple bus. This interrupt could go automatically into a "save files" routine on power failure. Whereas this kind of programming effort is appropriate on military and serious industrial computers, The Computer Cookbook is hard pressed to think of applications requiring this on the Apple where ordinary backup procedures, carefully applied, would not do the trick.

Printers

Computer printers come in different varieties, from slow, low-cost models using skinny, narrow paper and the cheapest of printing technologies, to laser-scanning devices that produce high-resolution typography. Talking about printers requires precision; the following definitions are a useful start:

[Printing Technologies]. There are several technologies by which printers put letters on papers. The best known of these are impact and thermal printing, but there are many others.

> Impact Printing. By far the most familiar is impact printing.
> This is familiar from typewriters and other devices. In
> impact printing, an inked ribbon is struck by a hammer, pin,
> or other hard metal part and leaves some ink on the paper.
> Impact printers can generally make carbons or use multipart
> forms.

Thermal Printers. Thermal printing is a low-cost alternative to impact printing in which special, heat-sensitive paper is used. Rather than strike the paper, the printing head heats it in a precise pattern, burning the letters in. Because thermal printers do not physically strike the paper, they are quieter in operation than impact printers. Apple Computer's "Silentype" is probably the best known thermal printer.

Electrostatic Printers. Another low-cost printing technology, less popular in recent years than it once was, uses special paper that is a sandwich of backing, dark ink, and aluminum finish. Rather than strike or heat the paper, the print head gives off a small electrostatic charge than melts the aluminum finish, exposing the ink beneath. The Axiom printer is perhaps the best known electrostatic.

Line Printers. Although "line printer" is sometimes used as a generic name for any high-speed printer, true line printers use high-speed belts or chains to print one full line at a time, a printing technology dating back to the old IBM 1403. Line printers are much faster and also more expensive than printers that only print a character at a time. The speed of line printers is measured in lines per minute, with 2000 being the highest achieved and 300 to 600 the mid-range. At very high speeds, line printers sometimes produce slightly wavy lines, often seen on checking statements or other mass-produced documents. Dataproducts (6219 DeSoto Ave., Woodland Hills, CA 91369) is the dominant supplier of line printers.

The first three technologies are dominant in personal computing; three others - ink-jet printing, xerographic printing, and laser printing - are used on mainframe systems. Ink-jet printing uses a technique in which a droplet of ink is fractured into tiny charged particles, which are then steered toward the paper by an electrostatic field. Ink-jet printers have slightly fuzzy results but are relatively fast at printing. Ink-jet printing may eventually become a high-quality, low-cost technology, competitive in price and speed with daisy wheel impact printing. There are several low-cost ink-jet printers in development, one by Apple's peripherals research group in Los Angeles.

Xerographic printing is an adaptation of the process used in Xerox copiers and is a high-speed, high-cost, high-quality technique. Xerographic printers are sometimes called intelligent copiers; the IBM 6670 Information Distributor is a typical example. This device uses a controller (originally developed for an ink-jet device) to guide a laser beam, which is then fed into the mechanism of an IBM Copier III. Xerographic printers are relatively high speed (100-200 characters per second) and offer sharper characters than ink-jet printers. Because their fonts are computer controlled, they can be switched rapidly during the printing process.

Laser printers are similar in that they use a laser beam, but they direct it at photographic film or paper, as in a conventional phototypesetting machines. Canon, the Japanese camera maker, introduced a relatively low-cost computer controlled typesetting machine in 1982 that uses laser technology.

[Daisy Wheel Printers]. Independent of the printing technology, there are several methods for forming characters on printers. Daisy wheel printers use a mechanism that is a descendant of the IBM Selectric golf ball mechanism. Daisy wheels were first introduced by Diablo in 1972, with its "Hy Type" printers. Qume (2350 Qume Drive, San Jose, CA 95150, 408-942-4000) is also a well-known manufacturer of daisy wheel printers, as is NEC, the Japanese company, although NEC uses a bent daisy called a thimble. Recently, several typewriter manufacturers have adopted daisy wheel technology, including Smith-Corona, for a low-cost ($600) device. C. Itoh, another Japanese company, has a low-cost daisy wheel printer competive with Qume and Diablo but slower.

A daisy wheel is a tiny plastic wheel about 3 inches in diameter with 96 spokes. Each spoke has on it a fully formed character. To print, the wheel is turned so the proper character faces the paper. It is then struck by the print hammer and hits the ribbon, which in turn leaves a mark on the paper. Daisy wheel printers produce the best quality of any computer-driven device short of a phototypesetting machine. The manuscript for this book was produced on a daisy wheel printer, a Diablo 1610. Daisy wheels are also interchangeable, meaning that legal, foreign language, special math, and APL wheels can be used. The table at the end of this section lists Qume daisy wheels; Diablo makes an equal variety and selection, as do some independent vendors.

Daisy wheels vary in: (1) sequence; (2) pitch; and (3) typestyle. Sequence is the order in which characters appear on the wheel. In general, it is best to think of 96-character wheels as a 1-to-1 map of the ASCII character set (DEL, a nonprinting character, usually maps to a bar negation sign often printed by control-Z), with other wheels varying the special characters therein. Thus "legal" wheels intended for law office word processing applications replace some of the ASCII characters used for programming, like "]","[", and so on, with special symbols for copyright (circled C), trademark (raised small TM or circled R), paragraph, etc. Likewise, wheels with Greek and math symbols are available, as are foreign language wheels.

Pitch refers to the number of characters per inch on a line. "10 pitch" simply means 10 characters per inch; "12 pitch" means 12. On typewriters, these spacings are sometimes called "pica" and "elite", with pica larger than elite. "PS" means that the character was designed for machines that proportional space, like the old IBM Executive typewriters. On a proportional space machine, an "i" is very skinny, and an "M" is fat. Newer model daisy wheel printers have built-in microprocessors that proportional space and justify lines.

Typestyle generally refers to font design. "Courier" is perhaps the standard computer printer font; it is a square-serif design that looks like it came from a typewriter. Serifs are the little tails on Roman lettering; sans serif, or nonserif faces include Gothic (used by many universities) and Orator, commonly used for projected presentations and slides. This book is set in OCR-B, an American National Standards Institute font, which can be machine scanned, and is nonserif. Square serifs give a typewriter look; rounded serifs give a weighty, typeset look and are popular for legal documents.

Artisan Legal 12   Part Number 303201-01

ABCDEFGHIJKLMNOPQRSTUVWXYZabcdefghijklmnopqrstuvwxyz

0123456789   ¼_¶™½¢!"#$%&°()*+,-./[®]©_':;§=†?@

Forms Gothic S-10   Part Number 38147

ABCDEFGHIJKLMNOPQRSTUVWXYZabcdefghijklmnopqrstuvwxyz

0123456789   ¬¢,.:;-+$#%{}[]()>=<~'^`?!@*/|\&"_

Manifold 10   Part Number 38103

ABCDEFGHIJKLMNOPQRSTUVWXYZABCDEFGHIJKLMNOPQRSTUVWXYZ

0123456789   ¬¢,.:;-+$#%{}⌈⌉()>=<¤'♭◊?!@:¨/|\&"_

Dual Gothic Legal 12   Part Number 38106-02

ABCDEFGHIJKLMNOPQRSTUVWXYZabcdefghijklmnopqrstuvwxyz

0123456789   ¼_¶™½¢!"#$%&°()*+,-./:;§=†?@[®]© '

OCR-A 10   Part Number 38144

ABCDEFGHIJKLMNOPQRZTUVWXYZabcdefghijklmnopqrstuvwxyz

0123456789   ¥ñ⌐.:;-+$£%ÄÜÆ&{}⊢=♪,'|.?|Ψ*/ÖØ&"_

OCR-B 10   Part Number 38146

ABCDEFGHIJKLMNOPQRSTUVWXYZabcdefghijklmnopqrstuvwxyz

0123456789   ¤£,.:;-+$#%{}[]()>=<~'^`?!@*/|\&"_

OCR-B 10 Scandia   Part Number 303405-01

ABCDEFGHIJKLMNOPQRSTUVWXYZabcdefghijklmnopqrstuvwxyz

0123456789   ,.:;-+¤#%äåÄÅ()>=<ü'üé?!É*/öö&"_

APL-10   Part Number 38150-01

α⊥∩∈_∇Δι∘'□|⊤○*?ρ⌈~↓∪ω⊃↑⊂ABCDEFGHIJKLMNOPQRSTUVWXYZ

0123456789   ¬•,.([+÷≤<={}←→∨∧:×;$]≥◊\¨≠/⊣⊢>)-

French Prestige Cubic 10   Part Number 38131

ABCDEFGHIJKLMNOPQRSTUVWXYZabcdefghijklmnopqrstuvwxyz

0123456789 |₣,.:;-+$£%éè°§()>=<¨'^`?!à*/ùç&"_

Russian Cubic 10   Part Number 38149

АБЦДЕФГЧИЖКЛМНОПЩРСТУВШХЫЗабцдефгчижклмнопщрстувшхыз

0123456789   ь',.:Э-+Ю#%йю[]()>=<_|Ъ`?!Я*/эяЙ"ь

Some ususual print wheels from the Diablo catalog

[Daisy Wheel Ribbons].   In general, there are two types of daisy wheel
ribbons: fabric and multistrike. Fabric ribbons are made of cloth, and they
loop continuously: the printing from them gets lighter and lighter. "Multi
strike" is something of a misnomer: actually, multistrike ribbons are only

struck once and provide high-quality output. These are comparable to "film" ribbons on typewriters. The highest possible quality is provided by so-called "single-strike" ribbons, not available for all machines.

Note that for "camera ready" copy, it is best to use a metal print wheel machine. Metal print wheels have higher mass and, to put it simply, hit the paper harder. They also produce sharper, darker images. However, plastic print wheels can also provide adequate camera copy - this book is an example. It helps, however, in offset printing to have the printer slightly overexpose the negatives of the originals. This will make light copy print darker and if done carefully will not result in extraneous shadows or other problems.

[Low-Cost Daisys]. 1980 saw the beginning of a "war of the daisys", in which several low-cost letter quality printers were introduced. Two came from C. Itoh, a Japanese manfuacturer. The "Starwriter I" is a $998 list price daisy whose only limitation is its slow speed, 25 characters per second. The Starwriter II is a 45-character version at $1348. Both have wide carriages as a standard feature, with 136 columns in 10 pitch and 163 columns in 12 pitch. Diablo Systems introduced a low-end daisy wheel printer, the 630, in April 1980.   The 630 can use either plastic or metalized print wheels interchangeably. The 630 has standard Diablo paper movement abilities, moving horizontally 120/units per inch and vertically 48/units inch. It uses HyType II ribbons. The price for the 630 is approximately $1700.

Brother Industries, Ltd., a Japanese company that has introduced a low-cost daisy wheel typewriter in the US, has a low-cost printer available from its US distributor, Dynax (333 South Hope St., Suite 2800, Los Angeles, CA 90071). The Brother device is compatible with the Qume Sprint 3 and can run as either a parallel or serial device.

In early 1982, Smith-Corona, the typewriter manufacturer, introduced an $800 daisy wheel printer the TP-1, for the personal computer market. This device is slow, with a speed of 12 to 15 characters per second, putting it in the range of converted IBM Selectric typewriters (see "Typewriters"), which print at a nominal top speed of 13.5 characters per second. However, the S-C device was designed from scratch to work with computers and offers a full ASCII character set (plus some fractions, like 1/2 and 1/4, and a cent sign), which converted Selectrics cannot. The S-C does not have many of the fancy features of more expensive daisys, like unit spacing, but seems adequate for many applications. It comes in both parallel and serial versions.

[ETX-ACK Protocol]. Daisy wheel printers that print at 30 to 45 characters per second have a problem in that their effective baud rate - that is, the rate at which they can accept and print characters with no waiting or wasted time - falls between the conventional 300- and 120- baud settings. A printer running at 300 baud will not run at full speed; one running at 1200 baud will eventually overrun its buffer.

Consequently, several software protocols have been developed to keep 1200-baud printers going at full speed but without losing characters or overruning buffers. The most important of these is the "ETX-ACK" protocol, in which an "End of Transmission" (hexadecimal 3) is placed into the data stream to the printer. When the ETX is removed from the print buffer (in the case of the Diablo 1610, the print buffer is 158 characters), the printer sends an ACK (hexadecimal 6) back to the computer.

A simple and effective technique is to insert an ETX after every CR (decimal 13) sent to the printer and to wait for the ACK character. Very little printer time is lost between waiting for the ACK and receiving it, although if CPU time is valuable, the best solution is to send 78-character lines followed by an ETX. When the host receives an ACK, it begins sending a 3rd message, thereby keeping the buffer full with between 78 and 157 characters.

The following is a simple ETX-ACK printer driver, used with North Star BASIC, which sends the character to be transmitted in the Z-80 C register, and returns 0 in the A register if transmission is successful:

```
        DRIVER  IN      A,(STATUS_BYTE) ; LOAD STATUS
                BIT     TXRDY,A         ; TEST TRANSMITTER RDY
                JR      Z,DRIVER        ; LOOP IF NOT RDY
                LD      A,C             ; LOAD CHAR TO SEND
                OUT     (DATA),A        ; SEND IT
                CP      ODH             ; IS IT A CR?
                JR      Z,ACK           ; IF SO, PROTOCOL
                XOR     A               ; IF NOT, CLEAR A
                RET                     ; AND RETURN
        ;
        ACK     IN      A,(STATUS_BYTE) ; MAKE SURE WE CAN OUTPUT
                BIT     TXRDY,A         ; WAIT FOR TRANSMIT READY
                JR      Z,ACK           ; BY LOOPING
                LD      A,03H           ; LOAD "ETX"
                OUT     (DATA),A        ; AND SEND IT
        ;
        WAIT    IN      A,(STATUS_BYTE) ; NOW READ RESPONSE
                BIT     RDRDY,A         ; WHEN RECEIVER READY
                JR      A,WAIT
                IN      A,(DATA)        ; PRINTER HAS SENT SOMETHING
                RES     7,A             ; PARITY MAY BE WEIRD
                CP      6               ; IS IT AN ACK?
                JR      NZ,ACK          ; IF NOT TRY ALL OVER
                XOR     A               ; OTHERWISE, RETURN
                RET
```

Apple uses a similar driver on its PROMs intended for use with 1200-baud ("Qume type") printers on its high-speed serial card.

[Dot Matrix Printers]. Most low-cost computer printers form letters out of a matrix (box) of dots. In the mid-1970s, the standard matrix for dots was 5 dots across by 7 dots down; the letter "A" looked like:

```
 XXX
X   X
X   X
XXXXX
X   X
X   X
X   X
```

In recent years, the resolution of dot matrix printers has improved. The standard of the early 1980s is 7 by 9 dots per character. Resolution of dot

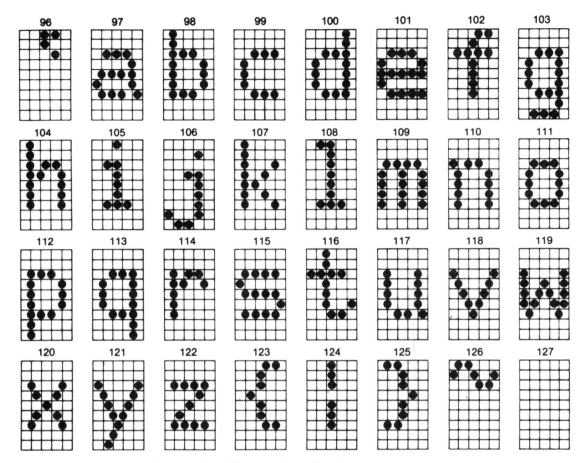

Epson MX-80 Dot Matrix Characters

matrix printers will continue to rise, because many non-Roman alphabets, such as Kanji (Japanese characters of Chinese origin) and Arabic, cannot be represented well with limited dots. The Epson MX-80, now an industry standard, uses a 7 by 9 dot matrix.

[Epson]. Seiko, the Japanese watch company, makes a family of 3 low-cost dot matrix printers that are perfect for personal computer systems, which it sells in the US under the trade name Epson. Since the introduction of Epson's MX-80 in late 1979, it has become the widest selling personal computer printer and was selected by IBM as the printer for its Personal Computer.

The Epson printers display many of the best features of Japanese product design. Centronics, the leading US computer printer manufacturer, made the world live with rough, 5 by 7 dot matrix characters; the Epson prints dense, excellent-quality letters that are often fully adequate for business use. The internal design of the Epson printer is elegant and simple: the parts count is low, improving reliability, and elements that wear, like the print head, snap out and are easily replaced. The printer was designed with the international market in mind: a switch selects it between Katakana, French, German, and English characters.

[Parallel Interfacing]. Most dealers have interface cards and cables that allow the Epson to be plugged in and used immediately. The MX-80 uses a Centronics compatible parallel interface; in general, the following steps must be taken to interface the MX-80 to various popular microcomputers:

TRS-80. The MX-80 was originally designed to work with the TRS-80 Model I and was in fact called the "TX" when first introduced in the fall of 1979. If the MX-80 is being used with a TRS-80, it plugs into the printer card edge on the expansion interface (Model I) or main console (Model III). The Radio Shack printer cable (26-4402) can be used, but an Epson-supplied cable allows some additional control over the printer and should be obtained if possible.

Apple. With the Apple II, the MX-80 uses the Centronics printer card (Apple part A2B0002X) and its cable and uses jumper block CB-01 on the board. In BASIC (and Pascal), the Apple sends both a carriage return and line feed automatically, so switches 1-2 and 1-3 on the MX-80 should be set to ON and switch 2-3 to OFF. The <Control I> feature of the Parallel Card must be used (in BASIC but not in Pascal) to set the print line to more than 40 characters and to return it to 40 after finishing with the printer and returning output to the screen. On the Apple ///, the Universal Parallel Interface card can be used, but a special cable may need to be wired.

IBM. The Epson printer plugs into the monochrome display card in the most popular (word processing) IBM configuration.

[The Epson RS-232 Interface]. Epson makes available, as an option, an RS-232-C interface board for its printer. This printed circuit board is about 4 by 5 inches and plugs onto the motherboard of the printer. The installation is relatively easy; the hardest thing is getting the top off the printer. The standard baud-rate settings for the printer are 1200 baud, no parity, and bit 8 grounded (always=0). Note that if the printer comes from your dealer this way, you will not have access to the TRS-80 graphic symbols or to the alternative alphabetic characters (Katakana, French, etc.). You may wish to specify a full 8-bit connection to get these.

The Epson RS-232 board also has a nice self-test feature, which allows easy check-out of installation and the printer. Pushing the self-test button in, and then turning on the printer, results in a memory diagnostic and a slew pattern of characters.

Epson's serial interface is nonstandard and really more of a half-serial, half-parallel connection. Furthermore, although most serial printers are implemented as terminal devices (DTE), the Epson serial card looks like a modem (DCE) to the computer.

The pins have the following meanings:

              pin 1   - chassis ground
              pin 2   - data into printer
              pin 3   - signal ground

pin 20 - "busy" (logic true)

Note that there is no data line back to the computer, so that a "hardware" handshake, not an ETX/ACK protocol as on some printers, is required to prevent overrun of the Epson's 2K buffer. This requires the following steps:

- The computer's software or UART must monitor pin 20, which goes high when the printer cannot take data. On some computer serial interfaces, this is done by looking at the CTS (Clear to Send) line - on others, the Data Set Ready (pin 6) or Data Carrier Detect (pin 8) lines.

- The cable between the computer and Epson must cross the proper pin of the computer to pin 20 of the Epson connector.

- The switches inside the Epson (S2-1 and S2-2) must be set to provide the proper polarity of the BUSY signal on pin 20. The signal can be inverted by setting a switch on the RS-232 board (S2-1 off and S2-2 on makes for BUSY*).

In general, BUSY should be inverted by setting the Epson's internal switches, pin 20 connected to pin 5 (CTS). Then, when the printer is busy, it will drive clear to send false (low) and prevent the UART from transmitting.

[Printing Abilities]. The MX-80 has the following special print modes:

DOUBLE WIDTH - prints characters extra wide to the
               end of the line, then resets;

DOUBLE STRIKE - the paper moves up 1/216 of an
                inch and overprints, giving an
                extra dark, "letter quality" look;

COMPRESSED - prints 132 characters on the line in
             a compressed format;

EMPHASIZED - an extra-force mode for multipart forms,
             carbons, etc.

As with other printers, these modes and other features on the MX-80 are manipulated from software by a set of control and escape codes. The following single-character control codes can be sent from BASIC with a LPRINT CHR$(n) or equivalent statement. Better results can sometimes be had by sending the control code plus 128 (e.g., sending the code with bit 7 set):

BEL (decimal 7) - Sounds bell.
LF (decimal 10) - Line feed.
VT (decimal 11) - Vertical tab.
FF (decimal 12) - Form feed.
CR (decimal 13) - Carriage return (CR).
SO (decimal 14) - Turn on double width mode..
SI (decimal 15) - Turn on compressed character mode.
DC1 (decimal 17) - Select printer, let it accept data.
DC2 (decimal 18) - Turn off compressed character mode.

```
        DC3 (decimal 19) - Deselect (turn off) printer.
        DC4 (decimal 20) - Turn off double width mode.
        CAN (decimal 24) - Cancel unprinted data. Reset to normal width.
        DEL (decimal 127) - Delete unprinted data. Reset to normal width.

        (Notes: CAN works only if switch 1-3 inside the printer is OFF.
         DEL, identical in function, works only if switch 1-4 is OFF).
```

The following escape sequences set the various modes on the MX-80. They require that the ASCII escape character (ESC, 27 decimal) be sent first, followed by a set of other characters. "A", "B", etc., refer to the capital letters:

```
        ESC A NUL (decimal 0) - Sets line spacing to 1/8" between lines.
        ESC A SOH (decimal 1) - Sets line spacing to 7/72" between lines.
                Defaults to 1/6" spacing (normal typing spacing).
        ESC B n1 n2 n3 NUL - Set vertical tabs at n1, n2, n3, where
                nx is the vertical line number + 128.
        ESC C n - Set form length to n lines.
        ESC D n1 n2 n3 NUL - Set horizontal tabs at character positions n1,
                n2, n3, where nx is the character position + 128;
        ESC E - Turn on EMPHASIZED MODE (very dark).
        ESC F - Turn off EMPHASIZED MODE.
        ESC G - Turn on DOUBLE STRIKE mode.
        ESC H - Turn off DOUBLE STRIKE mode.
```

Note that the set vertical and horizontal tab instructions really supply a list that must be terminated by a null, or the printer will continue to set tabs everywhere!

[Graphics]. The MX-80 has a standard graphics mode that derives from TRS-80 Model I block graphics. This mode uses codes 160 (e.g., 32+128) to 223 to define a graphics character set similar to that used on the TRS-80 screen. A 6 by 12 dot matrix is defined for each graphics character in the set. Note that Japanese Katakana characters, if enabled by switch 1-7 inside the printer, occupy this code space and will, if switched in, disable the TRS-80 graphics codes.

[Graphics from Dot Matrix Printers]. In addition to being able to print text, dot matrix printers offer varying degrees of graphics ability if the pins of the printhead can be individually controlled. The printer can be thought of as a type of raster device, with the programming limitation that the raster must be painted in "stripes" of 7 or 9 lines down, e.g.,

```
        ----------------direction of printhead---------->

        X X XX    X X   X X  XX XXXXXXXXXX XXXXXX XXXXX   dots from pin 1
        XXXXXX X XX X X X XX    XXX XXXX XXX XXX XXXX     dots from pin 2
        ....
        XX XXX XX XX XX XX XXX XXX XXX XXX XXXXXXXXXXX    dots from pin 9
```

Graphics ability is usually an optional feature of dot matrix printers. The Apple Silentype features graphics as a standard feature; a single control code sent to the Silentype will "dump" the high-resolution graphics page - that is, make a hard copy of what is seen on the Apple screen. The Silentype in this mode can be thought of as almost a Xerox machine.

Another machine aimed for the Apple II, Axiom's "MicroPlotter", provides a printout of either of the Apple's high-resolution graphics pages with a single keystroke command. As a printer, the EX820 is normally set for 40 columns. It will print all 96 ASCII characters and responds to the following control characters: BEL, LF, and CR. Wide characters, 20 per line, can be printed by sending a control-E to the EX820. Narrow characters, 80 per line, will be printed if a control-W is sent. Normal-width characters can be restored with a control-V. Reverse printing, which puts light characters on a black background, follows after sending a control-O. Control-N restores normal printing.

The Axiom can be set up for user-defined characters or custom plotting with a control-Z. Each print line on the EX820 has eight dots top to bottom. After a control-Z is received, each bit of subsequent ASCII codes controls a vertical dot. Vertical resolution is thus 8 # 8 or 64 lines per inch. Horizontal resolution in graphics mode can be either 128, 256, or 512 dots per line, as determined by a control-E, -V, and -W, respectively.

In addition to these control codes, the EX820 responds to a number of others that have been added specifically for use with the Apple. A control-T will "dump" the entire 24-line text screen of the Apple. A control-F will print the current high resolution graphics page. Page one is selected by a control-shift-M, and page two is selected with a control-shift-N.

[The Sanders Media 12/7]. In the US, the highest quality dot matrix printer has been the Sanders Media 12/7, introduced in 1979 by Sanders Technology, a financially troubled company founded by Royden Sanders. Sanders Technology should not be confused with Sanders Associates, a graphics terminal company founded by the same man. (Sanders might be called the Al Shugart of the printer business.) In 1982, Sanders Technology was reorganized and emerged on March 1 as Santec Corporation (9 Columbia Drive, Amherst, NH 03031, 603-882-1000). Santec still sells and services the Media 12/7.

The Sanders printer can put 13-mil (13/1000 of an inch) diameter dots within spaced 3.5 mils in the horizontal direction, and 8 mils in the vertical direction. This close placement means that the dots can overlap about 50% horizontally and 75% vertically, forming nearly solid lines. With several passes of its printhead, the Media 12/7 can create solid letters that approach the quality of typeset copy:

The Helvesan Italic typeface is part of the Helvesan family of fonts which
also includes Helvesan Regular and Helvesan Draft. The use of
an italic typeface is a nice way of highlighting
certain areas of text and is especially useful in document production. It prints
at the same pitch and speed as the Helvesan Regular typeface. This copy is printed
centered within the image area. The line
length is determined either automatically by the system of by the user inserting carriage
returns at the desired line ending.

[Kanji Printers].   In Japan, much effort is being made to develop Kanji printers capable of good-quality representations of the Chinese characters in the Japanese alphabet. Japan has 3 types of characters: Katakana, which is a phonetic alphabet used to render foreign words, in advertising, by children, and by data processing machines; Hiragana, a phonetic alphabet being slowly imposed on the younger generation by the Japanese Ministry of Education; and Kanji, the once Chinese characters that make up the bulk of written Japanese.

Although a 1-to-1 correspondence between ASCII and Katakana can be established, some American and European companies are unwilling to deal with Kanji and will ultimately pay for it in the market. Knowledge of Kanji characters is the key measure of literacy to the Japanese: basic literacy calls for knowledge of some 3000 different characters - 10,000 characters is perhaps the adult norm. True scholars may learn upwards of 50,000 characters.

Although to date the complexities of their alphabet have prevented the Japanese from developing effective word processing, time and technology is on their side. Improvements in the resolution of both video display devices and printers has made Kanji printing and display possible, and 16-bit computers make word processing and telecommunications with up to 32,000 characters much easier. The primary difficulty in Japanese word processing is, in fact, not display but data entry, because a Kanji keyboard must have multiple shift levels far beyond the ALT-CONTROL-SHIFT-P of the worse American models. This problem explains much of the Japanese research interest in voice recognition technology.

The following sample is from a Kanji printer introduced by IBM Japan in 1979:

例 外 番 号	例 外 事 項 メ ッ セ ー ジ
0 1	発注方針の指定が誤っている。
0 2	固定数での発注なのに数量が指定されていない。
0 3	発注方針Ｅ（ＬＵＣ），Ｆ（ＰＰＢ）が実行できない。
	（０１～０３の場合，正味所要量で処理される。）

[Printer Guide]. The following is a list of prices for various printers, and a list of various daisy wheel typestyles available:

SYSTEM	MANUFACTURER	DESCRIPTION/IDENTIFICATION	LIST	DISCOUNT
Printer	Anadex	Dot matrix 132 col. 9500	1650.00	1399.00
Printer	Anadex	Dot matrix 220 col. 9501	1650.00	1399.00
Printer	Anadex	Dot matrix DP8000	995.00	845.00
Printer	Centronics	Dot matrix parallel 737	995.00	845.00
Printer	Centronics	Dot matrix parallel 730	795.00	675.00
Printer	Centronics	Dot matrix parallel F/T 779	1350.00	995.00
Printer	Centronics	Dot matrix serial u/l case 737	1045.00	830.00
Printer	Centronics	Dot matrix serial 730	845.00	718.00
Printer	Diablo	Letter quality 630 Metal PW	2710.00	2425.00
Printer	Epson	Graphtrax+	65.00	53.00
Printer	Epson	MX-100, 136col, tractor, graf	995.00	695.00
Printer	Epson	MX-70	449.00	399.95
Printer	Epson	MX-80	549.00	440.00
Printer	Epson	MX-80 F/T	689.00	549.00
Printer	Epson	Serial Add-on IF, 2K buffer	149.00	120.00
Printer	IDS	Paper Tiger 440-G w/graphics	1149.00	950.00
Printer	IDS	Paper Tiger 445	795.00	675.00
Printer	IDS	Paper Tiger 445G	894.00	770.00
Printer	IDS	Paper Tiger 460-G w/graphics	1295.00	1100.00
Printer	IDS	Paper Tiger 560		
Printer	IDS	Prism 132 color w/graphics		1695.00
Printer	IDS	Prism 80 color w/graphics		1395.00
Printer	NEC	Dot matrix, 8023		565.00
Printer	NEC	Spinwriter 3510, 33cps,128col	2589.00	2019.00
Printer	NEC	Spinwriter 7710, 55cps,132col	3335.00	2449.00
Printer	NEC/Sellum	NEC 3510 w/16K buf, int	2789.00	2169.00
Printer	NEC/Sellum	NEC 7719 w/16K buf, bi-d, int	3535.00	2649.00
Printer	Okidata	Microline 80	600.00	449.00
Printer	Okidata	Microline 82	799.00	660.00
Printer	Qume	80075 GERMAN Elite 12		
Printer	Qume	80956 WP Letter Gothic 12		
Printer	Qume	80961 WP Theme 10 pt PS		
Printer	Qume	80962 APL 10 light italic 12		
Printer	Qume	80964 WP light italic 12		
Printer	Qume	80966 WP Courier 12		
Printer	Qume	80968 MULTI elite 12		
Printer	Qume	80973 WB Prestige Elite 12		
Printer	Qume	80974 AY Bookface Academic 10		
Printer	Qume	80981 COMMERICAL Documenty PS		
Printer	Qume	80982 ESA Pica 10		
Printer	Qume	80983 UKN Pica 10		
Printer	Qume	80984 ESA Elite 12		
Printer	Qume	80985 UKN Elite 12		
Printer	Qume	80986 ESA Courier 12		
Printer	Qume	80987 UKN Courier 12		
Printer	Qume	80988 ESA Letter Gothic 12		
Printer	Qume	80989 UKN Letter Gothic 12		
Printer	Qume	80994 LEGAL Documentary PS		
Printer	Qume	82050 WP Courier 10		
Printer	Qume	82051 WP Pica 10		
Printer	Qume	82052 WP Prestige Elite 12		
Printer	Qume	82053 BILINGUAL Courier 10		

Printer	Qume	82054 BILINGUAL Prestige Elite 12
Printer	Qume	82055 MULTI Pica 10
Printer	Qume	82056 UK Pica 10
Printer	Qume	82057 WP Orator 90% 10
Printer	Qume	82058 WP Prestige Pica 10
Printer	Qume	82059 WP Dual Gothic 12
Printer	Qume	82060 WP Courier Italic 12
Printer	Qume	82061 WP Bookface Academic 10
Printer	Qume	82062 A-N SYMBOL 1 Letter Gothic 12
Printer	Qume	82063 SYMBOL 2 Greek/Math 12
Printer	Qume	82064 ANSI OCR-A 10
Printer	Qume	82065 ANSI OCR-B 10
Printer	Qume	82066 BILINGUAL Letter Gothic 12
Printer	Qume	82067 MULTI Letter Gothic 12
Printer	Qume	82068 MULTI Courier 10
Printer	Qume	82069 WP Theme 11 Pt. PS
Printer	Qume	82070 WP Elite 12
Printer	Qume	82074 DEUTSCHLAND Pica 10
Printer	Qume	82075 SVERIGE/SUOMI 10
Printer	Qume	82076 ENGLAND Pica 10
Printer	Qume	82077 DANMARK/NORGE Pica 10
Printer	Qume	82078 FRANCE Pica 10
Printer	Qume	82079 SCHWEIZ Pica 10
Printer	Qume	82080 ITALIA Pica 10
Printer	Qume	82081 NEDERLAND Pica 10
Printer	Qume	82082 ESPANA Pica 10
Printer	Qume	82084 KATAKANA Gothic 10
Printer	Qume	82085 DEUTSCHLAND Courier 10
Printer	Qume	82087 ENGLAND Courtier 10
Printer	Qume	82088 ENGLAND Prestice Elite 12
Printer	Qume	82089 WP Letter Gothic L 12
Printer	Qume	82090 WP Gothic 15
Printer	Qume	82096 WP Polygo Pica 10
Printer	Qume	82098 ESA Pica L 10
Printer	Qume	82099 UKN Pica L 10
Printer	Qume	82150 DEUTSCHLAND Letter Gothic 12
Printer	Qume	82153 SVERIGE/SUOMI Prestige Elite 12
Printer	Qume	82154 DANMARK/NORGE Prestige Elite 12
Printer	Qume	82155 NASKH Arabic 10 Pt. PS
Printer	Qume	82156 FRANCE Prestige Elite 12
Printer	Qume	82157 DEUTSCHLAND Prestige Elite 12
Printer	Qume	82158 SCHWEIZ Prestige Elite 12
Printer	Qume	82160 NEDERLAND Prestige Elite 12
Printer	Qume	82161 ESPANA Prestige Elite 12
Printer	Qume	82162 WPS Thesis 10 Pt.
Printer	Qume	82164 LEGAL 2 Courier 10
Printer	Qume	82165 LEGAL 2 Prestige Elite 12
Printer	Qume	82166 LEGAL 2 Dual Gothic 12
Printer	Qume	82167 ASCII 96 Prestige Elite 12
Printer	Qume	82168 BILINGUAL Bookface Academic 10
Printer	Qume	82170 MULTI Bookface Academic 10
Printer	Qume	82180 WP Large Elite 12
Printer	Qume	82190 WPS Boldface 10 pt. PS
Printer	Qume	82191 WPS Boldface Italic PS

```
Printer    Qume        82193 WPS Arcadia 10 Pt. PS
Printer    Qume        82194 WPS Modern 10 Pt. PS
Printer    Qume        82195 WPS Title 10 Pt. PS
Printer    Qume        82196 WPS Essay Italic 10 Pt. PS
Printer    Qume        82197 SVERGI/SUOMI Letter Gothic 12
Printer    TI          Dot-Matrix 810              1995.00 1695.00
```

R

RS-232

Serial data ports are found on all but the most limited microcomputer systems. Ports, like port holes on a ship, are a microcomputer's windows on the outside world - the channels through which data flows in and out of the computer. In a parallel port, bits of data - 1s and 0s - move in and out of the computer together, in a parallel stream of eight.

In a serial port, data goes in and out of the computer one bit at a time. The bits are said to follow each other, like chapters in a soap opera, hence the name "serial".

Some things are more standardized than others in the microcomputer world. Fortunately, serial data transfer is relatively more standardized. In the 1960s, as timesharing developed in the US, it became desirable to have a standard method by which data terminals could attach to modems, which in turn could attach to mainframe computers.

After severals years of deliberation - much of which was spent studying the de-facto standards that had already developed in the industry - the Electronic Industries Association (EIA) came forth with its standard RS-232-C in October 1969. "RS" merely means "Recommended Standard"; "232" is the number of the standard; and "C" is the revision level, i.e., RS-232-C is the 3rd revision of the basic standard, the early versions being RS-232-A and RS-232-B. This US standard is close to ISO International Standard 2110-1972, although there are some pin assignment incompatibilities between the two.

[The DB-25]. In practical terms, saying that something has an RS-232 port means a 25-pin connector with 13 pins on top and 12 on the bottom. These connectors are called "DB-25s" and can be purchased at any Radio Shack store for about $5. Most terminals, modems, and computers have female connectors built into their frames; male-male DB-25s are required to connect them.

An RS-232 connection between a computer and, say, a terminal can have as few as 3 wires (transmit data, receive data, and ground: pins 2, 3, and 7). RS-232 cabling is thus by far the least expensive way to connect devices over distances of a few hundred feet. Ordinary inside telephone wire, which has 4 strands (red, green, yellow, black) can be used. RS-232 connections degrade above distances of 500 feet, depending on the baud rate; one should experiment, however, because connections of this length are possible.

[Getting the Pins Right]. Making RS-232 cables - or at least understanding how they are made - is a skill that most microcomputer owners should acquire. The basic situation is that there are 3 wires to connect to 2 DB-25s. On one wire, data bits are going in one direction. On the other, they are going in the oppsite direction. The 3rd wire is a reference ground for these two.

Consider the case of attaching a serial printer, like a Diablo or Qume, to a computer. The history of the RS-232 standard is important to remember. In it, devices - whatever they really are - fall into two classes, "modems" or data communications equipment (DCEs), and "terminals" or data terminal equipment (DTEs).

A terminal, or DTC, sends its data bits out on pin 2 of the DB-25 connector. If one takes a voltmeter and puts it on pins 2 and 7 of a sending device, the voltage on pin 2 should jump between 0 and +5 volts, with the speed of the jump dependent on the baud rate. A terminal expects to receive data on pin 3 of the DB-25.

Nearly all serial printers are set up to act like terminals, or DTCs. The computer port is usually - but not always - set up to act like a DCE. A DCE, by contrast, expects to find incoming data on pin 3 and puts outgoing data on pin 2. In short:

```
PIN       DTC (COMPUTER)                      DCE (PRINTER)
---       --------------                      --------------
 2        transmitted data -------------> received data
 3        received data <---------------- transmitted data
 7        ground <----------------------> ground
```

The symmetry, of course, is not accidental. This connection could be made with a "straight across" RS-232 cable - that is, one in which pin 1 of one connector is wired directly to pin 2 of the other. A "straight across" cable can be made using flat ribbon cable and the blue plastic slide-lock terminators available from Radio Shack for about $10; they sometimes cost upwards of $30 from computer stores.

If a printer is on receiving data, why hook up line 3 at all? Actually, most serial devices, even the so-called receive-only (RO), transmit a few characters back to the computer. ("RO" in printer company talk is the opposite of KSR, keyboard send-receive, and really means "keyboardless".) The ETX/ACK protocol, for example, which prevents the computer from transmitting faster than the printer can receive, has the printer send an ASCII "ACK" code to the computer over line 3 when its buffer is empty.

[Control Pins]. The 3-wire RS-232 connection described above has the simplest serial interface. Behind every serial interface, however, lies a UART, or Universal Asynchronous Receiver Transmitter. A UART is an integrated circuit designed to simplify building serial interfaces. Some UARTs commonly used on microcomputers, and their official names, are:

```
Intel 8251A
Signetics Programmable Communications Interface (PCI) 2651
Zilog Z-80 SIO Serial Input/Output Controller
Western Digital TR1602A Asynchronous Receiver/Transmitter
Motorola 6850
```

Anyone doing RS-232 interfacing should determine which UARTs are being used in their system and obtain the manufacturer's data sheets for the parts. Some time spent on reading connector schematics also helps.

Some UARTS, such as the Motorola 6850, require implementation of the so-called control lines on the RS-232 interface. These lines - pins 5, 6, 8 and 20 - are used to provide "hardware handshaking" between two RS-232 devices. RS-232 handshaking is similar to the "busy/acknowledge" handshaking done on parallel ports, and can simplify the software of RS-232 drivers.

Often, however, such coordination is unnecessary. At these times, it becomes necessary to defeat hardware handhaking by tying the control pins "high" - that is, to a +5-volt source. Thus the California Computer Products 7710 serial card for the Apple II will not work unless clear to send, pin 5, is tied to +5 volts. To connect the CCS card to a terminal or printer, for example, the following connector is needed at the CCS card end:

```
       CCS 7710
            2 <--------------- data to card
            3 ---------------> data from card

            4 ----|   CTS tied to RTS (always +5 V)
            5 ----|

            6 ----|   DTR tied to DSR (+5 V)
           20 ----|

            7 <--------------> ground
```

Note that by tying pins 2 to 3, it is possible to fool a UART into talking to itself. This item is called a loop-back connector and is useful in testing terminals. One should always be able to type and see characters on a working terminal with a loop-back connector on the back, because (1) the baud rate, (2) stop bits, and (3) parity setting for sending and receiving are almost always the same.

The full set of connections on an RS-232 connector can be considered as having the following levels of complexity:

PIN	NAME	FUNCTION	COMMENTS
GROUNDS:			
1	AA	PROTECTIVE GROUND	Bonded to chassis
7	AB	SIGNAL GROUND	Ground
DATA:			
2	BA	TRANSMITTED DATA	Data going to DCE

| 3 | BB | RECEIVED DATA | Data coming from DCE |

CONTROL SIGNALS:

4	CA	REQUEST TO SEND	Signal to DCE
5	CB	CLEAR TO SEND	Signal from DCE
6	CC	DATA SET READY	Signal from DCE
20	CD	DATA TERMINAL READY	Signal to DCE
22	CE	RING INDICATOR	From DCE
8	CF	RECEIVED LINE SIGNAL DETECTOR	From DCE
21	CG	SIGNAL QUALITY DETECTOR	From DCE
23	CH	DATA SIGNAL RATE (DTE)	To DCE
23	CI	DATA SIGNAL RATE SELECTOR (DCE)	From DCE

TIMING SIGNALS:

24	DA	TRANSMIT SIGNAL ELEMENT TIMING	
15	DB	TRANSMISSION SIGNAL ELEMENT TIMING (DCE SOURCE)	
17	DD	RECEIVER SIGNAL ELEMENT TIMING (DCE SOURCE)	

SECONDARY DATA:

| 14 | SBA | SECONDARY TRANSMITTED DATA | To DCE |
| 16 | SBB | SECONDARY RECEIVED DATA | From DCE |

SECONDARY CONTROL:

19	SCA	SECONDARY REQUEST TO SEND	
13	SCB	SECONDARY TRANSMITTED DATA	
12	SCF	SECONDARY RECEIVED LINE SIGNAL	

RESERVED OR UNASSIGNED:

9
10
25

[Asynchronous Serial Transmission]. Thus far, only the electrical connections for sending and receiving data have been described. Serial data can be sent over these lines 1 bit at a time, in one of two different ways: asynchronously or synchronously.

Of the two techniques, "asynch serial" is by far most commonly used on microcomputers. "Asynchronous" means without regard to time - that is, that characters are sent whenever they are ready. Clearly, this is the logical way for a device such as a terminal with a keyboard, to communicate, because the flow of characters from a typist's fingers is sporadic and, in computer time, slow.

For asynchronous transmission, however, some extra bits - "start" and "stop" bits - are needed to frame the character sent to the UART. The electrical line of a serial port is in the idle condition, or spacing, when its voltage is more positive (with respect to ground) than +3 volts. When the voltage goes low (below +3 volts), it is said to be marking. A mark is a "1", and a space is a "0".

In asynchronous transmission, a complete character is made up of:

```
             1 start bit, equal to 1;
             5, 6, 7 or 8 data bits, equal to 0 or 1;
             an optional parity bit, equal to 0 or 1;
             1, 1.5, or 2 stop bits, equal to 0.
```

The baud rate is the rate at which bits are sent over the interface. Baud
rates are set by initializing the UART chip from bootstrap software, and
sometimes by hardware switches. The most common baud rates are:

```
           110 - Teletype speed, 10 characters per second
           134.5 - a Western Union speed, stock exchange tickers
           300 - telephone communication, Bell 103A
          1200 - serial printers (Qume); Bell 212 modems
          2400 - computer-to-computer; some modems
          4800 - ditto
          9600 - ASCII terminals to computer, often top speed
        19,200 - sometimes available
```

Naturally the baud rate at which one UART sends should be the same at which
another UART is set to receive. Mismatching baud rates is one of the most
common problems of RS-232 connections failing to work. Usually, however, a
baud rate problem can be distinguished from a connection problem by the fact
that garbled characters will get through even at the wrong baud rate, whereas
nothing will get through if pins are connected wrong.

To understand UART operation, it is best to follow one through a cycle. The
receive data line (RxD) on a UART is normally in the spacing state, or high.
A falling edge on this line - that is, the start of a "1" - is taken as a
start bit, which indicates a character is coming.

Since it knows the baud rate, the UART knows how long to wait for the next
data bit. The UART has also been set to expect between 5 and 8 data bits.
These bits are "clocked in", least significant bit first, into an 8-bit
register. If less than 8 bits are expected, the high-order bits are filled
with 0s.

If a parity bit is expected, the bit after the last data bit is checked. Even
parity simply means that an even number of 1s have been received; odd parity,
than an odd number have. A "parity error" flag is set if parity is enabled
and does not match.

Past the parity stage - even, odd, or none - the UART expects the line to
return to its spacing, or 0, condition. Note that a "stop bit" is the same as
a quiet line. If the UART detects a 1 instead of a 0, it sets an error
condition called "framing error".

At this point, the character in the UART's 8-bit register is complete.
Usually, the UART has 2 such 8-bit registers, so one can be filled while the
other is offered to the computer. This is called "double buffering".
However, if a character is completely received off the line before the
computer gets around to reading, the character waiting is clobbered by the
new character, and an "overrun" error condition results.

[Synchronous Serial]. Synchronous serial data transfer differs considerably from asynchronous transfer. In the more familiar asynchronous serial format, the start and stop bits signal the receiving device (UART) that a character is coming, and they serve to signal when it is over. The bits that make up the character are clocked in relative to their position from the start bit according to the baud rate. Consider this typical 8-bit data, 1 start, 2 stop bit configuration:

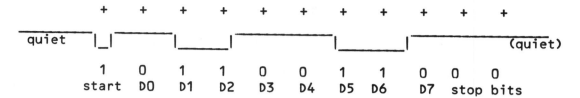

```
      +   +   +   +   +   +   +   +   +   +   +
  _____                      _____
 |quiet  |_| |‾‾‾‾|____|      |    |____|   |   (quiet)
      1   0   1   1   0   0   1   1   0   0   0
    start  D0  D1  D2  D3  D4  D5  D6  D7  stop bits
```

Here, the baud-rate clock comes into effect with the first stop bit, then ticks (symbolized by the + signs) to determine whether the voltage is high or low.

The problem with asynchronous serial communication is the overhead, the three extra bits of information needed with each byte of data. With 110 bits per second - at 110 baud - we are transmitting only 80 data bits, which is why we mentally divide baud rates by 10, not 8, to get the number of characters transmitted per second.

For large block transfers of data, as between computer mainframes, a more efficient system has been devised. Synchronous serial data transfer, like asynchronous serial transfer, needs few wires (unlike parallel transfers) and can work at long distance but communicates more efficiently if properly programmed.

In synchronous serial data transfers, there are no start or stop bits - merely a continuous stream of ones and zeros:

```
1 0 0 1 0 1 0 0 1 0 1 0 0 1 1 0 1 0 0 1 0 1 1 0 1 0 0 1 0 0 0 0
```

Although this stream looks almost meaningless, it actually contains a special bit pattern called the SYNC (or SYN) character. The sync character is a bit pattern of 0 1 1 0 1 0 0 1.

At the start of a sync serial transmission block, the sending device usually sends two sync characters. These must be recognized by the receiving device, which at that time should be in a state called the "hunt mode", in which it is on the lookout only for the sync character pattern.

The sync character is conceptually similar to the start bit. When the receiver finds the sync character, the UART locks in on the transmission and begins clocking the data bits for all bytes off the line, with no pause for start or stop bits. The difference in efficiency results from the fact that the data block clocked in can be several thousand bytes, a savings of, say, 3000 bits (1 start, 2 stop times 1000) at a cost of 16 (two sync characters). In most synchronous protocols, an ASCII End Of Transmission (EOT) character tells the receiver that the block is over.

There is one new problem, however. In asynchronous transmission, the transmitting computer sends when it has something to say. In synchronous transmission, it can't stop sending, because the receiving computer is depending on it. Thus a fill or pad character is necessary. Most synchronous UART chips will automatically send sync characters when the host computer cannot fill the transmitter buffer fast enough. (In receive mode, most UARTs strip these out automatically as well.)

[Control of a Synchronous Port]. The Motorola 6852 Synchronous Serial Data Adapter (SSDA) is a relatively typical synchronous serial chip, available on a California Computer Systems card (7712A) for the Apple II computer. A look at its control registers provides some clues as to how a sync serial interface is programmed.

The status word looks very much like an asynch serial status word. The following bits in the status word can be tested for these conditions:

```
BIT    CONDITION
---    ---------
 0 - received data is available to be read
 1 - transmitter register is available for data
 2 - one if Data Carrier Detect on (modem control)
 3 - one if Clear to Send on, else zero
 4 - transmitter is sending sync chars, not data
 5 - receiver overrun, not read before new byte in
 6 - parity error
 7 - interrupt request by SSDA
```

The SSDA has three different control words, which can be somewhat confusing. However, the types of control conditions that can be set include:

- word length, 6 to 8 bits long; even, odd, or no parity;
- send sync code on transmitter underflow;
- external sync mode (answer) or internal (originate);
- reset receiver or transmitter;
- strip sync characters from data stream automatically;
- interrupt on receive (or transmit buffer) data available;
- one or two character sync mode.

Various other UART chips, such as the Intel 8251, can be programmed for sync protocols. Consult the manufacturer's data sheet (normally available free from their Literature Departments - no, it's not college English).

[Bisync Protocol]. When two devices talk over a synchronous serial line, some protocol must be followed to ensure that the transmission is successful and complete. IBM's 2770 Bisync protocol is a (de-facto) industry standard. It goes like this:

[Transmitting Computer]. Wanting to send, sends ENQ
        (enquiry) to receiving computer.

[Receiving Computer]. Being ready to receive, sends
        a Data Link Escape (DLE).

[Transmitting Computer]. Sends STX (start of text),

the actual data, an ETB (end of block), and
two cyclic redundancy check (CRC) codes.

[Receiving Computer]. Sends DLE 1 indicating that
the CRC sum checks and an odd total of
blocks have been received.

[Transmitting Computer]. Sends STX, block, ETB as
above. If last block, ETX is sent instead
of ETB.

[Receiving Computer]. Sends acknowledgement saying
the last block has been received successfully.

[Transmitting Computer]. Sends end-of-transmission
(EOT) character and disconnects.

[Receiving Computer]. Receiving EOT, disconnects.

For more details, consult IBM System Reference Library Publication General
Information - Binary Synchronous Communications, File TP-09, Order No. GA27-
3004.2.

A firm that offers microcomputer data communications software is Winterhalter
& Associates, Inc. (3825 N. Zeeb Road, Dexter, Michigan 48130, 313-426-3029
or 313-665-5582). They advertise software that allows microcomputers to talk
the protocols of machines by DEC and Xerox (X.25); IBM 2770, 2780, 3270, 3741,
3780 (Bisync); and IBM 3767 (SDLC/SNA).

[RS-449]. The US government never liked the RS-232-C standard, primarily
because it combines electrical, functional, and mechanical characteristics.
In an effort to supercede RS-232-C, the US government, in a Federal Standard
published July 24, 1979, adopted the RS-449 interface, with an implementation
date of June 1, 1980. In theory, all "RS-232-like" terminal equipment bought
by the government after that time should be RS-449 compatible.

RS-449 separates the electrical from mechanical and functional specifications.
The interface calls for a 37-pin connector, plus a 9-pin secondary channel
connector. One competitor to RS-449 is the international networking standard,
X.21, developed by the International Telegraph and Telephone Consultative
Committee (CCITT). X.21 in theory uses a hardware interface called X.24, but
few people know what X.24 should look like. By default, a 15-pin connector is
now generally associated with X.21.

S

S-100 Computers

The S-100 bus has the singular honor of being the original microcomputer bus. A bus is a sort of public transportation for electrical signals: signals placed on a microcomputer bus are available to any card on that bus. While bus systems as found on the Apple II, IBM PC, and other computers add manufacturing cost to a computer, bus arrangements allow for far more flexible computers.

Credit for the design of the S-100 bus goes to Ed Roberts of MITS, the Alberquerque, NM, firm that introduced the Altair microcomputer in January 1975. Compared to Digital Equipment Corporation (DEC), which spent millions of dollars designing, testing, and redesigning its "Q-Bus" for its minis, Roberts and company just tossed together the S-100 bus. Surprisingly, once in the field, the S-100 bus had no more real technical drawbacks than a highly engineered bus like the Q-bus.

A board designed to fit into an S-100 bus has on it 100 connectors: 50 on one side of the printed circuit card, and 50 on the other. Pins 1 and 2 on this bus contain unregulated power (+8 and +16 volts, respectively), as do their partner pins on the other side of the board, 51 and 52. Pins 50 and 100 are ground. In between are data and address pins, clock lines, and a variety of other control lines.

A complete S-100 bus computer is typically made up of: (1) a large, flat motherboard with 12 slots or edge connectors for S-100 cards; (2) a power supply on the motherboard; (3) a CPU card with a Z-80, 8080, or other processor (few S-100 systems use the 6502 or 6800 microprocessors); (4) RAM memory cards, typically 16K or, more recently, 64K cards; (5) a serial communications port, to attach to an industry-standard ASCII terminal; (6) a floppy disk controller card.

The S-100 bus became a de-facto industry standard after its introduction by MITS. A second S-100 bus computer, the IMSAI, was introduced by a San Francisco Bay-area company of the same name in 1976. A number of companies with names like Parasitic Engineering began offering S-100 bus compatible replacement cards for Altari and IMSAI products, and the microcomputer

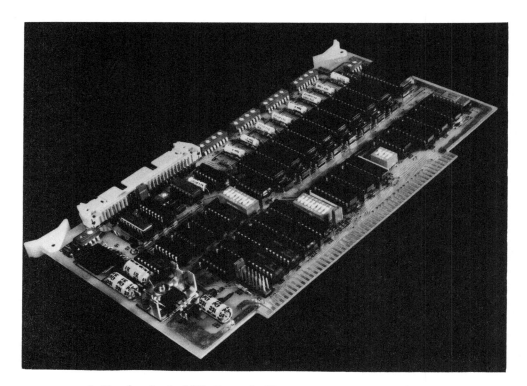

A Typical S-100 Board (Intersystems ADDA)

industry was born.

[The S-100 Industry].   Standards, like the de-facto S-100 bus standard, are usually very good for industries as a whole but often very bad for individual companies. When S-100 bus computer systems reached their peak in 1978-79 (in terms of percentage of new systems sold), MITS and IMSAI were on the ropes in bankruptcy and were soon followed by Processor Technology, maker of the SOL, another popular S-100 system in its day. At the same time, hundreds of small companies were making S-100 boards, ranging from bread-and-butter memory and processor boards to exotic video display processors and other devices.

In retrospect, the S-100 bus was, and to some extent still is, the first great "open system", around which independent designers could work and feel comfortable that there would be a large enough market for their products. The Apple II computer eclipsed the S-100 bus as such a "platform" for design in 1980-81, only to be eclipsed itself later by the IBM PC.

In 1978, a group began meeting to create a standard, now IEEE 696, for the S-100 bus. The proposed standard was published in Computer magazine (5855 Naples Plaza, Long Beach, CA) in its July 1979 issue. The politics of the S-100 bus standard are interesting: it was strongly backed by S-100 board companies like Morrow Designs and Godbout/CompuPro but got little cooperation from S-100 mainframe manufacturers such as North Star, Vector Graphic, and Cromemco. These no doubt felt that the existence of a standard could hurt them by encouraging consumers to mix 'n' match boards, rather than staying with brand products. (Use of technical incompatibility for account control, a practice pioneered by IBM and DEC, is nothing new in the computer industry.)

IEEE 696 has one other interesting feature: a provision for 16-bit and multiple processor operation. These features alone guarantee the S-100 bus several extra years of life in custom, high-performance OEM systems, in a nitch between the popular but inflexible micros and the minis.

In 1982, the most important S-100 bus computer companies were:

- Vector Graphic (Thousand Oaks, CA). Started in 1976 in a spare bedroom, Vector Graphic in 1982 was a $35 million per year company with 350 employees, and publicly traded stock. Vector Graphic early specialized in S-100-based word processing and business systems, generally using CP/M. The company now offers an 8/16-bit system, the Vector 4, which has both a Z-80B and Intel 8088.

- Cromemco (Palo Alto, CA). Cromemco, one of the early S-100 companies, has a reputation as the Hewlett-Packard of micros, offering scientific and laboratory systems. In 1982, in a departure from its usual line, Cromemco brought out a low-cost bundled system.

- North Star (San Leandro, CA). North Star introduced the "Advantage" single-board computer in 1981, but continues to sell its S-100 Horizon. The Horizon is known as a reliable machine (there is apparently one on every US nuclear submarine - something to do with sonar) and has a good BCD version of BASIC.

- Morrow Designs (San Leandro, CA). For many years a maker of S-100 boards, George Morrow's company now has a line of S-100 products as well as an integrated system, the Micro Decision, which at $1790 competes with the Osborne I and other low-cost, Z-80-based bundled systems.

- Alpha Micro (Irvine, CA). One of the 1st 16-bit micros, the Alpha Micro continues as a larger, minicomputer-like business computer.

- CompuPro (Oakland, CA). As with Morrow, a provider of S-100 boards, Bill Godbout's CompuPro now has its own computer.

- Seattle Computer (Seattle, WA). Seattle Computer has a very fast 8086 system and makes specialized 16-bit S-100 memory boards.

[North Star]. North Star was started in 1976 by Mark Greenberg and Charles Grant and for a time did business out of Greenberg's Berkeley, CA, garage as "Kentucky Fried Computers" (this was not long after release of "Kentucky Fried Movie"). The company's first product was a floating-point S-100 board, which is still available. Its second important product was its "Micro Disk System" (MDS), one of the first disk controllers for Shugart 5-1/4-inch drives. This product was very popular for use with the Processor Technology Sol computer, which had available only a full-sized 8-inch floppy.

In mid-1977, North Star brought out its "Horizon" computer. The Horizon appeared at the same time as a number of machines - Cromemco and Vector Graphic, to name two that have stayed around - but managed to carve a niche anyway. Both North Star and Cromemco were somehow "scientific" machines (this old distinction, never really appropriate, dates back to the pre-360 days when IBM had one line of "scientific" computers like the 7094, and another line of "business" computers like the 1130).

The Cromemco, however, was a "big" machine: it was physically bigger and had a metal case that made it weigh a ton; it had flanges with sharp edges for rack mounting making it need a wall and not a desktop and also making it clumsy to carry around; and it used 8-inch PerSci drives, not 5-1/4-inch floppies, and was generally more of a lab and industrial machine. The Horizon, by contrast, appealed more to "micro"-computer types.

Significantly, North Star wrote its own version of BASIC, which gave the computer a certain appeal to programmers. North Star's experience with disk drives was extremely important; its hard-sector minifloppies worked wonderfully well in an era when other disks, especially Cromemco's PerSci drives, were always flaking out. The Computer Cookbook has installed North Star systems that have been in round-the-clock operation for several years. By 1980, North Star was shipping some 1000 Horizons per month and in the spring of 1981 moved to expanded facilities out of Berkeley's "flatland" and into San Leandro. At the end of 1981, there was an installed base of about 40,000 Horizon systems.

On the negative side, North Star has always tended to "go it alone" in the microcomputer industry. The company was very late (1980) to embrace CP/M as an operating system and has resisted efforts to standardize the S-100 bus (the Horizon bus is more incompatible than most). North Star also came late to computer graphics, not bringing out its "Advantage" desktop until 1981.

In 1981, North Star made serious moves to consolidate and round out its Horizon line and also, of course, introduced its desktop computer with graphics, the "Advantage". The consolidation process involved making the 64K RAM, 2-quad drive system standard, discouraging sale of systems with (1) old 32- and 16-K RAM boards, and (2) double-density drives.

The new products, and of course the "TSS" software packages, were designed to make the Horizon a multi-user small business computer. The new 64K RAM board was designed for bank-switching among users and for the 4-port serial board to hook them up. The new disk drives and cartridge tape back-up system were also introduced primarily to support this configuration.

The North Star line is interesting from the OEM point of view. North Star's use of a 5-Mbyte Winchester in the space of a 2nd floppy makes for a very well-integrated package, especially on the Advantage. For applications requiring mass storage and graphics, the Advantage has it all in a nice desktop package - plus better computation speed than, say, the Apple III with the ProFile hard disk.

North Star is located at 14440 Catalina Street, San Leandro, CA 94577, 415-357-8500; their Telex is 910-366-7001. (For the name of an authorized dealer, call toll-free 800-447-4700, or 800-322-4400 in Illinois, or

800-447-0890 in Alaska and Hawaii.) The International North Star User's Group (INSUA), not directly affiliated with the company, publishes a newsletter called the Compass. Dues are $10 a year. Address: Box 1318, Antioch, CA 94509.

[S-100 Board and Price Guide]. The left-hand column is the generic name of the product (e.g., video monitors) or the target system (Apple II, TRS-80 Model III). The 2nd column is the actual manufacturer; note that for some systems (e.g., the IBM) there are many non-IBM vendors of compatible products. Field 3 provides as much identifying and descriptive information about the product as space permits, including the manufacturer's part number, if available. The 1st price given is the suggested list price; the 2nd price is the lowest observed discount price or sometimes the dealer or wholesale price. These should be used together to establish a high-low range for actual prices.

SYSTEM	MANUFACTURER	DESCRIPTION/IDENTIFICATION	LIST	DISCOUNT
S-100	CCS	16K static RAM 2016A 450ns	349.95	180.00
S-100	CCS	16K static RAM 2016B 300ns	389.95	190.00
S-100	CCS	16K static RAM 2016C 200ns	399.95	210.00
S-100	CCS	32K static RAM 2032A 450ns	710.00	603.00
S-100	CCS	32K static RAM 2032B 300ns	750.00	637.00
S-100	CCS	32K static RAM 2032C 200ns	810.00	688.00
S-100	CCS	64K dynamic RAM 2065A	700.00	595.00
S-100	CCS	CPU Z-80 2810A +serial	300.00	255.00
S-100	CCS	Disk controller 2422 w/CPM	400.00	340.00
S-100	CCS	Mainframe 2200A 12-slot	400.00	340.00
S-100	Compu/Time	Clock calendar board 102A	150.00	128.00
S-100	Computalker	Speech synthesizer board CT-1	525.00	446.00
S-100	Cromemco	CS-3 computer 2 8" drives	11190.00	9511.00
S-100	Cromemco	CS-3 computer 8" drive	7995.00	6795.00
S-100	Cromemco	Floppy 2 5" DS tandon	1295.00	1100.00
S-100	Cromemco	Floppy 5" DS Tandon	595.00	505.00
S-100	Cromemco	Floppy 5" SS in case	495.00	420.00
S-100	Cromemco	Floppy 8" DS PerSci	3695.00	3140.00
S-100	Cromemco	Hard disk 11 meg	6695.00	5945.00
S-100	Cromemco	Hard disk 22 meg	11995.00	10195.00
S-100	Cromemco	Motherboard & cage 8 slot	195.00	165.00
S-100	Cromemco	Motherboard & cage 12 slot	245.00	208.00
S-100	Cromemco	Motherboard & cage 21 slot	395.00	335.00
S-100	Cromemco	Z-2 HGS graphics system	14500.00	12325.00
S-100	Cromemco	Z-2 system	995.00	845.00
S-100	Cromemco	Z-2 w/hard disk	9995.00	8495.00
S-100	Hayes	Modem 103A	399.00	339.00
S-100	Heuristics*	Speech Recognizer Mod 50	399.00	339.00
S-100	IMSAI*	Computer 8080 w/MPU P/S	800.00	800.00
S-100	Ithaca	16K static RAM 250ns	495.00	420.00
S-100	Ithaca	64K dynamic RAM 250 ns	995.00	845.00
S-100	Ithaca	A/D D/A 8 bit	495.00	420.00
S-100	Ithaca	CPU Z-80 4MHz	395.00	335.00
S-100	Ithaca	EPROM board to 64K	295.00	250.00
S-100	Ithaca	Floppy cont SS DD DMA	495.00	420.00
S-100	Ithaca	I/O board 4P 2S INT	445.00	378.00

S-100	Morrow	16K static RAM "SuperRam"	319.00	271.00
S-100	Morrow	16K static RAM "Memory Mas"	389.00	330.00
S-100	Morrow	24K static RAM "Memory Mas"	499.00	424.00
S-100	Morrow	32K static RAM "SuperRam"	649.00	551.00
S-100	Morrow	Floppy cont 2D "Disk Jockey"	399.00	339.00
S-100	Morrow	Floppy cont Disk jockey	229.00	194.00
S-100	Morrow	Hard cont 10MB	695.00	590.00
S-100	Morrow	Hard cont 26MB	695.00	590.00
S-100	Morrow	I/O "Mult"	329.00	279.00
S-100	Morrow	I/O "Switchboard"	259.00	220.00
S-100	Morrow	Motherboard 12 slot	149.00	126.00
S-100	Morrow	Motherboard 20 slot	199.00	169.00
S-100	Morrow	Motherboard 8 slot "Wonderbuss"	124.00	105.00
S-100	Mountain	Clock 100,000 day	350.00	297.00
S-100	Mullen	Extender board w/logic probe	79.00	67.00
S-100	Mullen	Relay/Opto Isolator	179.00	152.00
S-100	N*	FPB-A (floating point board)	399.00	
S-100	N*	HDS-18	5374.00	
S-100	N*	HDS-BU	3895.00	
S-100	N*	HRAM-32 (1K bank selectable)	599.00	
S-100	N*	HRAM-64 (1K bank selectable)	1099.00	
S-100	N*	HRZ-1Q-64K-HD-18	9270.00	
S-100	N*	HRZ-1Q-64K-HD-5	6695.00	
S-100	N*	HRZ-2D-64K	4195.00	
S-100	N*	HRZ-DRV-D (double den drive)	569.00	
S-100	N*	HRZ-DRV-Q (quad den drive)	799.00	
S-100	N*	HSIO-4 (4 port serial board)	349.00	
S-100	N*	Horizon 1-User Op System	149.00	104.00
S-100	N*	Horizon 1Q-HD5	4999.00	3499.00
S-100	N*	Horizon HD5 upgrade	2399.00	1679.00
S-100	N*	Horizon Multi-User Op Sys	349.00	244.00
S-100	N*	MDS-CTRL (floppy controller)	565.00	
S-100	N*	MOTHER BD (Horizon 12-slot)	473.00	
S-100	N*	ZPB-A (Z80A processor board)	325.00	
S-100	Newtech	Music Board Model 6	100.00	85.00
S-100	Potomac	Modem 103A	399.00	339.00
S-100	SD	CPU Z80	384.00	326.00
S-100	SD	Floppy CONT	507.00	430.00
S-100	SD	I/O 4S	764.00	649.00
S-100	SD	Singleboard Z80 4MHz	471.00	400.00
S-100	SD	VDB IO-MAP 80X24	556.00	472.00
S-100	SDM	CPU CMOS 1802	375.00	318.00
S-100	SDM	Floppy cont 8010	140.00	119.00
S-100	SSM	CPU 8080	252.00	214.00
S-100	SSM	CPU Z80	344.00	292.00
S-100	SSM	EPROM programmer 2708/2716	265.00	225.00
S-100	SSM	I/O 2P	99.00	84.00
S-100	SSM	I/O 2P 2S	290.00	246.00
S-100	SSM	Music board	349.00	296.00
S-100	SSM	Prototype board	99.00	84.00
S-100	SSM	VDB IO-MAP	269.00	228.00
S-100	SSM	VDB mem-map	242.00	205.00
S-100	Scion	Graphics board "MicroAngelo"	1095.00	930.00
S-100	Series1	CPU 4MHz Z-80	245.00	208.00

S-100	Tarbell	Cassette I/O	175.00	148.00
S-100	Tarbell	Floppy DD	495.00	420.00
S-100	Tarbell	Floppy SD	325.00	276.00

[S-100 Video Display Boards]. Video display boards or VDBs are best thought of as stripped-down parasitic ASCII terminals that take their power supply and sometimes their memory from a microcomputer host rather than incur the hardware overhead required to duplicate these items in a stand-alone device. This saving on hardware can make VDBs much cheaper than terminals (although the mass production of low-price $995 terminals, such as the ADM-3 and SOROC 120, has made this much less true than it once was). Price aside, the key differences between VDBs and terminals are:

- Video Output. Although an ASCII terminal contains its own tube, a video display board needs its own monitor. Most VDBs offer standard composite video and ground as their output. This can be good or bad, depending on the application. For an additional information screen on a system, a VDB plus monitor is all that is required, there being no point in paying for an additional keyboard on a terminal. A video monitor may be more desirable anyway: terminals, for example, can't be hung from the ceiling the way monitors can.

- Fast Display. Most VDBs use the host computer's memory for their character storage. Although this typically eats ups 4K of the computer's RAM, it has the advantage of speed - a VBD's screen display can change with the computer's memory speed and usually gives the impression of being instantaneous. Word processors allowing insertion and deletion are especially nice on memory-mapped VDBs, because no waiting for page rewrites is required. This speed can also come in handy in time-critical systems where buffering terminal output is a nuisance or impossible.

- Character Sets. Nearly every VBD has on it a character generator chip and a character set defined in PROM. By changing PROMs, or having your own burned, custom character sets can be used, allowing Greek letters, APL symbols, etc. This makes VDBs very useful in engineering, foreign language, and other applications.

[Real VDBs]. The Computer Cookbook is familiar with the following VBDs:

- SD Systems VSB-8024. (SD Systems, PO Box 28810, Dallas, TX 75228, 214-271-4667). This video display board was designed for use in SD System's terminal-less S-100 computer systems. The board generates a 24 by 80 display and has its own on-board memory. It has a keyboard port. Recent price, $525.

- Matrox ALTR-2480. (Matrox Electronic Systems, Ltd., 2795 Bates Rd., Montreal, Quebec, Canada H3S 1B5, 514-481-6838). This board can be used to provide alphanumeric video to Matrox's ALT-256 or ALT-512 graphic display boards or as a stand-alone memory-mapped display. The Matrox board has its own 4K of RAM on the board and has no keyboard connectors. Recent list price, $295.

- SSM VB3. (SSM, formerly Solid State Music, 2116 Walsh Ave., Santa Clara, CA 92050, 408-727-4707). As with the SD Systems board, the SSM board has a keyboard port on board is intended for use as a naked terminal. The board can display up to 256 special characters and has a 160 by 204 resolution for graphics. Recent list price, $565.

- The Screen Splitter. (Micro Diversions, Inc., 8455-D Tyco Rd., Vienna, VA 22180, 703-827-0888). Micro Diversion's Screen Splitter was designed primarily for use in that company's package word processing system but is available as a separate board.

- Vector. (Vector Graphic, Westlake Village, CA 91362, 213-991-2302). Vector Graphic uses its VDB in its complete computer system and even builds a shell around it to make it look like an ASCII terminal. The board is available separately.

[How They Work]. The Matrox ALTR-2480 is a typical memory-mapped video display board. The board must be installed on a 4K boundary of the host computer's RAM, set by jumpers on the board. The 16-bit address of a character to be displayed has the following composition:

BBBBRRRR RCCCCCCC

where BBBB bits are the 4K RAM boundary, the five RRRRR bits determine the row 0-23 on the display screen, and the seven CCCCCCC bits determine the column 0-127. Actually, only columns 0-79 can be displayed, the extra 48 bytes on each line are free space. (A similar situation, incidentally, exists on the Apple II computer.) If the board were installed in the F block of memory, the letter A is placed on the upper-left corner of the screen in row 1, column 2 by writing the ASCII code for A (65 decimal) into the memory location with the following 16-bit address:

11110000 100000002

or F082 hex.

[Enhancement]. Nearly all video display systems use one bit, usually bit 7, of the ASCII code to determine if the display should be enhanced that is, set to one of the following modes: (1) blinking; (2) reverse (black characters on white background); (3) underlined, or (4) some combinations of these. Although the Matrox board has no underlining, it uses bit 7 to select normal, inverse, or blinking video, and bits 6-0 select the character to be displayed, as per the character generator table. A special enhancement mode can be jumpered that selects only 64 ASCII characters, but it gives software control over four simultaneous enhancement modes: normal (0,0); inverse (0,1); blink (1,0); and blink inverse (1,1).

[External Sync]. One of the advantages of using a VDB is the ability to mix the output video signal with other video. In particular, the Matrox ALT-2480 provides the following outputs on a 16-pin header:

PIN	SIGNAL	COMMENTS
1	DTC	dot clock (bi-directional)
2	HR	horizontal reset (bi)
3	VR*	vertical reset (invert, bi)
4	GC	graphic clock (for old 256 boards)
5	CSYNC*	composite sync
6	+5V	
7	HR*	horizontal reset
8	GND	ground
9	LVID	logic video (TTL level)
10		
11	VB*	vertical blank (invert)
12	HB*	horizontal blank (invert)
13	SV	vertical sync
14	SH	horizontal sync
15	ES	external sync
16	CVDO	composite video

These can be used to interface the character generator board into an external video system for titling and other functions. For example, the board can be synched with an external video source by adding a PLL-01 phase lock loop model, which takes the external sync signal and composite video as input, and which drives DTC, VR, and SH on the board as output. The composite video coming off the board is then the original video with characters superimposed.

[The SD Systems VDB-8024]. In contrast to the Matrox ALTR-2480, which is something of a plain-Jane display board, the SD Systems VDB-8024 board was designed to take over many of the functions usually associated with ASCII terminals. The VDB has a Z-80 on the board and, unlike other memory-mapped video display systems, uses I/O ports in a way that makes it look very much like a serial terminal device. To write to the board, an ASCII character is written to port 1, if the board is ready. The status is read from port 0.

Software Publishing

Despite increasing amounts of venture capital, the personal computer software publishing industry remains a difficult business in which to turn a profit, although the long-range prospect for the personal computer software market is excellent. A hybrid industry sprung to life in the 1980s, software publishing requires traditional, print-oriented houses to cope with the baffling complexity of computers, while exposing mainframe and minicomputer software operations to the unfamiliar pitfalls of the mass market.

Current trends in personal computer software publishing include:

(1) The emergence of a software-driven personal computer market

that will further strengthen the dominant position enjoyed by the major manufacturers: Apple, Tandy, and Atari. These companies, which emerged from the original hardware scramble with a large base of users, now enjoy the fact that new software is developed first for their machines, which increases their attractiveness to customers. Personal computer manufacturers outside this happy circle, such as Commodore and Texas Instruments, will continue to fall behind unless they make a significant commitment to closing the software gap for their machines.

(2) Despite the growing sales of personal computers, software publishers face serious economic, legal and technical challenges to viability. Personal computer software, once a cottage industry, now requires labor-intensive, high-price programming; expensive packaging; and aggressive advertising and marketing support. Cassette tapes, once the primary means of distributing personal computer software, are rapidly giving way to more expensive floppy disk distribution and to yet more expensive ROMs.

(3) As software costs increase, however, software piracy and the informal duplication of programs continues to hold down revenue for software publishers. Legal solutions, based on either patent or copyright law, to the piracy problem are nonexistent or inadequate. Technical solutions to software protection exist, but all have economic side effects at times worse than the disease.

[Publishing on Floppies]. Floppy disks are now the dominant mode of delivery in personal computer software publishing. Publishing on disk presents a variety of problems.

The first set of problems derives from the fragility of the floppy disk medium itself. Although floppy disks can often be used for years without wearing out, it is relatively easy to destroy them, either by physical abuse (cigarette burns, coffee spills, bending, folding, or other forms of mutilation) or by inadvertent erasure of their magnetic field.

As a result, there is a general desire in the field to have back up or duplicate copies of most important disks - in particular, any disk that one pays good money for. Most manufacturers, for example, advise users to immediately copy the system diskettes on which they receive their disk operating systems (DOS) and BASIC language interpreters and then to put the original disks away.

Furthermore, as programs are developed, and data files built up, good programming practice requires that backups be made constantly to prevent the loss of valuable program changes and data. Such a loss can entail hundreds of hours of time lost for reconstruction of programs or data.

In an effort to thwart pirates, however, most personal computer software publishers distribute uncopyable disks. Although most publishers have replacement policies for registered owners - send the old disk in, get a new one at cost - users of these programs are rightfully nervous about losing their programs or, more seriously, valuable data. MicroPro International, publisher of WordStar, a word-processing program that runs on larger microcomputers operating under CP/M, attempted a no backup policy on WordStar version 2.0, released August 1980, but found its users in revolt, so they quickly offered WordStar version 2.1 with the security feature removed.

In another instance, in late 1980, Lee Meador, of Arlington, TX, introduced a program to the personal computer marketplace called VCOPY, which was designed to make one backup copy - only - of Personal Software's popular VisiCalc financial modeling package. Meador argues that executives using VisiCalc can't afford the interruption caused by losing their disks, hence the justification for the copying program. (Personal Software, in a counter move, later announced that a registered user of VisiCalc who had sent in his warranty card could receive a backup disk for $30.)

[Piracy]. While VCOPY was, in fact, a friendly copying program (making only one copy that included the user's serial number) in late 1980 several programs, including "Locksmith" and "Nibbles Away", came onto the personal computer market. These were designed to copy anything, and could be used for illegal duplication.

An analysis of disk copying incidents shows that most disk copying takes places in the following situations: (1) small-scale copying between friends, resulting in perhaps one or two bootleg copies; (2) larger-scale copying by computer clubs, resulting in perhaps 10 or more copies, but without serious commercial motive; (3) copying by dealers, with the intent to under-report sales and keep profits to themselves; (4) commercial frauds or mix-ups, which usually involve lack of clear title to the software in question, and (5) international piracy, where programs are sold abroad unlicensed and the situation is complicated by language barriers and the distances involved.

Of these types of duplication, (1) and (2) are clearly the most important but at the same time the most difficult to pin down. Informal copying of disks by friends is by nature unpublicized but probably results in the greatest revenue loss for software publishers. Computer club copying is, in a sense, a slightly more organized version of such copying among friends, in which there is no blatant commercial motive.

In the other categories, a number of cases of software piracy have been publicized in the last year. A typical incident of dealer piracy emerged in Tucson in early 1981, in which Management Control Systems agreed to install a Dynabyte DB8/4 computer and various software for a small business. The computer did not work on delivery, and upon investigation the businessman discovered that the software provided was apparently illegally copied. (The manuals delivered were also Xerox copies.) When traced by the original software houses, none proved legitimate. In its defense, Management Control Systems claimed it had only delivered demonstration programs to its customer and would deliver licensed programs upon receipt of final payment, which was pending. The case is still in court.

Another incident, involving a confused rights situation, took place in November 1980, involving Compu-Net, a small firm based in Mt. Vernon, IA, which apparently purchased, from two mysterious gentlemen from CA exclusive rights to programs authored and owned by three other firms. In an international incident in 1979, Nestar Systems of San Jose, CA, has charged that its programmer's Toolkit ROM for the Apple was being illegally duplicated and sold in Europe. This is one of the few incidents reported of ROM piracy. In Japan, Lifeboat Associates has had a Japanese company, Kohjinsha, Ltd., sell its products and even copy its ad without any licensing or other agreement.

[Copy Protection of Disks]. In general, any disk on any computer can be copied. The true question is not absolute protection but the cost-effectiveness of copy protection. (One On the Apple computer, disks can be protected from duplication by the Apple's Disk Operating System (DOS) by one of several techniques. The most common involves introducing a false cyclic redundancy check (CRC) error on one or more of the disk tracks, which causes the simple disk copy program distributed with the Apple II to halt. The Apple II DOS, in short, thinks wrongly that it has a bad diskette and fails to copy it.

However, so-called bit copy programs, notably Locksmith, by Omega Software Products, Inc., copy disks one bit at a time, without regard to the CRC check. Bit copy programs are far from infalable, because they are highly sensitive to differences in the rotational speed of the disk drives involved in the copying operation. However, they do allow copying of a number of disks that were previously considered uncopyable by their publishers.

Although legal action against the authors of the bit copy programs appears impossible, informal pressure by software publishers led a number of microcomputer magazines to drop ads for Locksmith.

In general, the most sensible recommendations for publishing on floppy disks are: (1) if possible on a given machine, uncopyable disks should be distributed, which will discourage most amateur users from distributing copies to friends, etc.; (2) to quell dissatisfaction over backup, a liberal replacement policy - send in your old disk, get a replacement free - should be maintained; which entails registration of copies and some administrative expense; (3) manuals and other packaging should be used to encourage users to buy the original, not a copy. Color printing and packaging are very useful tools to this end.

Extremely expensive ($1000 plus) software packages can be protected by special hardware key devices. This involves distribution with the software of a hardware device, typically a small plug-in board. One such device, used by the Technical Analysis Group of New Orleans, which sells expensive ($1500) stock market and commodities analysis software, is an Apple II mini-card, which plugs into slot 2 of the 8 peripheral slots on the Apple. The card contains encoded into it a serial number that is periodically checked by the Technical Analysis Group program, which will not run if the card is not in place. The TAG group software is distributed on disk. These devices work well but generally require the design and manufacture of a custom PC board at a cost of at least $50 per unit.

[Apple's Special Delivery Software (SDS) Program]. Apple Computer Co., in addition to its authorized Apple software offerings, began in late 1980 to act as a distributor for software developed and tested by third parties. Apple has taken extreme measures to distance itself from the SDS software and includes an elaborate disclaimer with each program. Apple's rationale is this: it wants to increase the amount and quality of Apple software on the market without, however, involving its own in-house software development team, which is presumably overburdened.

Apple's initial rules for the SDS program are an interesting mix of agreements, as follows: (1) SDS programs are distributed only on disks, and require the Apple II Auto-Start ROM to operate; the disks run when plugged into the Apple, but the programs on them cannot be copied or modified; (2) customers are given a license agreement that provides that the programs may be used for personal use on a single computer; a different license entirely is needed for resale of the programs; (3) buyers may return any SDS software package with 7 days of receipt, for any reason; (4) SDS disks are copy protected; in theory, this prevents disks from being copied and returned or passed around; and (5) the physical floppy disk is guaranteed for 90 days, unless damaged by the customer or the computer.

In some sense, Apple's new program is simply an effort to enter the mail-order software market, without, at the same time, putting Apple's reputation and resources at risk. Whether Apple can do this remains to be seen. The SDS program also signals the growing importance of a new type of naive software buyer who merely wants put a disk into the drive, turn on the computer, and have the program run.

In the minicomputer industry, most computers have software-readable serial numbers built into the machine. When a program is purchased, it is modified before shipping to run only on the machine for which it was licensed.

Although this is a possible approach to the problem of software piracy, it seems unlikely that any single microcomputer manufacturer will be the first to design such a device into its machines due to risk of slowing down sales through lack of software. A trade industry agreement, under the auspices of the Microcomputer Industry Trade Association (MITA) or similar group, is more likely to spur the development of some standard hardware for this purpose, but in any event, given the anticipated 5-10 year lifespan of the microcomputer designs now on the market, hardware serial numbers are not likely to be widespread before the late 1980s, if then.

Although floppy disk and ROM technology will remain dominant for many years to come, several developments on the horizon may change software distribution techniques and software publishing.

In general, floppy disks, sometimes grouped with rotating memories, may give way to bubble memories, which are essentially chips that retain their memory after power is removed. Unlike ROMs, which in some aspects they closely resemble, bubbles can be written on and can be mastered on demand, giving them this important advantage of floppies.

However, bubble memory has consistently been more promising than real. Bubbles are about 5 or 6 years behind where many once predicted the technology to be, and Texas Instruments, once the leader in the bubble race, dropped its entire bubble memory effort in 1981. Intel, however, and several other U.S. and Japanese firms remain in the bubble dance, with Intel guaranteeing price reductions along an attractive curve in an effort to encourage systems designs that use its bubbles.

[Teledelivery]. Also promising as a delivery method but not yet significant is so-called teledelivery of software - namely, the transmission of software from one computer to another using telephone lines or, potentially, coaxial cable. CompuServe, operator of the MicroNet personal computer network, has for some time had some simple systems programs on its mainframe computers that can be sold to owners of Apples and other machines that log onto its system.

Unfortunately, teledelivery of software not only reproduces all the problems of hardware compatibility from which disk distribution now suffers, but creates the additional, nontrivial problem of error-free transmission. If executable object programs, as opposed to source programs, are to be transmitted, they must be entirely free of errors, because a single mistaken bit is sufficient to cause the received program to crash when the buyer attempts to run it. CompuServe and several other firms have complicated checksum and error-correcting code programs to combat this problem, but it remains serious. Furthermore, transmission costs to personal computers are still high, especially at the low baud rates (300 typical) at which most of them operate.

Teledelivery may piggyback on other commercial developments, however, in particular distribution of digital audio music, especially over cable. Here the error correction problem will remain, and in fact be more severe, given the high transmission rates necessary to make this type of music distribution practical. Although a missed bit will make relatively little difference in a symphony, it will in a transmitted program.

[Media Choice: RAM vs ROM?]. Consider a hypothetical educational publisher that decides to first implement its software - a music education program also requiring graphics (to represent musical notes, etc.) - on the Atari 400/800 computers, then on the Apple II, then the Texas Instruments 99/4, and then PET, in that order. Since the Tandy computers, other than the low installed base Color Computer, do not have sound, they have been eliminated.

The next key question confronting the publisher is this: what should be the distribution medium for the program? At the present state of technology, there are three major choices of magnetic media to consider:

- Cassette tapes, the earliest medium used in the field and among the least expensive to manufacture, are relatively inconvenient to use and are rapidly giving way to floppy disks;

- Floppy disks, 5-1/4-inch magnetic platters on which information is recorded like a turning record, are somewhat more expensive to manufacture than tapes (in quantity, disks cost at least $2 each) and are susceptible to damage in the hands of young or inexperienced users;

- ROM packs, which load easily, even by children, but which are relatively expensive to master, must be produced in high-volume runs to be economical. Unlike disks, however, ROM

packs cannot be copied; thus loss to informal copying and
software piracy is minimized.

[Publishing on ROM]. Although floppy disks, especially those used in word
processing applications, are now relatively familiar items, ROM is not. ROM
stands for Read Only Memory, which, as its name implies, is a type of computer
memory that can be read but not written on. Most personal computers are built
with some ROM inside them, typically 8K or 12K (1024 bytes), and also have the
better-known RAM or Random Access Memory in units of 16K, 32K, or 48K.

Personal computers lose their RAM memory whenever their power is turned off.
ROM, importantly, has its information permanently burned into its chips. When
the computer is turned back on, the memory in the ROM is immediately there,
unchanged from before. If a computer has only RAM, or is using a program that
runs in RAM memory, it must be reloaded from a disk or tape if it is to run
again. This reloading process can be time-consuming and inconvenient to the
user.

Physically, ROM packs consist of the ROM chips mounted on a printed circuit
board and enclosed in a plastic case. A plug with metal contacts of some sort
extends out of the bottom of the pack, with a mating connector found on the
computer itself, often at the bottom of a cartridge-like slot. ROM packs on
home video games are essentially identical to those on personal computers.

For most publishers, the situation presented in the case of ROM packs — the
inventory problem — is a familiar but deadly one in a time of high interest
rates, while the tape and disk options offer the increasingly popular option
of "on demand" publishing, thereby significantly reducing inventory and
carrying costs.

ROMs must be manufactured in batches. As with a press run, manufacture of a
ROM involves both a fixed setup charge, and a unit cost which declines as the
run increases but which must be weighed against carrying charges and the risk
of scrapping ("remaindering") an overrun.

Texas Instruments, for example, requires a minimum run of 1000 of its ROM
"Command Modules" for the 99/4 computer. Each run has a set-up charge of
$5000 per chip in the Command Modules, with a single module containing one to
five different chips. The unit price per chip is $2.95 and assembly of the
final package, regardless of the number of chips, costs $9.70 per module.
Naturally, the lower the chip count (each chip is 8K of program code or
tables, and the number of chips required varies by complexity of the program),
the lower the manufacturing cost.

Retail prices, therefore, for ROM-based software are generally higher than for
disk- and cassette-based equivalents. Most ROM-based software packages list
for a minimum of $20, whereas disks sell at a minimum of $15. Cassette-based
games often retail as low as $8 or $10.

[Software Development Using ROM]. There are additional nontrivial technical
problems involved in developing programs to run in ROM. Computer programs are
typically developed in a "debugging cycle" of revisions and corrections.
Although simple computer programs involving limited choices (like those for
games) can be made nearly 100% reliable, complex programs can never be

guaranteed "bug free."

With complex systems, committing a program to ROM becomes a serious step. Often, it is simply not possible to test all the potential branches of a program - although if there is a bug in a program, it will always be found by a user within the first week of release.

Furthermore, only certain types of computer programs can be successfully placed in ROM at all. Large computer programs, and programs that must cope with changing inputs and situations, are actually never finished but require constant "software maintainence", usually provided under contract by the original developer.

ROM, being fixed for all time, does not lend itself to overly complex programs or to those that must be customized or changed in varying environments. In general, ROM works well for fixed, simple, or very standard programs. In the microcomputer world, it has been used most successfully for games, which have fixed rules for legal inputs and outputs, and for system software, which must be highly standardized. ROM is not promising for accounting applications for example, because nearly all accounting systems must be altered slightly to fit the needs of individual businesses.

Because it must be fixed as perfect, the time required to develop ROM-based software can be significantly longer than the time required to develop disk- or cassette-based software. When under development, computer programs run through a constant cycle of correction and "de-bugging". On computers using random access memory (RAM), this process is relatively painless. In the final stages of developing ROM-based programs, however, the program code to be tested must be "burned in" to a special type of memory called an EPROM (Erasable Programmable Read Only Memory). This additional step of burning and re-burning PROMs can add a great deal of time to the debugging cycle - and naturally occurs at the end of projects when financial and scheduling pressures are greatest.

Furthermore, although disk- and cassette-based programs for personal computers can be developed using the same low-cost computers as those on which the programs will eventually run, ROM-based programs must often be developed on larger machines and then transferred, as a final step, to the smaller "target" computer.

In short, a ROM-based development program can require a considerable investment in extra hardware. For example, Texas Instruments encourages software houses to develop ROM-based modules for its 99/4 personal computer, which sells retail for about $1500. These modules, however, cannot be programmed on the 99/4. To develop them, a software house needs a TI DS-990 Model 8 minicomputer, which sells for $31,900. This computer comes with special programs and hardware that simulate the ROM of the 99/4, but which allow programming changes during development. When the program is finished, it can then be "burned" in to ROMs for "stand alone" testing on the 99/4.

[Legal Protection for Personal Computer Software]. In general, legal protection for personal computer software is weak, except in clear cases of large-scale, for-profit commercial frauds. Most importantly, legal measures to protect software cannot be counted upon, but they must be combined with technological and economic protections.

The three primary paths for protection of personal computer software are: (1) patent protection, which is difficult to obtain except in conjunction with a patentable piece of computer hardware; (2) copyright protection, which is routinely granted to program listings, but which has major shortcomings in the degree of protection; and (3) trade secrecy, which in some sense is the most practical means of legal/economic protection, but which can evaporate overnight and is at odds with copyright protection.

[Patent Protection]. In general, the US Supreme Court has held that software is not patentable. The Court's reasoning on this point - which many in the computer industry hold to be poor, and out of touch with the realities of the technical world - is that computer programs are akin to the theorems of pure mathematics. Patents, the Court has held, were created to stimulate technical inventions, not to regulate the discoveries of pure science and mathematics, which for the good of mankind are to be kept in the public domain.

The basic decision on this point remains the so-called "Benton" case (Gottschalk v Benton 1972), in which the court unanimously rejected a patent claim for an algorithm that converted information in binary-coded decimal (BCD) to pure binary. The Court held that the algorithm was an idea from the realm of pure mathematics; as Justice Douglas argued, "an idea of itself is not patentable".

The line of reasoning laid down in Benton has, effectively, denied patent protection to computer software. Recently, the Court's "hard line" position again software patents has begun to erode, as several recent decisions indicate (see below). This erosion appears to be taking place along two tracks: the first involves hybrid hardware/software combinations, the second involves nonmathematical (e.g., text processing) programs.

From the point of view of the software developer, patent protection for qualified computer programs would be highly desirable. Although copyrights protect the superficial expression of a work, such as a program listing or exact disk copies, patents protect the underlying concept. Thus, in a hypothetical situation, an "adaptation" of a highly original program to a different computer might not be a violation of the copyright notice on the original source listing but could be found to be a violation of patent law if the original program was patented.

Naturally, not every computer program should have a patent, and a cynical reading of the Court's decisions would hold that it is precisely the sifting, judging, and administrative burden that the Court and Patent Office wish to avoid. The key words in granting patents are "useful", "novel", and "nonobvious". Clearly, many software techniques seem to qualify under all three criteria.

Before these tests can be applied, however, the courts must first decide a more fundamental question - namely, is software statutory. In current patent law, an invention is patentable if it is a "process", "machine", "article of manufacture", or "composition of matter". The current problem in the patentability of software is not that it is not "useful", "novel", or "nonobvious", but that it is simple not "statutory" - that is, not among the types of novel things that are covered by patent law.

Several recent rulings have moved the Court closer to letting software into the magic circle of the statutory. In a March 1981 decision, Diamond v Diehr, the court denied a type of "infection" theory in which a total patent application, by having an unpatentable component (e.g., a computer program), was as a whole unpatentable. Thus, in the Diamond case, the Court ruled that "A claim drawn to subject matter otherwise statutory does not become nonstatutory simply because it uses a mathematical formula, computer program, or digital computer".

Along a second track, the courts have backpeddled on the Benton case and elaborated a test, the so-called "Two-Step Freeman Test", to see if some non-mathematical software can slide by Benton. The first of the Freeman tests is a severe test that says in effect that, if the program contains no mathematical language, such as add, subtract, multiply, or divide, it is patentable. If a program fails the first test, it may still be patentable, but only if the goal of the program is not to solve a mathematical problem. Finally, should it pass the Freeman Test, the program must then be found to be novel, useful, and non-obvious.

On July 1, 1980, Whitlow Computer Systems of Englewood Cliffs, NJ was issued a patent (#4,210,916) of a sorting program used primarily on IBM computers. In issuing the patent, the fact that the "SyncSort" was a data sorting program, and not a program for mathematical computation, was critical. Since the Benton case, the courts have granted other patents for software, deciding in the Johnson and Fluke cases that although patents could not be granted for programs that solved mathematical problems, they could be granted for other types of programs, such as those that do sorting.

[Copyright Protection]. In general, copyright protection is the technique of protection for computer software favored by the courts. In practice, however, copyright protection is effective only in cases of gross copying for commercial gain. Copyright protection is not as effective as trade secret protection and in some instances can nullify it.

The Courts have come to understand only slowly the unique protection problems surrounding computer software. Under the "old" Copyright Act of 1909 (replaced by the Copyright Act of 1976), computer software could not be copyrighted in its "object code" form.

(Computer programs exist in various forms and languages. Typically, a program is written in a half-English, half-mathematical computer language like FORTRAN, COBOL, BASIC, or Pascal. The listing of the program in one of these languages is called the source code of the program. This source code is then taken by a specialized computer program called a compiler then takes these English-language instructions and translates them into the detailed machine language that the computer understands. This compiled version of the program is called the object code of the program. Most computer software publishers distribute object code only for programs).

The classic horror story under the 1909 Copyright Act was the Data Cash case, decided in 1979 but under the terms of the old act. In this case, an Illinois judge ruled that a ROM used in a chess game and copied by a Hong Kong firm was a "machine part" and not subject to copyright law. The judge based his reasoning on a 1908 case involving piano rolls, which held that these were parts of the piano and not subject to the copyright protection normally afforded sheet music.

Data Cash made a large investment in the programming that went into the chess game, which it put on the market for $169 in 1977. The source code of the program was registered with the Copyright Office. The "copycat" version of the game was introduced by JS&A, of Chicago (more recently in trouble with the FTC) at $99 and used an electronically copied version of the ROM. The game itself was manufactured for JS&A in Hong Kong.

[CONTU]. The Copyright Act of 1976 contains, in a clause in Section 117, a stipulation that the new Act does not apply to "works used in conjunction with computers". Congressional unhappiness with this clause led to the creation of a National Commission on New Technological Uses of Copyrighted Words, better known as CONTU, who presented its final report on July 31, 1978. The CONTU report is the state-of-the-art legal thinking about copyright protection of computer firmware. It provides: (1) that Section 117 of the Act of 1976 is removed; (2) that computer programs can be copyrighted; and (3) that rightful owners of programs can copy and adapt them for their own use. The recommendation allows legal customization of software and backup of valuable disks, tapes, etc.

Although the CONTU recommendations are not overly specific about media, the report eliminates the treatment of ROMs as "machine parts" and puts them in the same class as other magnetic media such as tapes and disks.

The Computer Software Copyright Act of 1980, passed in the last days of the 96th Congress and signed by President Carter just before leaving office, revises Section 117 of the Copyright Act of 1976. The Computer Software Copyright Act implements the CONTU recommendations and encompasses both object and source code, defining a computer program as "a set of statements or instructions to be used directly or indirectly to bring about a certain result".

Unfortunately, there is a conflict between copyright protection and trade secret protection. Copyright protection implies some sort of publication, which of course is contrary to trade secrecy. The Copyright Act, as amended, holds that copyright registration negates claims under state trade secrecy laws. In short, the Federal copyright law requires a "trade" in the type of protection - a trade that may not be to a software publisher's advantage. Furthermore, secrecy of source code may be necessary in any event, because programs can be modified slightly to be nonidentical with the copied program. With patent protection, the "underlying" idea of an invention is covered; copyright, however, generally protects only the expression of a work, not the underlying concept.

Coincidentally, the status of software copyright in England is as ambiguous as it is in the U.S. In a pro-copyright decision in late 1980, an English court, invoking a law that allows confiscation of materials in violation of copyright, ordered various TRS-80 computer programs to be removed from the premises of an apparently unauthorized distributor of the programs in Chesterfield, Derby. This case, however, is not a strong test case, because rights to the software were not seriously contested but rather confused, as the result of bankruptcy of the original software developer.

[Trade Secret Protection]. Trade secrets are defined as formula, process, mechanism, compound, or compilation of data not patented but known only by certain individuals using it in business to obtain a commercial advantage. The classic example of a trade secret is the Coca-Cola formula, which has never been patented and is known only to selected Coke personnel.

For trade secrecy to be enforced, a bona fide "secret" must exist, and it must be a duty of those made privy to it not to disclose it. This generally means that employees or contractors must mutually sign a confidential disclosure agreement.

Trade secrecy can be easily lost. If a secret becomes widely public, protection is lost. Typically, secrets are lost by carelessness but also can be lost by their discovery by competitors. Publication of a trade secret, as is required by copyright registration, is evidence of secrecy being lost. In general, trade secrets are difficult to maintain where public sales are involved.

Sorting

The computers of the world spend a great deal of their time sorting business records of one kind or another. Sorting involves putting things in order, whether by number, by date, or by some other kind of sort key. Sorting consumes computer resources. This is best understood from the beginning: in sorting, like war, nobody wins; some just lose less than others.

The secret of implementing a successful sorting operation is to decide which resource (time, memory, disk space, programming effort) a system can spare and which is limited; then pick a sorting algorithm to strike an optimal balance of these factors.

[Indicies]. When people sort things - say, for example, a pile of papers - they almost always physically move the item they are sorting. When we get back cancelled checks from the bank, we usually sort them into ascending numerical order by putting a few down here, holding this one in our left hand, putting a few more down, and generally shuffling until the numbers are right.

Computers, of course, work with information, not physical objects. They can move information around - a computer can read a record from one part of a floppy disk and write it on another - but more often they work by sorting an index to the item.

If we sorted our bank checks the way a computer sorts, we would first take the checks just as they came from the bank and transcribe the numbers on a piece of paper. Then, perhaps drawing arrows to a second column on the paper, we would work out where each check belongs in the numerical sequence without actually moving the checks.

Only when we had a map telling us where each check should go would we actually physically move the checks to their proper position. If the bank sent us 20 checks, we'd have 20 positions on our list; after sorting, we might know, for example, that the check the bank sent us in position 1 actually belongs at the end, in position 20, and that the check in position 5 really belongs in position 3.

Now to rearrange the checks, we would spread them out in their old positions and shift them to new positions in one operation. To do this as the computer would do it, we go through each of the 20 positions, look up their new position on our index, and move the check directly to that position, i.e.:

```
    FROM BANK          MAPPING          SORTED ORDER
    ---------          -------          ------------
      1)   172         1  - > 20          1)   150
      2)   151         2  - >  2          2)   151
      3)   156         3  - >  5          3)   152
      4)   154         4  - >  4          4)   154
      5)   150         5  - >  1          5)   156
          etc.            etc.               etc.
     19)   171        19  - > 19         19)   171
     20)   157        20  - >  6         20)   172
```

In this example, we are using the check number as the sort key. The sort key is anything we use to compare two items: it can be a single number, as in this example, or a set of numbers (month, day, year, for example), or anything else that will tell us if one item in the file should come before, after, or in the same place as another. In general, the procedure for sorting a file on a floppy disk or magnetic tape is:

STEP 1. A pass is made through the file on the disk. For each record in the file, the sort key of that record is stored in an array A(N), where N is the total number of records in the file.

STEP 2. An array parallel to the array A is set up to hold a pointer to the record from which the sort key A(i) came. Call this array X(N). If the records in the file are numbered 1,2, 3, etc. then the values of X will originally be 1,2,3, i.e.,

```
FOR I=1 TO N
X(I)=I
NEXT I
```

STEP 3. The array A is sorted into either ascending or or descending order by one of the well-known sorting algorithms detailed below. However, each time an element of A is moved or switched to another place in A, the corresponding element(s) in X must also be moved.

STEP 4. The array X now contains, in sorted order, pointers to the records in the old file as they should go into the new file. If the old file is 1 and the new file is 2, then the file can be rewritten by this code:

```
FOR I=1 TO N
READ #1, location X(I) , [the record]
WRITE #2, location I, [the record]
NEXT I
```

Results: File 2 now contains a sorted version of file 1. File 1
    is unchanged.

[Application Notes]. For an efficient sort, you must have enough memory to
keep both the sort key array and the index array in memory. If both are
integers, it can take 2*5*1000 = 10 K of free memory to sort a 1000-item file
with a BASIC that uses 5 bytes per number. Step 4 requires a random access
file and, if files are large, two disks. The random access feature allows the
computer to go right to the record it wants, no matter where it is in the
file. Two disks - one for reading the old file, another for writing the new
file - will usually operate faster than reading and writing two files on the
same disk drive.

Note that most academic discussions of sorting neglect to mention the need to
carry an index pointer (if indeed not the whole record) along with the sort
key. However, sorting arrays of random numbers is not a terribly interesting
thing to do. In the following algorithms, it should be remembered that
every time A(i) is changed, X(i) must be changed along with it.

[Sorting Algorithms]. Sorting algorithms are like fancy restaurants: people
are always looking for one that is exotic or new or fashionable. The
following are strictly meat-and-potatoes-type algorithms. One of these should
work well in most any computer configuration that has the resources to do
sorting.

Sorting algorithms can be compared on the following points: speed, memory
use, programming difficulty, stability, and worst-case behavior.

Speed is usually the most important attribute of a sort, although at times,
when memory or disk space is tight, a slower in-place sort will be preferred.
The speed of any sort is a function of how many times are being sorted - what
function, however, varyies importantly among the different algorithms. Slower
sorts, like the bubble sort, have completion times proportional to the number
of elements being sorted squared (N*N). Faster sorts like Quicksort have a
running time proportional to N times the natural log (log(e)) of N. For large
N, this can be quite a difference. In a benchmark test on a Northstar
HORIZON, a Bubble Sort of a 1000 element array took 48 minutes, whereas a
Quicksort of the same array took 3.5 minutes.

Sorts that require no extra memory, except for that of the sort key array, are
called "in-place" sorts, because the items in the array are moved around on
top of each other in place. Some sorts, such as Quicksort (which is actually
a recursive sort) require extra memory for temporary storage. With Quicksort,
the size of the stack can be limited to 2*log2 of (N), which for a 1000-item
array is only 100 bytes. However, at other times an in-place sort may be
necessary.

Programming difficulty speaks for itself. In general, sorts should be
implemented as subroutines and checked out on arrays of random numbers. If

variable names and calling conventions are kept the same, several sort subroutines can be tried to see which works best.

[Stability]. The stability of a sort refers to whether two elements with identical sort keys will have the same relative position in the sorted file that they had in the unsorted file. In a file of business transactions, for example, it may be important to keep two transactions on the same day in the same relative position when the file is sorted later by date. Of the sorting algorithms given below, only the Bubble Sort is a stable sort.

["Worst-Case" Behavior]. Nearly all sorts degenerate badly under certain conditions. The Bubble Sort works best when its file is almost in order. The Quicksort, on the other hand, works best when the file is in complete disorder and works very poorly when it is almost ordered. In general, however, concern about worst-case behavior is misplaced. Worst-case conditions are worth worrying about only if there is a known consistent pattern in the input file, and even then there may be no simple solution possible. Sorting is an expensive operation in the best case, and people who worry about the worst case usually have yet to face up to this fact.

Three sorts - the Bubble Sort, the Shell Sort, and the Quicksort - are described below. The following table summarizes their properties:

SORT	SPEED	EXTRA SPACE?	PROGRAMMING DIFFICULTY	STABLE?	WORSE CASE
Bubble	slow	In place	Easy	Yes	random file
Shell	fast	In place	Moderate	No	hard to say
Quick	fast	Stack	Hard	No	file sorted

[Bubble Sort]. The Bubble Sort is among the easiest to program of all sorting algorithms. It is also one of the slowest, but there are some conditions under which the Bubble Sort is the best choice:

(1) Time not important. If a computer can be left on all night sorting, the Bubble Sort may be an easy-to-implement sort that will get the job done with a minimum of programming effort.

(2) File almost in order. If you need to sort files that are almost in order to begin with, the Bubble Sort may be the best sort (and Quicksort the worst!). Files that are almost but not quite in order are a common occurrence in the business world. A file of transactions may have new items posted to its end each day. The file will be almost sorted by date, with only a few items that need to bubble up into the file from the bottom end. A Bubble Sort would be the best choice there.

(3) Stable sort required. In some applications, the relative order of two items in a file must be preserved even if they have the same sort key. The best solution here may be to elaborate the sort key, but it may be easier to use a stable sort that will not switch equal items. The Bubble Sort is a stable sort.

BUBBLESORT

STEP 1. The array A is to be sorted in ascending order. A flag
F will be used to tell if any elements of the array have been
moved. Initially, we set the flag F to 0.

STEP 2. We now set I to 1. I will control our pass through A.

STEP 3. We compare elements of the array A(I) and the next
element, A(I+1). If A(I+1) is greater than A(I), the two
elements are in the right relative order, and we go on to Step
4. If not, we exchange A(I) and A(I+1) by using a temporary
variable T:

```
T=A(I)
A(I)=A(I+1)
A(I+1)=T
```

If a switch is made, we set the flag F to 1. Now we go on to
the next step.

STEP 4. We now set I to I+1. If the new value of I equals N,
the number of elements in the array, we have completed a pass
through the file and should go to Step 5. If I is less than
N, we should go back to Step 3. Notice that if A(I) was
switched in Step 3, it will be the new A(I) when we go back
and repeat the step again, and it will be pushed up until it
reaches its proper place. This bubbling up action gives this
sort its name.

STEP 5. We have now completed a pass through the array. If the
flag F is still 0, we know we have made a complete pass and
not had to switch any items - in other words, the array is in
order, and we can quit. If F equals 1, we switched at least
one item on the last pass. We should return to Step 1 and
make another pass until we find F=0.

This is the simplest version of the Bubble Sort. The sort can be improved in
several ways. On each pass, we essentially push the biggest item in the array
up to the bottom of the array - that is, to A(N) on the first pass, A(N-1) on
the second, and so on. When we reach A(N-1) on the third pass, there is no
reason to compare it with A(N), because we know these are now in order. We
can use a variable L (for last) to limit the search by making the following
changes:

STEP 0. Set L = N initially. We do this only once.

STEP 3. If we make an exchange, set K equal to I. K is the
point at which we've had to make an exchange.

STEP 4. Here we test to see if I equals L, not N. Pass 1 will
be the same as before; after that, the bottom part of the file
will be skipped, because we know it is in order.

STEP 5. At the end of a pass, if we are going back for another
pass, we now set L to K, our new bottom limit for comparisons.

A close relative of the Bubble Sort is the so-called Cocktail Shaker sort.
This is basically a double bubble - it bubbles items up and down at the same
time. The Cocktail Shaker sort is not much faster than the Bubble and is much
more complicated to program.

[The Shell Sort]. Shell's sort (it is named after a man, not after any
property of the sorting algorithm) is a good fast sort that is not as
difficult to program as the Quicksort and is only slightly slower. The Shell
sort also has the advantage of being an in-place sort, and not requiring extra
memory for a stack, as does the Quicksort algorithm.

STEP 1. The Shell sort works by splitting the array A into a
series of subarrays, sorting these, and then slowing merging
the sorted subarrays. The variable M contains the number of
elements in the subarrays. To begin the sort, set M=N, where
N is the total number of elements to be sorted in array A.

STEP 2. This step sets the new subarray size. Set:

$$M = INT(M/2)$$

If M now equals zero, the sort is finished. We can return to
the calling program or transfer beyond the sort.

STEP 3. This step establishes one of the subarrays. Set J equal
to 1. Set K equal to N-M.

STEP 4. This step prepares the loop that follows. Set I equal
to J.

STEP 5. This is a loop that tests elements in the subarrays and
switches them if necessary. Set L equal to I+M. Now test
A(I) against A(L). If A(I) is less than A(L), go to Step 7.
If A(I) is greater than or equal to A(L), exchange the two
using a temporary variable T, e.g.,

T=A(I) \ A(I)=A(L) \ A(L)=T

After exchanging, set I to I-M. If I is now less than 1, go
to Step 6. If I is still greater than one, repeat this step
(Step 5).

STEP 6. This step moves us to the next sublist. Set J equal to
J+1. If J <= K, then go to Step 4. Otherwise (J>K), go to
Step 2.

This version of the Shell sort works without FOR-NEXT loops, whose operation
depends on the particular version of BASIC being used. The following is a
listing of a version of the Shell sort good for arrays less than 8000 elements
long:

STEP 1. Set D equal to 8191.

STEP 2. Set K equal to 1.

STEP 3. Set D equal to INT((D-1)/2)

STEP 4. Set I equal to D + 1.

STEP 5. If I is greater than N, the sort is finished.

STEP 6. Set T equal to A(I).

STEP 7. Set J equal to I-D.

STEP 8. If J is less than 1, go to Step 10.

STEP 9. If T is greater than or equal to A(J), go to Step 11.
    If not, set A(J+D) to A(J). Set J equal to J - D. Go to Step
    8.

STEP 10. Set J back to J+D. Set A(J) equal to T. Set I equal
    to I+1. Go to Step 5.

STEP 11. Set A(J+D) to T. Set I equal to I+1. Go to Step 5.

If the array is be be sorted into descending order, the comparison between T
and A(J) in Step 9 should be less than or equal.

[Implementation Notes]. This version of the Shell sort can be coded using
FOR-NEXT loops, but requires an exit out of a loop in Step 9. In some BASICs,
e.g., North Star BASIC, this would have to be coded:

IF T=A(J) THEN EXIT [Step 11]

If Steps 7 and 8 are coded as a FOR-NEXT loop, the control variable J may or
may not need to be set to J+D in Step 10 depending on whether BASIC modifies J
when the test against 1 fails. On exit from the loop, J should never be less
than 1; if so, it needs to be set to J+D:

[Step 7 & 8] FOR J = I-D TO 1 STEP - D

[Step 9]   IF T>= A(J) THEN [Step 11]

             A(J+D) = A(J)
             NEXT J

[Step 10]   IF J<1 THEN J=J+D
             A(J) = T

[Quicksort]. Quicksort is a top-of-the-line fast sort that rquires some
programming and extra memory to implement. Quicksort is really a recursive
sort but is much slower if implemented that way. This version of Quicksort
uses a two-element stack S2(S1,2) whose first dimension, S1, is a function of
the number of elements N in the array:

$$S1 = INT(LOG(N)/LOG(2)+1$$

The variable S is used as a pointer to the stack. The comparand X is picked at random to avoid Quicksort's well-known worst-case problems:

STEP 1. Set S, the stack pointer, to 1. Set S2(1,1) to 1. Set S2(1,2) to N.

STEP 2. This step pops the stack. Set L to S2(S,1). Set R to S2(S,2). Set S to S-1.

STEP 3. Set I equal to L. Set J equal to R. Pick X at random between R and L as follows:

$$X = A(INT(RND(0)*(R-L)+.5)+L)$$

where RND(0) generates a random number between 0 and 1.

STEP 4. If A(I) is greater than or equal to X, go to Step 5, otherwise set I to I + 1 and repeat this step.

STEP 5. If X is greater than or equal to A(J), go to Step 6, otherwise set J to J-1 and repeat this step.

STEP 6. If I is greater than J, go to Step 7. Other- wise exchange A(I) and A(J) using a temporary variable T, e.g.,

$$T=A(I) \setminus A(I)=A(J) \setminus A(J)=T$$

and set I to I plus 1, J to J minus one. Go on to the next step.

STEP 7. If I is less than or equal to J, go to Step 4. If J-L is greater than R-I, go to Step 9. If I is greater than or equal to R, go to Step 8. If none of the above, push the stack by setting S to S+1, S2(S,1) to I, and S2(S,2) to R. Go on to the next step.

STEP 8. Set R equal to J. Go to Step 11.

STEP 9. If L is greater than or equal to J, then go to Step 10. Otherwise push the stack by setting S to S+1, S2(S,1) to L, S2(S,2) to J.

STEP 10. Set L to I.

STEP 11. If L is less than R, go to Step 3. If S is greater than zero, go to Step 2. If S equals zero, the sort is finished.

Speech Synthesis

Speech synthesizers are interesting and increasingly important output devices. Talking computers are not just curiosity items: computers and video games are slowly becoming expected to talk. The attraction of having in the home talking companions that you can turn off is not to be overlooked.

[Talking Printers]. Speech synthesizers are probably easiest thought of as printers that talk their output rather than write it. The Votrax Type 'n' Talk, introduced in mid-1981, is probably the best example of such a device. The Type 'n' Talk connects to a computer over an RS-232-C line and accepts any text string.

As output devices, there are two problems for synthesizer units: translation of English text to "phonemes", the sounds of speech; and production of the phonemes themselves. Most languages have about 50 distinct phonemes or sounds. In all the languages of the world, there are about 80 or so different sounds. These 80 sounds can be thought of as the full repertoire of the human vocal tract. In linguistics, each of these sounds is assigned a symbol in the IPA, or International Phonetic Alphabet. IPA symbols - many of them Greek letters - are the strange-looking characters found in many dictionaries.

The fact that many IPA symbols are special characters makes the IPA unsuited for use on computers. A transliteration of IPA symbols to 2-letter ASCII symbols was done in the 1960s for the US Defense Advanced Research Projects Agency, DARPA, and is cometimes called the "ARPAbet". In any event, the IPA or the ARPAbet should be the reference set of phoneme work.

[Votrax Phonemes]. Votrax, a US company with a long history of involvement in speech synthesis, uses its own set of phonemes that is slightly different from the ARPAbet but works on similar principles. The Votrax phonemes, which are adequate to represent (Midwest Ohio) American English, lack some sounds from foreign languages. The number following some codes, especially vowels, indicates duration, with higher numbers having shorter duration:

VOTRAX PHONEME	DURATION (MS)		VOTRAX PHONEME	DURATION (MS)
EH3	59		A	185
EH2	71		AY	65
EH1	121		Y1	80
PA0	47 (pause)		UH3	47
DT	47		AH	250
A2	71		P	103
A1	103		O	185
ZH	90		ɪ	185
AH2	71		U	185
I3	55		Y	103
I2	80		T	71

I1	121		R	90
M	103		E	185
N	80		W	80
B	71		AE	185
V	71		AE1	103
CH	71		AW2	90
SH	121		UH2	71
Z	71		UH1	103
AW1	146		UH	185
NG	121		O2	80
AH1	146		O1	121
OO1	103		IU	59
OO	185		U1	90
L	103		THV	80
K	80		TH	71
J	47		ER	146
H	71		EH	185
G	71		E1	121
F	103		AW	250
D	55		PA1	185 (pause)
S	90		STOP	47 (stop)

Note that of these 64 combinations (they map 1 to 1 with the ASCII set starting at "ə", hex 40), many are the same phoneme but with different duration. Thus EH is 185 ms, and EH3 lasts only 59 ms.

[Text to Speech Conversion]. As most foreigners know, written English bears a very rough correlation to spoken English. The process of taking a sentence and coming up with its phonemes is called "text-to-speech conversion". Using an example from the Computalker, a speech synthesizer popular in the late 1970s, a sentence "Can you make me say something?" has to be translated to:

```
Can     you   make   me    say    something?
KAE4N   YUW1  MEYK   MIY   SEY3   SAHMPTHIHNX?
```

This translation process is not trivial, nor will it ever be 100% accurate. The foundation work on translation of English to speech is a January, 21, 1976 paper by Honey Sue Elovitz et al., called "Automatic Translation of English Text to Phonetics by Means of Letter-To-Sound Rules". (The paper is sold by NTIS as AD-A021 929.) This work, conducted at the Naval Research Laboratory, produced a set of about 500 text-to-speech rules. These rules have been modified by Texas Instruments for use with its speech synthesizer. Votrax apparently developed its text-to-speech algorithm in-house.

[Text to Speech With the Type 'N' Talk]. The $389 Votrax Type 'n' Talk can be used as a stand-along processor to convert text files into phoneme strings, according to its algorithm. To do this, a 2-way serial link between the host computer and the Type 'n' Talk must be established. A hardware handshake must be used to prevent overrun of the TNT buffer, because conversion is slow.

The following interface works bi-directionally between the California Computer Systems CCS 7710A serial card for the Apple II and the Votrax Type 'N' Talk. This interface has the advantage of being able to send a line of text to the TNT using the PSEND "on" mode and recover a line that is the converted phoneme string generated by the TNT. Note, however, that for slower computers, the baud rate setting should be about 300 for best results.

```
           CCS PIN                              TNT
           -------                              ---
              7         signal ground            7
              2         <---data-----            2
              3         ----data---->            3
              5         -----RTS---->            4
              4         <----CTS-----            5
              8         +12v-RSD---->            8
             20         <----DTR--+12v           20
```

The use of the CTS and RTS "handshake" lines prevents the relatively slow Type 'N' Talk from being "overrun" by the computer. When the Type 'N' Talk's buffer is full, pin 5 on the TNT goes low, indicating that it is not clear to send. Conversely, when the TNT is sending a phoneme stream back to the computer, a low on CCS pin 5 tells the TNT that the computer is not ready to receive. The pair of pins 8 and 20 establishes that the two devices both have power; neither will work unless these pins are at "high" (+12 V) voltage levels.

[TI's Allophones]. Texas Instruments, in its speech synthesis system, uses a different unit, the "allophone", from the phoneme. Allophones are somewhat more exact units than phonemes, although there is less agreement about just which allophones are valid. A plosive "p", as in pin, is an aspirated sound, whereas a nonplosive "p", as in spin, is not. In TI's system, these are considered two different allophones, even though they are the same phoneme. The TI system uses 128 allophones, compared to Votrax's 64 phonemes. It produces better-sounding speech than the Votrax but requires more work in software. TI's version of the NRL text to speech work uses 650 rules, which take 7 Kbytes of storage. These rules chose phonemes correctly 97% of the time and allophones correctly 92% of the time, according to TI benchmarks.

[Speech Construction]. The job of producing high-quality speech is far from over once a string of phonemes or allophones has been produced. In the TI system, a second software step, called speech construction, post-processes the allophone string to improve the quality of the impending output. In speech construction: (1) energy levels between allophones are smoothed to make speech smoother; (2) stress is added to the allophone string; and (3) pitch changes, and intonation is taken into account.

[Speech Production]. Speech production is the process by which digital data finally becomes sound. Both the Votrax and the Texas Instruments systems use what is essentially a model of the human vocal tract, although the techniques of modeling are extremely different.

The Votrax model has three fundamental parts: a pair of signal sources, a set of filters, and an amplification section. In Votrax speech, a variable frequency oscillator generates a base noise for speech. To this tone, some pseudo-random noise is added to simulate the sound of rushing air common in human speech. This pseudo-random noise is a fricative source. Votrax phonemes fall into several categories and can be either voiced, voiced and fricative, voiced stops, fricative stops, fricatives, or nasal:

VOICED		VOICED FRICATIVE	VOICED STOP	FRICATIVE STOP	FRICATIVE	NASAL
E	AW	Z	B	T	S	M
Y	UH	ZH	D	DT	SH	N
I	O	J	G	K	CH	NG
EH	OO	V		P	TH	
A	R	THV			F	
AE	ER				H	
AH	L					

The output from the voiced and fricative generator is then chopped into 4 bands, which simulate the vocal cavities, by a bank of filters. The output of the filter bank is mixed and sent to the audio amplifier. The Votrax chip offers circuitry that makes attaching either A, B, or C type amplifiers easy.

Vowels become stressed (long) in the Votrax system by being doubled as phonemes. Thus the word "system" sounds best as:

S I1 I3 S T EH3 M

where the two "I" sounds combine to make a long, stressed one. "Warning" is likewise W-01-02-R-N-I3-NG.

[Linear Predictive Coding]. Linear Predictive Coding (LPC), uses a more abstract model of the human vocal tract. LPC is built out of a filter network.

[Analog Voice]. Computer-controlled speech need not always be synthesized speech. One simple method of producing speed under computer control is to use conventional analog recording on one track (or two for stereo, etc.) and digital timing and addressing information on another parallel track. This is commonly done on professional audio recording for broadcast and movie work.

In playback, however, these tape systems have the usual problem of tape: slow, serial access. One interesting solution is used in CDC's Plato system, whose terminals have an audio disk similar in concept and layout to a floppy disk. Each disk has 128 concentric tracks, each 10 seconds long. Each track is subdivided into 32 sectors, for a total of 4096 different points. Access time to any point on the disk is less than a second. The head mechanism, unlike a floppy drive head, is pneumatic.

Unfortunately, even 1 second access time creates pauses between words as the disk skips from word to word. A vocabulary of 4096 words is also limited.

[Digital Recording]. One alternative to analog recording is to make a digital recording of speech and to use it. Digital recording is becoming popular in high-cost offices of the future, as in some of the Wang products, where it allows "voicegrams" to be sent to others on the network and allows incorporation into the workstation of the old-fashioned Dictaphone.

To digitize speech well, a basic sample rate of 100K bits per second is needed. A Fourier analysis can then extract speech parameters, reducing the data to about 10K bits per second. When re-expanded, this information will sound extremely lifelike.

[Phoneme Synthesis]. In recent years, the tendency in synthesis work has been to place phoneme devices on chips. These devices have the advantage of being able to produce almost any human sound if programmed correctly - although that becomes a major problem. Votrax, a long-established firm in speech synthesis, has a synthesizer chip, the VC-01, which produces 64 phonemes.

Spreadsheets

Spreadsheets are a type of computer program that might be called numeric word processors. Everyone knows that computers can add, subtract, and do arithmetic. With spreadsheets, however, they do it in front of you.

Like a word processor, a spreadsheet allows constant revision and change of the data and gives clean, freshly calculated versions of the results. Spreadsheet programs are highly interactive and one of the best uses of microcomputers: when a user hits a key, magic seems to happen.

The best-known spreadsheet is "VisiCalc", the product of VisiCorp (formerly Personal Software, 2895 Zanker Rd., San Jose, CA, 95134). VisiCalc was 1st introduced at the Boston Computer Show in October 1979, and rapidly gained popularity. In 1981, VisiCalc began selling Apples, because people wanted had to buy the computer to go with it the piece of software.

Naturally, VisiCalc has attracted a number of imitations, informally known as visiclones. Of these, CP/M-based "SuperCalc" is the most important. VisiCalc was revised once in August 1981, when VisiCorp brought out VisiCalc 3.3, an upgraded version of the original VisiCalc with added Boolean operations (greater than, less than, etc.) and an edit feature for changing formulas. "SuperCalc" from Sorcim (405 Aldo Ave., Santa Clara, CA 95050) makes further improvements on VisiCalc, offering varying column widths (useful for labels) a help command, and other features. Other visiclones: include "CalcStar", from Micropro International, the publishers of "WordStar", and compatible with that word processor; "Multiplan", from MicroSoft; and "Migicalc" from Peachtree.

[What a Spreadsheet Does]. A spreadsheet is a 2-dimensional matrix of cells that can be thought of as boxes on a large sheet of paper. In each box goes either a number, a short label, or - and here is the secret of the power of computer-driven spreadsheets - a formula, defining the value of the box to be equal to the value of other boxes.

In nearly all systems, the spreadsheet is lettered across the top, and numbered down. Thus a VisiCalc spreadsheet looks like:

	A	B	C	D	E	F
1						
2	23.4	30.0	53.4			
3						
4						
5						

Here, cell A1 is a constant, but cell C2 has been defined as "A2+B2". Thus, if we move the cursor over cell A2, and change the value from 23.4 to 25.1, cell C2 will also change - as if by magic - to 55.1.

[VisiCalc Commands]. VisiCalc is especially interesting if one looks at it as a programming language that nonprogrammers have taken to using. Raw VisiCalc "programs" are called "templates"; there is now a small but growing market in standardized templates for tax forms, and so on. A fleshed-out VisiCalc program is called a "model"; a VisiCalc user might have 20 or 30 models in his or her library.

Like any programming language, VisiCalc has a syntax. Commands to VisiCalc are typed on top of the cursor position. One moves around the spreadsheet by using the cursor arrows on the computer's keyboard (on the Apple II, the arrows and the space bar are used in combination). A "jump" to a particular cell in the spreadsheet can be made by the right arrow command:

        >C43

sends VisiCalc to column C, row 43.

Entities in VisiCalc are either "labels" or "values". Labels are used in VisiCalc to provide short descriptions of numeric items, e.g., "COST". Values are either constants or simple formulae. A label starts with any letter of the alphabet or the quote symbol ". A value starts with a numeric digit, or one of the arithmetic operators +,-,(,., or @.

Commands in VisiCalc start with a slash, /, followed by a letter. The following is the VisiCalc command set:

    /B   - blank out the cell under the cursor. Can
                be aborted if any key other than CR or
                a cursor move follows the B.

    /C   - clear sheet: erases the entire sheet. Requires
                a 'Y' to confirm.

    /D   - delete row (requires "R") or column ("C").

    /E   - edit. Brings menu choice of label ("L") or
                value ("V"). Puts entry on edit line.
                Escape deletes a character to the left
                of the cursor; the left and right arrow
                keys move the cursor; and anything else,
                except CR, is inserted.

    /F   - format of cell display. Subchoices: D defaults
                to global format of current window; G
                general format; I integer; L left justify;
                R right justify; $ dollar and cents; .
                integer values as stars for bar graphs.

    /G   - global formatting commands. A number N>=3 sets
                the column width; OR sets recalculation

-277-

by rows (A1 to AK1, then A2 to AK2, etc.)
OC sets recalculation order to columns.
/GRA sets automatic recalculation; /GRM
sets manual calculation that must be
triggered with the ! command (this is a
timesaver on large models). /GF sets the
format of any unformatted entries in the
current window.

/I   - Insert. /IR inserts a row, /IC a column.

/M   - Move. Moves a row or column.

/P   - Print. A menu comes up: file writes to a file;
        slot # gives printer card slot. The sheet
        is printed from the current cursor location,
        taken as the top left, to a specified bottom
        right position. Printer set-up strings are
        allowed.

/R   - Replicate. Allows formulae to be replicated across
        rows and columns.

/S   - Storage (disk) commands. /SL loads a model; /SS saves
        one; /SD deletes a model from the disk and
        must be confirmed; /SI initializes a disk; /SQ
        boots from a slot number (Apple II command);
        # data commands.

/T   - Titles.

/V   - Shows copyright notice and version.

/W   - Window. The screen can be set to various size windows,
        which can be scrolled against each other.

/-   - repeat a label across column width.

[Related Visi-Products]. In mid-1981, VisiCorp introduced a series of additional products, including:

VisiPlot - A plotting program compatible with VisiCalc files.
    VisiPlot can plot up to 16 different series of data, with a
    maximum limit of 645 total plot points. An individual data
    series can contain up to 150 plot points. Line charts, bar
    charts, area charts, pie charts, scatter charts and
    combinations are permissible. Requires Apple II with DOS 3.3,
    48K, and two disk drives. List price, $180.

VisiTrend - Generates trend series from VisiCalc data, including
    trendline forecasting, linear multiple regressions, etc.
    VisiTrend generates output data ready for plotting by
    VisiPlot and is sold combined with that package. The
    VisiPlot/VisiTrend combination is $259.95.

VisiDex - A card index scheme using VisiCalc files. VisiDex
allows easy cross-referencing of information and "pulls" all
related files when a card is accessed. VisiDex also has a
built-in date and calendar routine valid for every month of
the 20th century, which makes this program particularly useful
for authors doing research, etc. Requires an Apple II with
DOS 3.3, 48K, and one disk drive. List price, $199.95

VisiTerm - A terminal communications package for use with either
the Apple serial card + modem, D.C. Hayes modem, or other
device. Uses hi-res, definable text fonts and has a built-in
font editor. Requires Apple II with DOS 3.3, 48K, one disk
drive. List price, $149.95

[Packaged Templates]. VisiCalc templates sold on disk are available for
standard business models. A company called Agrisoft (Suite 202, 1001 East
Walnut, Columbia, MO 65201) sells agricultural models like "Crop Comparison".
Apple itself sells a series called "Real Estate Analyst". Tax models are
available from Professional Software Technology, Inc., (180 Franklin St.,
Cambridge, MA 02139).

[Further Information]. Several newsletters have popped up during the last few
years for the serious VisiCalc user. SATN, a bimonthly, is published by
VisiCalc's creators, Software Arts (POB 494, Cambridge, MA 02139) and is $30
a year for 6 issues. Visitips is a newsletter from a VisiCalc users group,
VisiGroup (POB 254, Scarsdale, NY 10583). Membership in VisiGroup costs $25
and includes 1 year's subscription to the newsletter. A book published by
Osborne/McGraw-Hill, VisiCalc: Home and Office Companion, by David Castlewitz
and Lawrence Chisauski, is full of VisiCalc models.

The Stock Market

Stock market information is like the water we drink. It has so many apparent
sources that, as long as it is clean, few people care, and only a few experts
know, exactly where it comes from.

Actually, investors using computers should take time to understand the source
of various forms of financial information. At times, this seems like tracing
the Nile up the Amazon - or something equally confusing. The headwater of
stock trading information, appropriately enough, is at 55 Water Street in New
York City, in the Wall Street area. This is the headquarters of SIAC, the
Securities Information Automation Corporation, a wholly owned subsidiary of
the New York and American Stock Exchanges.

When trades take place on the Stock Exchange floor at 11 Wall Street, they are
recorded on special mark sense forms. These forms - something like test forms
used in schools - are fed into readers just off the main floor, and the
information is transmitted a few blocks away to SIAC's computers - big IBM
mainframes. On the average, less than a minute elapses between trade time and

report time. One agreement of the exchanges calls for 90% of all trades to be reported in less than 90 seconds.

Once in SIAC's computers, trade reports are filtered for obvious errors and then formatted and displaced over one of two "networks" or outgoing lines - network "A", which contains only New York Stock Exchange (NYSE) trades, and network "B", which contains American Stock Exchange (AMEX) and regional stock exchange reports. SIAC in New York actually takes feeds from such places as the Pacific Stock Exchange (PSE) in San Francisco, turns them around, and sends them back out over Network "B"; the other regional exchanges feeding into Network "B" are the Boston Stock Exchange (BSE), Midwest Stock Exchange (MSE), and Philadelphia Stock Exchange (PHLX).

The outgoing lines from SIAC are 4800-baud lines. One combined line, commonly called the "C" line, has both Network A and B data combined on it. This high-speed line typically feeds to "vendors" - companies such as Quotron, GTE, Reuters, and so on, each of which resells the data to their customers. The Exchanges are somewhat fussy about selling their data, because information charges are the 2nd largest source of its revenue, after member fees. Vendors pay the exchanges a monthly fee (about $55) per customer and must report how many customers they have and who they are.

For most brokerage offices, getting real-time stock market quotations consists of signing up with one of the major vendors and taking data from their network. Quotron, for example, the largest vendor, has offices in New York that receive the NYSE line, as well as commodity exchange tickers and the like, and packages the results into a 9600-baud combined outgoing line, which runs to Quotron regional computer centers, which in turn service Quotron customers over 1200-baud lines. The United Press International, another vendor, captures the stock data for transmission to its member newspapers. There are perhaps 50 different vendors attached to the basic SIAC lines.

The basic charge for the "C" consolidated last sale line is $600/month - $300/month if obtained indirectly from another licensed subscriber. In addition, the subscriber must pay communications charges to his or her site from 55 Water Street in New York - another $1000 per month or higher. Finally, the Exchange levies a fee based on the intended use of the information. The Exchange classified computer programs into these categories: (1) open to interrogation by users, e.g., the user punches in a symbol, and get the current price; (2) stock table compilation, as for newspapers, $500; (3) operations control programs, $500; (4) analysis programs, as might be used by active investors and traders, $500; and (5) market making programs, $3000. Fitting a program to these definitions is usually done on a case-by-case basis by the exchange. These usage charges apply whether information is taken in a direct feed from 55 Water Street or indirectly through another vendor.

[The Bid/Ask and NASD line]. The Consolidated Last Sale line has most, but not all, of the stock information in the US. Whereas the Last Sale line reports trades after they take place, the Bid/Ask line reports bids and offers off the floor of the exchange. Because many bids and asks are made that are not consummated in trades, the Bid/Ask line is even busier than the Last Sale line. A 9600-baud line is used for Bid/Ask data, which costs $252 per month (not counting communications) direct from the Exchange, and $126 if obtained indirectly.

The National Association of Securities Dealers, based in Washington, DC (1735 K St., NW, Washington, DC 20006) reports sales in the over-the-counter (OTC) market. The NASD data line actually originates in Stamford, CT, and is a 2400-baud synchronous line. The typical format for a bid/ask quotation on NASD is:

SYN SYN SHO M AAAAA $$$$F FS $$$$F ETX HPC

where SYN, SHO, FS, and EXT are ASCII characters of the same name. M is a message type identifier; AAAAA is the security identifier; the first $$$$F field is the best bid quote, with a fraction; the second $$$$F, after the field separator (FS), is the best ask quote, with a fraction.

[The Low-Speed Lines]. The high-speed vendor lines date from the 1970s and were designed to work in a computer-to-computer fashion. The traditional stock exchange ticker, meant to be read by humans, is still very much in existence and offers a possible method to obtain current trading data. The low-speed lines run at 135 baud and frequently clog up when trading is active, running perhaps 8-10 minutes behind the market on a normal close and much longer if volume is heavy. Note that the Exchange requires that Registered Representatives have a quotation system whose information derives from the high-speed line, so that the quotes they provide their customers are fresh. However, offices with two systems - say, a Quotron for current prices, and a low-speed ticker feeding into a computer for analysis - get considerable price breaks on data received over the second system.

The low-speed line is available both in real time and 15 minutes delayed. If delayed, there is a lower charge for the data, which the exchanges at that point consider uninteresting. This 15-minute delayed line is the one seen scrolling across the bottom of cable TV channels. Brokerage offices with moving ticker displays usually have the real-time, low-speed line.

[Interfacing to the Low-Speed Ticker]. The low speed stock exchange lines, which are carried by Western Union, use the so-called "900" series ticker code, which is best described as a 6 level, as opposed to 5 level, Baudot code. This code uses 6 data bits, 2 stop bits, and is transmitted at 135 baud. (In early 1982, the NYSE altered its transmissions to only 1 stop bit.) Counting the start bit, 9 bits are required by each character, making the effective rate 15 characters per second. A bit time is 7.4 ms, and a character time is 66.6 ms.

When Western Union installs a ticker line, it terminates it with an ugly gray box sometimes called a Line Interface Box (LIB), and sometimes called a Data Line Termination (DLT). For use with computers, it is important to specify to WU that EIA levels are desired as output from the box; otherwise, they will usually install a damaging 60-mA current loop. (This change can be made in the field by the WU installer and is free). With the proper output levels, two strands of wire can be run from the screw-type terminals (2 and 3) in the LIB to pins 2 and 7 of a RS-232-C serial interface. If the baud rate and stop bits on the UART are set correctly, the computer will read data.

[Low-Speed Ticker Code]. The 6-level code used on the low-speed ticker gives 64 possible values. Some of these have very special meanings assigned by the stock exchanges. There are special, 1 character codes for fractions, like

3/8, and codes for "when issued", and so on. A table mapping these codes as they are received over a line:

CODE	CHAR	CODE	CHAR
0	(blank)	32	.
1	E	33	5
2	. (Filler Dot)	34	c (cash)
3	A	35	1
4	Pr (Preferred)	36	.
5	S	37	s (100s shares)
6	I	38	9
7	U	39	spare
8	WI when issued	40	0
9	D	41	4
10	R	42	. end announcement
11	J	43	. begin announcement
12	N	44	spare
13	F	45	6
14	C	46	3
15	K	47	spare
16	T	48	1/8
17	Z	49	7/8
18	L	50	ss (10s shares)
19	W	51	1/2
20	H	52	8
21	Y	53	3/4
22	P	54	ST (stopped trading)
23	Q	55	1/4
24	O	56	spare
25	B	57	2
26	G	58	7
27	&	59	B
28	M	60	$
29	X	61	5/8
30	V	62	3/8
31	RT (rights)	63	rubout

[Ticker Symbols]. Ticker tape symbols are always 3 letters but may be modified by suffixes and, less often, by a prefix. Typical symbols are:

GFD	Guilford Mills Inc.
WTA	Welded Tube Co of America

Suffixes that modify symbols are:

.A	Class A	.STPD	Stopped Stock
.B	Class B	.UR	Under Rule 783
.CT	Certificate	.V	Voting Trust Certificate
.CV	Convertible	.WD	When Distributed
.F	Subject to Interest Equalization Law	.WI	When Issued
		.WS	Warrants
.N	New	.WW	With Warrants
.ND	Next Day	.XC	Ex-coupon

```
.OPD      Delayed Opening          .XD      Ex-dividend
.P.Pr     Prior Preferred          .XI      Ex-interest
.Pr       Preferred                .XR      Ex-rights
.R        Rights                   .XW      Without Warrants
.REOP     Reopening Trade
.SLD      Delayed sale
.SLD.LAST Delayed is also last
```

Suffixes can be strung together: "CLQ Pr C" means California Life Corporation preferred stock series C, and "BNK WS C" means Bangor Punta Corporation series C warrants.

Prefixes are found less often. "Q" before a symbol means the company is in receivership or in bankruptcy proceedings, e.g., "QXYZ" means XYZ is sunk.

[Low-Speed Ticker Syntax]. The low-speed ticker lines (both the New York and the American) were designed to be read by humans, not computers. The Computer Cookbook strongly recommends that persons interested in getting stock market data directly from the Exchange use the high-speed, 4800-baud line, despite its extra cost. This so-called vendor line, which is used by organizations such as Quotron, Bunker-Raymo, and GTE as the source of their quotes, uses an IBM bisync protocol and will produce highly accurate results. It is, of course, expensive, especially to run to areas outside New York.

Each report of a trade, or "tick", has the following basic syntax:

                        SYMBOL VOLUME PRICE

A clever feature of the 6-level Baudot code used on the low-speed ticker is that all letters (alpha characters) have a low-order bit equal to 0, and all numbers have it equal to 1. Printing ticker devices use this bit to print above the line or below it. Thus a classic piece of tickertape looks like:

```
        ABC         XYZ
        2000s45     4s10
```

This means that 2000 shares of ABC sold at a price of 45. (The small "s" or share symbol is considered a numeric or lower case pallet code.) The conventions for reporting volume are:

        100 share trades: volume always omitted
                ABC45 = 100 shares @ 45

        200 to 900 shares: only the 100s digit used
                ABC9s45 = 900 shares @ 45

        1000 to 9900 shares: volume shown in full
                ABC9900s45 = 9900 shares @ 45

        10000 to 999900 shares = shown in full with figure dots
                ABC10.000.s.45 = 10000 shares @ 45

Multiple trades make the syntax even more complicated. The whole number portion of a 2nd and 3rd trade are dropped when the additional trade ends in a fraction, and the whole number portion is the same as the intitial trade:

ABC 45 1/4 1/2 3/8
= 3 trades of 100 shares @ 45 1/4, 45 1/2, and 45 3/8

When the 1st trade does not end in a fraction, the prices are separated by a figure dot, as it does if the 2rd or 3rd trade is not a round 100 share lot:

ABC45.1/4
= 100 shares @ 45, and 100 shares @ 45 1/4
ABC45 1/4.1000s1/2
= 100 shares @ 45 1/4, 1000 shares @ 45 1/2

Only 100 share units are ever assumed. Thus ABC1000s45 1/4 1/2 means 1000 shares at 45 1/4, and 100 shares at 45 1/2.

Prices are not always simple either. Things can trade in units other than eights: thus, GHI10.000.s.16.32 means 10000 shares of GHI at 16/32nds.

If these rules are not complicated enough, there are various modes of operation for the low-speed line. Digits deleted mode means that only the units digit and the fractional part of the price is transmitted, e.g., ABC 45 1/4 becomes ABC 5 1/4. Digits deleted mode is very common. When a stock crosses a price boundary, say from 49 to 50, the full price is given. Volume deleted mode means that all volume figures are deleted for trades of less than 5000 shares. This mode is also very common and prevents accurate volume figures from being taken off the low-speed line. Entire trades are deleted in "ticker deletion" mode if they involve less than 5000 shares and took place at the same price as the last trade. This mode of reporting is similar to the "tick" (price changes only) reporting used in commodities markets.

Full specifications on the low-speed line format can be obtained from the NYSE Market Data Communications department, 11 Wall Street, New York, NY 10005. The pertinent document is called "Consolidated Tape System General Information".

[Low Speed Line Software]. Several vendors sell softwar that allows interfacing to the low-speed ticker line. The best established of these systems is "Tickertec", originally developed for the North Star Horizon and then moved to the various TRS-80 models, including the Model II and III. Tickertec is marketed by Max Ule & Company (6 East 43rd St., New York, NY 10017, 800-223-6642, 212-687-0705). A fully loaded Tickertec software package costs about $7000, with the bare bones version costing $2000. Tickertec has a market monitor function that will set off an indicator if stock prices go above or below preset limits.

Marketview Microsystems (59 Leicester St., Brighton, MA 02135, 617-787-9794) sells an Apple II software package that would provide a scrolling tickerline from any of several exchanges and last price information in a continuous display of 16 items. The Marketviewer system works not only with the NYSE and AMEX low-speed lines but also with the low-speed commodity lines from the CBT, CEC, and CME. A company called First Flight Data Systems (PO Box 555, Kitty Hawk, NC 27949, 800-334-4773, 919-441-6480) introduced a product called "The Monitor" in 1981, which uses the Apple II. The Monitor can watch 8 different portfolios of up to 30 stocks each, keeps an advance/decline indicator and a tick index, and can give quotes on up to 4000 stocks, although it comes with a basic library of 1600. The Monitor costs $2300.

[Interfacing Through a Vendor]. In general, the vendors of stock quote machines such as Quotron do not like the idea of people attaching personal computers to their systems. Quotron has an Apple II interface available but keeps it quiet. A company called National Stockwatch Corporation (1238 Ortiz SE, Albuquerque, NM 87108, 505-265-7571) has timesharing computers set up in a number of states and retransmits a 15 minute delayed ticker to TRS-80s, Apple IIs, and two of its own private label computers on a continuous basis.

[The Dow Jones Average]. The Dow Jones Average of 30 industrials (DJII) is by far the most familiar index of stock prices to the American public. This is the index reported each night on the television news (the inflections of various newscasters as they root for the index to rise might suggest that TV personalities always buy long and never sell short). The index 1st appeared on July 3, 1884, in Charles Henry Dow's "Customer's Afternoon Letter", a 2-page news bulletin that was the precursor of the Wall Street Journal, which started publication in 1890.

The stocks making up the average varied in the early days, with the index gradually shifting focus from railroad stocks to industrials. In October 1896, an industrial average became a daily feature of the Journal. The average was just that, a simple mathematical average. Over time, however, some of the stocks making up the average began to split - that is, issue 2 shares at a lower price for 1 of their old, in an effort to keep per share prices within reach of small investors. This created a number of problems with the continuity of the index and led, in 1928, to a method where a divisor was used. When stocks split, or when one issue replaces another in the average, the divisor is changed to make yesterday's index equivalent to the new.

[How to Compute the Index]. The current divisor for the Dow Jones Index, and a list of stocks making up the list of 30 industrials, 15 utilities, and so on, is published every Monday in the Wall Street Journal. The method of calculating the index is simple once the prices of the stocks and the divisor is known:

30 STOCKS MAKING UP THE DOW JONES INDUSTRIAL AVERAGE (DJII)
FRIDAY, MAY 14, 1982

Allied Corporation	AlldCp	37.500
Aluminum Co.	Alcoa	26.625
American Brands	ABrand	42.375
American Can	AmCan	27.125
American Tel. & Tel.	ATT	54.750
Bethlehem Steel	BethStl	20.750
DuPont	duPont	36.000
Eastman Kodak	EsKod	73.875
Exxon	Exxon	29.000
General Electric	GenEl	62.625
General Foods	GnFds	36.250
General Motors	GMot	44.000
Goodyear	Goodyr	23.625
Inco	INCO	10.750
IBM	IBM	63.625
International Harvester	IntHarv	4.750

```
Inter Paper                    IntPaper        36.750
Manville Corp.                 Manvill         12.250
Merck                          Merck           75.000
Minnesota M&M                  MMM             55.500

Owens-Illinois                 OwenIll         27.125
Procter & Gamble               ProctG          84.750
Sears Roebuck                  Sears           20.250
Standard Oil of California     StOilCl         34.500
Texaco                         Texaco          31.500
Union Carbide                  UnCarb          47.000
United Technologies            UnTech          40.250
US Steel                       USSteel         24.875
Westinghouse Electric          WestgE          25.750
Woolworth                      Wolwth          19.875
                                               ------
Total                                         1127.50
/ 1.314 = DJII average                         858.07
```

T

Tandy

Since its introduction in 1977, Tandy's TRS-80 has become the best-selling computer in history. By the end of 1982, close to 600,000 TRS-80s of various models were in the field, and Tandy Corporation, once a leather crafts store and now the owner of the 6200-store Radio Shack chain, had taken a place alongside IBM in the computer field.

[History of the TRS-80]. In the beginning, Radio Shack wanted to build a small "hobby" computer kit in its stores. This unit would have been like the KIM or RCA VIP - that is, a microprocessor on a printed circuit board with various LEDs and front panel lights.

By the fall of 1976, Tandy had decided that it really wanted a computer that could programmed in a higher level language. Tandy began investigating "Tiny Basic", which had then been implemented on a number of 8-bit microprocessors. At first, Radio Shack considered using the National Semiconductor PACE microprocessor, with its interest then moving to National's SC/MP ("Simple Cost Effective Microprocessor"). Tandy recruited Steve Leininger, then in National's microprocessor design group, to work on Tandy's new computer project. Leininger, more than anyone, is the "father" of the TRS-80.

From the SC/MP, Radio Shack's attention turned to the Intel 8080 and Motorola 6800 microprocessors. These MOS microprocessors were the standby of the first generation of microcomputers, notably the Altair and the IMSAI. Upon investigation, however, Tandy found Zilog willing to make a very competitive arrangement with its new Z-80. Tandy chose that chip for the TRS-80's CPU. By February 1977, a breadboard edition of the TRS-80 was ready. Memory was then relatively expensive: the breadboard version had 2K ROM and 1K of RAM.

By September 1977, the first models (much expanded) of the TRS-80 were in production, although it was not until early 1978 that they appeared in most Radio Shack stores. At first, the Tandy's TRS-80 and Commodore's PET (both then selling for $595) were neck-and-neck in competition at the low end of the microcomputer scale, but by the latter part of 1978, Tandy had clearly won out by virtue of better marketing and support of its system, especially in the area of perhiperals. Sadly, Charles Tandy, the founder of the company, failed to live to see the success of the TRS-80. He died in his sleep at age 60 on November 4, 1978.

[Overview of the TRS-80]. In general, the TRS-80 is an adequate low-cost computer. The following is a survey of the various components of the TRS-80 system.

[CPU]. The TRS-80 Model I has its central processing unit (CPU) inside the plastic keyboard case. The Model I TRS-80 uses the Zilog Z-80 CPU, but runs it at slower than top speed (at 1.77 mHz, 563 ns, derived from the video timing chain) to make it work with slower memory chips. The Models II and III run the Z-80 at the usual 4 mHz.

[Keyboard]. Radio Shack's full-size keyboard was an important advantage in the machine's early competition with the PET. In the TRS-80, the keys of the keyboard are connected to certain memory locations (387F-3840), which are then scanned by software to see if a key has been depressed. One problem that results from this approach is "bounce" on the keyboard, meaning that multiple characters can appear on screen when a key is pressed. There are several software and hardware corrections for bounce, and the new versions of TRS-80 disk operating system (DOS 2.2, DOS 3.0, and Apparat's NEWDOS) all contain "debounce" software.

[BASIC]. The TRS-80 has its system software, Level I BASIC and Level II BASIC, in 2 ROM (Read Only Memory) chips at the center of the logic board inside the computer. Level I BASIC should be seen as a learning tool for those unfamiliar with the language. When a user has mastered Level I, however, he should upgrade his machine to Level II, which means taking it to Radio Shack and having them change the ROMs. The current cost of this modification is $120. Note that the software in ROM is proprietary, and although the ROMs can be purchased separately, it is best to "keep it legal" and let RS make the changes.

[Expanding the TRS-80]. Radio Shack has allowed for expansion of the TRS-80 with the "expansion interface". The interface is a plastic box connected to the keyboard unit by a thick ribbon cable. The TV monitor is designed to sit on top of this box, getting it partly out of the way. (Most TRS-80 systems tend to be a maze of wires and connections, a design drawback corrected only in the TRS-80 Model II.)

[Memory Expansion]. 16K or 32K of RAM memory (usually in addition to 16K of RAM in the keyboard unit) will plug easily into the expansion interface. The RAM chips needed (usually Japanese) are sold by many independent vendors for around $120, and by Radio Shack for $149.

[Disk System]. Radio Shack uses the Shugart SA-400 mini-floppy disk drive in a single-sided, single-density mode. The first disk drive in the system must, unfortunately, always house a system disk and has 55K of "free storage" on the disk after allowing room for TRSDOS and Disk BASIC. Up to four disks can be chained together for a total mini-floppy capacity of 310K bytes. Several vendors, notably PerCom in Texas, sell higher, 77-track (vs. 35 normal) drive systems for the TRS-80, and full-size floppies and hard disks are also available, the latter from Parasitic (Albany, CA) and Corvus Systems.

[Printers]. Printers can be added to the TRS-80 by one of several methods.
On Level II machines, a special connector can be attached to the back of the
keyboard, where the Expansion Interface cable would normally go, and then run
to a Centronics-compatible parallel printer. This cable, which Radio Shack
sells for $59, saves the expense of having the EI. Alternately, an RS232 or
current loop device can be connected using an add-on product like the Small
Systems Hardware TRS232. Small Systems also includes a driver routine in
BASIC for the interface. Many firms are now selling printers that have
built-in TRS-80 interfaces.

[RS-232 Interface]. The Expansion Interface has a place for a RS232C card
($99) that gives the TRS-80 an industry standard RS232 port. Radio Shack
generally intended the RS232 port connect to a modem; however, with proper
driver software, the RS232 board can drive a Diablo-like printer or printing
terminal. Tandy computers are generally designed for a Centronics-type
parallel printers.

[TRS-80 Flaws]. Most of the faults in the TRS-80 design can be traced back to
Radio Shack's decision to make a low-cost system that almost anyone could use,
and one that would keep bringing the customers back for one item at a time.
The TRS-80 is like a lobster trap: once you get into it, you have to go a
little deeper. It is also, of course, a salesperson's dream and a smart bit
of marketing on the part of Radio Shack.

The Color Computer, which now sells for under $300, should be looked at as an
educational toy for adults, not as a computer that can perform serious
business accounting tasks. The computer is fine for people who want
to learn BASIC programming by doing (which is the only real way to learn it)
and to provide "hands on" experience with computers.

[The TRS-80 Model II]. Radio Shack has implicitly recognized many of the
TRS-80's problems and solved them in the TRS-80 Model II, which it announced
in the spring of 1979, and which appeared in stores that fall. The TRS-80
Model II uses the same Z-80 microprocessor as the TRS-80, but runs it at the
full rated speed of 4 mHz, twice as fast as the old model. The Model II's
memory chips are correspondingly faster, and are sold only in 32K units. The
video display has full upper and lower case characters and a larger, CRT-type
24 line by 80 character screen. Up to 4 full-sized Shugart SA-800 floppy disk
drives can be used, with the system disk mounted next to the video display and
the other 3 rack-mounted vertically under the $350 desk. Finally, Radio Shack
has put the entire $3450 Model II in a single piece of furniture, eliminating
the old TRS-80's familiar maze of connectors.

[The Model III]. The TRS-80 Model III was introduced in mid-1980 as a
replacement for the Model I. One interesting thing about the Model III is its
external I/O bus which is an open invitation, so to speak, to interface
devices to the machine. The I/O bus allows input and output through the 256
I/O ports on the Z-80 microprocessor (actually, ports 00H-7FH, since ports
80H-0FFH are reserved for the TRS-80). The lines on the I/O bus are defined
as follows:

    Address lines. Eight lines, A0-A7, determine the I/O port
       address (00-7F).

Data line. A 1-byte data channel is available, lines DB0-DB7.

Control lines. These lines help the Model III's Z-80 do the
    right thing while I/O is in
            progress from the bus. The lines are:

IN*-Z80 - input is in progress;

OUT*-Z80 - output is in progress;

RESET* - resets system;

IOBUSINT* - if Z-80 interrupts are enables, interrupts CPU;

IOBUSWAIT* - forces wait states on CPU if I/O bus is enabled;

EXTIOSEL* - input to CPU that latches the I/O bus input for an IN
    instruction;

M1* and IORQ* - see Z-80 definition.

The external I/O bus is enabled for input only if bit 4 of port 0ECH is set to
one. In Microsoft BASIC is an OUT 236,16 instruction. If external devices
are to generate interrupts, the address of the user interrupt service routine
must be placed in locations 403E and 403F, because the Z-80 Mode 1 locations
(memory 0-60, etc.) are used by the Model III's Level II ROMs. Bus
interrupts are enabled only if bit 3 of Port EOH is set to one.

Telesoftware

Both the terms "downloading" and telesoftware have rapidly become buzzwords of
the new electronic era. Some use the "download" term so loosely that anything
that is transmitted is downloaded.

An attempt to make a precise technical definition of downloading follows.
Downloading is the loading of a program or other information into a remote
computer over a communications link by another machine.

Several implications follow out of this definition. The idea of loading
the remote computer means that the receiving machine must have storage of some
kind. (It is inappropriate, therefore, to talk of downloading information
to memory-less terminals, because information can be displayed on them, but
not stored in them.)

Second, downloading implies computer-to-computer (and often unattended)
operation. Downloading is concerned only with transmission and storage;
display of the information at human reading speed can take place later, after
the communications link is cut. Although downloading can take place at any
speed, the concept suggests a high-speed, machine-to-machine transfer of some
kind.

Clearly, downloading becomes increasingly important as falling microprocessor and memory costs make local storage and processing of information feasible. In the evolution of terminal devices, intelligent terminals have replaced dumb terminals; these intelligent terminals, which have microprocessors and random-access memory, will, in turn, eventually be replaced by general-purpose personal computers, which they already resemble.

[Telesoftware].   Although textual material and numerical data can be downloaded to a personal computer, the transmission of personal computer programs is generally referred to as "telesoftware".   There is an ascending degree of difficulty in the successful downloading of text, numeric data, and program data:

  - Text is clearly the easiest material to download to a computer.
    If the text material is to be read off the computer screen,
    minor transmission errors can be ignored. A simple criterion
    that determines whether a system is downloading or merely
    displaying information is this: is the human's reading time
    greater than the connect time? Tandy's turnkey videotext
    system, which uses special $399 terminals, employs a technique
    commonly called dump and disconnect, in which the transmission
    takes place uninterrupted, at high speed; the host
    disconnects; and the reader browses, off-line, at the received
    material. Note that in this nearly one-way transmission, it
    is assumed that the human reader can reconstuct any garbled
    text.

  - Numeric computer data, as opposed to text, presents greater
    problems, because the requirement for accuracy is higher.
    Most systems for downloading numeric data use checksums and
    allow retransmission requests by the receiving computer.

  - Programs. Although numeric data, especially critical financial
    data, requires error-free transmission, transmission errors
    will not cause the remote system operating on that data to
    crash. If control of the remote machine is handed over to a
    downloaded program, however, a transmission error is more than
    likely to cause the remote unit to crash. If the remote unit
    is unattended, resetting the unit can be a serious difficulty.

[Current Telephone-Based Efforts].   At present, telesoftware is an experimental and yet-to-be-successful method of distributing software.

The most ambitious effort involving telephone distribution of software in the US has been made by Texas Instruments through TEXNET, TI's adjunct to The Source.   TI has made a big effort to place software for its 99/4 Home Computer on TEXNET (Attachment I-A), including programs that use the 99/4's voice synthesizer and color graphics display.

However, TI's TEXNET telesoftware appears to be heavily subsidized and seems to exist to encourage sales of the TI computer.   Two other telesoftware operations, those run by CompuServe and The Source, appear equally unprofitable.

CompuServe is the Columbus, OH-based operator of MicroNet. CompuServe offers user-written software in a software exchange and also distributes free a short executive program that turns a TRS-80 Model I or III computer into a simulated Tandy Videotex terminal (the Videotex terminal, a specialized Tandy product, has a modem, RF modulator, and low-cost keypad, and sells at $399).

Although the executive downloading program has some appeal to TRS-80 owners (it is a free program, after all), the User Software Exchange appears poorly maintained and infrequently used. Its software offerings, like those of many computer club software exchanges, are unsophisticated and amateurish, particularly in contrast to those of TI.

Finally, The Source, owned by Reader's Digest, offers a limited number of programs in its User Publishing section. The Source disclaims any responsibility for these offerings.

In Europe, personal computer software has been downloaded over Prestel, the UK's public timesharing service. In September 1980, the Council on Educational Technology (CET) of the UK formulated a proposed standard for distribution of program listings (usually BASIC programs in ASCII) over Prestel (Attachment I-D). This transmission protocol used a parity check on individual characters and a CRC-type check on blocks on code. Individual terminals could request a finite number of retransmissions of blocks found to have parity or CRC errors.

[Mainframe Transmission Protocols]. In its telephone downloading efforts, the microcomputer world is duplicating techniques relatively well-established in the big computer or mainframe world. A number of communications protocols have been devised to ensure error-free transmission of files between computers. IBM's 2770 Bisync protocol is typical:

```
              IBM 2770 BISYNC PROTOCOL
              ------------------------


          transmitting computer   receiving computer
          ---------------------   ------------------

  { phase 1 - initial are you there inquiry}

            sends ENQ inquiry      responds w/DLE 0
```

The receiving computer always reponds with a DLE, followed by a 0 or 1. The last bit of this ASCII character indicates whether the receiving computer has received an even or odd number of blocks from the sending computer.

```
  { phase 2 - 1st and subsequent data blocks}

            sends STX start of text
            sends data characters
            sends ETB, end text block
            sends 2 CRC characters

                              if CRC checks, sends
```

                                        DLE 1, indicating
                                        an odd number of blocks
                                        received

    This sequence continues for n data blocks.

    { phase 3 - last data block}

            sends STX
            sends DATA
            sends EXT, end of text
            sends CRC
                                        responds in usual way

    { phase 4 - final sign-off}

            sends EOT, end of transmission

Many transmission protocols also feature timeouts, which effect a
retransmission if no acknowledgement is received in say, 10 seconds, on the
theory that the transmission was completely lost.

[Downloading over 1-way Video Channels].   Downloading over 1-way video
channels is considerably more difficult than downloading over a 2-way
telephone channel. The basic problem is that the receiving computer cannot
ask for retransmission, an ability assmued in almost all 2-way telephone
downloading protocols.

There are two basic technologies used for transmitting computer data over
video channels:

    - Vertical blanking interval (VBI) techniques, common from
      broadcast and cable-carried teletext. Teletext decoders, in
      these schemes, are conceptually identical to modems. Most can
      deliver an effect baud rate of 300 or 1200 baud, although some
      claim the ability to transmit at 9600 baud. Full-field
      teletext uses the same encoding and decoding technique but
      uses 200 or so horizontal scan lines in a full TV channel
      rather than 2 or 3.

    - Audio subcarriers. An alternate technique, similar to SCA
      transmission of data, involves use of the 5 or 6 audio
      subcarriers available on television channels. A 5 kHz audio
      subcarrier is capable, with appropriate encoding and decoding
      equipment, to transmit at an effect baud rate of 19,000 bps.
      Some newer digital stream devices promise rates of up to 56K
      baud on 7.5 kHz channels.

In addition to difficulties created by decoding hardware, a number of
problems in teletext transmission of software are created by the fact that
teletext was designed to transmit text information, not binary data.   In
particular, problems that arise with both the BBC (British) Teletext
specification and the AT&T (North American) specification are:

- Transmission is in 7-bit ASCII characters with odd parity. The natural unit for computer-to-computer communication is an 8-bit byte;

- Text transmission can tolerate errors, but transmission of binary machine code cannot. An error of one bit in thousands, although merely producing a typo in text, is quite likely to cause a downloaded program to crash.

- Personal computer programs can be large, typically running 32K and 48K, and growing larger with the increasing use of sound, speech, and elaborate graphics. Absolute transmission time is a problem, especially over VBI systems or with slow decoders. Furthermore, text transmission has always worked with relatively short pages of information. Long programs must be broken among pages, and the position of these program segments must be optimized in the teletext carousel.

Subcarrier audio techniques are used by Playcable, a joint venture of Mattel, the toymaker, and General Instruments, the electronics company and cable TV supplier.

Only a few protocols for 1-way teletext transmission have been developed, one by the author. John Hedger, of the Independent Broadcast Authority (IBA) in England, has also experimented with downloading programs via teletext.

[Protocol for Teletext Software Downloading]. The following protocol for point-to-multipoint software transmission has been developed by William Bates. Teletext systems have been designed to transmit text using 7-bit ASCII code. The transmission of nontext information - whether binary numbers or program code - using teletext transportation systems remains a difficult problem. Point-to-multipoint transmission over one-way links does not allow the receiving device to make retransmission requests, as is common with land line protocols; the 7 bit/8 bit problem is a nuisance; and, unlike text, binary data, especially executable machine code, must be 100% accurate.

This proposed protocol for transmitting machine code object programs has the advantages of being compatible with both the AT&T "North American Broadcast Teletext Specification" (June 22, 1981) and with the BBC standard, as well as being compatible with the two major teletext decoders on the North American market, the Zenith "Virdata" decoder and the Norpak "Mark IV". This form of one-way downloading can also be used (and was in fact originally developed) for use on Western Union point-to-multipoint land lines using ordinary modems.

1-WAY DOWNLOAD PROTOCOL
----

(1) Transportation. For any transmission system allowing 7 data bits, odd parity can be used. Note that although even parity is the de-facto standard of telephone and timesharing systems, odd parity is used by teletext systems. Historically teletext decoders have had to recover bit-rate clocks from data waveforms; odd parity ensures that there will be at least one data level transition every 14 bit-times (consider even parity

with all "0s" transmitted — there could be long stretches of
"dead air", e.g., all zeros).

(2) Nibble Stream. The function of the teletext decoder is to
deliver a continuous stream of 7-bit plus odd parity bytes
over an interface (RS-232-C or parallel) to the personal
computer. When received by the personal computer, each
7-data, odd-parity byte produces one Hamming-protected 4-bit
nibble when decoded using the "Bates bit-switch" technique
outlined below.

(3) This nibble stream is interpreted according to the AT&T
protocol for DATA PACKETS. DATA PACKETS can carry DATA GROUPS
that are either Type 0 (displayable teletext) or, in this
case, Type 1 (download record). It is assumed that the
teletext decoder will route Type 1 records over an interface
toward the personal computer, whereas Type 0 records
(broadcast teletext) will be directly displayed by its
character generator/PLP software. Note that the personal
computer with appropriate software can be used for both
functions but at a loss of 1/2 bandwidth for teletext
transmission (but better accuracy).

(4) Up to 16 Type 1 DATA GROUPS create an object-code overlay of
57,120 bytes, an adequate memory image for most microcompters.
The continuity index of the DATA GROUP header is monitored to
detect loss of a data group. Because a single DATA GROUP size
is so small (7K) relative to the number of bytes needed for
microcomputer programs, the continuity index is used as a type
of high-order address nibble.

(5) The actual data is contained in 4-byte independent segments
that occur naturally on DATA BLOCK (scan line) boundaries. It
is assumed here that the decoder will reject bad packets
(e.g., individual scan lines). Each scan line is made up of 7
4-byte groups ADDRH,ADDRL,DATAH,DATAL. The first two bytes
indicate the location in memory of the following two bytes.
The executive program receiving this data and stuffing it into
memory must protect itself from possible overlapping addresses
contained in the downloaded program. Note that, because
2-byte units are being addressed at a time, bit 0 of ADDRL is
always 0. In the future, this bit may be used to extend
addressing to a 128K absolute address space. Also note that
this scheme allows noncontiguous memory to be easily addressed
and allows data tables to be dynamically updated.

(6) A transmission is considered complete when 16 data groups, as
indicated by the continuity index, have been received, and
none of the data groups have been "broken" — that is, none
contained fewer DATA BLOCKS than indicated in the count in
their header. Note that because of segmentation, "broken"
data blocks do not damage the memory image, although they may
result in unfilled gaps. If fewer than 16 DATA GROUPS are
required to fill memory, as is likely, null (0 DATA BLOCKS

long) DATA GROUPS must be sent.

(7) The repetition index allows easy overlay and correction of "broken" data GROUPS. A DATA GROUP, once received correctly, stays correct, even if the subsequent DATA GROUP with the same number is received "broken".

(8) If the personal computer does not receive 16 unbroken data groups within a set (0-15) number of repetitions, the download is considered unsuccessful, and the personal computer program aborts. A clock time abort mechanism and/or manual reset may be necessary on very noisy lines.

[The Bates Bit-Switch Technique]. The Bates bit-switch technique makes a slight modification of Hamming encoding to allow transmission of 8-bit (used to encode 4 "hard" message bits) Hamming codes over serial links restricted to transmitting 7 data bits, odd parity, e.g., most 1-way teletext links.

[Encoding Algorithm]. The input to the algorithm is a 4-bit nibble with value 0-F in hexadecimal. The preliminary output is a 7-bit byte, described by the following table:

INPUT NIBBLE		OUTPUT (B7-B1)
0	0000	0010101
1	0001	0000010
2	0010	0001001
3	0011	0011110
4	0100	0100100
5	0101	0110011
6	0110	0111000
7	0111	0101111
8	1000	1010000
9	1001	1000111
A	1010	1001100
B	1011	1011011
C	1100	1100001
D	1101	1110110
E	1110	1111101
F	1111	1101010

The output can be thought of as the conventional Hamming encoding with the most significant bit (bit 8), a message bit, moved to the position of B7, a check bit. What was B7 will not be generated by the encoding software but rather by a hardware UART (below).

This output word is then transmitted by a UART set for 7 data bits, odd parity. The UART can be counted on to generate B8 as follows:

INPUT	PARITY BIT (B8)
0	0

1	0
2	1
3	1
4	1
5	1
6	0
7	0
8	1
9	1
A	0
B	0
C	0
D	0
E	1
F	1

[Transmission]. The full byte is transmitted in the usual fashion. Output transmission should generate two stop bits; receiving UARTS should be set to 1 stop bit. This allows for "jitter" in the baud rate clocks of potentially several thousand receiving devices in the field.

[Decoding Algorithm]. The receiving UART can be set at either 7 data, odd parity, or at 8 data, no parity. In either case, reception should be considered complete after 1 stop bit is received (this is a hardware characteristic of most UARTs). The following description of the decoding algorithm assumes that the UART is set at 7 data, odd parity, and generates a status indication PARITY ERROR. Note that this technique can suffer a PARITY ERROR and yet recover all 4 message bits accurately. Conversely, absence of a PARITY ERROR does not guarantee the data; further tests (Hamming tests "A", "B", and "C") must be made.

BATES-MODIFIED HAMMING DECODING ALGORITHM

{action depends on the status of the UART}

if PARITY_ERROR then

    begin

        {make the following tests}

        A:=B7 XOR B6 XOR B2 XOR B1;
        B:=B7 XOR B4 XOR B3 XOR B2;
        C:=B6 XOR B5 XOR B4 XOR B2;

            case (A,B,C) of

        {"correct" inverts the specified bit}
        {"accept" means B7,B6,B4,B2 taken as message bits}

            0 0 1 correct(B7); accept;

```
                    1 1 1   accept;
                    0 1 0   correct(B6); accept;
                    1 1 0   accept;
                    1 0 0   correct(B4); accept;
                    1 0 1   accept;
                    0 1 1   correct(B2); accept;

              end;

          if not PARITY_ERROR then

            begin

              {make the same tests}

              A:=B7 XOR B6 XOR B2 XOR B1;
              B:=B7 XOR B4 XOR B3 XOR B2;
              C:=B6 XOR B5 XOR B4 XOR B2;

              {options}

              if (A and B and C) = 1, then accept
                 else reject

            end;
```

This transmission scheme has the full capabilities of the Hamming technique. It is capable of correcting single bit errors in transmission and of detecting an even number (2, 4, or 6) of bit errors. An odd number of bit errors (3, 5, or 7) result in bad message bits being accepted. A completely inverted byte (8-bit errors) will also be accepted.

Teletext and Videotext

"Teletext" and "videotext" are terms around which a conspiracy seems to have formed to keep their meanings confused.

Teletext is the transmission of digital information at high speeds (e.g., megabaud type rates) in television pictures, sometimes in the vertical blanking interval (VBI), and sometimes in the entire video frame (full-frame teletext). In England, the BBC and ITV have had a commercial teletext service operational for 6 or 7 years. In the United States, Time Incorporated is running full-frame teletext tests in Coral Gables, FL, and in San Diego, CA.

Videotext is the use of telephone lines for 2-way communication. Videotext, therefore, is a development out of computer timesharing (there are those who say videotext, per se, doesn't really exist) and is differentiated only by a low-cost terminal. Two-way cable TV systems can be used as a low-speed substitute for the phone system. In this case, a cable-distributed system (as used by Dow Jones in Englewood, NJ, and at a Colorado site) is videotext, not teletext. The LA Times-Mirror test in Southern California is also videotext, not teletext.

[Videotex]. "Videotex", without the final "t", is sometimes used as a generic term to cover the fields of both teletext and videotext (The Computer Cookbook believes this usage to be confusing). A Videotex Industry Association was created in February 1982 to "promote and encourage the development of videotex and teletext in the U.S.; to educate the public about the applications and benefits of videotex and teletext; to serve as a conduit for the exchange of information, opinions and analysis within the industry; to represent the interests of the videotex and teletext industry before local and national regulatory and legislative bodies."

[Prestel]. The British Prestel system, one of the largest videotext services, has become something of an international news provider. Presel began offering commercial service in the US from a Boston computer center in February 1982 and, through a company called Logica in New York, offered an Apple II Prestel board.

From the US, users can access the 210,000-page Prestel database over Telenet. More than 15,000 users are connected to Prestel, and about 900 information providers are using system for electronic publishing and mail. Information providers - akin to publishers - using Prestel include Merrill Lynch, American Express, Holiday Inn, Frost & Sullivan, Newsweek, TWA, and Official Airlines Guide. US companies using the system on a closed user group basis include DuPont, ABC-TV, and Digital Equipment (DEC). Prestel uses Zenith terminals ($1250) and Wolfdata and Radofin decoders.

Information providers to the Prestel world service pay: (1) standing charge of $10,000 per year; (2) charge of $10 per page per year, with a 100-page minimum; (3) communications costs estimated at $0.15/min via Telenet; (4) free unlimited editing time; and (5) billing charge of 5% of page price is charged for handling frame revenue billing.

Users of the Prestel world service pay: (1) standing charge of $50 per month; (2) connect time of $0.30/min (3) communications charges of $0.15/min for Telenet; and (4) a per-page charge, as set by each information provider. Subscriber information about Prestel can be obtained from Logicia (NY) or from British Videotex & Teletext (1730 N Lynn St., Suite 400, Arlington, VA 22209, 703-841-9308), a sort of lobbying group in the US.

[The Tandy-CompuServe Agreement]. In their early 1981 catalog, Radio Shack advertised their VideoTex information terminal at $399. This device included a telephone modem and screen for this price, as well as one free hour of time on CompuServe. In addition to the VideoTex terminal, Tandy offers software packages for tying in to CompuServe - even one program for the Apple II. At present, Tandy's videotex offerings include:

Model I/Model III VideoTex Package (26-2220)	$29.95
Model II VideoTex Package (26-2221)	$29.95
TRS-80 Color Computer Package (26-2222)	$29.95
"Dumb Terminal" emulator	$19.95
Apple II VideoTex Package (26-2223)	$29.95

[The LA Times-Mirror]. In a joint venture announced in January 1982, Times Mirror Videotex Services announced plans to start 20 videotext systems in US between 1983 and 1985. The Times-Mirror venture began field tests on two systems, one using two-way cable TV and the other telephone-based, in Southern California in March 1982 at Mission Viejo and Verdes. Like Time Incorporated and Knight-Ridder, Times-Mirror plans to involve both local newspapers and cable operators in setting up its systems. Among services offered in the field test are teleshopping from Sears, home banking from Bank of America, Ticketron reservations, and airline information.

[1982 Teletext Experiments]. Teletext is an expensive technology that to date has been developed primarily by the central post office and telephone authorities (PTT's) of European countries. In early 1982, the FCC seemed faced with the problem of choosing either the British, French, or Canadian systems for teletext. In February 1982, the FCC decided instead upon an open-entry policy for teletext rather than imposing a uniform teletext standard on the US. Naturally, each foreign country, and their corporate allies in the US, had hoped their standard would be the one imposed.

Various teletext experiments in the US continued in 1982. A Washington, DC, teletext trial run by WETA-TV and the Alternative Media Center moved into 2nd test phase in January 1982, shifting its focus from hard news to a bulletin board, electronic art display, and analysis of events. The 1st phase of the study showed that Washington Post news pages, entertainment, and weather were most widely read. In February 1982, KIRO-TV Seattle launched a teletext experiment, installing several receivers in public places to get exposure and comment.

Building a teletext decoder is no joke. A number of firms have attempted to build teletext decoders that would work with satellite and cable transmission. Southern Satellite Systems (SSS), of Tulsa, OK, is the carrier of Ted Turner's WTBS "Superstation" out of Atlanta, GA. In the late 1970s, SSS decided to utilize the excess capacity of the vertical interval of WTBS for 1-way, point-to-multipoint data transmission. The vertical interval could carry the equivalent of about 800 low-speed, 300-baud lines and offer instant, nationwide coverage.

SSSs first attempted to have a decoder built under contract with MicroTV, a Philadelphia, PA-based firm. Their boxes, according to SSS, didn't work. Southern Satellite then went to Scientific Atlanta, a big supplier of satellite dishes and cable converters. Their attempt to make a teletext decoder also failed.

At NCTA in 1979, Zenith, which had decided that it wanted to be in the cable TV business but wasn't sure how, had on display a number of items culled from their lab. Among these was a teletext decoder that had been built with British chips. Zenith's booth was across the aisle from Southern Satellite's, and a relationship was born.

Video Data Systems and Oak Industries have also had unsuccessful decoder projects. The decoders built by Wegner for United Video, which use audio subcarriers, are said to have reliability problems. The only other firm with a Vertical Blanking Interval (VBI) scheme is Tocom, which has a system that puts data in lines 17 and 18 at the headend. It is designed to allow cable operators to offer a teletext service from their local station. Cable systems with this service cannot also carry SSS's satellite transmissions, because the Tocom scheme clears lines 17 and 18 prior to insertion.

[Physical Description]. Zenith's teletext decoder is a low flatbox 19 inches wide by 20 inches deep by 4 inches high. It is designed to be rack-mounted with other video equipment. The box is very large for home use and has sharp edges on the rack mount flanges. There are 2 cutouts on the back for RS-232 DCE ports, although only 1 connector is implemented. The RS-232 does not allow the mating connector to be screwed into the box, making the connection insecure over long use.

Revision 2.0 (mid-1981) "production" models of the decoder are designed to make it difficult for the cable operator to modify in order to illegally access other services. Whereas the older versions of the box had three rotary switches allowing easy setting to any teletext service, the new boxes are "set" at the factory and otherwise not touched. There are no user options, except for a single (not 3) digit page select wheel and for a reset button on the back of the unit.

At the Eastern Cable show in Atlanta, GA, in August 1981, Southern Satellite had a revision V 2.0 of the decoder motherboard, dated 5-1-81. There was an "I Forgot" card mounted on the motherboard correcting a problem with the video sync separator. Also, the Dow Jones unit, which arrived at the show direct from Zenith, apparently had a bad trace on the PC board that prevented the UART parity enable from working. Zenith has a revised motherboard that went to layout in August, 1981. It corrects the synch separator and the trace problem. The Mullard (UK) teletext chip in the box uses lines 15 and 16. Line 14 would be the next to be used.

[Teletext Page Assignment and Selection]. A 3-position rotary switch on the front of the old models, which allows dialing from one service to another, has been replaced by a single rotary switch, which allows dialing only the last (decimal) page digit in a group of 10. The hundred's and ten's digit is set inside the unit by strapping. The strapping technique is strange and involves putting the pins of a diode array IC in and out of the socket.

Pages are numbered 100 to 800. Page 100-109 are used for SSS diagnostics and other items. The current index is:

                103 - "clock cracker" diagnostic
                110 - UPI
                113 - a cat's face graphic
                120 - Reuters
                210 - Dow Jones

In general, pages above 200 are reserved for RS-232 services.

In the diode array square, the channel's most significant decimal digits are selected by strapping a chip with the BCD representation of the digit. Pins 1-4 represent the ten's digit, and pins 5-8 set the hundred's digit. UPI is strapped as follows:

```
1 - pin out = 0
2 - pin out = 0        BCD 4
3 - pin in  = 1
4 - pin out = 0

5 - pin out = 0
6 - pin in  = 1        BCD 2
7 - pin out = 0
8 - pin out = 0
```

To get Dow Jones, this was changed to: 1000 - 0100, or BCD 12.

[RS-232 Options]. The RS-232 port is, in theory, fully strappable. The device uses an Intel 8251 UART. The strapping is controlled by an IC in the second row, third from left in an 8-socket field.

[Teletext Chip UART Operation]. The Mullard chips searches the incoming bit stream off lines 15-16 for its proper page identifier at a 5-megabit rate. When it finds the proper prologue as determined by the page setting of the unit, the device clocks 22 bytes into a data buffer. The Zenith unit then clocks these out the RS-232 port at the selected speed. As long as more packets of information are not received by the teletext chip prior to the buffer going empty, there is no overrun.

The effective baud rate of the Mullard chip depends on how fast you send it data packets, not on any switch setting inside the unit. Thus it is essentially controlled from the headend. As long as the RS-232 port is set at a speed greater than or equal to the effective baud rate, giving it time to clear the buffer before the next packet arrives, the unit will not overrun.

Texas Instruments

Texas Instruments, the giant semiconductor manufacturing company, announced its home computer on June 1, 1979, in anticipation of its unveiling at the Summer Consumer Electronics Show in Chicago, June 3-6, 1979. The first machines were seen in stores in August of 1979 and were not available in quantity until late that year.

The 99/4 took a great deal of abuse from the microcomputer community, much of it deserved. But by 1982, TI - always known for running well in a straight line - had dropped the price, with rebate, to under $300, and had overtaken all but Commodore in "home" computer sales.

The 99/4 has a long history. As early as 1977, Texas Instruments commissioned several market research studies of the home computer market, including one by the Gallup poll organization. These studies indicated that the home computer market was not yet ripe but that it might explode in the early 1980s. TI, whose success in calculators came from its ability to club competitors on the head in high volume manufacturing, waited.

Texas Instruments also had both technical and marketing reasons for delaying the introduction of its home computer. On the technical side, TI already had "on the shelf" a good 16-bit microprocessor, the 9900, that it could use in a small computer system. On the other hand, the firm had no 8-bit microprocessor of its own and, should it have decided to bring out an 8-bit machine, would have been placed in the embarrassing position of buying parts from Motorola, MOS Technology, Zilog, or Intel, its competitors, or funding a new R&D program to develop its own 8-bit processor when this product was far past its prime. TI apparently chose to believe that it was "ahead of the market" with its 16-bit 9900 and waited.

On the marketing side, TI appears to have gone after the elusive "consumer" market that, if anyone has, Apple has. TI originally priced its machine right under the Apple II at $1150 and included, in addition to the keyboard/computer unit, its own Zenith color monitor - leaving the TV free for watching TV.

In addition to 16-color graphics, the 99/4 has all the other "video game" enhancements associated with the Apple II, including a tone generator with a 5-octave range, and (optional) game paddle controls. An interesting twist to the system is that TI apparently wants to make an adapted version of its "Speak and Spell" voice synthesizer standard equipment. The components of the system are:

- Console Unit. As on the Tandy TRS-80, the central processor
  and main memory of the TI-99/4 is inside the keyboard
  enclosure. The keyboard itself is highly simplified in
  comparison to standard ASCII keyboards. TI thinks that so
  much of its applications software will be in ROM that
  relatively little RAM will be needed. The machine is not
  really portable, weighing 42 pounds with monitor.

- Video Monitor. TI is supplying a Zenith 13" color video
  monitor with its system. Standard screen display is 24 lines
  of 32 characters - narrower than that of the Apple II.
  Characters are displayed on an 8x8 dot matrix, and the ability
  to custom-program 256 characters appears to be standard. For
  graphics, the screen is 192 x 256 pixels.

[Software]. While the TI machine has a disk, the TI computer also uses plug-in "ROM packs" for applications software. On the TI machine these slide into a tray on the right-hand side of the keyboard. These contain up to 30 kilobytes of ROM, depending on the application. TI calls these ROM packs "Solid State Software" (its trademark) and suggests they retail between $19.95 and $69.95.

Tymnet and Telenet

Packet-switched networks are the least understood yet most important aspects of any telecommunications system.

[Telenet]. Telenet was acquired by General Telephone & Electronics (GTE) in 1979. In 1978, as a separate company, Telenet's revenues came to $8.9 million. At the time of GTE's acquisition, the Federal Communications Commission ruled that Telenet must be handled at "arm's length" from GTE's other telephone businesses.

Telenet's president since 1973 was Lawrence G. Roberts. Roberts, who began his career at MIT's Lincoln Laboratory, and who holds a PhD from that institution had directed ARPANET from 1966 serving as director of information processing techniques. ARPANET was the first large-scale application of packet-switching technology. Telenet, modeled on it, went operational in mid-1975.

[Telenet Numbers]. GTE/Telenet provides local network access in US cities of 50,000 population or more. IN-WATS access is available in other locations. 1200 BPS access numbers require the use of Bell 212- or Vadic 3405-compatible modems, as noted by the following codes: (B) = BELL 212, (V) = VADIC 3405, (B/V) = either Bell 212 or Vadic 3405. < > indicates the actual location of telenet facilities. In some cases, local access may require extended metro telephone service or involve message unit charges.

		300 BPS		1200 BPS
AL%205	BESSEMER	326-3420	<BIRMINGHAM>	(B/V) 326-3420
AL%205	BIRMINGHAM	326-3420		(B/V) 326-3420
AL%205	FLORENCE	766-9101		(B/V) 766-9101
AL 205	HUNTSVILLE	539-2281		(B/V) 539-2281
AL%205	MOBILE	432-1680		(B/V) 432-1680
AL 205	MONTGOMERY	265-1500		(B/V) 265-1500
AL%205	SHEFFIELD	766-9101	<FLORENCE>	(B/V) 766-9101
AK 907	ANCHORAGE	276-0271		(B/V) 276-0271
AK 907	JUNEAU	586-9700		(B/V) 586-9700
AR%501	LITTLE ROCK	372-4616		(B/V) 372-4616
AZ%602	MESA	254-0244	<PHOENIX>	(B/V) 254-0244
AZ%602	PHOENIX	254-0244		(B/V) 254-0244
AZ%602	SCOTTSDALE	254-0244	<PHOENIX>	(B/V) 254-0244
AZ%602	TEMPE	254-0244	<PHOENIX>	(B/V) 254-0244
AZ 602	TUCSON	745-1666		(B/V) 745-1666
CA 213	ALHAMBRA	507-0909	<GLENDALE>	(B/V) 507-0909
CA 714	ANAHEIM	558-6061	<SANTA ANA>	(B/V) 558-7078
CA 805	BAKERSFIELD	327-8146		(B/V) 327-8146
CA 415	BURLINGAME	595-0360	<SAN CARLOS>	(B/V) 591-0726
CA%213	CANOGA PARK	306-2984	<MARINA DEL REY>	(B/V) 306-2984
CA%714	COLTON	824-9000		(B/V) 824-9000

```
CA%408 CUPERTINO            294-9119 <SAN JOSE>              (B/V) 294-9119
CA%714 ES CONDIDO           743-1210                        (B/V) 743-1210
CA 213 EL MONTE             507-0909 <GLENDALE>             (B/V) 507-0909
CA 714 FULLERTON            558-6061 <SANTA ANA>            (B/V) 558-7078
CA 209 FRESNO               233-0961                        (B/V) 233-0961
CA 714 GARDEN GROVE         898-9820                        (B/V) 898-9820
CA%213 GLENDALE             507-0909                        (B/V) 507-0909
CA#415 HAYWARD              881-1382                        (B/V) 881-1382
CA 213 HOLLYWOOD            689-9040 <LOS ANGELES>          (B/V) 624-2251
CA#213 HOLLYWOOD            937-3580 <LOS ANGELES>          (B/V) 937-3580
CA 714 HUNTINGTON BEACH     558-6061 <SANTA ANA>            (B/V) 558-7078
CA 213 INGLEWOOD            689-9040 <LOS ANGELES>          (B/V) 624-2251
CA#213 INGLEWOOD            937-3580 <LOS ANGELES>          (B/V) 937-3580
CA 213 LOS ANGELES          689-9040                        (B/V) 624-2251
CA#213 LOS ANGELES          937-3580                        (B/V) 937-3580
CA%415 LOS ALTOS            856-9995 <PALO ALTO>            (B/V) 856-9995
CA%213 LONG BEACH           548-6141 <SAN PEDRO>            (B/V) 548-6141
CA%213 MARINA DEL REY       306-2984                        (B/V) 306-2984
CA 209 MODESTO              576-2852                        (B/V) 576-2852
CA%415 MOUNTAIN VIEW        856-9995 <PALO ALTO>            (B/V) 856-9995
CA 714 NEWPORT BEACH        558-6061 <SANTA ANA>            (B/V) 558-7078
CA%415 OAKLAND              836-4911                        (B/V) 836-4911
CA 805 OXNARD               659-4660 <VENTURA>              (B/V) 656-6760
CA%415 PALO ALTO            856-9995                        (B/V) 856-9995
CA 213 PASADENA             507-0909 <GLENDALE>             (B/V) 507-0909
CA 415 REDWOOD CITY         595-0360 <SAN CARLOS>           (B/V) 591-0726
CA%714 RIVERSIDE            824-9000 <COLTON>               (B/V) 824-9000
CA%916 SACRAMENTO           448-6262                        (B/V) 448-6262
CA%408 SALINAS              443-4940                        (B/V) 443-4940
CA%714 SAN BERNADINO        824-9000 <COLTON>               (B/V) 824-9000
CA%415 SAN CARLOS           591-0726                        (B/V) 591-0726
CA 714 SAN DIEGO            231-1922                        (B/V) 233-0233
CA 415 SAN FRANCISCO        362-6200                        (B/V) 956-5777
CA%408 SAN JOSE             294-9119                        (B/V) 294-9119
CA 415 SAN MATEO            595-0360 <SAN CARLOS>           (B/V) 591-0726
CA%213 SAN PEDRO            548-6141                        (B/V) 548-6141
CA 714 SANTA ANA            558-6061                        (B/V) 558-7078
CA 805 SANTA BARBARA        682-5361                        (B/V) 682-5361
CA%408 SANTA CLARA          294-9119 <SAN JOSE>             (B/V) 294-9119
CA%213 SANTA MONICA         306-2984 <MARINA DEL REY>       (B/V) 306-2984
CA%408 SUNNYVALE            294-9119 <SAN JOSE>             (B/V) 294-9119
CA%213 TORRANCE             548-6141 <SAN PEDRO>            (B/V) 548-6141
CA 213 WOODLAND HILLS       992-0144
CA%415 WOODSIDE             856-9995 <PALO ALTO>            (B/V) 856-9995
CA%805 VENTURA              656-6760                        (B/V) 656-6760
CO%303 AURORA               337-6000 <DENVER>               (B/V) 337-6060
CO%303 BOULDER              337-6000 <DENVER>               (B/V) 337-6060
CO%303 COLORADO SPRINGS     635-5361                        (B/V) 635-5361
CO%303 DENVER               337-6000                        (B/V) 337-6060
CO%303 LAKEWOOD             337-6000 <DENVER>               (B/V) 337-6060
CT 203 DANBURY              794-9075                        (B/V) 794-9075
CT 203 GREENWICH            348-0787 <STAMFORD>             (B/V) 348-0787
CT 203 HARTFORD             522-0344                        (B/V) 247-9479
CT%203 MILFORD              624-5954 <NEW HAVEN>            (B/V) 624-5954
```

```
CT%203  NEW HAVEN          624-5954                        (B/V)  624-5954
CT%203  STAMFORD           348-0787                        (B/V)  348-0787
CT 203  WEST HARTFORD      522-0344 <HARTFORD>             (B/V)  247-9479
DC%202  WASHINGTON         429-7896                        (B/V)  429-7800
DE 302  WILMINGTON         454-7710                        (B/V)  454-7710
FL 813  CLEARWATER         323-4026 <ST. PETE>             (B/V)  323-4026
FL 305  FT. LAUDERDALE     764-4505                        (B/V)  764-4505
FL%904  JACKSONVILLE       356-2264                        (B/V)  356-2264
FL%305  MIAMI              372-0230                        (B/V)  372-0230
FL 305  ORLANDO            422-4088                        (B/V)  422-4088
FL 813  ST PETERSBURG      323-4026                        (B/V)  323-4026
FL*904  TALLAHASSEE        224-6824                        (B/V)  224-6824
FL 813  TAMPA              224-9920                        (B/V)  223-1088
FL 305  W PALM BEACH       833-6691
GA 404  ATLANTA            577-8911                        (B/V)  523-0834
GA 912  SAVANNAH           236-2605
HI 808  HONOLULU           524-8110                        (B)    524-8221
IA 319  CEDAR RAPIDS       364-0911                        (B/V)  364-0911
IA 402  COUNCIL BLUFFS     341-7733 <OMAHA, NE>            (B/V)  341-7733
IA 515  DES MOINES         288-4403                        (B/V)  288-4403
ID 208  BOISE              343-0611                        (B/V)  343-0611
IL 312  ARLINGTON HEIGHTS  938-0500 <CHICAGO>              (B/V)  938-0600
IL 217  CHAMPAIGN          384-6428 <URBANA>              (B/V)  384-6428
IL 312  CHICAGO            938-0500                        (B/V)  938-0600
IL 312  CICERO             938-0500 <CHICAGO>              (B/V)  938-0600
IL 314  EAST ST LOUIS      421-4990 <ST LOUIS, MO>         (B/V)  421-4990
IL 312  OAK PARK           938-0500 <CHICAGO>              (B/V)  938-0600
IL 309  PEORIA             637-8570                        (B/V)  637-8570
IL 312  SKOKIE             938-0500 <CHICAGO>              (B/V)  938-0600
IL 217  SPRINGFIELD        753-1373                        (B/V)  753-1373
IL 217  URBANA             384-6428                        (B/V)  384-6428
IN*812  EVANSVILLE         424-5250                        (B/V)  424-5250
IN*219  FT. WAYNE          426-4022                        (B/V)  426-4022
IN 219  GARY               882-8800                        (B/V)  882-8800
IN 317  INDIANAPOLIS       635-9630                        (B/V)  634-5708
IN 219  MISHAWKA           233-7104 <SOUTH BEND>           (B/V)  233-7104
IN 219  OSCEOLA            233-7104 <SOUTH BEND>           (B/V)  233-7104
IN 219  SOUTH BEND         233-7104                        (B/V)  233-7104
KS 816  KANSAS CITY        221-9900 <KANSAS CITY, MO>      (B/V)  221-9900
KS 913  TOPEKA             233-9880                        (B/V)  233-9880
KS 316  WICHITA            262-5669                        (B/V)  262-5669
KY*502  BOWLING GREEN      843-9026                        (B/V)  843-9026
KY%502  FRANKFORT          875-3920                        (B/V)  875-3920
KY 606  LEXINGTON          233-0312
KY%502  LOUISVILLE         589-5580                        (B/V)  589-5580
LA 504  BATON ROUGE        343-0753
LA 318  MONROE             387-6330
LA%504  NEW ORLEANS        524-4094                        (B/V)  524-4094
LA 318  SHREVEPORT         221-5833                        (B/V)  221-5833
ME 207  AUGUSTA            623-5136                        (B/V)  623-5136
MD 301  ANNAPOLIS          266-6886
MD 301  BALTIMORE          962-5010                        (B/V)  727-6060
MD%202  BETHESDA           429-7896 <WASH., D.C.>          (B/V)  429-7800
MD 301  DUNDALK            962-5010 <BALTIMORE>            (B/V)  727-6060
```

```
MD%202 ROCKVILLE        429-7896 <WASH., D.C.>      (B/V) 429-7800
MD%202 SILVER SPRING    429-7896 <WASH., D.C.>      (B/V) 429-7800
MD 301 TOWSON           962-5010 <BALTIMORE>        (B/V) 727-6060
MA 617 ARLINGTON        338-1400 <BOSTON>           (B/V) 338-7495
MA 617 BOSTON           338-1400                    (B/V) 338-7495
MA 617 BROOKLINE        338-1400 <BOSTON>           (B/V) 338-7495
MA 617 CAMBRIDGE        338-1400 <BOSTON>           (B/V) 338-7495
MA 413 CHICOPEE         781-3811 <SPRINGFIELD>      (B/V) 781-3811
MA 413 HOLYOKE          781-3811 <SPRINGFIELD>      (B/V) 781-3811
MA#617 LEXINGTON        863-1550                    (B/V) 863-1550
MA 617 MEDFORD          338-1400 <BOSTON>           (B/V) 338-7495
MA 617 NEWTON           338-1400 <BOSTON>           (B/V) 338-7495
MA 617 QUINCY           338-1400 <BOSTON>           (B/V) 338-7495
MA 617 SOMERVILLE       338-1400 <BOSTON>           (B/V) 338-7495
MA 413 SPRINGFIELD      781-3811                    (B/V) 781-3811
MA 617 WALTHAM          338-1400 <BOSTON>           (B/V) 338-7495
MA%617 WORCESTER        755-4740                    (B/V) 755-4740
MI 313 ANN ARBOR        996-0351                    (B/V) 996-5995
MI 616 BATTLE CREEK     968-0929                    (B/V) 968-0929
MI 313 DETROIT          964-5538                    (B/V) 964-2989
MI 313 FLINT            233-3050                    (B/V) 233-3050
MI 616 GRAND RAPIDS     458-1200                    (B/V) 774-0966
MI 616 KALAMAZOO        385-0160
MI%517 LANSING          372-5400                    (B/V) 484-2067
MI 517 SAGINAW          790-5166
MI%313 WARREN           575-9480                    (B/V) 575-9480
MN%218 DULUTH           722-1719                    (B/V) 722-1719
MN%612 MINNEAPOLIS      341-2459                    (B/V) 341-2459
MN%612 ST. PAUL         341-2459 <MINNEAPOLIS>      (B/V) 341-2459
MO 314 FLORISSANT       421-4990 <ST. LOUIS>        (B/V) 421-4990
MO 816 KANSAS CITY      221-9900                    (B/V) 221-9900
MO 314 ST. LOUIS        421-4990                    (B/V) 421-4990
MS#601 JACKSON          969-0036                    (B/V) 969-0036
MT 406 HELENA           443-0000
NE*402 LINCOLN          475-8392                    (B/V) 475-8392
NE 402 OMAHA            341-7733                    (B/V) 341-7733
NH 603 CONCORD          224-8110                    (B/V) 224-1024
NH 603 PORTSMOUTH       431-2302
NV 702 LAS VEGAS        733-2158                    (B/V) 737-6861
NJ 609 ATLANTIC CITY    348-0561
NJ 201 BAYONNE          623-6818 <NEWARK>           (B/V) 623-0469
NJ 201 JERSEY CITY      623-6818 <NEWARK>           (B/V) 623-0469
NJ 609 MARLTON          596-1500                    (B/V) 596-1500
NJ 201 MORRISTOWN       455-0275                    (B/V) 455-0275
NJ 201 NEW BRUNSWICK    246-1090
NJ 201 NEWARK           623-6818                    (B/V) 623-0469
NJ 201 PASSAIC          777-0952
NJ 201 PATERSON         684-7560                    (B/V) 684-7560
NJ*609 PRINCETON        683-1312                    (B/V) 683-1312
NJ 609 TRENTON          989-8847                    (B/V) 989-8847
NJ 201 UNION CITY       623-6818 <NEWARK>           (B/V) 623-0469
NM 505 ALBUQUERQUE      243-7701                    (B/V) 243-4479
NY%518 ALBANY           465-8444                    (B/V) 465-8444
NY 607 BINGHAMTON       772-6642                    (B/V) 772-6642
```

```
NY  716 BUFFALO            847-0600                               (B/V) 847-1440
NY#516 DEER PARK           667-5566                               (B/V) 667-5566
NY  516 HEMPSTEAD          292-0320                               (B/V) 292-3800
NY#212 NEW YORK            785-2540                               (B/V) 785-3860
                           736-0099                               (B/V) 947-9600
NY%914 POUGHKEEPSIE        473-2240                               (B/V) 473-2240
NY  716 ROCHESTER          454-3430                               (B/V) 454-1020
NY%518 SCHENECTADY         465-8444 <ALBANY>                      (B/V) 465-8444
NY  315 SYRACUSE           472-5503                               (B/V) 472-5583
NY%518 TROY                465-8444 <ALBANY>                      (B/V) 465-8444
NY  315 UTICA/ROME         797-0920                               (B/V) 797-0920
NY  914 WHITE PLAINS       328-9199                               (B/V) 328-9199
NC  704 ASHEVILLE          253-3517                               (B/V) 253-3517
NC  704 CHARLOTTE          374-0371                               (B/V) 332-3131
                                                                  (B/V) 377-6865
NC%919 DAVIDSON            549-8139 <RESEARCH TRI. PARK>          (B/V) 549-8139
NC%919 DURHAM              549-8139 <RESEARCH TRI. PARK>          (B/V) 549-8139
NC  919 GREENSBORO         273-2851                               (B/V) 273-2851
NC  919 HIGH POINT         899-2253                               (B/V) 889-2253
NC%919 RALEIGH             549-8139 <RESEARCH TRI. PARK>          (B/V) 549-8139
NC%919 RESEARCH TRI.PARK   549-8139                               (B/V) 549-8139
NC  919 WINSTON-SALEM      725-2126                               (B/V) 725-2126
OH  216 AKRON              762-9791                               (B/V) 762-9791
OH  216 CANTON             452-0903
OH%513 CINCINNATI          579-0390                               (B/V) 579-0390
OH%216 CLEVELAND           575-1658                               (B/V) 575-1658
OH  614 COLUMBUS           463-9340                               (B/V) 463-9340
OH%513 DAYTON              461-5254                               (B/V) 461-5254
                                                                  (B/V) 535-8541
PA  215 KING OF PRUSSIA    337-4300                               (B/V) 337-4300
PA  412 PENN HILLS         288-9950 <PITTSBURGH>                  (B/V) 288-9974
PA  215 PHILADELPHIA       574-0620                               (B/V) 574-9462
PA  412 PITTSBURGH         288-9950                               (B/V) 288-9974
PA  717 SCRANTON           961-5321
PA  215 UPPER DARBY        574-0620 <PHILADELPHIA>                (B/V) 574-9462
PA  717 YORK               846-6550                               (B/V) 846-6550
RI%401 PROVIDENCE          751-7912                               (B/V) 751-7912
RI%401 WARWICK             751-7912 <PROVIDENCE>                  (B/V) 751-7912
SC%803 CHARLESTON          722-4303                               (B/V) 722-4303
SC%803 COLUMBIA            254-0695                               (B/V) 254-0695
SC%803 GREENVILLE          233-3486                               (B/V) 233-3486
SD  605 PIERRE             224-6188                               (B/V) 224-6188
TN%615 CHATTANOOGA         756-1161                               (B/V) 756-1161
TN  615 KNOXVILLE          523-5500                               (B/V) 523-5500
TN%901 MEMPHIS             521-0215                               (B/V) 521-0215
TN  615 NASHVILLE          244-8310                               (B/V) 244-5099
TX%915 ABILENE             676-8545                               (B/V) 676-8545
TX  512 AUSTIN             928-1130                               (B/V) 928-1130
TX  512 CORPUS CHRISTI     884-9030                               (B/V) 884-9030
TX  214 DALLAS             748-0127                               (B/V) 748-6371
TX  915 EL PASO            532-7907                               (B/V) 532-7907
TX  817 FORT WORTH         336-7791                               (B/V) 332-4307
TX  713 GALVESTON          762-3308                               (B/V) 762-3308
TX%713 HOUSTON             227-1018                               (B/V) 227-1018
```

```
TX%512 LACKLAND            225-8004 <SAN ANTONIO>           (B/V) 225-8004
TX%713 NEDERLAND           724-6717                         (B/V) 724-6717
TX%915 SAN ANGELO          944-7621                         (B/V) 944-7621
TX%512 SAN ANTONIO         225-8004                         (B/V) 225-8004
UT%801 SALT LAKE CITY      359-0149                         (B/V) 359-0149
VA%202 ALEXANDRIA          429-7896 <WASHINGTON, D.C.>      (B/V) 429-7800
VA%202 ANNANDALE           429-7896 <WASHINGTON, D.C.>      (B/V) 429-7800
VA 804 CHESAPEAKE          625-1186 <NORFOLK>               (B/V) 625-1186
VA%202 FAIRFAX             429-7896 <WASHINGTON, D.C.>      (B/V) 429-7800
VA%202 FALLS CHURCH        429-7896 <WASHINGTON, D.C.>      (B/V) 429-7800
VA 703 HERNDON             435-3333
VA 804 NEWPORT NEWS        596-6600                         (B/V) 596-6600
VA 804 NORFOLK             625-1186                         (B/V) 625-1186
VA 804 PORTSMOUTH          625-1186 <NORFOLK>               (B/V) 625-1186
VA 804 RICHMOND            788-9902                         (B/V) 788-9902
VA%202 SPRINGFIELD         429-7896 <WASHINGTON, D.C.>      (B/V) 429-7800
VA%202 VIENNA              429-7896 <WASHINGTON, D.C.>      (B/V) 429-7800
VA 804 VIRGINIA BEACH      625-1186 <NORFOLK>               (B/V) 625-1186
VT*802 BURLINGTON          864-7942                         (B/V) 864-7942
VT 802 MONTPELIER          229-4966
WA%206 AUBURN              939-9982                         (B/V) 939-9982
WA 206 BELLEVUE            447-9012 <SEATTLE>               (B/V) 625-9612
WA 206 LONGVIEW            577-5835
WA 206 SEATTLE             447-9012                         (B/V) 625-9612
WA%509 SPOKANE             455-4071                         (B/V) 455-4071
WA%206 TACOMA              627-1791                         (B/V) 627-1791
WA 509 WENATCHEE           662-1901                         (B/V) 662-1901
WI%608 MADISON             257-5010                         (B/V) 257-5010
WI%414 MILWAUKEE           271-3914                         (B/V) 271-3914
WV 304 CHARLESTON          345-6471                         (B/V) 345-6471
WY%307 CHEYENNE            638-4421                         (B/V) 638-4421
IN-WATS 800               424-9494                         (B/V) 424-9494
```

[Tymnet]. Tymnet extended its coverage to Alaska and Hawaii. In Alaska, Tymnet charges are $6.50 per connect hour, plus $0.30 per 1000 characters transmitted. In Hawaii, charges were $3 per hour, plus $0.20 per 1000 characters.

```
TYMNET ACCESS SORTED BY STATE              9/01/1982
NODE   CITY                 STATE           DEN   ACCESS #        MODEM
----   ------------------   -------------   ---   -------------   -----------
2246   BIRMINGHAM           ALABAMA         HIGH  205/942-4141    (VADIC 3467)
1642   HUNTSVILLE           ALABAMA         MED   205/539-3753    (VADIC 3467)
1050   MOBILE               ALABAMA         MED   205/432-3382    (VADIC 3467)
2246   MONTGOMERY           ALABAMA         LOW   205/834-3410    (VADIC 3467)
 367   ANCHORAGE            ALASKA          INTL  907/278-3511    (VADIC 3467)
 442   JUNEAU               ALASKA          INTL  907/586-6611    (VADIC 3467)
2364   PHOENIX              ARIZONA         HIGH  602/254-5811    (VADIC 3467)
1336   TUCSON               ARIZONA         HIGH  602/790-0764    (VADIC 3467)
1207   FT SMITH             ARKANSAS        LOW   501/782-3210    (VADIC 3467)
2412   JONESBORO            ARKANSAS        LOW   501/932-6886    ( 212A )
2412   LITTLE ROCK          ARKANSAS        MED   501/372-5780
2412   LITTLE ROCK          ARKANSAS        MED   501/376-3768    ( 212A )
```

1207	SPRINGDALE	ARKANSAS	LOW	501/756-2201	(VADIC 3467)
1406	ALHAMBRA	CALIFORNIA	MED	213/572-0999	
1210	ALHAMBRA	CALIFORNIA	MED	213/280-1103	(212A)
2346 *	ANTIOCH	CALIFORNIA	LOW	415/757-6855	(VADIC 3467)
1406	ARCADIA	CALIFORNIA	LOW	213/574-7636	
1210	ARCADIA	CALIFORNIA	LOW	213/574-8834	(212A)
2475	BURLINGAME	CALIFORNIA	LOW	415/583-6950	(212A)
2447	EL SEGUNDO	CALIFORNIA	HIGH	213/640-1281	(212A)
2470	FRESNO	CALIFORNIA	LOW	209/442-4141	(VADIC 3467)
2346 *	HAYWARD	CALIFORNIA	LOW	415/785-3431	(VADIC 3467)
1024	LONG BEACH	CALIFORNIA	LOW	213/435-7088	(VADIC 3467)
1144	LOS ANGELES	CALIFORNIA	HIGH	213/626-2400	(212A)
1144	LOS ANGELES	CALIFORNIA	HIGH	213/626-3030	(212A)
1406	LOS ANGELES	CALIFORNIA	HIGH	213/623-8500	(1200 VADIC)
1406	LOS ANGELES	CALIFORNIA	HIGH	213/629-3001	(1200 202S)
2447	MARINA DEL REY	CALIFORNIA	LOW	213/821-2257	(212A)
1406	MISSION HILLS	CALIFORNIA	LOW	213/365-2013	
1210	MISSION HILLS	CALIFORNIA	LOW	213/365-9277	(212A)
2346 *	MODESTO	CALIFORNIA	LOW	209/578-4236	(VADIC 3467)
1017	MT VIEW/PALO ALTO	CALIFORNIA	MED	415/941-8450	(212A)
1210	NORTHRIDGE	CALIFORNIA	MED	213/998-3331	(212A)
1406	NORTHRIDGE	CALIFORNIA	MED	213/998-4872	(212A)
1210	NORWALK	CALIFORNIA	LOW	213/865-0555	(212A)
1406	NORWALK	CALIFORNIA	LOW	213/865-2066	(212A)
2346 *	OAKLAND	CALIFORNIA	HIGH	415/836-8700	(VADIC 3467)
1025	PALM SPRINGS	CALIFORNIA	LOW	714/320-0772	
2361	PALO ALTO/MT VIEW	CALIFORNIA	MED	415/966-8550	(VADIC 3467)
1210	PASADENA	CALIFORNIA	LOW	213/577-8696	(212A)
1406	PASADENA	CALIFORNIA	LOW	213/577-8722	(212A)
2346 *	PLEASANT HILL	CALIFORNIA	LOW	415/798-2093	(VADIC 3467)
1025	RANCHO BERNARDO	CALIFORNIA	LOW	714/485-1990	
1055 *	RIVERSIDE/COLTON	CALIFORNIA	HIGH	714/370-1200	(VADIC 3467)
2702	SACRAMENTO	CALIFORNIA	HIGH	916/448-8151	(VADIC 3467)
2456 *	SALINAS	CALIFORNIA	LOW	408/443-4333	(VADIC 3467)
1024	SAN CLEMENTE	CALIFORNIA	LOW	714/498-3130	(VADIC 3467)
1025 *	SAN DIEGO	CALIFORNIA	HIGH	714/296-3370	(VADIC 3467)
1126	SAN FRANCISCO	CALIFORNIA	HIGH	415/986-8200	
2475	SAN FRANCISCO	CALIFORNIA	HIGH	415/788-7955	(212A)
2475	SAN FRANCISCO	CALIFORNIA	HIGH	415/397-4300	(1200 VADIC)
2470	SAN JOSE/CUPERTINO	CALIFORNIA	HIGH	408/980-8100	(VADIC 3467)
1155	SAN JOSE/CUPERTINO	CALIFORNIA	HIGH	408/446-6932	(1200 202S)
2456	SAN JOSE/CUPERTINO	CALIFORNIA	HIGH	408/257-0593	(CCITT)
1210	SAN PEDRO	CALIFORNIA	MED	213/518-3773	(212A)
2447	SAN PEDRO	CALIFORNIA	MED	213/830-0775	(212A)
1024 *	SANTA ANA	CALIFORNIA	HIGH	714/662-0514	(VADIC 3467)
1705	SANTA BARBARA	CALIFORNIA	MED	805/682-9641	(VADIC 3467)
2361	SANTA CRUZ	CALIFORNIA	MED	408/426-8400	(VADIC 3467)
2702	SANTA ROSA	CALIFORNIA	LOW	707/575-0160	(VADIC 3467)
1406	VAN NUYS	CALIFORNIA	LOW	213/986-9503	
1007	VENTURA/OXNARD	CALIFORNIA	HIGH	805/486-4811	(VADIC 3467)
1025	VISTA	CALIFORNIA	LOW	714/727-6011	
2346 *	WALNUT CREEK	CALIFORNIA	LOW	415/932-0116	(VADIC 3467)
1406	WEST COVINA	CALIFORNIA	LOW	213/331-3954	
1210	WEST COVINA	CALIFORNIA	LOW	213/915-5702	(212A)

2415	COLORADO SPRINGS	COLORADO	MED	303/475-2121	(VADIC 3467)
2414	DENVER	COLORADO	HIGH	303/830-9210	(VADIC 3467)
1445	BRIDGEPORT	CONNECTICUT	MED	203/367-6021	(VADIC 3467)
2357	DANBURY	CONNECTICUT	LOW	203/743-1340	(212A)
2653	DARIEN	CONNECTICUT	HIGH	203/965-0000	(VADIC 3467)
2357	HARTFORD	CONNECTICUT	HIGH	203/242-7140	
2357	HARTFORD	CONNECTICUT	HIGH	203/242-7417	(212A)
2357	NEW HAVEN	CONNECTICUT	MED	203/789-0579	
2357	NEW HAVEN	CONNECTICUT	MED	203/787-1702	(212A)
2653 ★	STAMFORD	CONNECTICUT	HIGH	203/965-0000	(VADIC 3467)
2357	WATERBURY	CONNECTICUT	LOW	203/755-1153	
2436	WASHINGTON	DC	HIGH	703/442-3900	
2251	WASHINGTON	DC	HIGH	703/734-3900	
2436	WASHINGTON	DC	HIGH	703/442-7800	(212A)
2251	WASHINGTON	DC	HIGH	703/734-8370	(212A)
2436	WASHINGTON	DC	HIGH	703/442-3960	(VADIC 3467)
2544 ★	WASHINGTON	DC	HIGH	703/691-8200	(VADIC 3467)
2450 ★	WILMINGTON	DELAWARE	MED	302/429-0112	(VADIC 3467)
1412	DAYTONA BEACH	FLORIDA	LOW	904/252-4481	
2336	FT LAUDERDALE	FLORIDA	MED	305/467-3807	(VADIC 3467)
1061	JACKSONVILLE	FLORIDA	MED	904/721-8100	
1066	MELBOURNE	FLORIDA	LOW	305/725-8011	
1066	MELBOURNE	FLORIDA	LOW	305/724-9972	(212A)
2336	MIAMI	FLORIDA	HIGH	305/624-7900	(VADIC 3467)
1412	ORLANDO	FLORIDA	HIGH	305/851-3530	
1412	ORLANDO	FLORIDA	HIGH	305/859-7670	(212A)
1050	PENSACOLA	FLORIDA	LOW	904/434-0134	(VADIC 3467)
1404	SARASOTA	FLORIDA	LOW	813/365-3526	(212A)
1066	ST PETERSBURG	FLORIDA	MED	813/535-6441	
1066	ST PETERSBURG	FLORIDA	MED	813/535-1446	(212A)
1404	TAMPA	FLORIDA	HIGH	813/977-2400	(212A)
2336	W.PALM BEACH	FLORIDA	MED	305/627-5410	(VADIC 3467)
2477 ★	ATLANTA	GEORGIA	HIGH	404/659-1600	(212A)
1061	SAVANNAH	GEORGIA	LOW	912/352-7259	
2477	SAVANNAH	GEORGIA	LOW	912/236-1904	(VADIC 3467)
2324 ★	HONOLULU	HAWAII	LOW	808/524-8450	(212A)
2565 ★	BOISE	IDAHO	MED	208/343-0404	(VADIC 3467)
2362	CHICAGO	ILLINOIS	HIGH	312/346-4961	
2362	CHICAGO	ILLINOIS	HIGH	312/368-4607	
2362	CHICAGO	ILLINOIS	HIGH	312/368-4700	
1205	CHICAGO	ILLINOIS	HIGH	312/641-1630	(212A)
2362	CHICAGO	ILLINOIS	HIGH	312/372-0391	(1200 VADIC)
2362	CHICAGO	ILLINOIS	HIGH	312/368-0022	(1200 202S)
1147	FREEPORT	ILLINOIS	LOW	815/233-5585	
1205	JOLIET	ILLINOIS	LOW	815/723-9854	(212A)
2362	PEORIA	ILLINOIS	LOW	309/673-2156	
1147	ROCKFORD	ILLINOIS	MED	815/398-6090	
1546	SPRINGFIELD	ILLINOIS	HIGH	217/753-7905	(VADIC 3467)
1201	EVANSVILLE	INDIANA	LOW	812/423-6885	
1202	FT WAYNE	INDIANA	LOW	219/424-5162	
2362	HIGHLAND	INDIANA	LOW	219/836-5452	
1202 ★	INDIANAPOLIS	INDIANA	HIGH	317/257-3461	(212A)
1202	MARION	INDIANA	LOW	317/662-0091	
2362	MERRILLVILLE	INDIANA	LOW	219/769-7254	

1156	SOUTH BEND	INDIANA	HIGH	219/233-4163	
1400	CEDAR RAPIDS	IOWA	LOW	319/363-2482	
1400	CEDER RAPIDS	IOWA	LOW	319/363-9019	(212A)
1400	DAVENPORT	IOWA	LOW	319/322-5642	
1400	DAVENPORT	IOWA	LOW	319/324-7197	(VADIC 3467)
1400	DES MOINES	IOWA	MED	515/288-6640	
1400	DES MOINES	IOWA	MED	515/288-8097	(212A)
1400	IOWA CITY	IOWA	MED	319/354-7371	
1400	IOWA CITY	IOWA	MED	319/354-9532	(212A)
1400	WATERLOO	IOWA	LOW	319/233-9227	(212A)
2501	SHAWNEE MISSION	KANSAS	MED	913/677-2833	
2501	SHAWNEE MISSION	KANSAS	MED	913/677-0707	(212A)
2501	TOPEKA	KANSAS	LOW	913/233-0690	
2413	WICHITA	KANSAS	HIGH	316/265-1241	(VADIC 3467)
1331	LEXINGTON	KENTUCKY	HIGH	606/253-3463	
1331	LEXINGTON	KENTUCKY	HIGH	606/253-3498	(212A)
1201	LOUISVILLE	KENTUCKY	HIGH	502/361-3881	
1201	LOUISVILLE	KENTUCKY	HIGH	502/361-3821	(212A)
1046	BATON ROUGE	LOUISIANA	HIGH	504/292-4050	
1046	BATON ROUGE	LOUISIANA	HIGH	504/292-2650	(212A)
1444	LAFAYETTE	LOUISIANA	MED	318/237-9500	(VADIC 3467)
1050	NEW ORLEANS	LOUISIANA	HIGH	504/524-4371	(VADIC 3467)
2177	SHREVEPORT	LOUISIANA	LOW	318/688-4666	(VADIC 3467)
2554 *	PORTLAND	MAINE	LOW	207/774-2654	(VADIC 3467)
2354 *	BALTIMORE	MARYLAND	HIGH	301/547-8100	(VADIC 3467)
2660	ROCKVILLE	MARYLAND	MED	301/770-1680	
2377	BOSTON	MASSACHUSETTS	HIGH	617/482-4677	
2377	BOSTON	MASSACHUSETTS	HIGH	617/482-5605	
2416	BOSTON	MASSACHUSETTS	HIGH	617/482-7035	(VADIC 3467)
2377	BOSTON	MASSACHUSETTS	HIGH	617/482-2170	(1200 202S)
2365 *	SPRINGFIELD	MASSACHUSETTS	HIGH	413/781-6830	(VADIC 3467)
2377	WORCESTER	MASSACHUSETTS	LOW	617/754-9451	
2377	WORCESTER	MASSACHUSETTS	LOW	617/755-5601	(212A)
1005	ANN ARBOR	MICHIGAN	HIGH	313/665-2627	
1005	ANN ARBOR	MICHIGAN	HIGH	313/662-8282	(212A)
1104	CADILLAC	MICHIGAN	LOW	616/775-1261	(VADIC 3467)
2454	DETROIT	MICHIGAN	HIGH	313/963-3388	
2454	DETROIT	MICHIGAN	HIGH	313/963-8880	(212A)
2454	DETROIT	MICHIGAN	HIGH	313/963-2353	(1200 VADIC)
2454	DETROIT	MICHIGAN	HIGH	313/963-4676	(1200 202S)
2360	FLINT	MICHIGAN	LOW	313/732-7303	(212A)
1104	GRAND RAPIDS	MICHIGAN	MED	616/459-5069	(VADIC 3467)
1057	JACKSON	MICHIGAN	MED	517/787-9461	
1104	KALAMAZOO	MICHIGAN	MED	616/385-3150	(VADIC 3467)
1104	LANSING	MICHIGAN	MED	517/487-2040	(VADIC 3467)
1104	MANISTEE	MICHIGAN	LOW	616/723-8373	(VADIC 3467)
2360	PLYMOUTH	MICHIGAN	MED	313/459-8900	
2360	PLYMOUTH	MICHIGAN	MED	313/459-8100	(212A)
2360	SOUTHFIELD	MICHIGAN	MED	313/569-8350	
1104	ST JOSEPH	MICHIGAN	LOW	616/429-2568	(VADIC 3467)
1104	TRAVERSE CITY	MICHIGAN	LOW	616/946-0002	(VADIC 3467)
2520	MANKATO	MINNESOTA	LOW	507/625-1684	(212A)
2520	MINNEAPOLIS	MINNESOTA	HIGH	612/339-5200	
2520	MINNEAPOLIS	MINNESOTA	HIGH	612/339-8086	

2520	MINNEAPOLIS	MINNESOTA	HIGH	612/339-2415	(212A)
2520	ROCHESTER	MINNESOTA	LOW	507/282-3741	(212A)
1046	JACKSON	MISSISSIPPI	MED	601/944-0860	
1046	JACKSON	MISSISSIPPI	MED	601/969-5141	(212A)
1433	PASCAGOULA	MISSISSIPPI	MED	601/769-6502	
1433	PASCAGOULA	MISSISSIPPI	MED	601/769-6673	(212A)
1043	BRIDGETON	MISSOURI	LOW	314/731-2304	
2501	COLUMBIA	MISSOURI	MED	314/875-1150	
1043	JEFFERSON CITY	MISSOURI	LOW	314/634-3273	(212A)
1207	JOPLIN	MISSOURI	LOW	417/782-3037	(VADIC 3467)
2501	KANSAS CITY	MISSOURI	HIGH	913/677-2833	
2501	KANSAS CITY	MISSOURI	HIGH	913/677-0707	(212A)
2501	SPRINGFIELD	MISSOURI	LOW	417/831-0566	(212A)
2501	ST JOSEPH	MISSOURI	LOW	816/232-0624	(212A)
1043	ST LOUIS	MISSOURI	HIGH	314/421-5110	
1043	ST LOUIS	MISSOURI	HIGH	314/621-4660	(212A)
2565 *	BUTTE	MONTANA	LOW	406/494-4637	(VADIC 3467)
453	LINCOLN	NEBRASKA	LOW	402/475-8659	(VADIC 3467)
453 *	OMAHA	NEBRASKA	HIGH	402/397-0414	(VADIC 3467)
1431	LAS VEGAS	NEVADA	MED	702/293-0300	(VADIC 3467)
765	RENO/CARSON CITY	NEVADA	MED	702/882-7810	(VADIC 3467)
1464	MANCHESTER	NEW HAMPSHIRE	LOW	603/623-8855	(VADIC 3467)
1464	NASHUA	NEW HAMPSHIRE	MED	603/882-0435	(VADIC 3467)
2665	ENGLEWOOD CLIFFS	NEW JERSEY	MED	201/894-8250	(VADIC 3467)
1300 *	JERSEY CITY	NEW JERSEY	LOW	201/432-0792	
1073	LYNDHURST	NEW JERSEY	HIGH	201/460-0100	
1073	LYNDHURST	NEW JERSEY	HIGH	201/460-0180	(212A)
2417	MOORESTOWN	NEW JERSEY	MED	609/235-3761	
2417	MORRISTOWN	NEW JERSEY	LOW	201/267-3997	(212A)
1415 *	NEW BRUNSWICK	NEW JERSEY	MED	609/452-1018	(VADIC 3467)
1300	NEWARK/UNION	NEW JERSEY	HIGH	201/483-5937	
1300	NEWARK/UNION	NEW JERSEY	HIGH	201/483-4878	(212A)
1211	PISCATAWAY	NEW JERSEY	HIGH	201/981-1900	(VADIC 3467)
1415 *	PRINCETON	NEW JERSEY	HIGH	609/452-1018	(VADIC 3467)
1300	RIDGEWOOD	NEW JERSEY	LOW	201/447-6175	(212A)
1053	WAYNE	NEW JERSEY	HIGH	201/785-4480	
1171	ALBUQUERQUE	NEW MEXICO	MED	505/843-6301	(VADIC 3467)
2357	ALBANY	NEW YORK	MED	518/463-3111	
2357	ALBANY	NEW YORK	MED	518/434-2633	(212A)
1003	BUFFALO	NEW YORK	HIGH	716/845-6610	
1003	BUFFALO	NEW YORK	HIGH	716/847-0500	(212A)
1241 *	CORNING	NEW YORK	MED	607/962-4481	(VADIC 3467)
1003	ELMIRA	NEW YORK	LOW	607/737-9010	(212A)
2476	HEMPSTEAD L.I.	NEW YORK	MED	516/872-6500	(VADIC 3467)
2476	HUNTINGTON L.I.	NEW YORK	MED	516/549-2780	(VADIC 3467)
1714 *	ITHICA	NEW YORK	MED	607/257-6601	(VADIC 3467)
2476	MINEOLA	NEW YORK	LOW	516/222-1423	(212A)
2471	NEW YORK	NEW YORK	HIGH	212/532-0437	
2471	NEW YORK	NEW YORK	HIGH	212/685-4414	
2476 *	NEW YORK	NEW YORK	HIGH	212/269-6985	(VADIC 3467)
2476	NEW YORK	NEW YORK	HIGH	212/785-5400	(VADIC 3467)
2471	NEW YORK	NEW YORK	HIGH	212/689-8850	(1200 202S)
1003	NIAGARA FALLS	NEW YORK	LOW	716/285-6691	
1003	NIAGARA FALLS	NEW YORK	LOW	716/285-3114	(212A)

2664	POUGHKEEPSIE	NEW YORK	LOW	914/471-6100	(VADIC 3467)
2452	ROCHESTER	NEW YORK	HIGH	716/248-8000	
2452	ROCHESTER	NEW YORK	HIGH	716/248-8350	(212A)
2351	SYRACUSE	NEW YORK	MED	315/437-7111	
2351	SYRACUSE	NEW YORK	MED	315/437-1117	(212A)
1405	WHITE PLAINS	NEW YORK	MED	914/328-9580	(VADIC 3467)
2664	WHITE PLAINS	NEW YORK	HIGH	914/684-6075	(VADIC 3467)
1313	ASHEVILLE	NORTH CAROLINA	LOW	704/255-0021	(212A)
1542	CHARLOTTE	NORTH CAROLINA	HIGH	704/376-2545	
1542	CHARLOTTE	NORTH CAROLINA	HIGH	704/376-2544	(212A)
2451	DURHAM	NORTH CAROLINA	HIGH	919/549-0441	
2451	DURHAM	NORTH CAROLINA	HIGH	919/549-8910	(212A)
1447	GREENSBORO	NORTH CAROLINA	MED	919/379-0470	(VADIC 3467)
1313	HIGH POINT	NORTH CAROLINA	LOW	919/885-0171	(VADIC 3467)
2451	RALEIGH	NORTH CAROLINA	LOW	919/832-6592	(212A)
1313	WINSTON-SALEM	NORTH CAROLINA	MED	919/725-9252	(VADIC 3467)
1237	AKRON	OHIO	MED	216/535-1861	(VADIC 3467)
1071 *	CINCINNATI	OHIO	HIGH	513/489-2100	
1071 *	CINCINNATI	OHIO	HIGH	513/489-2200	(212A)
1071 *	CINCINNATI	OHIO	HIGH	513/489-2300	(VADIC 3467)
2502	CLEVELAND	OHIO	HIGH	216/781-7050	
2502	CLEVELAND	OHIO	HIGH	216/861-5383	(212A)
1026	COLUMBUS	OHIO	HIGH	614/421-7270	
1026	COLUMBUS	OHIO	HIGH	614/421-1650	(212A)
1042 *	DAYTON	OHIO	HIGH	513/223-3847	(VADIC 3467)
1026	MARYSVILLE	OHIO	LOW	513/642-2015	(212A)
2454	TOLEDO	OHIO	MED	419/243-3144	
2454	TOLEDO	OHIO	MED	419/255-2946	(212A)
2435	YOUNGSTOWN	OHIO	LOW	216/744-5326	(212A)
1101	OKLAHOMA CITY	OKLAHOMA	HIGH	405/947-6387	(VADIC 3467)
1207	TULSA	OKLAHOMA	HIGH	918/582-4433	(VADIC 3467)
2540 *	PORTLAND	OREGON	HIGH	503/226-0627	(VADIC 3467)
2417	ALLENTOWN	PENNSYLVANIA	MED	215/433-6131	
2417	ALLENTOWN	PENNSYLVANIA	MED	215/432-5926	(212A)
2435	ALTOONA	PENNSYLVANIA	LOW	814/946-8888	(212A)
1703	DOWNINGTON	PENNSYLVANIA	LOW	215/269-9861	(VADIC 3467)
1003	ERIE	PENNSYLVANIA	LOW	814/453-7161	
2354	HARRISBURG	PENNSYLVANIA	MED	717/233-8531	(VADIC 3467)
1703	KING OF PRUSSIA	PENNSYLVANIA	MED	215/337-9900	(VADIC 3467)
2417	PHILADELPHIA	PENNSYLVANIA	HIGH	215/561-6120	
2417	PHILADELPHIA	PENNSYLVANIA	HIGH	215/567-1381	(212A)
2435	PITTSBURGH	PENNSYLVANIA	HIGH	412/765-1320	
2435	PITTSBURGH	PENNSYLVANIA	HIGH	412/261-4151	(212A)
2450	VALLEY FORGE	PENNSYLVANIA	HIGH	215/666-9190	
2450	VALLEY FORGE	PENNSYLVANIA	HIGH	215/666-0930	(212A)
1556	YORK	PENNSYLVANIA	MED	717/846-3900	(VADIC 3467)
1174	MAYAGUEZ	PUERTO RICO	INTL	809/833-4535	(VADIC 3467)
1174	PONCE	PUERTO RICO	INTL	809/840-9110	(VADIC 3467)
1174	SAN JUAN	PUERTO RICO	INTL	809/792-5900	(VADIC 3467)
2657	PROVIDENCE	RHODE ISLAND	HIGH	401/273-0200	(VADIC 3467)
1542	CHARLESTON	SOUTH CAROLINA	LOW	803/577-2179	(VADIC 3467)
2477	COLUMBIA	SOUTH CAROLINA	MED	803/252-0840	
1542	COLUMBIA	SOUTH CAROLINA	MED	803/256-5238	(212A)
2477	GREENVILLE	SOUTH CAROLINA	MED	803/271-2418	

1542	GREENVILLE	SOUTH CAROLINA	MED	803/271-9967	
1313	SPARTANBURG	SOUTH CAROLINA	LOW	803/585-2637	(VADIC 3467)
1325	CHATTANOOGA	TENNESSEE	MED	615/756-5856	
1325	CHATTANOOGA	TENNESSEE	MED	615/756-0561	(212A)
1330	KNOXVILLE	TENNESSEE	MED	615/637-3118	(VADIC 3467)
2412	MEMPHIS	TENNESSEE	HIGH	901/529-0170	
2412	MEMPHIS	TENNESSEE	HIGH	901/529-0183	(212A)
1330	NASHVILLE	TENNESSEE	HIGH	615/367-9382	(VADIC 3467)
1045	AUSTIN	TEXAS	HIGH	512/444-3280	(VADIC 3467)
2247	BAYTOWN	TEXAS	LOW	713/427-5856	
2247	BEAUMONT	TEXAS	LOW	713/832-2589	
1335	CORPUS CHRISTI	TEXAS	MED	512/883-8050	(VADIC 3467)
2453	DALLAS	TEXAS	HIGH	214/638-8888	(VADIC 3467)
2401	DALLAS	TEXAS	WATS	IN-TEXAS WATS	(VADIC 3467)
2401	DALLAS	TEXAS	WATS	NATIONAL WATS	(VADIC 3467)
1171	EL PASO	TEXAS	HIGH	915/533-1453	(VADIC 3467)
2177	FT WORTH	TEXAS	MED	214/263-4581	(VADIC 3467)
2247	HOUSTON	TEXAS	HIGH	713/977-4080	
2245	HOUSTON	TEXAS	HIGH	713/977-7671	(212A)
2245 *	HOUSTON	TEXAS	HIGH	713/975-0500	(VADIC 3467)
2177	LONGVIEW	TEXAS	LOW	214/758-1756	(VADIC 3467)
1014	LUBBOCK	TEXAS	LOW	806/762-0136	
1014	MIDLAND	TEXAS	MED	915/683-5645	
1014	MIDLAND	TEXAS	MED	915/683-9833	(212A)
1014	ODESSA	TEXAS	LOW	915/563-3745	
1102	SAN ANTONIO	TEXAS	HIGH	512/225-8002	(VADIC 3467)
1021	SALT LAKE CITY	UTAH	HIGH	801/582-8972	
1021	SALT LAKE CITY	UTAH	HIGH	801/582-6060	(212A)
2554	BURLINGTON	VERMONT	LOW	802/658-2123	(VADIC 3467)
2544	FAIRFAX	VIRGINIA	HIGH	703/691-8200	(VADIC 3467)
2451	LYNCHBURG	VIRGINIA	LOW	804/528-0021	(212A)
2616	MIDLOTHIAN	VIRGINIA	HIGH	804/744-4860	(VADIC 3467)
1563	NEWPORT NEWS	VIRGINIA	MED	804/596-7609	(VADIC 3467)
2251	NORFOLK	VIRGINIA	MED	804/625-8301	(212A)
2616	RICHMOND	VIRGINIA	HIGH	804/744-4860	(VADIC 3467)
1313	ROANOKE	VIRGINIA	LOW	703/345-4730	(VADIC 3467)
2503 *	ENUMCLAW	WASHINGTON	LOW	206/825-5121	(VADIC 3467)
2503 *	OLYMPIA	WASHINGTON	LOW	206/754-3900	(VADIC 3467)
2564	RICHLAND	WASHINGTON	MED	509/375-3367	(VADIC 3467)
2503 *	SEATTLE	WASHINGTON	HIGH	206/285-0109	(VADIC 3467)
1461	SPOKANE	WASHINGTON	MED	509/747-4105	(VADIC 3467)
2503 *	TACOMA	WASHINGTON	LOW	206/473-7810	(VADIC 3467)
1026	CHARLESTON	WEST VIRGINIA	LOW	304/345-2908	(212A)
1026	HUNTINGTON	WEST VIRGINIA	LOW	304/522-6261	
2440 *	APPLETON	WISCONSIN	LOW	414/735-9390	(VADIC 3467)
2440 *	BROOKFIELD	WISCONSIN	LOW	414/785-1614	(VADIC 3467)
2520	EAU CLAIRE	WISCONSIN	LOW	715/834-7863	(212A)
2440 *	GREEN BAY	WISCONSIN	LOW	414/437-9897	(VADIC 3467)
1157	MADISON	WISCONSIN	HIGH	608/221-4211	
1157	MADISON	WISCONSIN	HIGH	608/221-0891	(212A)
2440 *	MILWAUKEE	WISCONSIN	HIGH	414/785-1614	(VADIC 3467)
1562	NEENAH	WISCONSIN	MED	414/722-5580	(VADIC 3467)
2440 *	OSHKOSH	WISCONSIN	LOW	414/235-1082	(VADIC 3467)
2440 *	RACINE	WISCONSIN	LOW	414/632-3006	(VADIC 3467)

NOTE: * DENOTES NEW/CHANGED SERVICE IN THE LAST 90 DAYS
MODEM: IF NOT MARKED THEN 300 BELL COMPATIBLE
        212A = 300/1200 BELL
        VADIC 3467 = 300/1200 BELL & VADIC 1200
        VADIC 1200 = VADIC 3400

        1200 202S = 1200 BELL HALF DUPLEX ONLY (ENSURE DESTINATION HOST
            INTERFACE WILL ACCEPT TRUE HALF DUPLEX OPERATION...MOST WILL NOT!)
        CCITT = 1200 EUROPEAN
        DENSITY MARKED AS INTL WILL INCURE AN ADDITIONAL CHARGE

[Uninet]. Uninet is developing as a third network, but as yet does not have
the coverage of Tymnet and Telenet. However, Uninet's plant is modern, and
often offers better service than the Time and Newsweek of packet-switching.

09/08/82   UNINET SERVICE NUMBERS
                 COMMON NETWORK ACCESS PHONE NUMBERS BY STATE
                   INFORMATION LAST UPDATED ON 09/03/82

| STATE | CITY | AREA | 10 TO | | OTHER | |
CITY	DENS	CODE	30 CPS	120 CPS	SERVICES	COMMENTS
ALABAMA						
BIRMINGHAM	HI	205	322-2751	322-2751		
MOBILE	HI	205	438-5926	438-5926		
MONTGOMERY	HI	205	264-6602	264-6602		
OPELIKA	LOW	205	749-2095			
ARIZONA						
PHOENIX	MED	602	258-1693	258-1693		
TUCSON	MED	602	747-4856	745-8201		
ARKANSAS						
LITTLE ROCK	MED	501	374-5036	371-0064		
CALIFORNIA						
BAKERSFIELD	HI	805	322-1075	322-1075		
BEVERLY HILLS	HI	213	857-1171	857-0466	930-0376	4800 RB 208
DEL MAR	HI	714			453-1076	4800 RB 208
EL SEGUNDO	HI	213	640-3600	640-3330		
FRESNO	HI	209	225-1354	225-1354		
FULLERTON	HI	213			576-0388	4800 RB 208
HAYWARD	HI	415	481-2520	481-2520		
LONG BEACH	HI	213	432-0461	432-0461		
LOS ANGELES	HI	213	688-0901	688-0901		
LOS GATOS	HI	408			358-3377	4800 RB 208
MONROVIA	HI	213	358-3241	358-3241		
MONTEREY	HI	408	373-0651	373-0651		
NEWPORT BEACH	HI	714	752-9231	851-9681	851-6390	4800 RB GDC
NEWPORT BEACH	HI	714			851-8007	2400 RB SYN
OAKLAND	HI	415	839-7459	839-7459		
OXNARD	MED	805	487-7880	483-9508		
PALO ALTO	HI	415	964-8350	962-0870	494-3743	4800 RB 208
POMONA	MED	714	623-6419	623-3196		
RIVERSIDE	HI	714	781-6272			
SACRAMENTO	HI	916	442-8303	442-8303		

SAN BERNARDINO	HI	714	888-4623	885-3554		
SAN CARLOS	HI	415	592-9848	592-9848		
SAN DIEGO	MED	714	571-8550	571-8550		
SAN FRANCISCO	HI	415	397-3810	397-3810		
SAN JOSE	HI	408	998-7331	998-7331	294-8208	4800 RB 208
SAN MATEO	HI	415	349-6131	349-6131		
SAN RAPHAEL	HI	415	459-4250	459-4250		
SANTA BARBARA	MED	805	963-7797			
STOCKTON	HI	209	464-7351	464-7351		
SUNNYVALE	HI	408	737-1675	737-1675		
SUNNYVALE	HI	408			733-7523	4800 RB GDC
VALLEJO	LOW	707	643-1311	643-4504		
WALNUT CREEK	HI	415	937-2868	937-2868		
COLORADO						
COLORADO SPRINGS	MED	303	576-4660	576-8850		
DENVER	HI	303	779-0919	779-0919	740-9401	4800 RB 208
GRAND JUNCTION	LOW	303	245-6902	245-3502		
CONNECTICUT						
BRIDGEPORT	MED	203	334-4451	334-4451		
DANBURY	HI	203	748-1980	749-1980		
GREENWICH	MED	203	661-3934			
HARTFORD	MED	203	522-1873	549-0137		
NEW HAVEN	MED	203	787-0699	865-6420		
NEW LONDON	LOW	203	443-2243	442-6492		
STAMFORD	HI	203	357-0655	348-1704	964-0184	4800 RB 208
WATERBURY	MED	203	755-4808			
DELAWARE						
WILMINGTON	MED	302	658-9797	658-9590		
DISTRICT OF COLUMBIA						
WASHINGTON	HI	703	821-6770	821-0138	893-8410	4800 RB 208
FLORIDA						
AVON PARK	MED	813		453-7700		
BOCA RATON	MED	305	368-4245			
CAPE CANAVERAL	LOW	305	783-4385			
FORT LAUDERDALE		305	462-0910	462-1101	772-6891	4800 RB 208
FORT MYERS	MED	813	337-2288	337-2288		
JACKSONVILLE	MED	904	725-5605	725-5605		
LAKELAND	MED	813	688-5619			
LEESBURG	LOW	904	787-8189			
MIAMI	MED	305	948-6815	948-6815		
NAPLES	MED	813		263-4522		
ORLANDO	MED	305	894-3771	894-3220	896-4079	4800 RB 208
SAINT PETERSBURG	MED	813	822-1411		821-2514	4800 RB
SARASOTA	MED	813	366-7778	366-7778		
TALLAHASSEE	MED	904	222-0081	222-0081		
TAMPA	MED	813	223-9431	228-7575	229-2750	4800 RB
WEST PALM BEACH	MED	305	659-2884	655-4344	832-1708	4800 RB 208
GEORGIA						
ATLANTA	HI	404	256-4904	256-1090	252-3087	4800 RB 208
ILLINOIS						
BLOOMINGTON	HI	309	663-5381	663-9418		
CHICAGO	HI	312	663-4404	663-4404	663-0106	4800 RB 208
EVANSVILLE	HI	618	853-2312	853-2312		
PEORIA	HI	309	637-0470	637-0470		

```
ROCKFORD          HI    815 229-5132    229-5132
SPRINGFIELD       HI    217 522-1283    522-1283
URBANA            HI    217 328-2867    328-2867
INDIANA
 EVANSVILLE       HI    812 464-5769    464-5769
 FORT WAYNE       MED   219 482-4620    482-3541
 GARY             HI    219 882-1661    882-1661
 INDIANAPOLIS           317 635-5265    635-5265
 SOUTH BEND       HI    219 232-3347    232-3347
IOWA
 CEDAR RAPIDS     HI    319 364-8185    364-8185
 DAVENPORT        HI    319 322-5989    322-5989
 DES MOINES       HI    515 224-1842    224-1842
 GRINNELL         HI    515 236-5473
KANSAS
 ATCHINSON        HI    913 367-3282
 COFFEYVILLE      MED   316 251-4190
 FORT HAYES       HI    913 628-1950
 HUTCHINSON       LOW   316 662-2379
 SALINA           LOW   913 825-6554
 TOPEKA           HI    913 232-0486    232-0486
 WICHITA          LOW   316 262-3523    265-7866
KENTUCKY
 COVINGTON        MED   606 491-2944    491-3427
 FRANKFORT        MED   502 223-2144
 LEXINGTON        MED   606 276-3531    276-5431
 LOUISVILLE       MED   502 589-0370    585-5883
LOUISIANA
 BATON ROUGE      LOW   504 344-4002    344-3110
 LAFAYETTE        LOW   318 232-8990    235-5239
 NEW ORLEANS      MED   504 568-1481    522-8330
MAINE
 AUGUSTA          HI    207 622-1891    622-1891
MARYLAND
 BALTIMORE        HI    301 837-4150    685-5610
MASSACHUSETTS
 ANDOVER          HI    617 475-7960
 BOSTON           HI    617 890-6100    890-1063   890-0563   4800 RB 208
 CAMBRIDGE        HI    617 661-7160
 NORTHAMPTON      MED   413 586-5965
 SPRINGFIELD      HI    413 734-6447    734-6447
 WALTHAM          HI    617 890-6100    890-1063   890-0563   4800 RB 208
 WORCESTER        HI    617 791-8448    791-9588
MICHIGAN
 ANN ARBOR        MED   313 662-1298    662-1298
 DETROIT          HI    313 352-5930    352-5981
 GRAND RAPIDS     LOW   616 241-2694    241-2694
 JACKSON          MED   517 788-2275    787-0910
 KALAMAZOO        LOW   616 388-6182    388-6182
 LANSING          HI    517 321-1660    321-1660
 MUSKEGAN               616 728-9144    728-9144
MINNESOTA
 MINNEAPOLIS      MED   612 546-4582    546-4582
MISSOURI
```

JEFFERSON CITY	MED	314	634-2112	634-2112			
KANSAS CITY	HI	816	474-4000	474-1016	474-4250	2000 RB SYNT
KANSAS CITY	HI	816			421-6531		VOTR
KANSAS CITY	HI	816			421-5864	4800 RB 208
SAINT LOUIS	MED	314	434-1212	434-8855	576-0503	4800 RB 208
NEBRASKA						
COLUMBUS	MED	402	564-4877			
LINCOLN	MED	402	474-6132	474-5791		
OMAHA	MED	402	346-2340	346-7758		
NEVADA						
LAS VEGAS	HI	702	383-5988	383-5988		
RENO	HI	702	322-7001	322-7001		
NEW HAMPSHIRE						
CONCORD	HI	603	224-5800	224-5800		
HANOVER	MED	603		643-6390		
MANCHESTER	LOW	603	669-7988			
MERRIMACK	HI	603	424-6171			
NEW JERSEY						
BRANCHBURG	HI	201	685-1654	722-7783		
CARTERET	HI	201	541-5120	541-5120		
CHERRY HILL	MED	609	667-9071	667-9071		
CRANFORD	LOW	201			272-8929	4800 RB 208
EDISON	LOW	201			494-5008	4800 RB 208
FORDS	HI	201	738-0367	738-0367		
FORT LEE		201	461-3430	461-3430	944-8005	4800 RB 208
MONTVALE		201			573-8546	4800 RB 208
MORRISTOWN	HI	201	267-8139	267-8139		
NEWARK	HI	201	624-1986	624-1986		
PARSIPPANY	MED	201	335-4050	263-4792	263-4670	4800 RB 208
PISCATAWAY		201				
PRINCETON	HI	609	921-8826	921-8826		
RIVER EDGE	HI	201	967-7530	262-6805		
ROSELAND	HI	201	228-9301	228-1370		
SOMERVILLE	LOW	201			722-2730	4800 RB 208
TRENTON	HI	609	394-9028	394-9028		
WOODBRIDGE	HI	201	636-5950	636-7080	750-1484	4800 RB 208
NEW MEXICO						
ALBUQUERQUE	MED	505	842-8897	842-8897		
NEW YORK						
BABYLON	HI	516	669-2570	669-2570		
BUFFALO	MED	716	842-6770	842-6770		
JOHNSTOWN	HI	518	762-7274			
LATHAM	HI	518	785-1522	785-1522		
MINEOLA	HI	516	741-5554	741-5554		
NEW YORK	HI	212	868-8338	736-6819	736-6573	4800 RB 208
PLAINVIEW		516	935-5035	935-5035		
ROCHESTER	HI	716	473-8560	473-0410		
SCHENECTADY	LOW	518	382-0096	382-0096		
SENECA FALLS	HI	315	568-6282	568-6282		
SYRACUSE	HI	315	476-1800	476-1800		
WHITE PLAINS	HI	914	328-0824	684-6152		
NORTH CAROLINA						
BEAUFORT		919				
CHARLOTTE	MED	704	365-4520	365-4570		1200 FD 212A

DURHAM	MED	919 471-1541	477-7327			
GREENSBORO	MED	919 274-1129	274-1129			
RALEIGH	MED	919 781-6350	781-6364			
TARBORO	MED	919 823-0124	823-3937			
WINSTON-SALEM	MED	919 748-1805	748-8370			
NORTH DAKOTA						
BISMARK	LOW	701 222-4720	258-1905			
OHIO						
AKRON	MED	216 376-5652	376-5652			
CANTON	MED	216 453-6144	453-6144			
CINCINNATI	MED	606 491-2944	491-3427			
CLEVELAND	MED	216 447-0950	447-0950			
DAYTON	MED	513 228-1729	228-1729			
DELAWARE	LOW	614 548-5141				
INDEPENDENCE	MED	216 447-0950	447-0950			
MANSFIELD	LOW	419 522-2800				
TOLEDO	MED	419 255-2520	255-2520			
WORTHINGTON	MED	614 885-2012	436-8241			
OKLAHOMA						
BARTLESVILLE	MED	918 336-5474	336-3095	336-4394	4800 RB	208
OKLAHOMA CITY	MED	405 843-9981	843-4743	840-5773	4800 RB	208
TULSA	MED	918 582-4313	582-8070	599-7558	2400 RB	SYNT
TULSA	MED	918		582-8139	4800 RB	GDC
VINITA	MED	918 256-7103				
OREGON						
ALBANY	MED	503 926-1610	926-1610			
HOOD RIVER	LOW	503 386-3433				
PORTLAND	LOW	503 228-6360	228-6360			
WOODBURN	MED	503 981-3395	981-3395			
PENNSYLVANIA						
ALLENTOWN	HI	215 395-8050	395-8050			
CARLISLE	HI	717 249-1610				
COATESVILLE	HI	215 383-7878	383-6018			
COLLEGEVILLE	HI	215 489-1040				
DANVILLE	LOW	717	275-1060			
FORT WASHINGTON	HI	215 628-4830				
HARRISBURG	HI	717 232-2681	232-2681			
PHILADELPHIA	HI	215 963-0206	963-0206	568-6450	4800 RB	208
PITTSBURGH	MED	412 931-8283	931-8950	931-8191	4800 RB	208
READING	HI	215 376-5781	376-5575	372-7006	4800 RB	208
YORK	MED	717 843-0837	843-9925	848-1936	4800 RB	
RHODE ISLAND						
PROVIDENCE		401 272-4970	272-9720			
SOUTH CAROLINA						
COLUMBIA	MED	803 254-0323				
SPARTANBURG	HI	803 583-9364				
TENNESSEE						
BRISTOL	LOW	615 968-7774	968-7754			
CHATTANOOGA	HI	615 265-6767	265-6767			
JOHNSON CITY	LOW	615 477-8183				
KNOXVILLE	HI	615 971-5894	971-5894			
MEMPHIS	MED	901 527-3057	527-3057			
NASHVILLE	MED	615 242-2870	242-2870			
TEXAS						

AMARILLO	LOW	806 372-7416	373-7976			
ATHENS	HI	214 675-1370	675-2569			
AUSTIN	LOW	512 447-6467	441-3053	479-0637	4800 RB 208
CORPUS CHRISTI	HI	512 241-4232				
DALLAS	HI	214 363-3101	361-8590	369-0560	4800 RB 208
EL PASO	HI	915 544-2912	544-2912			
GRAND PRAIRIE	HI	214 263-6471	263-4161			
HOUSTON	HI	713 626-4240	552-0773	961-3860	4800 RB 208
HOUSTON	HI	713		626-9586	2400 RB S201
MIDLAND	LOW	915 683-6156				
SAN ANGELO	LOW	915 944-8668	944-0515			
SAN ANTONIO	MED	512 684-6330	681-2474			
TYLER	LOW	214 597-5094				
UTAH						
SALT LAKE CITY	MED	801 328-8001	364-2299			
VERMONT						
RUTLAND	HI	802 775-1973	775-1973			
VIRGINIA						
CHARLOTTESVILLE	HI	804 977-4265				
COVINGTON	MED	703 962-2264				
FALLS CHURCH	HI	703 821-6770	821-0138	893-8410	4800 RB 208
NORFOLK	MED	804 623-6008				
RICHMOND	MED	804 226-4458	226-4458			
WASHINGTON						
BELLINGHAM	MED	206 733-8800				
EVERETT	LOW	206 353-7750				
RICHLAND	MED	509 946-4071				
SEATTLE	MED	206 644-2840	644-2840	625-6947	4800 RB 208
SPOKANE	MED	509 838-3727	838-3727			
WISCONSIN						
APPLETON	MED	414 733-7372				
MADISON	MED	608 837-4559				
MILWAUKEE	MED	414 475-9011	475-0996			
RACINE	MED	414 632-2747	636-3055			
SHEBOYGAN	MED	414 452-0508				
SUN PRAIRIE	MED	608 837-4559	837-2847			

Typewriters

Microprocessors are proving both a blessing and a curse to the manufacturers
of typewriters – including IBM. The days of the complex, elaborately
engineered electromechanical typewriter, including IBM's classic Selectric,
are clearly numbered by the lower parts count made possible by
microprocessor-controlled machines and simpler, daisy wheel printing
mechanisms.

In the meantime, however, traditional typewriter manufacturers face a
sluggish market, high research-and-development costs, and questionable public
desire for enhanced typewriter features such as random-access memory, floppy

disks, and single-line displays.

Instead, competition from more advanced word processing equipment seems to be splitting the traditional typewriter in two, into its printing element, which becomes indistinguishable from, and in competition with, letter-quality computer printers, both daisy-wheel and dot-matrix, and into its keyboard element, which is increasingly attached to a video display device, not a hardcopy printer. In the long run, the typewriter, except as an ill-used office convenience, seems destined to become an adjunct to interlinked word processing systems and is desirable only where video workstations and centralized hard copy printing is somehow not convenient or economical.

[The End of the Electromechanical]. In 1980, microprocessors led to a new kind of typewriter, the electronic typewriter. The electronic typewriter differs from the electric typewriter in that the electronic uses circuitry to replace many of the complicated mechanical linkages of the older, electrical-driven typewriters. For the sake of clarity, what the general public calls electric typewriters, should be called electromechanical, to emphasize their reliance on complicated mechanical linkages.

In theory, electromechanical typewriters are doomed to be replaced by electronic typewriters. A typical electromechanical typewriter, such the classic IBM Selectric II, has approximately 3000 parts, many of them moving parts. An electronic typewriter, by contrast, may have as few as 1000 parts and even fewer moving ones. Given similar levels of assembly automation and the declining prices of chips, the electronics seem to be clear-cut, long-term winners in the evolution of these devices.

The long term matters only if one survives the short run, and in the short run, some traditional typewriter manufacturers may be dead. Most have had serious problems meeting escalating labor costs, sluggish demand, and the high (for their industry) research and development costs required to gain entry into the electronic age.

Many famous names in the history of office equipment have barely survived into the 1980s: Remington Rand closed its last US factory in the mid-1970s, shifting production to Canada, and filed a Chapter 11 bankruptcy petition for purposes of reorganization in March 1981. Royal Business Machines closed its Hartford, CT, plant in the mid-1970s. As a US subsidiary of Triumph-Adler, itself a money-losing subsidiary of Volkswagenwerk AG, Royal has continued to report losses.

In September 1981, Triumph-Adler laid off 2800 of its 8700 employees and closed one of its four plants in Germany. Another German firm, Olympia Werke AG, has been reported to be on the auction block, with ITT possibly interested in picking it up. In the meantime, competition in both low-cost electromechanicals and electronic typewriters from the Japanese has increased. At the Hanover fair in August 1981, Tokyo Juki Industrial Co. introduced a $400 imitation of the IBM Selectric, and Japan's Brother Industry has introduced similar models.

IBM has been well aware that its Selectric, undoubtedly one of the most successful products of all time, is in the golden years of its life cycle. In 1979, IBM, perhaps spurred to early action by competition, introduced its own electronic typewriters, the Models 50, 60, and 75, which are designed to slowly take over by upward migration, the considerable base of Selectric users. On April 3, 1981, IBM formally discontinued the classic Selectric II, although it continues to sell the newer electromechanical Selectric III. With many of its patents on the Selectric golf-ball typing element expired, IBM has also cut prices on all its typewriters in an effort to meet competition, particularly from Olivetti and the Japanese.

[Electronics]. The microprocessor-controlled typewriter has opened up new possibilities but also created new headaches for all traditional manufacturers. Of these, only a few, including IBM and Olivetti, have had the research depth to develop microprocessor controlled typewriters without undue strain. In part the problem lies with the fact that rather than being used to reduce costs, both of manufacturing and for the consumer or office product user, the introduction of electronics has sparked an expensive features war, which no manufacturer has won, and which is of questionable benefit to end users.

Once a typewriter is controlled by a chip and contains random-access memory, it is a matter of programming to introduce other features, such as searching, block moves of text, automatic centering and underlining, and so on. Because the electronic typewriters do more than their older counterparts, typewriter manufacturers have concluded that consumers should pay more for them - which consumers, from sales figures, have not seemed so willing to buy. In particular, the sorts of features now commonly found on electronic typewriters include:

> Auto Centering: lines are centered on the page by the
>   microprocessor;
>
> Auto Underscore: a word or line can be marked at beginning and
>   end for underlining;
>
> Auto Carriage Return: while typing, the right margin is ignored.
>   The typewriter inserts a word to the right if it fits, or
>   breaks it down to the next line if not;
>
> Auto Erase Backspace: characters backed over are erased;
>
> Decimal alignment: numbers typed in columns, as in accounting or
>   statistical typing, are automatically aligned;
>
> Auto Column Layout: multiple columns per page;
>
> Auto Headers/Footers: titles for top and bottom of pages,
>   respectively;
>
> Auto Paper Feed: insert of paper;
>
> Auto Word Wraparound: allows insertions and deletions inside
>   paragraphs, with a newly formatted paragraph automatically
>   produced;
>
> Phrase Storage and Recall: commonly used words and phrases can
>   be stored in the typewriter's memory, and recalled with
>   special function keys or special codes;

Proportional spacing: as on the old IBM Executive typewriter;

Right Justification: pads the line with space to flush out the
right margin;

Multilingual printout: sometimes requires a manual change of
typing element or daisy wheel;

Sub/Superscripts: half-line move up or down allows chemical
formula, exponents, etc., to be automatically produced;

Global Search/Replace: phrases can be corrected through the full
range of the document in the typewriter's memory;

Text Insert/Delete: allows insertion of blocks of text, for
example, new paragraphs, within a document;

Document Assembly/Merge: allows creation of documents from
multiple sources, such as form letter generation from a letter
template and list of names and addreses.

It should come as no suprise that the companies best coping with the new
typewriter are those with computer and word processing backgrounds or
high-tech, research-and-development operations, such as Exxon's Qyx division.
The new typewriter is essentially a nondisplay word processor. Ironically, it
is the typewriter's limitations - its convenience in light typing operations,
such as file folder labels, notes, and what not - that may keep it by every
desk in the future, when heavy typing operations are taken over by Wangs,
Displaywriters, and the like.

[Communications].   Despite   the   problems   of   some   of   the   traditional
manufacturers, as a whole the typewriter market is stable and mature. There
are 40 million typewriters installed in the US, which are being replaced at a
stable rate of 1.5 million per year (as in 1978) and never dropping much below
1.3 million (as in 1976). The fundamental outlook for the basic typewriter
market is neither especially favorable nor especially unfavorable. The number
of college-age students, traditionally the strongest market for portable and
low-cost machines, will decline in the 1980s. At the same time, however,
there is a long-term, general secular growth in sales and sophistication of
office equipment, which should improve typewriter sales.

On this calm, flat base of traditional sales, then - especially of lower-cost
electromechanical and manual portable machines - the upper reaches of the
office typewriter market will undergo stormy seas. In general, the office
typewriter market will merge with the word processing market, with the
following noticeable trends:

(1) Shared Resources. The all-in-one typewriter, such as Exxon's
Level 5 Qyx, which has a microprocessor, floppy disks, and
printing mechanism, will not be able to compete with display
word processing systems or with systems that share expensive
resources, like the printer. Printing mechanisms and disk
storage, floppy or hard, will always be relatively high

compared to the price of microprocessor chips and memory. The clear trend in office networking is for multiple workstations to share disks and printers while providing individual keyboards and displays.

(2) Divorce of Keyboard and Printer. The typewriter, as designed in the 19th century, is based on the translation of a keystroke into an impression on paper. The introduction of memory and electronics breaks this direct linkage. In future designs keyboards for typing, will function independently of printer mechanisms for printing. Sony's Typecorder is perhaps the best example of this trend: like a dictation device, it is designed to function as a keyboard with only magnetic memory (either cassette tapes or microfloppies), to be portable and only later, by attachment to a printer back at the office, to allow for hardcopy.

(3) Competition with Computer Printers. A corollary of the above separation of functions is that whatever a typewriter can do, a computer printer can probably do better. Although many typewriter manufacturers have learned from computer printer manufacturers how to incorporate microprocessors and how to reduce costs and parts, a computer printer will always be cheaper than a typewriter, because the former need not have the keyboard mechanism. The true market for typewriters in the office word processing environment is as convenience devices, for which the handiness of having hardcopy at a desk, say for notes, etc., justifies the expense of redundant hardware. The same thing holds in the personal computer environment: although a typewriter with RS-232 interface can be made to function as a low-cost computer printer, a computer printer using the same mechanism presumably will always be cheaper. Because practically every personal computer system already has a keyboard, the issue is whether convenience actually justifies the cost of a second one.

[IBM]. IBM (corporate headquarters in Armonk, NY) makes, in addition to the Selectric electromechanical typewriter, three electronic typewriters: the Model 50, 60, and 75. The Model 50 has proportional spacing, like the old IBM Executive, and the Model 60 has dual (10 and 12 characters per inch) spacing. The Model 60 has automatic carriage return and a phrase storage of 736 characters, which can be divided into 10 bins. This feature makes it useful for form typing and other repetitive tasks.

The IBM 75 is an upgraded version of the Model 60 with 7500 characters of storage. It allows revision of documents that can be stored within its memory. The Model 175 has 15,500 characters of memory, about 7 pages of text. Current prices: Selectric III (electromechanical) $810-1035; Models 50 & 60 (electronic) $1430.

[IBM Electronic Modifications]. Northern Telecom (PO Box 1222, Minneapolis, MN 55440, 612-932-8000), a major manufacturer of telephone equipment, makes the Intelligent Remote Input Stand (IRIS), which attaches to either the IBM Model 50, 60, or 75. IRIS has a large RAM memory, starting at 16K and expandable to 48K, a 40-character display, and block move and insert features. An optional expansion is a built-in, 300-baud, Bell 103A-type modem, which turns the device into a buffered terminal for timsharing access or workstation-to- workstation electronic mail. The 16K version is $1400; 48K version $1900; modem option is $200.

Alcotech, Inc. (5169 Douglas Fir Rd., Calabasas, CA 91302, 213-992-7590) makes Wordfile 60, a device similar to that of Northern Telecom, but which incorporates a mini-cassette recorder as well. Documents up to 16,000 characters (8 pages) can be stored on these removable cassettes. Retail price is about $2655.

Mediamix (PO Box 67B57, Los Angeles, CA 90067) makes a $500 black box with 2000 characters of memory that connects to any of the IBM 50, 60, or 75 models. California Micro Computer (9323 Warbler Ave., Fountain Valley, CA 92708, 714-968-0890) makes a circuit board and cable that converts any of the Models 50, 60, or 75 into either a: (1) RO printer or (2) a KSR terminal.

[Qyx]. Qyx (a division of Exxon Enterprises, 101 Gordon Dr., Lionville, PN 07932) makes a complete line of intelligent typewriters, starting with a Level 1 machine and working up to its top-of-the-line Level 5. Prices for memory typewriters (Level I) start about $1400. Those with floppy disks (Level 3 and above) leap upward into the $3000 range, with the Level 5 running about $7000.

[Olivetti]. Olivetti, the large Italian firm (US office: 155 White Plains Rd., Tarrytown, NY 10591) makes a floppy-disk word processing system that uses its 201/222 electronic typewriters. The Olivetti 201 has a 2-character display, and the 222 has a 15-character display. Olivetti introduced a Z8000 based microcomputer system with word processing option in 1982.

The Olivetti TES 401 and 501 have 7500 character memory. Prices: Praxis 30 (single-pitch electronic portable) $595; Praxis 35 (triple-pitch electronic portable) $695; 201 (limited display, 16K RAM memory) $2800.

[Vertical Data Systems]. Vertical Data (1215 Meyerside Dr., Unit 2A Mississauga, Ontario Canada, L5T 1H3 416-671-1752) makes a box that gives the Olivetti Praxis 35 typewriter either an RS-232, IEEE-488, or parallel interface. A KSR option turns the typewriter into a printing terminal. Prices for the box start at $275.

[XYMEC]. XYMEX (177901 Sky Park Circle, Irvine, CA 92714 714-557-8501) makes a computer printer out of the Olivetti 201 and 221 electronic typewriters. The Xymec printer has either a Centronics parallel interface or an optional RS-232 interface. Prices start about $2650.

[Conitronix]. Contitronix (3848 Marquis Dr., Garland, TX 75042, 214-276-0555, Telex 73-2524 CONTITRON), a company whose first product was a dual-language (Arabic and English, or Arabic and French) typewriter, and which is affiliated with the Middle Eastern Najjar group, makes a sophisticated electronic typewriter called the Eight-K. Conitronix also makes a receive-only terminal (Model 1100) out of its printer mechanism, which uses Qume printwheels. Recently, Contitronix introduced a combined display word processor and microcomputer programmable in BASIC.

[Olympia]. Olympia (Box 22, Somerville, NJ 08876) makes low-end electronic typewriters, the ES 100 and ES101, which use daisy wheel technology but have limited 8-byte internal buffers.) Olympia's more expensive 6010 and 6020 memory typewriters have 4000 and 8000 bytes of memory storage, respectively.

[Palomar Computer Products]. Palomar (910-105 W. San Marcos Blvd., San Marcos, CA 92069, 714-744-7314) makes an adaptor for the Olympia ES100 electronic typewriter. The adaptor gives the typewriter a parallel or RS-232 port, making it a receive-only printer. Without the interface, the ES100 typewriter only is $1095. With the interface, it is $1395.

[Royal]. Adler (Adler-Royal Business Machines, 1600 Rt. 22, Box 1597 Union, NJ 07083) makes a floppy disk-based text-editing word processor, the SE 6000. It has a 3-character display and 4000 byte internal memory, and connects to dual floppy disks with 64K bytes storage each.

[Smith-Corona]. SCM Corporation's Smith-Corona Typetronic is another simplified typewriter using ultrasonic waves to transmit keystrokes to the typing element. It is priced at about $900.

[Juki]. Juki (3186 Airway Ave., Suite G Costa Mesa, CA 92626, 213-328-6826), a Japanese manufacturer of sewing machines and computer peripherals, introduced a low-cost ($395) electromechanical typewriter designed to compete with the IBM Selectric.

[IBM Selectrics]. Converting IBM Selectrics into printers is an inexpensive means of obtaining a high-quality printer for a computer or word processing system. However, converting Selectrics into computer printers involves a number of compromises. The Selectric is an excellent piece of office equipment. It was not designed, however, to be a piece of computer equipment.

In general, it is a better idea not to convert a Selectric unless it is available free. Smith Corona now makes a low-cost typewriter that can run directly off personal computer, and heavy-duty, dot matrix printers such as the Epson MX-80 produce excellent quality output for all but the most exacting camera-ready applications.

[How It Works]. The Selectric is the original "golf ball" typewriter. The Selectric type ball, or typing element, as IBM likes to call it, has 4 horizontal rings of 22 characters each, providing a total of 88 different characters. Note that most computer printers offer 96 printing characters. There is not a 1-to-1 correspondence between Selectric wheels and ASCII.

The characters are laid out on the Selectric ball in a way that reduces the total motion the ball has to make. Two motions control the ball: a tilting motion that selects the proper horizontal ring, and a rotation that selects the right character from the 22 rows on the rings.

In the standard office Selectric, six moving "bails" in the base of the machine control the tilting and rotation of the ball by a complicated mechanical (not electronic) process. The bails are called T1, T2, R1, R2, R2A, and R5. T1 and T2 provide, proper amount of "tilt" to the ball; R5 rotates the ball 90 degrees clockwise; R1, R2, and R2A rotate the ball to one of the five positions to the right of the "home" position. The shift on the

Selectric rotates the ball 180 degrees - lower case letters normally face the paper, and upper case characters normally face the typist.

[Modifying the Selectric]. It is possible to get into the base of the Selectric and control the bails (which are small rods) with a set of electrically driven magnets. In addition to the 6 magnets that are needed to control the motion of the type ball (actually 7 if shift is counted), other magnets, for a total of 10, are needed to control the space, the carriage return, and the print cycle clutch.

Several reputable firms, such as ESCON, Inc., of Pleasant Hill, CA, make a full-time business of modifying used Selectrics or providing kits to those who want to do it themselves. The cost of converting a used Selectric into a computer printer is about $600, depending on the type of connection desired to the computer (an RS-232-C interface, the most popular, is also the most expensive). This cost of modifying the typewriter is, of course, in addition to the value of the machine. A new Selectric, modified for computer printing, usually runs about $1800, depending on interface options.

[Selectric I/Os]. In addition to the Selectrics I, II, and III, which are office typewriters, IBM and several other companies under license from IBM have, in the past, made printers and terminals that used the Selectric mechanism. Unlike the office typewriter, these have the electromagnets built into them. A number of these Selectric Input/Output Keyboard Printers, or Selectric I/Os as they are generally known, are available on the surplus market at prices ranging from $700 on up.

[BCD vs Correspondence Code]. Some Selectric I/Os that were built for computer use employ the BCD (Binary Coded Decimal) coding system and use special typing elements. BCD code is a limited, 62-character, all-capitals code with special computer symbols, which was offered in place of the Correspondence coding scheme used on the normal office Selectric.

In general, avoid BCD machines. Correspondence elements can be used on BCD machines, but to utilize all 88 characters, a conversion must be programmed. Here is the layout of Correspondence ("C") and BCD machines. Note that a number of locations on the BCD element are unused (unu). The strange special characters on the BCD ball are represented in the chart by 3-letter codes.

BCD TO CORRESPONDENCE CODE CONVERSION

RING:	TOP		UPPER		LOWER		BOTTOM	
	C	BCD	C	BCD	C	BCD	C	BCD
	1/2	unu	X	unu	M	unu	G	unu
	'	unu	U	unu	V	unu	F	unu
	&	unu	D	unu	R	unu	:	unu
	*	unu	C	cro	A	bar	,	?
	$	@	L	%	0	*	?	squ
	Z	>	T	\	1/4	;	J	<
	@	unu	N	unu	.	unu	+	unu
	%	unu	E	unu	"	unu	P	unu
	cnt	unu	K	unu	I	unu	Q	unu
	)	:	H	arc	S	]	Y	[

(	chk	B	hsh	W	del		cro
!	1	x	/	m	J	g	A
3	3	u	T	v	L	f	C
7	5	d	V	r	N	;	E
8	7	c	X	a	P	,	G
4	8	1	Y	o	Q	/	H
z	0	t	t	j	–	j	&
2	2	n	S	.	K	=	B
5	4	e	U	'	M	p	D
6	6	k	W	i	O	q	F
0	9	h	Z	s	R	y	1
9	'	b	,	w	S	–	.

[Versions of the Correspondence Typeball]. IBM has several versions of its relatively universal Correspondence typing element. These differ by what is over the "1" key and by what is on the key directly to the right of "P" and, in the legal versions, by what is over the "6" and "2". The following table is of the versions of the Correspondence typing elements. These different versions should not be confused with the style of the typing element, which refers to the type face--italic, Gothic, Courier, etc. Most versions are available in several styles:

VERSIONS OF THE CORRESPONDENCE ELEMENT

American Standard
  - top left key is ! over 1
  - key to right of P is 1/4 over 1/2

Bracket
  - top left key is [over]
  - key to right of P is o over !

Fraction
  - top left key has +- over 1
  - key to right of P is 1/4 over 1/2

Degree
  - top left key has +- over 1
  - key to right of P is o over !

Legal (R-3177)
  - top left key has o over 1
  - "2" key has paragraph symbol over 2
  - "6" key has section symbol over 6
  - key to right of P has [over]

Legal (R-3178)
  - same but "1/4 1/2" to right of P

Legal (R-3017)
  - same but o ! to right of P

TM/R (R-3304)
  - key to right of P has TM over R

[Using Selectrics with Computers]. Selectrics are adequate as printing devices in situations where low volumes of high-quality output are needed - in a small legal office or for a not-too-prolific writer. Because the metal typing element has a high mass, the print quality of the Selectric is better than that of plastic daisy wheel printers. Metal daisy wheel printers (e.g., the Diablo 630, about $1800) are comparable in quality.

A Selectric linked to a computer will normally need: (1) a power cord to the Selectic; (2) another power cord to the interface box (this drives the magnets inside the Selectric); and (3) a cable to the serial or parallel port of the computer. In most configurations, the Selectric looks like a printer to the computer.

Several cautions about using Selectrics with computers need to be made. 1st, a computer runs a Selectric harder than a human does in the course of normal office typing. The machine may wear quickly, especially the platen. IBM will generally offer service contracts convering only the IBM parts of converted machines.

Second, although the Selectric is fine for word processing and other applications, programmers should keep in mind that Selectrics are not ASCII devices. The ASCII character set has 96 printing characters. The Selectric has only 88 characters, and a number of these are given to traditional typewriter keys, like 1/4 over 1/2. As a result, the Selectric is missing a number of special characters from the ASCII set that are needed in program listings: >,<,[,],{,},\,~,`,^,|.

[Alternatives to the Selectric]. The usual trade-up from the Selectric in word processing applications is to a plastic or metal "daisy wheel" printer such as the Diablo or Qume or to a "thimble" printer such as the NEC Spinterm. Many of the dense dot matrix printers are on the verge of letter quality printing and may be satisfactory in some applications.

V

Video Games

Any reader of the business press in 1982 could not help but become aware of the boom in both arcade video games and in home video game sales. Video games represent not so much a revolution in chip prices but in "ergonomics" - a buzzword that has come to stand for the ability of ordinary, untrained people to use complicated, confusing devices.

Video games are the first microprocessor controlled product that ordinary people can actually operate. If we discount clocks, as found in microwave ovens, thermostats, and VCRs, there are still, almost 8 years into the IC revolution, very few microprocessors in the average home - unless that home happens to have a video game, as almost 15 million households in the US do.

If consumers enjoy the sense of power and control that working with a computer can provide, as do many programmers, video games become not just a way of zapping aliens but the entering wedge of computers into the mass market. Games show that in the consumer market less is more - the more simple, the better. Once thought of as a distraction from "real" computing, video games have in fact brought a number of advances to the industry, including the use of joysticks and similar user-friendly controls, improved graphics, and the widespread use of ROMs as a medium for program distribution.

Contrary to accepted opinion, the consumer has a number of applications in which he or she could use a home computer: game playing, home education, home banking and shopping, and various types of data base management. The barrier to consumer use is technological: of these applications, only game playing and, to a lesser extent, home education have been simplified enough. Home shopping, when it arrives, will not involve calling The Source, inputting a long log-on sequence, and paging past menus on Comp-U-Card; it will be a cross between zapping aliens and playing "The Price is Right".

[Distribution Trends]. In comparing video games and personal computers there is a simple but important difference in retailing patterns. Video games can be bought at a store - any store - taken home, plugged in, and used.

Personal computers, by contrast, require support. They are not well suited for discount, move-it-in/move-it-out selling. Apple Computer Co., for example, in 1982 cracked down on dealers who were making mail-order sales of its products, on the theory that Apple users need walk-in stores where they can get support. Such education is expensive. If required, it clearly eliminates the K-Mart and stereo-type stores as sellers of Apples and nearly eliminates such established retailers as Sears, Wards, and Macy's.

By contrast, the distribution trend of game-type computers such as the TI 99/4A, Atari 400, and Commodore VIC-20 has clearly been toward discount and mass market retail outlets. These machines will often have one suggested list price and a deep-dish discount or "street" price, possibly including a manufacturer's rebate. Not much extra support is offered the consumer buying these machines, and usually none is expected.

The advantage to such a retailing strategy is that there is no limit to the number of outlets that can handle such products. In 1982, TI signed up its 8000 store, making it more widely available, at least as measured by outlets, than Radio Shack products.

[Trends in Video Game Hardware]. Trends in video game hardware can be determined by looking at: (1) new products announced for 1982-83 introduction; and (2) trends within the various component elements of video games. Of new video game products, the Coleco console has excellent graphics. Coleco's own software - not its Atari- or Mattel-compatible software - for arcade games like "Zaxxon" is excellent. Coleco has also taken the important step of adding an "Atari adapter" which will allow Atari VCS software to be played on its machine. The new Atari 5200 "supergame," rivals the graphics of the Coleco machine.

Although the Coleco and Atari supergames represent major improvements in dedicated video game hardware, the Commodore Max, announced in the spring of 1982 for fall shipments is a combined computer and home video game, even more than Commodore's VIC-20,. Commodore is touting the Max as a "3-in-1" machine, meaning that it combines: (1) a video game; (2) a home computer; and (3) a music synthesizer. The Max has a 40-column by 25-line screen, 16 colors, and graphics; it comes with 2.5K of RAM and a membrane keyboard similar to the Sinclair ZX-81. The Max has a suggested retail price of $179.95, which makes it competitive with video games - the Atari VCS, for example, currently lists at $149.95 - and with computers, including Commodore's own VIC-20, currently about $249.

The Max uses a new 6510 microprocessor developed by Commodore's subsidiary, MOS Technology, which designed the 6502 microprocessor used in Apple and Atari computers, as well as Commodore's earlier "PET" series. Another Commodore-designed chip, the 6581, is a 3-voice music synthesizer, each voice having a 9-octave range. The 6581 has programmable envelope generators for each voice (attack, sustain, release, decay), filters, and resonance. The Max has an optional BASIC cartridge with a full version of BASIC, including strings, 9-digit numbers, and built-in math functions.

[Component-by-Component Trends]. In general, video games must be inexpensive, high-volume items. As such, they lend themselves to the use of semiconductor parts but not electromechanical devices, such as printers and floppy disks. Some peripheral functions, like speech synthesis - a speech synthesizer, as an output device, is essentially a "talking printer" - can be implemented with chips and low-cost hardware, making them candidates for home game systems. Because manufacturing runs in games are so high, any personal computer peripheral that can be rendered in chip form is a potential game peripheral.

[CPUs and RAM]. In video games, as in personal computers, the trend is clearly toward faster processors and increased RAM memory. The Coleco game uses 3 Z-80 microprocessors, 1 for control, 1 for graphics, and 1 for sound. Intellivision uses a 16-bit 8088. Specialized video display processors, such as the ANTIC chip used in the Atari series, are another co-processor trend. Another distinct possibility in game design is the use of computers-on-a-chip, because these reduce parts count, improve reliability, and reduce interface requirements. They are practical primarily for high-volume applications like game consoles.

[Graphic Resolution]. In home games, there is clearly a trend toward increased resolution. However, the principal upcoming limit in the evolution of game consoles is the color quality possible on home television sets. In the NTSC system used on all North American sets, vertical resolution is limited to a maximum of 484 visible lines. Resolution at this level requires use of interlacing fields of video, a difficult-to-implement technique only emerging on expensive raster terminals coming on the business market. Currently, 240 vertical lines is typical maximum vertical resolution for NTSC equipment.

Horizontal resolution of NTSC equipment has an upper limit of 448 horizontal dots for video information received in over-the-air broadcast. Most home sets, however, can display only 100 to 200 distinct horizontal points, or "pixels". Prototype - not commercially available at any price - Panasonic shadow-mask tubes have the following resolutions, providing an upper range:

20 inch tube	920 horizontal
18 inch tube	890 horizontal
16 inch tube	790 horizontal
14 inch tube	750 horizontal

In practice, 620 horizontal resolution - the resolution of the IBM personal computer in black-and-white mode - is the maximum that can be hoped for with commercially available, high-quality shadow mask monitors.

These limits on resolution are for raster-scan, as opposed to vector, display tubes. Atari's "Asteroids" overcame the limitations of raster-scan devices by an expensive black-and-white vector monitor. One small company, General Consumer Electronics Corp., of Santa Monica, CA, has suggested the same approach in the home video game field. The company, founded by ex-Mattel executives, showed at the June, 1982 CES show a $300 home console game that included a 9-inch, black-and-white, X-Y vector display tube.

[Keyboards]. The item of greatest uncertainty in the future of home video games is the keyboard. Although the Odyssey 2 has had a membrane keyboard since its introduction, Mattel's keyboard unit has stood on the verge of introduction for years, and it now appears to be dead, to be replaced by a different Mattel computer in 1983. Atari has shown little interest in a keyboard for either its VCS or its supergame to be introduced in late 1982.

[Joysticks]. The general concensus is that Atari and Odyssey are best. Atari controllers are interchangeable. Odyssey and Intellivision are hard-wired. Trak balls, used on Atari arcade games like "Centipede", give most accurate levels of control. The Bally arcade joystick with built-in trigger allows fire without removing the hand from stick. Larger buttons, as on the Atari but not on the Intellivision, are preferred, because in some space action games like "Space Armada" and "Astromash", your fingers become tired. Special joysticks have been suggested for complex games like "Defender" and "Asteroids". Mattel's Intellivision controller has 12 keys, 4 buttons, and a disk - some think it too complicated. Odyssey controllers are the best, with their ball-in-socket design.

Left-handed joysticks for the Atari VCS are available from Irata Repairs, 2562 E. Glade, Mesa, AZ 85204, for $12.95 plus $2 shipping and handling. A replacement, arcade-style controller for the Atari VCS is available from Starplex Electronics, (E. 23301 Mission, Liberty Lake, WA 99019, 509-924-3654).

[Speech Synthesis]. Speech synthesis, at one time a novelty, is on the verge of becoming a standard feature of home video games. Both Mattel and Odyssey have announced speech synthesizer "cartridges" for their games; these plug into the usual cartridge slot and allow a game to "piggy-back" onto the speech cartridge itself. Cost of each cartridge is in the $100 range. Both companies have announced game software that takes advantage of speech abilities for late 1982. Astrovision has also announced a speech option for its console.

[Music Synthesis]. Both Mattel and Commodore have moved into the realm of "home music synthesis". Mattel has a programmable drum set - a stand-alone electronic toy unrelated to its Intellivision system - and Commodore has a custom music synthesis chip, the MOS Technology 6581, built into its Max and VIC-20 systems. The Commodore chip features 3 independently controlled voices. Similar but less powerful chips from other manufacturers include the General Instruments AY-3-8910 Programmable Sound Generator (PSG) and the Texas Instruments SN/76489N. General Instruments "Stick 3" chipset, likely to show up in Mattel products in the 4th quarter of 1983, includes an advanced multivoice music chip.

[Storage]. For low-cost home systems, floppy disks, even "micro" (3-inch) floppies, remain prohibitively expensive for most home systems. Floppies are not especially useful for the distribution of software, in that they can, with enough effort, be copied. In home systems, the trend is away from floppies toward RAM memory for storage, with the computer being simply left on, or with the memory backed up by a recharging battery. Bubble memory offers another possible technology for temporary storage of moderate amounts of consumer information, such as checkbook records.

[The Software Industry]. In the video games, one of the important trends of 1981-82 was the development of third-party software houses for the major game consoles. The leading third-party software house was Activision, a Mountain View, CA-based company with total sales of $66 million (from 10 Atari VCS cartridges) in its first fiscal year, which ran from April 1, 1981 to March 31, 1982. Activision posted earnings of $12.9 million on those sales.

Activision was founded in October 1979 by James Levy, a former recording company executive, and 4 software designers from Atari who had, by the time they left Atari, had designed over half of Atari's cartridges. Activision has venture capital money from Sutter Hill - which means that its well-publicized growth figures must be taken with a slight grain of salt - and has invested heavily in advertising, including network TV. Activision recently settled out-of-court with Atari, which had sued the company for $20 million, claiming that one of its games, "Dragster", had been developed while the designers were still at Atari. At the June 1982 CES show in Chicago, Activision announced that it would begin to make cartridges for Mattel's Intellivision.

Imagic, Inc., based in Saratoga, CA, is a similar start-up software venture. Imagic has announced publicly that it will produce software for all 3 major console systems, including the Atari VCS, Mattel Intellivision, and Odyssey 2. Other companies with cartridges on sale for the Atari VCS include US Games and Games By Apollo. At the June 1982 CES show, a half-dozen or so other companies jumped on the VCS bandwagon, including Coleco, which has announced a home console (with an Atari VCS cartridge adapter) of its own, and Mattel, which made its surprising announcement at the April, 1982 Toy Fair in New York. A partial list of third-party software suppliers for the Atari VCS:

Activision - Santa Clara, CA
Imagic - Saratoga, CA
Parker Brothers - CT
Mattel - Hawthorne, CA
Spectravision - NY
Games By Apollo - Richardson, TX
Coleco - Hartford, CT
Fox Video Games - Saratoga, CA
US Games - CA

[Analysis]. Third-party software develops when the installed base of a particular machine reaches some critical mass. In the case of video game consoles, the Atari VCS has an installed base of almost 5 million units. If Activision sales are any indication, this base is ample for a profitable after-market in cartridge sales. A general estimate of 1982 cartridge shipments by vendor is:

Atari	20m
Mattel	12m
All Other	28m

Total 1982	60m

Although VCS, Intellivision, and Odyssey are at present associated with consoles by particular manufacturers, they should be increasingly thought of as akin to "formats" in the recording industry, such as VHS, Beta, or 8-track. Odyssey is in the dangerous position of having its format pushed out of the market, leaving it with two: VCS and Intellivision. Fortunately, rather than knock all competing formats out of the market, Atari has decided to leave VCS behind, introducing a new, more capable format for its "supergame". Nevertheless, the association of a cartridge format with a manufacturer will soon fade, just as the association of Beta format with Sony has faded.

Third-party software places the hardware or console manufacturer in a peculiar position. As a hardware manufacturer, the more software available for a machine, the better. This lesson is very clear from the personal computer industry. Apple has never sold much of its own software for the Apple II computer; independent vendors have sold far more.

By contrast, Texas Instrument's home computer, the 99/4, suffered poor sales for many years as TI slowly, and at considerable expense, built a library of TI-produced software. IBM, while licensing and selling some third-party software for its PC has taken the approach of actively encouraging outside software development on the theory that it neither can nor wants to develop all software itself.

The software market is lucrative and not about to be given up by the console manufacturers - that would be like Gillette deciding to sell only razors, not blades. Yet Atari is almost unique in being a manufacturer of console games and computers that also is its own major software provider for its machines.

[Licensing Wars]. Along with the entry of new companies in the software field has come a general escalation of bidding for established or "pre-sold" properties, including proven coin-op games, comic-book characters, and movie titles.

In the arcade rights field, the most dramatic event in this battle has been a February, 1982 coup by Atari in which it scored rights for 4 Centuri co-op games ("Phoenix", "Challenger", "Vanguard", and "Round Up") after Coleco had announced, obviously prematurely, that it had licenses for the games. Coleco was, in fact, showing sample cartridges of the game at the time of the Atari-Centuri announcement. Atari has also acquired home rights to several successful arcade games by Williams Electronics ("Defender") and Stern ("Berzerk").

Several of the new console manufacturers have aggressively bought successful coin-op titles in an effort to win immediate acceptance for their machines. Thus Commodore, for its VIC-20 computer/game, has acquired home rights for Bally/Midway's "Gorf", "Omega Race", and "Super Alien". Coleco, despite its setback from Atari, has rights to Nintendo's "Donkey Kong" and Sega's "Zaxxon". Gabriel, the toymaker subsidiary of CBS, Inc., has announced that it is entering the software market with an exclusive 4-year license of all new Bally/Midway arcade games.

[Movie Tie-Ins]. Of movie titles, most important is clearly Disney's "Tron", a July 9, 1982 release that was accompanied by simultaneous appearance of both an arcade game (from Bally/Midway) and two home games (from Mattel). Other important movie tie-ins include an arrangement by Atari to license titles from Lucasfilm, Ltd., for home games of "Raiders of the Lost Ark". Parker Brothers has rights to "Return of the Jedi" (upcoming as the 3rd film in the "Star Wars" saga and scheduled for May 1983 release).

Rights for "Star Wars: The Empire Strikes Back," are also owned by Parker Brothers, which has a VCS game based on that film. Other titles owned by Parker Brothers include "James Bond"; "Spiderman", based on the Marvel Comics figure; and "Frogger".

In 1982, several film companies have announced entry into the home game software market, notably 20th Century-Fox, which has formed a subsidiary, Fox Video Games, Inc., to develop games with the Atari VCS, and MGM, which has announced, but not detailed, plans to enter the game business.

[Analysis]. The trend toward licensing "presold" games must be seen as part and parcel of the increasing advertising expenditures necessary to introduce new software: rather than spend money to advertise an uncertain new game, it may be wiser to spend it licensing an already established title. In this, the game industry is no different from the paperback book industry, which licenses successful hardback titles, or the movie industry, which licenses successful paperbacks.

There are, however, some differences. Books and movies have a relatively limited "shelf life" - somewhere between milk and yogurt. Game cartridges must achieve relatively high sales to justify manufacturing runs. Consequently, mainly safe and timeless titles - e.g., "Superman" - have been licensed to date. As cartridges begin to appear at the same time as paperback novelizations - e.g., a few weeks before release of the film - the risk of licensing a flop increases.

Furthermore, there is no persuasive evidence that movies and, increasingly, arcade games, can be successfully translated to the home console medium. Playing "Defender" on the Atari home VCS cartridge as opposed to playing the fast-action arcade game is like seeing "Star Wars" on a Betamax as opposed to seeing it in 70 mm with Dolby sound. As arcade games have rapidly become more sophisticated, this gap is increasing. Consumers seem to be well aware of the difference between playing the arcade version of a game and the home version.

Cartridges of movies seem analogous to novelizations and soundtrack albums. These are generally bought as a sort of souvenir of the movie experience, not for their stand-alone, intrinsic entertainment value. It is hard to judge how a "Tron" game, say, with little play-value would stand up over a period of a year to a better, nonmovie game title. In publishing terms, it is very important for a software (game) publisher to have a strong backlist to amortize far higher R&D and manufacturing costs than exist in the book publishing industry.

[The Arcade Game Market]. The arcade game market is large, with a gross of about $5 billion in 1981, dwarfing the film industry ($2.6 billion). As in the film industry, the gross is far from the net. Manufacturers typically sell games to distributors for approximately $2-3000 per machine. These are then placed in arcades and other store locations for a cut of the take, which can be as much as $15,000 per year for a popular game in a good location.

Six manufacturers hold approximately 95% of the arcade game market. Total industry revenues, at the level of sales to distributors, have climbed from $50 million in 1977 to $800 million in 1981. The major companies are:

COMPANY	EST. 1981 SALES
Midway (Bally Mfg.)	$300 million
Atari (Warner)	210 million

Williams Electronics	120 million
Stern Electronics	70 million
Sega Ent. (Gulf & West.)	60 million
Centuri	60 million

[Company Profiles]. Bally Manufacturing is the major maker of pinball and slot machines in this country. Atari, now owned by Warner Communications and making a substantial contribution to that company's growth, was founded in the early 1970s with "Pong", the original video game. Williams Electronics was formerly owned by Seeburg Corporation, a now-bankrupt manufacturer of jukeboxes. Stern is a 1976 Chicago start-up venture created by a bankruptcy lawyer, Gary Stern, out of Chicago Dynamic Industries, better known as "Chicago Coin". Sega is a subsidiary of Gulf+Western, also the parent corporation of Paramount Pictures. Centuri is a Florida company headed by Edward Miller, formerly with the Japanese "Space Invaders" company, Taito.

[Development of Arcade Game Software]. Several of the most successful arcade games, including "Space Invaders" and "Pac-Man", were originally developed in Japan, where the games have been popular longer than in the US. Japanese developers, notably Taito ("Space Invaders") and Namco ("Galaxian" and "Pac-Man"), license US manufacturers for 5-10% royalty on the gross sales price of the game machine (e.g., $200 per machine sold). The games can in turn be sublicensed and merchandised: Bally, which owns the US license for "Pac-Man" (except for the home cartridge, which was directly licensed by Namco to Atari) has sublicensed 30 other "Pac-Man" products, including a "Pac-Man" board game to be produced by Milton Bradley.

The mushrooming of the US market - far larger than the Japanese market - has led Japan to experience what might be called a "game brain drain". Centuri, for example, has hired away 5 video game development experts from Taito and set them up in their own laboratory in Bensenville, IL. Recently, unhappy with merely receiving royalties, several Japanese firms have announced plans to go it alone in the US arcade market. Nintendo, a Japanese maker of playing cards and another amusement items, is building a $10 million manufacturing plant near Seattle for its "Donkey Kong" game. Taito has a recently enlarged plant in Chicago for its new offering, "Qix" (pronounced "kicks" like the Exxon typewriter). Universal Co., another Japanese company, has a factory in Santa Clara, CA, and Namco has an option on a facility in Sunnyvale.

[History of Arcade Games]. "Space Invaders" holds the honor of being the first superstar arcade video game. The original version of "Space Invaders" was developed in Japan by Taito and was so popular there that in 1978 the government was forced to mint additional 100 yen pieces (about 20 cents) to feed the games. During the big years of "Space Invaders", Taito earned some $150 million in profits. The company remains, along with Namco, originator of "Pac-Man", one of several successful Japanese game think tanks, actively licensing other games to US manufacturers. "Pac-Man" was licensed to Bally Manufacturing for arcade games and to Atari for home cartridges.

A number of "knock-off" versions of "Space Invaders" quickly appeared, setting a pattern for the industry. "Apple Invaders" for the personal computer of the same name, is a typical example, resembling the original game with a few minor variations (the user's cannon can hide behind crumbling barricades, for example).

"Galaxian", developed by Namco and licensed to Bally, was a direct
evolutionary offshoot of "Space Invaders", varying in the fact that the
invaders, rather than march relentlessly (and boringly) down the screen, peel
off and swoop down on the target. There are a number of personal computer
versions of "Galaxian", including "Apple Galaxian", "Alien Typhoon", and
others.

Atari, the US subsidiary of Warner Communications, has created a number of
original arcade games that it typically makes available for its $130 home
video game and its 400 and 800 home computers. Familiar Atari games include
"Asteroids", (fast action game played on a field, rather than from a static
position); "Missile Command" (defend cities from smart MIRVs); and
"Battleground" (a you-are-there tank game).

[Game R&D]. Successful arcade games, as with hit movies, require creativity,
technical skill, timing, and luck to bring off. As in the movie business, all
eyes tend to be on the blockbusters - the "Pac-Mans" and "Raiders of the Lost
Ark" - rather than the games and films that lose money.

As in movie special-effects budgets, an increasing amount of money is being
spent on game R&D by the major companies and by would-be entrants. New arcade
games feature X-Y vector rather than raster screens, and many have voice
synthesizers and elaborate musical and sound effects.

However, some large portion of the R&D effort is wasted and must be written
off. Bally, for example, maintains three teams of 25 (total) engineers,
artists, and programmers working on games. The assembly-language programming
of the microprocessors used in the arcade games can be deadly, and cause
programmer burn-out.

[Game Cartridge List]. In the following table, the left-hand column is the
generic name of the product (e.g., video monitors) or the target system (Apple
II, TRS-80 Model III). The 2nd column is the actual manufacturer; note that
for some systems, e.g., the IBM, there are many non-IBM vendors of compatible
products. Field 3 provides as much identifying and descriptive information
about the product as space permits, including the manufacturer's part number,
if available. The 1st price given is the suggested list price; the 2nd price
is the lowest observed discount price or sometimes the dealer or wholesale
price. These should be used together to establish a high-low range for actual
prices.

SYSTEM	MANUFACTURER	DESCRIPTION/IDENTIFICATION	LIST	DISCOUNT
5200	Atari	**Master Component	299.95	
Astro	Astrocade	**Master Component	249.95	
Astro	Astrocade	Amazin' Maze/Tic-Tac	24.95	
Astro	Astrocade	Astro Battle	24.95	
Astro	Astrocade	Bally Pin	29.95	
Astro	Astrocade	Baseball/Tennis/Hockey/Handball	29.95	
Astro	Astrocade	Bingo Math/Speed Math	24.95	
Astro	Astrocade	Bio Rhythm Calendar	29.95	
Astro	Astrocade	Black Jack/Poker/Acey Ducey	29.95	
Astro	Astrocade	Clowns/Brickyard	29.95	
Astro	Astrocade	Coloring Book (w/LP)		

Astro	Astrocade	Cosmic Raiders	
Astro	Astrocade	Dog Patch	24.95
Astro	Astrocade	Football	29.95
Astro	Astrocade	Galactic Invasion	29.95
Astro	Astrocade	Grand Prix	29.95
Astro	Astrocade	Letter Match/Spell 'n Score	29.95
Astro	Astrocade	Munchie	
Astro	Astrocade	Panzer Attack/Red Baron	24.95
Astro	Astrocade	Pirate's Chase (4/82)	29.95
Astro	Astrocade	Quest for the Orb	
Astro	Astrocade	Seawolf/Missle	24.95
Astro	Astrocade	Space Fortress	29.95
Astro	Astrocade	Space Fortress	
Astro	Astrocade	Star Battle	24.95
Astro	Astrocade	The Wizard	
Astro	Astrocade	Zzzap/Dogem	24.95
Astro+K	Astrocade	**Z-Grass Computer	479.95
Astro+K	Astrocade	Bally Basic Demo	29.95
Astro+K	Astrocade	Bally Basic Old	29.95
Astro+K	Astrocade	Clue/Flying Ace	10.95
Astro+K	Astrocade	Max/Horserace	10.95
Astro+K	Astrocade	Music Maker I (fall 82)	59.95
Atari 400	Arcade Plus	Arcade Pro Football	
Atari 400	Arcade Plus	Ghost Hunter	
Atari 400	Arcade Plus	Night Rally	
Atari 400	Atari	Star Raiders	
Atari 400	K-Byte (CBS)	Krazy Shoot-Out	
Coleco	Coleco	**Master Component	234.99
Coleco	Coleco	*Atari Conversion Module	89.99
Coleco	Coleco	*Controller	32.99
Coleco	Coleco	Carnival	33.99
Coleco	Coleco	Challenger Chess	
Coleco	Coleco	Cosmic Avenger (10/82)	33.99
Coleco	Coleco	Dimensional Puzzels	
Coleco	Coleco	Donkey Kong	33.99
Coleco	Coleco	Head to Head Baseball	
Coleco	Coleco	Head to Head Football	
Coleco	Coleco	Horse Racing	33.99
Coleco	Coleco	Las Vegas (10/82)	33.99
Coleco	Coleco	Mouse Trap	33.99
Coleco	Coleco	Ripcord	
Coleco	Coleco	Sidetrack	
Coleco	Coleco	Skiing	
Coleco	Coleco	Smurf Action	33.99
Coleco	Coleco	Space Fury (10/82)	39.99
Coleco	Coleco	Spectar	
Coleco	Coleco	Tunnels & Trolls	
Coleco	Coleco	Turbo + Shift & Foot Pedal	89.99
Coleco	Coleco	Venture	33.99
Coleco	Coleco	Zaaxon	59.99
Mattel	Coleco	Carnival	35.99
Mattel	Coleco	Donky Kong	35.99
Mattel	Coleco	Mattel Turbo (10/82)	35.99
Mattel	Coleco	Mattel Zaaxon (11/82)	35.99

Mattel	Coleco	Mouse Trap	35.99	
Mattel	Coleco	Night Stalker		
Mattel	Mattel	**Intellivision Console	299.95	249.95
Mattel	Mattel	ABPA Backgammon	20.99	
Mattel	Mattel	Armor Battle	29.99	
Mattel	Mattel	Astrosmash		
Mattel	Mattel	Auto Racing	24.99	
Mattel	Mattel	Boxing		
Mattel	Mattel	Checkers	15.99	
Mattel	Mattel	Elect. Co. Math Fun	15.99	
Mattel	Mattel	Elect. Co. Word Fun	15.99	
Mattel	Mattel	Frog Bog		
Mattel	Mattel	HGL Hockey	24.99	
Mattel	Mattel	Horse Racing	24.99	
Mattel	Mattel	Las Vegas Poker & Black Jack	15.99	
Mattel	Mattel	Las Vegas Roulette	15.99	
Mattel	Mattel	Major League Baseball		
Mattel	Mattel	NASL Soccer	24.99	
Mattel	Mattel	NBA Basketball	29.99	
Mattel	Mattel	NFL Football	29.99	
Mattel	Mattel	Night Stalker		
Mattel	Mattel	PGA Golf	24.99	
Mattel	Mattel	Sea Battle	34.99	
Mattel	Mattel	Snafu	24.99	
Mattel	Mattel	Space Armada	29.99	
Mattel	Mattel	Star Strike		
Mattel	Mattel	Tennis	24.99	
Mattel	Mattel	Triple Action	24.99	
Mattel	Mattel	Tron I		
Mattel	Mattel	Tron II		
Mattel	Mattel	US Ski Team Skiing	29.99	
Mattel	Mattel	USAC Auto Racing		
Mattel+S	Mattel	B-17 Bomber		
Mattel+S	Mattel	Bomb Squad		
Mattel+S	Mattel	Space Spartans		
ODYSSEY2	Odyssey	**Console	139.95	
ODYSSEY2	Odyssey	Alien Invaders	22.95	
ODYSSEY2	Odyssey	Alpine Skiing	22.95	
ODYSSEY2	Odyssey	Armored Encounter/Sub Chase	22.95	
ODYSSEY2	Odyssey	Baseball	22.95	
ODYSSEY2	Odyssey	Blastout	22.95	
ODYSSEY2	Odyssey	Bowling/Basketball	22.95	
ODYSSEY2	Odyssey	Computer Golf	22.95	
ODYSSEY2	Odyssey	Computer Intro	29.95	
ODYSSEY2	Odyssey	Conquest of the World	49.95	
ODYSSEY2	Odyssey	Cosmic Conflict	22.95	
ODYSSEY2	Odyssey	Dynasty	14.95	
ODYSSEY2	Odyssey	Football (American)	22.95	
ODYSSEY2	Odyssey	Freedom Fighter	29.95	
ODYSSEY2	Odyssey	Great Wall Street Fortune Hunt	49.95	
ODYSSEY2	Odyssey	Helicopter Rescue/Out of World	22.95	
ODYSSEY2	Odyssey	Hockey/Soccer	22.95	
ODYSSEY2	Odyssey	I've Got Your Number	14.95	
ODYSSEY2	Odyssey	Invaders from Hyperspace	22.95	

ODYSSEY2	Odyssey	KC Munchkin	22.95
ODYSSEY2	Odyssey	Las Vegas Blackjack	22.95
ODYSSEY2	Odyssey	Matchmaker/Logic/Buzzword	22.95
ODYSSEY2	Odyssey	Math-A-Magic/Echo	22.95
ODYSSEY2	Odyssey	Message Center	22.95
ODYSSEY2	Odyssey	Monkeyshines	29.95
ODYSSEY2	Odyssey	Pachinko	22.95
ODYSSEY2	Odyssey	Pocket Billiards	22.95
ODYSSEY2	Odyssey	Quest for the Rings	49.95
ODYSSEY2	Odyssey	Showdown in 2100 AD	22.95
ODYSSEY2	Odyssey	Slot Machine	22.95
ODYSSEY2	Odyssey	Take the Money and Run	14.95
ODYSSEY2	Odyssey	Thunderball	22.95
ODYSSEY2	Odyssey	UFO	22.95
ODYSSEY2	Odyssey	Volleyball	22.95
ODYSSEY2	Odyssey	War of Nerves	22.95
TI	TI	**Console	299.97
TI	TI	A-Maze--Ing	
TI	TI	Blackjack and Poker	
TI	TI	Blasto	
TI	TI	Car Wars	
TI	TI	Connect Four	
TI	TI	Football	
TI	TI	Hangman	
TI	TI	Hunt the Wumpus	
TI	TI	Hustle	
TI	TI	Indoor Soccer	
TI	TI	Mind Challengers	
TI	TI	Munchman	
TI	TI	Music Maker	
TI	TI	TI Invaders	
TI	TI	TI Logo	
TI	TI	The Attack	
TI	TI	Tombstone City: 21st Century	
TI	TI	Video Chess	
TI	TI	Video Games I	
TI	TI	Yahtzee	
TI	TI	ZeroZap	
VCS	ACTIVISION	Barnstorming	22.95
VCS	ACTIVISION	Bridge	22.95
VCS	ACTIVISION	Checkers	22.95
VCS	ACTIVISION	Chopper Command	
VCS	ACTIVISION	Drag Race	22.95
VCS	ACTIVISION	Fishing Derby	22.95
VCS	ACTIVISION	Freeway	22.95
VCS	ACTIVISION	Galactic Invasion	
VCS	ACTIVISION	Grand Prix	
VCS	ACTIVISION	Kaboom!	
VCS	ACTIVISION	Laser Blast	
VCS	ACTIVISION	Skiing	22.95
VCS	ACTIVISION	Stampede	
VCS	ACTIVISION	Starmaster	
VCS	ACTIVISION	Tennis	22.95
VCS 1082	ACTIVISION	PITFALL	?????

VCS	1082	ACTIVISION	MEGAMANIA	?????	
VCS	682	APOLLO	LOCH JAW (SHARK ATTACK)	31.95	
VCS	682	APOLLO	LOST LUGGAGE	31.95	
VCS	682	APOLLO	RACKETBALL	31.95	
VCS	682	APOLLO	SKEET SHOOT	31.95	
VCS	682	APOLLO	SPACE CHASE	31.95	
VCS	682	APOLLO	SPACE CAVERN	31.95	
VCS	982	APOLLO	KYPHUS	31.95	
VCS	982	APOLLO	GUARDIAN	31.95	
VCS	982	APOLLO	INFILTRATE	31.95	
VCS	982	APOLLO	FINAL APPROACH	31.95	
VCS	982	APOLLO	WABBIT	31.95	
VCS	982	APOLLO	LABYRINTH	31.95	
VCS	982	APOLLO	BAT'S INCREDIBLE	31.95	
VCS	982	APOLLO	SQUOOSH	31.95	
VCS		ATARI	**Console	149.95	119.95
VCS		ATARI	AIR-SEA BATTLE	22.95	
VCS		ATARI	BACKGAMMON	26.95	
VCS		ATARI	BASIC PROGRAMMING	26.95	
VCS		ATARI	BASEBALL	37.95	
VCS		ATARI	BASKETBALL	22.95	
VCS		ATARI	Bowling	22.95	
VCS		ATARI	BRAIN GAMES	22.95	
VCS		ATARI	Breakout	22.95	
VCS		ATARI	Canyon Bomber	22.95	
VCS		ATARI	Circus ATARI	26.95	
VCS		ATARI	Codebreaker	22.95	
VCS		ATARI	Combat	22.95	
VCS		ATARI	Concentration	22.95	
VCS		ATARI	Defender	37.95	
VCS		ATARI	Dodge 'Em	22.95	
VCS		ATARI	Football (American)	12.95	
VCS		ATARI	FROG POND		
VCS		ATARI	Golf	22.95	
VCS		ATARI	Hangman	22.95	
VCS		ATARI	Haunted House	26.95	
VCS		ATARI	Home Run	12.95	
VCS		ATARI	Human Cannonball	12.95	
VCS		ATARI	Indy 500		
VCS		ATARI	Maze Craze	26.95	
VCS		ATARI	Missle Command	31.95	
VCS		ATARI	Night Driver	26.95	
VCS		ATARI	Othello	22.95	
VCS		ATARI	Outlaw	22.95	
VCS		ATARI	Slot Racers	22.95	
VCS		ATARI	Space Invaders	31.95	
VCS		ATARI	Space War		
VCS		ATARI	Street Racer	12.95	
VCS		ATARI	Super Breakout	31.95	
VCS		ATARI	Superman	31.95	
VCS		ATARI	Surround		
VCS		ATARI	Video Checkers	29.95	
VCS		ATARI	Video Chess	26.95	
VCS		ATARI	Video Olympics	22.95	

```
VCS      ATARI       VOLLEYBALL                 37.95
VCS      ATARI       Video Pinball              31.95
VCS      ATARI       Warlords                   31.95
VCS     *ATARI       3-D TIC-TAC-TOE            22.95
VCS     *ATARI       CASINO                     31.95
VCS     *ATARI       PELE'S SOCCER              31.95
VCS     *ATARI       SKY DIVER                  22.95
VCS8 1281 ATARI      ASTEROIDS                A 37.95
VCS   482 ATARI      PAC-MAN                    37.95
VCS8  682 ATARI      ADVENTURE                  31.95
VCS   882 ATARI      BERSERK                  A 31.95
VCS4  882 ATARI      YAR'S REVENGE              31.95
VCS4  982 ATARI      RAIDERS OF THE LOST ARK    37.95
VCS4  982 ATARI      STAR RAIDERS               37.95
VCS? 1182 ATARI      ADVENTURE I                37.95
VCS  1182 ATARI      ADVENTURE II               37.95
VCS  1282 ATARI      FOX BAT                    37.95
VCS4 1282 ATARI      E.T.                     M ?????
VCS4 1182 CABALLERO  CUSTER'S REVENGE         X 49.95
VCS4 1182 CABALLERO  BACHELOR PARTY           X 49.95
VCS4 1182 CABALLERO  BEAT 'EM AND EAT 'EM     X 49.95
VCS4 1282 CBS        WIZARD OF WOR            A ?????
VCS4 1282 CBS        GORF                     A ?????
VCS4 1282 CBS        ?????                    ? ?????
VCS4  782 COLECO     DONKEY KONG                33.95
VCS4  882 COLECO     CARNIVAL                   33.99
VCS4  882 COLECO     VENTURE                    33.99
VCS4  982 COLECO     MOUSE TRAP                 33.99
VCS4  982 COLECO     SMURF ACTION               33.99
VCS4 1082 COLECO     TURBO                      33.99
VCS4 1082 COLECO     ZAAXON                     33.99
VCS   582 COMMAVID   COSMIC SWARM               34.95
VCS   782 COMMAVID   ROOM OF DOOM               34.95
VCS  1082 COMMAVID   MINES OF MINOS             34.95
VCS  1082 COMMAVID   MISSION OMEGA              34.95
VCS4 1282 COMMAVID   UNDERWORLD                 34.95
VCS4 1082 DATA AGE   ENCOUNTER NL5              31.95
VCS4 1082 DATA AGE   SSSNAKE                    31.95
VCS4 1082 DATA AGE   WARP LOCK                  31.95
VCS4 1082 DATA AGE   AIRLOCK                    31.95
VCS4 1082 DATA AGE   SURVIVAL RUN               31.95
VCS4 0183 FOX        9 TO 5                   M 31.95
VCS4 0183 FOX        M*A*S*H                  M 31.95
VCS4 0183 FOX        PORKY'S                  M 31.95
VCS4 0183 FOX        BONNIE AND CLYDE         M 31.95
VCS4 0183 FOX        TOUGH ENOUGH             M 31.95
VCS4 1182 FOX        MEGAFORCE                M 31.95
VCS4 1182 FOX        ALIEN                    M 31.95
VCS4 1282 FOX        FANTASTIC VOYAGE         M 31.95
VCS   682 IMAGIC     DEMON ATTACK               31.95
VCS   682 IMAGIC     STAR VOYAGER               31.95
VCS   682 IMAGIC     TRICK SHOT                 24.95
VCS4  682 IMAGIC     VIDEO ACTION CENTER        29.95
VCS4  782 IMAGIC     ATLANTIS                   31.95
```

VCS	782	IMAGIC	COSMIC ARK	31.95
VCS4	782	IMAGIC	FIREFIGHTER	24.95
VCS4	782	IMAGIC	RIDDLE OF THE SPHINX	31.95
VCS	682	MATTEL	ASTROBLAST	34.95
VCS	682	MATTEL	BIG LEAGUE BASEBALL	34.95
VCS	682	MATTEL	FROGS & FLIES	30.95
VCS	682	MATTEL	PRO FOOTBALL	34.95
VCS	682	MATTEL	SPACE ATTACK	34.95
VCS	682	MATTEL	TANK BATTLE	34.95
VCS	882	MATTEL	TRON DEADLY DISCS	40.95
VCS	982	MATTEL	DARK CAVERN	40.95
VCS	982	MATTEL	INTERNATIONAL SOCCER	34.95
VCS	1082	MATTEL	LOCK 'N CHASE	40.95
VCS	183	PARKER	JAMES BOND: 007	39.95
VCS	183	PARKER	SKY SKIPPER	39.95
VCS	183	PARKER	JAWS	39.95
VCS	882	PARKER	STAR WARS: EMPIRE STRIKES BACK	39.95
VCS	982	PARKER	FROGGER	39.95
VCS	982	PARKER	TUTANKHAM	39.95
VCS	1082	PARKER	AMIDAR	39.95
VCS	1082	PARKER	SUPER COBRA	39.95
VCS	1082	PARKER	REACTOR	39.95
VCS	1082	PARKER	SPIDERMAN	39.95
VCS	682	SEARS	STEEPLECHASE	
VCS	682	SEARS	STELLER TRACK	
VCS	782	SPECTRAVISION	GANGSTER ALLEY	29.95
VCS	782	SPECTRAVISION	PLANET PATROL	29.95
VCS	882	SPECTRAVISION	CROSS FIRE	29.95
VCS	882	SPECTRAVISION	CHINA SYNDROME	U 29.95
VCS	882	SPECTRAVISION	TAPE WORM	29.95
VCS4	982	STARPATH	PHASER PATROL	69.95
VCS4	0183	STARPATH	DRAGON STOMPER	14.95
VCS4	0183	STARPATH	ESCAPE FROM THE MIND MASTER	14.95
VIC-20		Commodore	**Computer/console	229.00
VIC-20		Commodore	Gorf	
VIC-20		Commodore	Jupiter Lander	24.95
VIC-20		Commodore	Midnight Driver	24.95
VIC-20		Commodore	Omega Race	
VIC-20		Commodore	Super Alien	24.95

Voice Recognition

Voice recognition is a relatively new computer technology with great potential
for making computers easier for everyone to use. At the current state of the
art, computers can understand human speech only under the following limited
conditions:

- Speaker Dependence and Training. Most systems must go through
    a training cycle before they can accurately recognize words.
    On most systems, the same person whose voice is to be
    recognized must do the training.

- Limited Vocabulary. Most commercial voice recognition devices can recognize between 32 and 128 different words. Larger vocabularies require additional computer memory and greater processing time, and they carry an increased probability of error.

- Discrete Speech. Although some advanced equipment can recognize words in continuously flowing human speech, most equipment requires a break in the voice pattern to signal the end of words or phrases. Typically, a phrase must be between 100 milliseconds and 1.5 seconds in duration, but no longer.

In commercial environments, voice recognition systems are used for such things as sorting items on conveyor belts or specialized types of data entry. United Airlines, the largest airline in the US, uses voice recognition equipment for sorting baggage. In the United Airlines application, each device is trained to understand the codes for cities used as flight destinations, e.g., "JFK" for John F Kennedy airport in New York, or "SFO" for San Francisco airport in California. A video display allows the operator to check that the voice command has been correctly understood by the computer, and headset microphones keep the operator's hands free for handling moving bags.

Voice recognition devices are either parametric or nonparametric. Parametric devices examine incoming electrical signals for phonetic information and parameters common to human speech. Nonparametric devices simply try to match incoming sound patterns, which could well be musical tones, without any concern for the so-called parameters of speech.

Human speech has a number of characteristic sound patterns called "formants". Each of 10 or so formants can be characterized by unique combinations of frequency and amplitude. Voiced speech, for example, generates a high frequency sound but low amplitude. Unvoiced speech, like "f" and "s", generates low frequency but greater amplitude.

Time problems present other difficulties for speech recognition equipment. Some words, like "eight", have microperiods of silence, perhaps 80-90 ms. A minimum time period is needed to prevent clicks and pops from being interpreted as words. Most words have a duration of 300-1000 ms. Most equipment that takes discrete speech samples will normalize the sample - that is, transform it into equal periods. This ensures that a word said slowly will be equivalent to a word spoken rapidly.

In the training mode, a speech recognition device will store an internal bit pattern resulting from its analysis of the sound. A device might, for example, use a bandpass filter to divide input into two sets of frequencies, say 100-900 Hz and 900-5000 Hz, and record exact frequency and amplitude information about both bands over, say, 16 sample periods of time. This information forms a basic table or template against which subsequent words are matched.

In recognition mode, new words are matched against the table of stored templates, and the best match taken. If no template is within a certain tolerance, no match results. Matching algorithms can be quite complex and also depend highly on the exact nature of the stored speech information. Note that two types of error are possible: a false negative (no match when there should be) and a false positive (wrong word match). Words that are close in sound - or in extracted speech parameters, and which may not sound alike at all - may need to be retrained until the batting average of the device improves.

[Continuous Speech]. Continuous speech presents many more problems than discrete speech. NEC, the Japanese company, makes a discrete speech recognition device for $67,000 that uses multiple, parallel microprocessors to make complex comparisons of speech patterns. In particular, the NEC device can compensate for nonuniform contractions or prolongations of speech.

W

Word Processing

In early 1982, the author of The Computer Cookbook was commissioned to compare the "big 3" personal computers for a New York company interested in getting word processors for its research department. Telecommunications and the ability to incorporate communicated documents into research, was vital, as was the ability to eventually expand the system to a local area network.

This survey did not consider the Osborne, a cost-effective word processor with no network and not much communications capability at the time; nor did the survey consider Wang, Datapoint, or other larger systems, although these have some serious advantages in terms of user-friendly software. One conclusion, based on this company's previous experience with personal computers, was that there are two related problems in adding personal computers in many offices: staff acceptance and its corollary, underutilization.

Many companies have bought a single personal computer, such as an Apple II, because it seemed time that they did so; but although there are undoubtedly some educational benefits in having a machine like the Apple around, as a piece of capital equipment, personal computers are often underused.

The specific list of needs for this company was:

  (1) word processing (typewriter replacement) for the research
      staff - that is, the ability to type notes and letters and
      to draft reports on their own machines. Final-camera ready
      work should be left to the production department, which uses a
      Wang. Research department members should be able to transmit
      draft reports to the Wang to eliminate wasteful retyping and
      speed turnaround.

  (2) terminals, to access the major on-line services like NewsNet,
      CompuServe, the Source, Dow-Jones, and possibly Prestel.

  (3) electronic publishing, a vague thought of expanding to offer
      clients an on-line videotex service, in which clients would

call the computer and receive the latest gossip, newsletters, etc.

Finally, there was a need for an additional, stand-alone Wang for the marketing department to handle mailing lists and correspondence. The company was happy with its other Wang equipment, and this choice was generally uncontested.

[Word Processing]. The emphasis on word processing made the selection somewhat simpler. All machines needed to be desktop units - floppy disk, keyboard, and screen in one package. All needed upper and lower case displays, full ASCII keyboards, if possible word processing function keys, and conventional word processing software. The specific systems and types of systems considered were:

(1) Apple /// with one 5" drive, "Applewriter ///" or the Pascal editor, and the SCRIPT /// formatting package;

(2) the IBM Personal Computer with 2 mini-floppy drives and Easywriter;

(3) the TRS-80 Model II with 8" floppy drive and SCRIPTSIT;

(4) CP/M-based machines, like the Xerox 820, running WORDSTAR;

(5) low-end, stand-alone word processors like the Wangwriter.

The jury found for the TRS-80 Model II. The reasoning behind the choice of the TRS-80 went as follows:

(1) Ease of Use. SCRIPTSIT, which was written for secretaries and small businessmen, is the easiest word processor to learn and actively use. It is better than Easywriter; IBM's word processor was surprisingly weak considering the company (it was not written by IBM, of course, but rather by IUS, and its the same "Easywriter Pro" available on the Apple). SCRIPTSIT's "fancy" features and options are better than the others: spelling corrector, mail list merge, etc. Finally, Radio Shack sells an audio (cassette tape) training course to take people through SCRIPTSIT.

(2) Keyboards. All had some minor problems. The Apple /// has a programmer's keyboard, not a typist's. IBM's, as might be expected, has the most solid "feel" but a badly misplaced shift key. The TRS-80 keyboard is a little noisy and has a cheap feeling.

(3) Communications interfacing. Although all the computers can have RS-232 ports added and modems attached thereto, only the Model II had an existing "communicating word processor" hardware and software package available. Both the Apple /// and the IBM would have required interfacing headaches.

(4) Expandability. The TRS-80 Model II can be the basis of a

turnkey videotex service should this be desired. The additional hardware and software required is about $10,000. Tandy also has available a local network software (ARCNET, based on Datapoint's local network system), a hard disk and, if necessary, a 16-bit processor upgrade. Although Apple and IBM have some of the above, only Tandy has all of the above.

The TRS-80 configuration should include a "loaded" central station with printer, double disks, system desk, etc., and as many 1-disk personal workstations as the budget can afford. At least $1,000 should be reserved for software goodies for the central station, such as VisiCalc. A purchase of this sort should not be considered without buying one legal, licensed copy of SCRIPTSIT per machine.

[Tandy Systems]. Word processing was difficult, if not impossible, on Tandy's original TRS-80 Model I system, because that computer, like the Apple II, was designed to use only upper case. The 1979 edition of The Computer Cookbook, in fact, carried a recipe for adding lower case to the machine. Later that year, Tandy announced a Lower Case Kit for the Model I (26-1104, $59), and its service centers began to support the modification officially.

Radio Shack's word processor is called SCRIPTSIT (a trademark). Actually, there are at least four versions of SCRIPTSIT: the Model I version (26-1563, $100); SCRIPTSIT 2.0 (26-4531, $400), designed for Radio Shack's bigger business computer, the Model II; the standard Model III version (26-1563, $100); and the so-called Super SCRIPTSIT (26-1590, $200), an enhanced version for the Model III that has many features of the version sold for the Model II.

These versions have a number of features in common. First, all will work on one-disk systems. The master SCRIPTSIT disk is designed to be cloned into many SCRIPTSIT disks, each with the SCRIPTSIT program, and some documents on it. On the full-sized floppies of the Model II, the SCRIPTSIT program takes up only 4% of the disk, leaving the rest for writing. The SCRIPTSIT program takes up a higher percent of the smaller mini-floppies on the Model III.

The interesting features of SCRIPTSIT 2.0 and Super SCRIPTSIT are tab alignment features and use of graphic characters as markers on the screen, this latter a feature of Wang-type specialized word processors but rarely seen on microcomputer-based machines. Of the 24 lines of the TRS-80 Model II's screen, the bottom two are reserved for status information, the bottom line giving the document name, page number, and so on, and the line above it giving the margin settings something like this:

The braces ({ and }) indicate the outer margins; the small o shows the indent for normal paragraphs. The plus sign + shows where, as on a typewriter, a regular tab has been placed; and the @ sign is a special kind of tab, called a decimal align tab, that allows columns of figures to be lined up automatically.

SCRIPTSIT also uses braces for some other nice features. {D} inserts the date, spelled out, in a letter or note. {P} inserts the current page number (when a document is modified, repaging is automatic), and {T} even inserts the current time. When used with the Profile II program, SCRIPTSIT will merge names, addresses, and even billing information into form letters. In this case, the information to be inserted would be identified by a field name, such as {FNAME}{LNAME}. The letter might start Dear {FNAME}, - if, of course, you are on a FNAME basis.

For such merge operations, a two-drive system is required. There are no other special hardware requirements for Model II word processing: Tandy's daisy printer is made by C. Itoh, prints at 43 characters per second, and is only $100 more than its dot matrix printer. This printer might be attractive to non-TRS-80 owners, too, except for the fact that it has a Radio Shack-type parallel interface - not the usual RS-232 interface found on Diablo, Qume, and NEC printers - and would require some knowledgeable hardware hacking to connect. (Consider using a parallel to serial buffer box, giving RS-232 data in, parallel data out).

[Spelling Correctors]. Spelling correction programs began to appear on the microcomputer market around 1981. The theory behind spelling correctors is simple: sentences are taken apart into words and the words looked up in a dictionary. If a word appears wrong, the computer flags it and asks for verification.

Spelling correctors, then, are usually interactive, not automatic, which makes it imperative that they be easy to use. Some of the programs on the market need to be told every little step to do and almost create more work than they save.

Spelling correctors can work either with dictionaries of literal word lists or use suffixes and prefixes. In the first type of dictionary, "friend" and "friendly" would each have entries, but in the second, only "friend" would be listed. Whichever technique is used, the corrector will flag words not on its list. The following output from a mainframe (Dailcom) spelling corrector gives the general idea:

```
              Prefix-Suffix Matches:
              BOXING BOX
              DRAGONS DRAGON
              DUNGEONS DUNGEON
              SHORTENS SHORTEN
              TUNNELS TUNNEL

              Near Misses:
              ADAPTER ADAPTED
              BALLY BALMY       Bally
              IRATA IRATE
              MATTEL MATTER
              MISSLE MISSILE       Missile
              PUZZLES PUZZLED
              REPARIS REPAIRS       repairs
              SIMULTANELUSLY simultaneously
              SPECTAR SPECTER
              STRATEGO STRATEGY
              TAPPED TAPED
```

```
          Unknown Words:
          ACTIVISION
          ACTIVISION'S
          APOLLO
          ARACADE      arcade
          ARACDE       arcade
          ARCADE
          ARMADA
          ASTEROIDS
          ASTRO
          ASTROMASH
          ATARI
          ATARI'S
          AZ
          BARNSTORMING
          BERZERK
          CAMMAND      Command
      ...etc...
```

[How the Computer Cookbook Was Produced]. Since 1980, the full text of The Computer Cookbook has been maintained on a Apple II system with a Corvus hard disk. The Pascal text editor is used exclusively to create and edit the text, which takes up approximately 1.2 Mbytes of the 10-Mbyte disk. Floppies are used as back up.

A "typesetting" program justifies the text for output by inserting space, in units of 1/120-inch, between words. (Individual letters within words are monospaced, as on a typewriter, at 10 characters per inch). The typesetting program was written in Pascal by the author. The text is printed on a Diablo 1610 with plastic print wheel. The font is OCR-B.

From the same base of Pascal text files, an "electronic" edition of this book is transmitted to NewsNet, the business information service. Users of NewsNet can search the text of the book for keywords, and receive updates to the book as they are written by the author. A Novation Apple-CAT modem is uesd for telephone communications. The computer, like a teenager, has its own phone. The telephone modem is also used to transmit the text of the book via Tymnet to a translator in Japan.

The following list of 500 companies in the microcomputer industry has been selected by the author on the basis of general importance, or by virtue of having a unique or unusual product (e.g., "The Word" Bible concordance). All judgements are that of the author. Companies which would like to be considered for listing in the next edition of The Computer Cookbook should send product information and press releases to William Bates at GPO Box 2139, New York, NY 10116. No calls, please.

2500 AD Software, Inc.
Suite 100, 2950 S. Jamacia Ct.
Aurora, CO 80014
303 752 4382

80 Microcomputing
Pine St.
Peterborough, NH 03458
80 Microcomputing is Wayne Green's TRS-80 publication. Green, one of the founders of Byte, also publishes Microcomputing (formerly Kilobaud).

80 NW Publishing
3110 North 31st Street
Tacoma, WA 98407

ACCU-SORT Systems, Inc.
511 School House Rd.
Telford, Pa 18969
215 723 0981

ADDS (Applied Digital Data Systems)
100 Marcus Blvd.
Hauppauge, NY 11787
516 231 5400
510 227 9886

ALF Products, Inc.
1448 Estes
Denver, CO 80215
303 234 0871
ALF is best-known for their music synthesizer boards for the Apple II computer.

AMDEK Corporation
2420 East Oakton St., Suite E
Arlington Heights, Il 60005
AMDEK, originally a company specializing in low-cost video monitors popular on the Apple II,

has branched out into other peripherals, including printers and floppy disk drives. (10/82)

ANPA Research Institute
1350 Sullivan Trail
PO Box 596
Easton, PA 18052
215 253 1655
The Research Institute of the American Newspaper Publisher Association publishes a number of clearly written guides to word processing and telecommunications topics. (11/82)

Ace Computer Products
1640 NW 3rd St.
Deerfield Beach, FL 33441
305 427 1257

Addison-Wesley Publishing Co.
Software Sales
Reading, MA 01867
617-944-3700
Addison-Wesley software, a part of the large El-Hi and technical book publisher, offers Micro-DSS/FINANCE and Micro-DSS/ANALYSIS, "decision support systems" that transcend spreadsheets like VisiCalc in both power and price. (11/82)

Adtrak, Inc.
1901 Old Middlefield Way
Mountain View, CA 94043
415 965 7473
Adtrak is an interesting service that tracks advertising in 20 or so microcomputer publications. (10/82)

Advanced Computer Products, Inc.

1310B E. Edinger
Santa Ana, CA 92705
714-558-8822
A company with close ties to Vista,
ACP offers low-ball prices on disk
drives (Siemens FDD100-8, $249) and
other products. (11/82)

Advanced Micro Devices
901 Thompson Pl.
Sunnyvale, CA 94086
408-732-2400
AMD is a semiconductor company that
emphasizes specialty chips, like its
9115 Arithmetic Processor. (11/82)

Advanced Micro Techniques
1291 E. Hillsdale Bldv., Suite 209
Foster City, CA 94404
415-349-9336
AMT sells Western Union Telex
software for CP/M based systems with
modems. (11/82)

Advanced Micro Techniques
1291 E. Hillsdale Blvd., Suite 209
Foster City, CA 94404
415 349 9336

Advanced Operating Systems
450 St. John Road
Michigan City, IN 46360
800 348 8558
219 879 4693

Advanced Operating Systems
Division of Howard W. Sams, Inc.
4300 West 62nd St.
POB 7092
Indianapolis, IN 46206
AOS sells a line of software for the
Apple II. (11/82)

Adventure International
Box 3435
Longwood, FL 32750
305-830-8194
Scott Adams's company is well-known
for its S.A.G.A. series of
adventures. (11/82)

Adwar Video
100 Fifth Avenue
New York, NY 10011

212-691-0976
Adwar is a video company that makes
the ProMark board that improves
color output of the Apple II, and an
frame buffer system that lets the
Apple generate broadcast-quality
NTSC video. (11/82)

Alien Group
27 W. 23rd St.
New York, Ny 10010
212-741-1770
Alien Group makes a speech
synthesizer, the "Voice Box", for
the Atari computer. (11/82)

Allenbach Industries, Inc.
2101 Las Palmas, Suite A
Carlsbad, CA 92008
800-854-1515 (outside CA)
714-438-2258
Allenback sells blank floppy disks,
and offers quantity disk duplication
services. (11/82)

Alpha Logic Business Systems, Inc.
4119 North Union Rd.
Woodstock, IL 60098
815-568-5166
Alpha Logic makes a VisiCalc patch
called "VC-Expand" that works with
the Saturn 128K RAM board for the
Apple II and gives VisiCalc 176K
free on that system. (11/82)

Alpha Micro Products
17881 Sky Park North
Irvine, CA 92714
714-957-1404
Alpha Micro makes an S-100 bus micro
with the power of a small mini.
(11/82)

AlphaByte Computer Products
31245 La Baya Drive
Westlake Village, CA 91362
213-706-0333 (voice)
213-883-8976 (modem orders)
Alpha Byte sells memory boards that
include an RS-232 interface for the
IBM PC. (11/82)

Altos Computer Systems
2360 Bering Drive

San Jose, CA 95131
408 946 6700
TELEX 171 562

Amaray Corporation
2251 Grant Rd.
Los Altos, CA 94022
415-966-2840
Amaray sells an interlocking file
systems for floppy disks. The
system can be built up in
increments. (11/82)

American Business Systems, Inc.
3 Littleton Rd.
Westford, MA 01886
617 692 2600

American Telephone & Telegraph
1776 On The Green
Morristown, NJ 07960
201-540-6821
ATT is the major phone company in
the U.S.A. (11/82)

American Word Processing Company
18730 Oxnard St.
Tarzana, CA 91356
213 705 2245
800 423 5220 (toll free)
TWX 910 493 2295
CABLE: AMWORD
American Word Processing sells word
processing supplies by mail. Write
for catalog. (11/82)

Ammicro
122 East 42nd St., Suite 1700
New York, NY 10168
212-254-3030
Ammicro sells the "Microwriter",
which is an Olivetti Paraxis daisy
wheel typewriter with parallel
interface. $750. (11/82)

Analog Devices
Route 1 Industrial Park
PO Box 280
Norwood, MA 02062
617 329 4700

Analog Technology Corporation
15859 E. Edna Place
Irwindale, CA 91706

213 960 4004

Anderson Jacobson, Inc.
521 Charcot Ave.
San Jose, CA 95131
408 263 8520

Anderson Publishing Co.
Simi Valley Business Park
PO Box 3534
Simi Valley, CA 93063
805 581 1184

Angel Systems, Inc.
dist. by American Business
Products, Inc.
155 N. Dean St.
Englewood, NJ 07631
201-569-0853
Angel Systems is the author of
PARSEC, Parish Secretary, a software
system for churches. PARSEC runs
under CP/M. Ask for Angel's
booklet, "Pastor's Guide to Choosing
a Microcomputer". Divine! (11/82)

Animation Graphics, Inc.
11317 Sunset Hills Rd.
Reston, VA 22090
703-471-0740
Animation Graphics makes the
"Illustrator's Library" package for
the Apple II. (11/82)

Apparat, Inc.
6000 E. Evans, Bldg. 2
Denver, CO 80222
303 758 7275

Apple Computer Co., Inc.
10260 Bandley Drive
Cupertino, CA 95016
406 996 1010

Applied Software Technology
14125 Capri Drive
Los Gatos, CA 95030
408 370 2662

Aries Computer Products
PO Box 7932
Eugene, OR 97401
503 687 0625

Arkansas Systems, Inc.
8901 Kanis Rd., Suite 206
Little Rock, Arkansas 72205
501 227 8471

Arrow Micro Software
11 Kingsford
Kanata, Ontario
K2K 1T2 Canada
613 592 4609

Artsci
5547 Satsuma Ave.
North Hollywood, CA 91601
213-985-2922
Artsci sells "Magic Window II", a
word processor for the Apple II, and
"Magicalc", an 80-column spreadsheet
program. (11/82)

Ashley, Allen
395 Sierra Madre Villa
Pasadena, CA 91107
213 793 5748

Ashton-Tate
9929 Jefferson Ave.
Los Angeles, CA 90230
213-204-5570
Ashton-Tate is the publisher of
dBASE II, a very popular data base
manager for the Apple II and other
computers. (11/82)

Aspen Software
PO Box 339 W
Tijeras, NM 87059
505 281 1634
Aspen Software publishes RATFOR, a
structured FORTRAN, and has rights
to the Random House Dictionary.
(11/82)

Atari
1265 Borregas Ave.
Sunnyvale, CA 94086
800-538-8547 (outside CA)
800 672 1404 (inside CA)
Atari, a division of Warner
Communications, makes arcade video
games, home video games, and home
computers. (11/82)

Auricle, Inc.

20823 Stevens Creek Blvd.
Cupertino, CA 95014
408-257-9830
Auricle makes a voice recognition
device. (11/82)

Avalon-Hill Game Co.
4517 Hartford Rd.
Baltimore, MD 21214
301-254-5300
Avalon-Hill specializes in war game
simulations, and publishes a number
for microcomputers. (11/82)

Axiom Corp.
5932 San Fernando Rd.
Glendale, CA 91202
213 245 9244
TWX 910 497 2283

Axlon
170 N. Wolfe Rd.
Sunnyvale, CA 94086
408-730-0216
Axlon makes add-on products for the
Atari, including a RAM expansion.
(11/82)

Azurdata, Inc.
Richland Skypark
PO Box 926
Richland, WA 99352
509-946-1683
TELEX 32 6340
Azurdata makes a portable RS-232
data collection terminal. (11/82)

BMC Computer Corporation
860 East Walnut St.
Carson, CA 90746
213 323 2600

BPI Systems
3423 Guadalupe
Austin, TX 78705
512 454 2801

BSR (USA) Ltd.
X 10 Products
Route 303
Blauvelt, NY 10913
914 358 6060

BUSS

325 Pennsylvania Ave., S.E.
Washington, DC 20003
202 544 0484

Beagle Brothers
4315 Sierra Vista
San Diego, CA 92103
800-854-2003 x827 (outside CA)
800-522-1500 x827 (inside CA)

Beehive International
4910 Amelia Earhart Drive
Box 25668
Salt Lake City, UT 84125
801 355 6000
TWX 910 925 5271

Benson Varian
385 Ravendale Drive
Mountain View, CA 94043
415 965 9900
TELEX 345 579 BENVAR MNTV

Bible Research Systems
8804 Wildridge Dr.
Austin, TX 78759
512-346-2181
Bible Research sells "THE WORD
Processor", which is a King James
Bible on a disk, including search
software, for $160. (11/82)

Bolt Beranek and Newman, Inc.
33 Moulton St.
Cambridge, MA 02238
617 491 1850

Book Company
11223 South Hindry Ave.
Los Angeles, CA 90045
800-421-3931 (outside CA)
213-417-3003
The Book Company has a line of Apple
II and Atari books. (11/82)

British Microcomputer Trade Assoc.
Computer Workshop Leeds
251 Otley Road, Leeds LS16 5LQ
England

Broderbund Software
1938 Fourth St.
San Rafael, CA 94901
415-456-6424

Broderbund sells a number of popular
Apple II games, including
"Choplifter" and "The Arcade
Machine", a game-construction game.
(11/82)

BudgeCo
428 Pala Ave.
Piedmont, CA 94611
415 658 8141
BudgeCo., Bill Budge's company,
sells the "Raster Blaster" pinball
game for the Apple II, and a pinball
game construction kit. (11/82)

Burroughs Corp.
Burroughs Place
Detroit, MI 48232
313 972 7000

Byte Publications, Inc.
70 Main St.
Peterborough, NH 03458
603 924 9281

C. Itoh Electronics, Inc.
5301 Beethoven St.
Los Angeles, CA 90066
213 390 7778

CUssP
PO Box 784
Palo Alto, CA 94302

Calcomp
3320 E. Lapalma Ave.
Anaheim, CA 92806
714 632 5245

California Computer Systems
250 Caribbean Drive
Sunnyvale, CA 94086
408 734 5811

California Digital Engineering
Box 526
Hollywood, CA 90028
213 661 2031

California Pacific
1615 5th St.
Davis, CA 95616

Canon USA, Inc.

One Canon Plaza
Lake Success, NY 11042
516 488 6700

Cap'n Software
PO Box 575
San Francisco, CA 94101
415 540 0202

Casheab
5737 Avenida Sanchez
San Diego, CA 92124
714 277 2547

Centronics Data Computer Corp.
Hudson, NH 03051
Route 111
603 883 0111
TWX 710 228 6505

Checks To Go
8384 Hercules St.
Box 425
La Mesa, CA 92041
714 460 4975

Cherry Electrical Products Corporation
30600 Sunset Ave.
Waukegan, IL 60085
312 689 7600

Co-op Software
PO Box 432
West Chicago, IL 60185
312 231 0912

Commercial Mailing Accessories, Inc.
1335 Deimar
St. Louis, MO 63108,
314 231 6006

Commodity System Reports
335 Bryant St., Suite 500
Palo Alto, CA 94301
415 326 1461

Commodore Business Machines, Inc.
950 Rittenhouse Rd.
Norristown, PA 19403
215 666 7950

CommuniTree Group
470 Castro, Suite 207 3002
San Francisco, CA 94114

415 474 0933

Communications Research Corporation
1720 130th Avenue, N.E.
Bellevue, WA 98005
206 881 9550

Compu/Time Computer Watch
PO Box 5343
Huntington Beach, CA 92646
714 536 5000

CompuServe
5000 Arlington Centre Blvd.
Columbus, OH 43220
614 457 8600

Compucolor Corp.
5965 Peachtree Corners East
Norcross, GA 30071
404 449 5961

Compugraphic
80 Industrial Way
Wilmington, MA 01887
617 944 6555

Compukids
PO Box 874
Sedalla, MO 65301

Compumotor Corporation
1310 Ross St.
Petaluma, CA 94952
707 778 1244

Compusoft Publishing
A Division of CompuSoft, Inc.
8643 Navajo Rd.
San Diego, CA 92119

Computalker Consultants
PO Box 1951
Santa Monica, CA 90406
213 828 6546

Compute!
PO Box 5119
Greensboro, NC 27403

Computer Assisted Bible Study
19 Huntington Lane
Willingboro, NJ 08046
609 877 8847

Computer Furniture and Accessories
1441 West 132nd St.
Gardena, CA 90249
213 327 7710

Computer Interface Technology
Unit C, 201 W. Dyer Rd.
Santa Ana, CA 92707
714 979 9920

Computer Numerical Control Corp.
460 New Boston Park
Woburn, MA 01801
617 933 0091

Computer Shopper
PO Box F
Titusville, FL 32780
303 269 3211

Computer Stations, Inc.
11610 Page Service Drive
St. Louis, MO 63141
314-432-7020 (tech assist)
800-325-4019 (orders)
Computer Station sells a variety of
interesting add-ons and software for
the Apple II. (11/82)

Grover & Assoc.
Creekside Center, Suite D116
7 Mount Lassen Drive
San Rafael, CA 94603

Hawkeye Grafix
23914 Mobile St.
Canoga Park, CA 91307
213 348 7909
213 881 4382

Hayden Book Co., Inc.
50 Essex St.
Rochelle Park, NJ 07662
201 843 0550
TWX 710 990 5071 (HAYDENPUB ROPK)

Hazeltine Corp.
Computer Terminal Equipment
Greenlawn, NY 11740
516 549 8800

Heath Company
Benton Harbor, MI 49022

616 982 3411 (phone orders)
616 982 3285 (computer sales)

Hendrix, Inc.
670 North Commercial St.
Manchester, NH 03101
603 669 9050

Hewlett Packard Co.
Inquiries Manager
1507 Page Mill Rd.
Palo Alto, CA 94304
415 857 1501

High Technology Software Products, Inc.
PO Box S 14665
8001 N. Classen Blvd.
Oklahoma City, OK 73113
405 840 9900

Hitachi America, Ltd.
Electronic Devices Sales
707 W. Algonquin Rd.
Arlington Heights, IL 60005
312 593 7660

Hitachi Sales Corporation of America
401 West Artesia Blvd.
Compton, CA 90220
213 537 8383

Honeywell, Inc.
Honeywell Plaza
Mineapolis, MN 55408

Houston Instruments
Div. Bausch & Lomb
One Houston Square
Austin, TX 78753
512 837 2820
TWX 910 874 2022

IDSI
Box 1658
Las Cruces, NM 88004

INDUSTRIAL DATA TERMINALS CORP.
173 HEATHERDOWN DRIVE
WESTERVILLE, OH 43081
614 882 3282

IXO, Inc.
6041 Bristol Parkway
Culver City, CA 90230

213 410 0455

Identiprint
2550 Boulevard of the Generals
Jeffersonville, PA 19403
215 539 4400

InfoSoft Systems, Inc.
25 Sylvan Rd. S.
Westport, CT 06880
203 226 8937

Infocom
55 Wheeler St.
Cambridge, MA 02138

Information Dialogues, Inc.
Suite 205
7850 Metro Parkway
Minneapolis, MN 55420
612 853 9200

Information Unlimited
146 N. Broad St.
Griffith, IN 46319
219 924 3522

Information Unlimited Software, Inc.
2401 Marinship Way
Sausalito, CA 94965
415-331-6700
IUS is the publisher of
"EasyWriter", "EasySpeller", "Easy
Filer", and "EasyPlanner", as well
as a series of financial management
software. (11/82)

Insoft
10175 SW Barbur Blvd., Suite 202 B
Portland, OR 97219
503 244 4181

Institute for Computers in Jewish Life
Hewbrew Theological College
7135 North Carpenter Rd.
Skokie, IL 60077

Instrumentation Laboratory
One Burtt Rd.
Andover, MA 01810
617 470 1790

Integral Data Systems
14 Tech Circle

Natick, MA 01760
617 237 7610

Integrand
8620 Roosevelt Ave.
Visalia, CA 93291
209-733-9288
Integrand makes S-100 frames and
furniture. Frames include power
supply, card cage and guides, fan
and reset switches. (10/82)

Intel
Literature Dept.
3065 Bowers Ave.
Santa Clara, CA 95051
408 987 8080

Interactive Computer Systems, Inc.
6403 DiMarco Rd.
Tampa, FL 33614

Interface Age Magazine
PO Box 1234
Cerritos, CA 90701
213 926 9544

Intermec
PO Box N
Lynnwood, WA 98036
206 743 7036

International Business Machines (IBM)
Personal Computer Division
PO Box 1328
Boca Raton, FL 33432

International Business Machines (IBM)
Corporate Headquarters
Old Orchard Rd.
Armonk, NY 10504

International Memories, Inc. (IMI)
10381 Bandley Dr.
Cupertion, CA 95014
408 446 9779

International Micro Systems
6445 Metcalf
Shawnee Mission, KS 66202
913 677 1137

International Minicomputer Accessories
2465 Augustine Dr.

Santa Clara, CA 95051
408 727 1970

JRT Systems
1891 23rd Ave.
San Francisco, CA 94122
415-566-5100
JRT sells a $29.95 version of Pascal
that runs under CP/M. (11/82)

Interstate Electronics Corp.
P.O. Box 3117
1001 E. Ball Rd.
Anaheim, CA 92803
714 635 7210

D/Punch Co.
POB 201
Newton Hlds., MA 02161
D/Punch kits are templates for
making "flippy" (reverse side)
disks. D/Punch also sells hub
reinforcers and other items. (11/82)

Durant Software
2532 Durant Ave., Suite 250
Berkeley, CA 94704
415-540-0912
Durant makes a CP/M file management
aide called "SimpliFile". (11/82)

Dynatech
7847 N. Caldwell Ave.
Niles, IL 60648
800-621-4109 (outside IL)
312-470-0700
Dynatech makes a program for the
Apple II that allows Applesoft BASIC
to write VisiCalc files. (11/82)

Executive Peripheral Systems, Inc.
800 San Antonio Rd.
Palo Alto, CA 94303
415-856-2822
EPS makes a fancy $400 keyboard with
function keys and numeric pad for
the Apple II. (11/82)

XCOMP
7566 Trade St.
San Diego, CA 92121
619-271-8730
TLX 182786
XCOMP makes one of the lowest-price

5 1/4" Winchester drives. (11/82)

Fox & Geller, Inc.
POB 1053
Teaneck, NJ 07666
201-837-0142
Fox & Geller several products,
including dGRAPH, to aid in use of
Ashton-Tate's dBASE II. (11/82)

Guage Group
POB 34082
Phoenix, AZ 85067
602-279-1533
The Guage Group makes a software
print spooler for the IBM PC, which
it calls "SoftCable". $60 (11/82)

Graphic Software, Inc.
POB 367 Kenmore Station
Boston, MA 02215
617-491-2434
Graphic Software makes "Chartman", a
business graphics package for the
IBM PC. (11/82)

ISO World
Box 880
375 Cochituate Rd.
Framingham, MA 01701
800-343-6474
Formerly Computer Business News, ISO
World is a micro-to-minicomputer
magazine published by International
Data Corp., publisher of Computer
World and InfoWorld. (11/82)

InfoWorld
530 Lytton Ave.
Palo Alto, CA 94301
415-328-4602
InfoWorld is a weekly newspaper for
the microcomputer industry. (11/82)

Link Systems
1640 19th St.
Santa Monica, CA 90404
213-453-1851
Link Systems specializes in Pascal
software for the Apple II, ///, and
IBM PC. (11/82)

Osborne Computer Corporation
800-772-3545 x905 (inside CA)

800-227-1617 x905 (outside CA)

Hayes Microcomputer Products, Inc.
5835 Peachtree Corners East
Norcross, GA 30092
404-449-8791
Hayes, formerly D.C. Hayes
Associates, is best-known as a maker
of modems, including a popular one
for the Apple II, and a 1,200 baud
"Smartmodem". (11/82)

Intertec Data Systems
2300 Broad River Rd.
Columbia, SC 29210
803 798 9100

Intex Micro Systems Corp.
755 West Big Beaver Rd., Suite 1717
Troy, Michigan 48084
313 362 4280

Ithaca Intersystems
1650 Hanshaw Rd.
PO Box 91
Ithaca, NY 14850
607 257 0190
TWX 510 255 4346

J B Engineering
1405 Marshall, Suite 705
Redwood City, CA 94063
415 367 1137

Jade Computer Products, Inc.
4901 W. Rosecrans
Hawthorne, CA 90250
213 679 3313

Japan Microcomputer Club
Rm 313, 3 5 8 Shibakoen
Minato Ku, Tokyo 105
Japan {Keigo Aono}

KPG Incorporated
Suite 204, Cosmopolitian Center
6075 Barfield Rd NE
Atlanta, GA 30328

Kaia Systems
PO Box 11461
Oakland, CA 94611
415 654 8671

Kertech Corp.
10 Babson Park Ave.
Babson Park, MA 02157
617 235 5964

Keytronic
PO Box 14687
Spokane, WA 99214
509 928 8000
510 773 1885

Konan Corporation
1434 N. 27th Ave.
Phoenix, AZ 85009
602 269 2649

Krell Software Corp.
1320 Stony Brook Rd.
Stony Brook, NY 11790

Kybe Corporation
132 Calvary St.
Waltham, MA 02154
617 899 0012
TELEX 94 0179

LJK Enterprises, Inc.
PO Box 10827
St. Louis, MO 63129
314 846 6124

Laboratory Microsystems
4147 Beethoven St.
Los Angeles, CA 90066
213-306-7412
Laboratory Microsystems sells a
variety of FORTH packages, including
FORTH running under CP/M; 8086 FORTH
under CP/M-86; and PC/FORTH for the
IBM PC. (10/82)

Language Resources
Janet L. Myers
4885 Riverbend Road
Boulder, CO 80301
303 449 8087

Leading Edge Products, Inc.
225 Turnpike Street
Canton, MA 02021
617 828 8150
Telex 951 624

Lear Siegler, Inc.

714 N. Brookhurst
Anaheim, CA 92803
714 774 1010

Lexisoft, Inc.
Box 267
Davis, CA 95616
916 758 3630

Lifeboat Associates
1651 Third Ave.
New York, NY 10028
212 860 0300

Lightning Software
Box 11725
Palo Alto, CA 94306
415 327 3280

Link Systems
1640 19th St.
Santa Monica, CA 90404
213 453 1851

Lobo Drives International
935 Camino Del Sur
Goleta, CA 93017
805 685 4546

Local Network Standards Committee
IEEE
PO Box 500
Beaverton, OR 97077
503 644 0161

Lockheed Information Systems
3460 Hillview Ave.
Palo Alto, CA 94304
800 277 1960 (toll free outside Califo
800 982 5838 (inside California)
415 493 4411, X 45412

Logica, Inc.
666 3rd Ave., 19th Floor
New York, NY 10017
212 599 0828

Logical Machines Corporation
1294 Hammerwood Ave.
Sunnyvale, CA 94086
408 744 1290
TWX 910 3399206

Lomas Data Products, inc.

729 Farm Road
Marlboro, MA 01752
617 481 2822

Lotus Development Corp.
Cambridge, MA
Lotus, a new company, publishes
"1-2-3" for the PC IBM, supposedly
the next VisiCalc. (11/82)

Lovell's
4205 Biltmore
Corpus Christi, TX 78418
512 852 3096

Lowell Ssytems, Inc.
150 Industrial Ave. East
Lowell, MA 01852
617 459 4930

Lucidata Ltd.
P.O. Box 128
Cambridge, CB2 5EZ
England

MACROTECH International Corp.
22133 Cohasset St.
Canoga Park, CA 91303
213-887-5737
MACROTECH makes a 256K byte S-100
bus memory board, which it sells for
$1,379. IEEE-696 compatible.
(10/82)

MuSYS
1752 B Langley
Irvine, CA 92714
714-662-7387
TWX 910-595-1967
MuSYS makes S-100 board computers
that can be used as independent
slaves. (11/82)

MicroArt Corporation
200 Market Bldg., Suite 961
Portland, OR 97201
800-642-7627 (outside OR)
506-692-3950
MicroArt makes a $295 business
graphics package for Zenith
computers. (11/82)

M&R Enterprises
PO Box 61011

Sunnyvale, CA 94088

MBP Software and Systems Technology, In
7700 Edgewater Drive, Suite 626
Oakland, CA 94621
415 632 1555

MJK Associates
122 Saratoga Ave., Suite 11
Santa Clara, CA 95050
408 247 5102

Maine Manufacturing Company
46 Bridge St.
Nashua, NH 03060
603 882 5142
800 258 1768 (toll free)

Marinchip Systems
16 Saint Jude Road
Mill Valley, CA 94941
415 383 1545

Mark Williams Co.
1430 West Wrightwood Ave.
Chicago, IL 60614
312 472 6659

Marketview Microsystems
59 Leicester St.
Brighton, MA 02135
617 787 9794

Matrix Software
1041 N. Main St.
Ann Arbor, MI 48104
313 663 6677

Matrox Electronic Systems, Inc.
2795 Bates Rd.
Montreal, QUE H3S 1B5
Canada
514 481 6838 or 735 1182
05 825651

Maxell Corp. of America
Data Products Group
60 Oxford Dr.
Moonachie, NJ 07074
201 440 8020

Measurement Systems & Controls, Inc.
867 North Main St.
Orange, CA 92668

714 633 4460

Memorex Corp.
Computer Media Group
2400 Condensa St.
Santa Clara, CA 95052

Metrologic Instruments
143 Harding Ave.
Bellmawr, NJ 08031

Micro Control Systems, Inc.
230 Hartford Turnpike
Vernon, CT 06066
203 643 4897

Micro Data Base Systems, Inc.
PO Box 248
Lafayette, IN 47902
317 742 7388

Micro Diversions, Inc.
8455 D Tyco Rd.
Vienna, VA 22180
703 827 0888

Micro Futures
PO Box 2765
Livonia, MI 48154
313 422 0914

Micro Mike's Inc.
905 South Buchanan
Amarillo, TX 79101

Micro Networks Corp.
324 Clark St.
Worcester, MA 01606
617 852 5400

Micro Peripherals Inc.
21201 Oxnard St.
Woodland Hills, CA 91367
213 999 2870

Micro Works
PO Box 1110
Del Mar, CA 92014
714 942 2400

MicroPro International Corp.
1299 4th St., Suite 400
San Raphael, CA 94901
415 457 8990

Microcom
1400A Providence Hwy.
Norwood, MA 02062
Microcom sells communications
software, including Telex emulators,
for the Apple II, ///, and IBM PC.
(11/82)

Microcom, Inc.
1400A Providence Highway
Norwood, MA 02062
617 762 9310

Microcomputer Consultants
PO Box T
Davis, CA 95617
800 824 5952
916 756 8104

Microcomputer Investors Association
902 Anderson Drive
Fredericksburg, VA 22401

Microcomputer Technology, Inc.
3304 W. MacArthur Blvd.
Santa Ana, CA 93704
714 979 9925

Microlab
3218 Skokie Valley Road
Highland Park, IL 60035
312 433 7550

Micromation
1620 Montgomery St.
San Francisco, CA 94111
415 398 0289
TWX 910 372 6101

MicroMotion
12077 Wilshire Blvd., #506
Los Angeles, CA 90023
213-821-4340
MicroMotion sells FORTH-79 for the
Apple II and Z-80 systems. (11/82)

Micromotion
12077 Wilshire Blvd., Suite 506
Los Angeles, CA 90025
213 821 4340

Micropolis
7959 Deerling Ave.
Canoga Park, CA 91304

213 703 1121

Microsoft Consumer Products
400 108th Ave., N.E., Suite 200
Bellevue, Washington 98004
206 454 1315

Microsoft, Inc.
10800 NE Eighth St.
Bellevue, WA 98004
206 454 1315

Microstuf, Inc.
1900 Leland Drive, Suite 12
Marietta, GA 30067
404 952 0267

Microtrend USA
1900 Plantside Drive
Louisville, KY 40299
800 626 6268

Microware
PO Box 79
Kingston, MA 02364
617 746 7342

Miller Microcomputer Services
61 Lake Shore Rd.
Natick, MA 01760
617 653 6136

Mokuraicherlin
PO Box 1131
Mount Shasta, CA 96067

Morrow Designs
600 McCormick St.
San Leandro, CA 94577
415-430-1970
George Morrow's company makes a
low-cost CP/M system, the Decision,
as well as S-100 boards and disk
drives. (11/82)

Microsystems
One Park Avenue
New York, NY 10016
212-725-7957
Now owned by Ziff-Davis Publishing,
Microsystems is dedicated to S-100
bus and CP/M products. $24.97/yr.
(11/82)

IMSAI
Fischer-Freitas Corp.
910 81st Ave., Bldg. 14
Oakland, CA 94621
415-635-7615
IMSAI lives! Maker of one of the
popular early S-100 bus computers,
IMSAI went down in 1979, only to be
rescued by Fischer-Freitas. The
IMSAI computer, which FF sells and
services, is a 8080-based machine
with front panel. (11/82)

Motorola Semiconductor Products
POB 20912
Phoenix, AZ 85036
602 244 5714

Mountain Computer
300 Harvey West Blvd.
Santa Cruz, CA 95060
408 429 8600

Mountain View Press, Inc.
PO Box 4656
Mountain View, CA 94040
415 981 4103

Muse
330 N. Charles St.
Baltimore, MD 21201

Mycroft Labs, Inc.
PO Box 6045
Tallahassee, FL 32301
904 385 2708

NCR Corp.
Dayton, OH 45479
513 449 2150

NEC Information Systems, Inc.
5 Militia Drive
Lexington, MA 02173
617 862 3120

National Information Utilities Corp.
1616 Anderson Rd.
McLean, VA
703 734 7000

National Semiconductor Corp.
2900 Semiconductor Drive
Santa Clara, CA 95051

National Software Co.
Chamber of Commerce Bldg., Suite 117
Baltimore, MD 21202
301 539 0123
800 638 7563

Naval Publications and Forms Center
5801 Tabor Ave.
Philadelphia, PA 19120

Nestar Systems, Inc.
430 Sherman Ave.
Palo Alto, CA 94306
415 327 0125

Network Consulting Inc.
A106   1093 W. Broadway
Vancouver, BC
Canada V6H 1E2
604 738 3500

New York Times Information Service
1719 A Route 10
Parsippany, NJ 07054

Newtech Computer Systems, Inc.
230 Clinton St.
Brooklyn, NY 11201
212 625 6220

Nikrom Technical Products
25 Prospect St.
Leominster, MA 01453
800 835 2246

Non-Pareil Industries
1890 Marietta Blvd.
Atlanta, GA 30318
404 352 1522

North Star
14440 Catalina St.
San Leandro, CA 94577
415 357 8500

North Star Users Group
PO Box 1318
Antioch, CA 94509

Novation
18664 Oxnard St.
Tarzana, CA 91356
213 996 5060
800 423 5410

Telex 80 4294 Answerback SPEDEX ATL

OSI User Group, Independent
PO Box 518
Newton Corner, MA 02158

Ohio Scientific
1333 South Chilicothe Rd.
Aurora, OH 44202
216 562 3101
800 321 6850 (toll free)

Okidata Corporation
111 Gaither Drive
Mt. Laurel, NJ 08054
609 235 2600
TWX 710 897 0792

Omni Communications Co., Inc.
200 W. County Line Rd., Box 200
Jackson, NJ 08527
201 928 1477

Olivetti
Docutel Olivetti Corp.
155 White Plains Rd.
Tarrytown, NY 10591
800-431-1366 (outside NY)
914-631-8100
Olivetti, the Italian typewriter
manufacturer, has a Z8000-based 16
bit computer, the M20. (11/82)

On-Line Systems
36575 Mudge Ranch Rd.
Coarsegold, CA 93614
209 683 6858

Onyx Systems, Inc.
73 E. Trimble Rd.
San Jose, CA 95131
408 946 6330

Open Systems, Inc.
430 Oak Grove, Suite 409
Minneapolis, MN 55403
612 870 3515

PAIA Electronics
1020 W. Wilshire Blvd.
Oklahoma City, OK 73116
405 843 9626

PCD Systems, Inc.

PO Box 143
Penn Yan, NY 14527
315 536 3734

Peachtree Software Inc.
3445 Peachtree Rd., N.E.   8th floor
Atlanta, GA 30326
404 266 0673

HumanSoft
661 Massachusettes Ave.
Arlington, MA 02174
617-641-1880
HumanSoft makes a dBASE II utility
for sorting and file compression.
(11/82)

Pearlsoft
PO Box 13850
Salem, OR 97309
503 363 8929

Penguin Software
830 4th Ave.
Geneva, IL 60134
312 232 1984

People's Computer Co.
1263 El Camino Real
Box E
Menlo Park, CA 94025
415 323 3111

Per Sci, Inc.
12210 Nebraska Ave.
West Los Angeles, CA 90025
213 820 3764

Percom Data Company, Inc.
211 N. Kirby
Garland, TX 75042
214 272 3421
800 527 1592 (toll free)

Perfect Software, Inc.
1400 Shattuck Ave.
Berkeley, CA 94709
415 974 6661

Personal Computer World
Sportscene Publishers (PCW) Ltd.
14 Rathbone Place
London W1P 1DE
001 631 1433

Phase One Systems, Inc.
7700 Edgewater Drive, Suite 830
Oakland, CA 94621
415 562 8085
TWX 910 366 7139

Philadelphia Consulting Group, Inc.
PO Box 102
Wynnewood, PA 19096
215 649 1598

Pirates Harbor
POB 8928
Boston, MA 02114
617-738-5051 (modem)
Pirates Harbor makes a $150 Apple II
board called "Crack-Shot" that takes
a snapshot of memory and dumps it to
disk. (11/82)

Pickles & Trout
PO Box 1208
Goleta, CA 93017
805 967 9563

Potomac Micro Magic, Inc.
5201 Leesburg Pike, Suite 604
Falls Church, VA 22041
703-379-9660
PMMI makes a low-cost S-100 board
modem competitive with the Hayes
S-100 board. (10/82)

Practical Programming
Box 3069
North Brunswick, NJ 08902

Predex Corporation
1345 Ave. of the Americas
New York, NY 10019
212 977 9090

Prime Computer, Inc.
40 Walnut St.
Wellesley Hills, MA 02181
617 879 2960

Professional Systems Corp.
3858 Carson St., Suite 220
Torrance, CA 90503
213 316 5345

Protocol Computers
6430 Variel Avenue #107

Woodland Hills, CA 91367

Q Kits, Div. J.R. Conwell Corp.
PO Box 35879
Tucson, AZ 85740
602 299 9831

Q.T. Products Division
Compatible Computer Corp.
3330 South Third St. West
Salt Lake City, UT 84115
801-974-0999
The QT line of S-100 mainframes and
disk drives is distributed by a
number of companies, including
Priority One (Chatsworth, CA
800-423-5922) and Compatible
Computer (NY 212-221-7900). (11/82)

Qantel Corp.
3525 Breakwater Ave.
Hayward, CA 94545
415 783 3410
TELEX 337 776

Quality Software
6660 Reseda Blvd., Ste. 105
Reseda, CA 91335

Quark Engineering
1433 Williams, Suite 1102
Denver, CO 80218

Quick Brown Fox
548 Broadway
New York, NY 10012
800-547-5995 x194
212-925-8290
Quick Brown Fox makes a word
processor for the Commodore VIC-20
and 64. (11/82)

Qume, Inc.
2350 Qume Drive
PO Box 50039
San Jose, CA 95150
408 942 4000
TWX 910 338 0232

RC Electronics, Inc.
7265 Tuolumne Dr.
Goleta, CA 93117
805 968 6614

RH Electronics
566 Irelan
Buellton, CA 93427
805-688-2047
RH sells the "Guardian Angel", a
$595 uninterruptable power source
for the Apple II. (11/82)

RR Software
POB 1512
Madison, WI 53701
608-244-6436
RR Software sells Janus, an Ada
compiler that runs under CP/M,
CP/M-86, and MS-DOS. (10/82)

RTR Software, Inc.
P.O. Box 12351
El Paso, TX 79912

Rainbow
19517 Business Center Drive
Northridge, CA 91324

Remark International
4 Sycamore Drive
Woodbury, NY 11797
516 367 3806

Remote Computing
1044 Northern Blvd.
Roslyn, NY 11576
516 484 4545

Research Press, Inc.
Box 8137 P
Prairie Village, KS 66208

SAVVY
100 South Elisworth St., 9th floor
San Mateo, CA 94401
415 340 0335

SDC Search Service
System Development Corporation
2500 Colorado Ave.
Santa Monica, CA 90406

SOROC Technology, Inc.
165 Freedom Ave.
Anaheim, CA 92801
714 992 2860
800 854 0147 (toll free)

SSM Microcomputer Products, Inc.
2190 Paragon Drive
San Jose, CA 95131
408-946-7400
SSM (originally Solid State Music)
makes a variety of boards for the
Apple II and other computers. It
also sells a communications package
called "Transend". (11/82)

Sandhu Machine Design, Inc.
308 S. State
Champaign, IL 61820
217 352 8485

Sat Trak International
c/o Computerland of Colorado Springs
4543 Templeton Gap Rd.
Colorado Springs, CO 80909
303 574 4150

Scanmark
Markem Corporation
Keene, NH 03431
603 352 1130

Static Memory Systems, Inc.
15 So. Van Buren Ave., Suite 209
Freeport, IL 61032
815-235-8713
SMS makes a memory board using
byte-wide, electrically eraseable
PROMS (E2PROMS) very useful in
firmware development. (10/82)

Santa Clara Systems, Inc.
560 Division St.
Campbell, CA 95008
408-374-6972
Santa Clara Systems sells hard disk
systems for microcomputers. (11/82)

Scotia Software
P.O. Box 197
Armdale, NS
Canada B3L 4J9
902 425 3879

Scott Instruments
815 North Elm
Denton, TX 76201
817 387 1054

Seattle Computer

1114 Industry Drive
Seattle, WA 98188
800-426-8936
An S-100 company with close ties to
MicroSoft, Seattle Computer sells a
8 MHz 8086 computer called the
"Gazelle" for $6000. (11/82)

Seiko
dist. by Intech Systems Corp.
2025 Royal Lane
Dallas, TX 75229
800-368-5010
Intech is distributor for the Seiko
8600 business computer system.
(11/82)

Select Information Systems, Inc.
919 Sir Francis Drake Blvd.
Kentfield, CA 94904
415 459 4003

Semiconductor Industry Association
20380 Town Center Lane, Suite 155
Cupertino, CA 95014
408 255 3522

SemiDisk Systems
POB GG
Beaverton, OR 97075
503-642-3100
SemiDisk Systems sells RAM memory
boards for the S-100 bus, TRS-80
Model 2, and IBM PC that emulate
floppy disk drives, and speed some
operations (sorts) considerably.
(10/82)

Semionics Associates
7530 Brompton St. #896
Houston, TX 77025
713 661 3565

Sensible Software
6619 Perham Dr.
W. Bloomfield, MI 48033
313 399 8877

Sentient Software, Inc.
PO Box 4929
Aspen, CO 81612
303 925 9293

Sextant

Dept. G, 716 E. St., S.E.
Washington, DC 2000?
202 544 0900

Shugart Associates, Inc.
435 Oakmead Parkway
Sunnyvale, CA 94086
408 733 0100

Strobe Inc.
897-5A Independence Ave.
Mountain View, CA 94043
415-969-5130
Strobe makes a low-cost ($795) pen
plotter.

Select Information Systems, Inc.
919 Sir Francis Drake Blvd.
Kentfield, CA 94904
415-459-4003
Select sells the "Select" word
processor. (11/82)

Scripps Data Systems, Inc.
9747 Businesspark Avenue
San Diego, CA 92131
714-695-1540
Scripps sells a Job Cost System for
the IBM PC. (11/82)

Siemens Corp.
OEM Data Products Division
240 Palais Rd
Anaheim, CA 92805
714 991 9700

Sierra On Line
36575 Mudge Ranch Rd.
Coarsegold, CA 93614

Sinclair Research Ltd.
2 Sinclair Plaza
Nashua, NH 03061
800 543 3000 #509

Sir-tech
6 Main St.
Ogdensbury, NY 13669

Sirius Software, Inc.
10364 Rockingham Dr.
Sacramento, CA 95827

Small Computer Company, Inc.

40 West Ridgewood Ave.
Ridgewood, NJ 07450
201-445-5643
The small Computer Company publishes
a data base manager called "filePro"
for the NEC PC-8000A computer.
(11/82)

SofTech Microsystems
16885 West Bernardo Drive
San Diego, CA 92127
714-451-1230
TWX 910 335 1594
SofTech Microsystems is a software
house that hold the major license on
UCSD's p-system. (11/82)

Software Affair
858 Rubis Dr.
Sunnyvale, CA 94086

Software Consultants
7053 Rose Trail
Memphis, TN 38134
901 377 3503

Software Publishing
1901 Landings Dr.
Mountain View, CA 94043

Software Sorcery, Inc.
7927 Jones Branch Dr., Suite 400
McLean, VA 22102
703 385 2944

Sola Corp.
1717 Busse Rd.
Elk Grove, IL 60007
312 439 2800
TELEX 28 0538

Solid Software
Suite 501
5500 Interstate North Parkway
Atlanta, GA 30328
404 952 7709

Sorcim
405 Aldo Avenue
Santa Clara, Ca 95050
408 727 7634

Source, The
1616 Anderson Rd.

McLean, VA 22102
703 821 6660

Southeastern Software
6414 Derbyshire Drive
New Orleans, LA 70126
504 246 8438

Southwest Technical Products Corp.
219 W. Rhapsody
San Antonio, TX 78216
512 344 0241

Southwestern Data Systems
PO Box 582
Santee, CA 92071
619-562-3221
Southwestern makes several excellent
terminal programs, including P-Term
The Professional, a Pascal program
for the Apple II. (11/82)

Spectrum Software
690 W. Fremont Ave.
Sunnyvale, CA 94087
408 738 4387

Springer Verlag
175 5th Ave.
New York, NY 10010

Standard Software of America
10 Mazzeo Drive
Randolph, MA 02368
800 343 0852
617 963 7220

Standards Administration Office
Institute for Computer Sciences and Tec
National Bureau of Standards
Washington, DC 20234

Stoneware
50 Belvedere St.
San Rafael, CA 94901

Strategic Simulations
465 Fairchild Dr., Suite 108
Mountain View, CA 94043
800 227 1617
800 772 3545 (CA)

Strictly Soft Ware
PO Box 338

Granville, OH 43023
800 848 5253
614 587 2938

Structured Systems Group
5208 Claremont Ave.
Oakland, CA 94618
415 547 1567

SubLogic
713 Edgebrook Dr.
Champaign, Il 61820

Summagraphics
35 Brentwood Ave.
Box 781
Fairfield, CT 06430
203 384 1344
TELEX 96 4348

Sun Research, Inc.
Box 210
New Durham, NH 03855
603 859 7110
510 297 4444

Supersoft
POB 1628
Champaign, IL 61820
217 359 2112

Sybex
2344 Sixth St.
Berkeley, CA 94710
415 848 8233
TELEX 336311

Synergistic Software
830 N. Riverside Dr. Suite 201
Renton, WA 98055
206 226 3216

Syntauri, Ltd.
3506 Waverly St.
Palo Alto, CA 94306

Systems Formulate Corp., USA
231 E South Whisman Rd.
Mountain View, CA 94041
415 969 7499

Systems Plus, Inc.
1120 San Antonio Road
Palo Alto, CA 94303

415 969 7047

TCS Software
3209 Fondren Rd.
Houston, TX 77063
713 977 7505

TNW Corporation
3351 Hancock St.
San Diego, CA 92110
714 225 1040
TWX 910 335 1194

TSD Display Products
35 Orville Drive
Bohemia, NY 11716
516 589 6800

Tandon Magnetics, Inc.
9333 Oso Ave.
Chatsworth, CA 91311
213 993 6644

Tandy (Radio Shack)
One Tandy Center
Fort Worth, TX 76102

Tarbell Electronics
950 Dovlen Place, Suite B
Carson, CA 90746
213 538 4251
213 538 2254

Technical Systems Consultants
111 Providence Rd.
Chapel Hill, NC 27514
919 493 1451

Technico, Inc.
9051 Red Branch Rd.
Columbia, MD 21045
301 995 1995
800 638 2893 (toll free)

Tecmar, Inc.
23414 Greenlawn Ave.
Cleveland, OH 44122
216 382 7599

Telecon Systems
90 E. Gish Rd., Suite 25
San Jose, CA 95112
408-275-1659
Telecon sells C compilers that run

on the 6809 (Flex), PDP-11 (RT-11),
and under CP/M and MS-DOS. (10/82)

Telcon Industries, Inc.
1401 N.W. 69th St.
Ft. Lauderdale, FL 33309
305 971 2250
510 956 9412

TeleVideo Systems, Inc.
1170 Morse Ave
Sunnyvale, CA 94086
800 538 8725
408 745 7760

Teletek
9767F Business Park Drive
Sacramento, CA 95827
916-361-1777
Teletek makes S-100 bus products,
including a 1-board computer that
includes CPU, serial and parallel
ports, and floppy disk controller.
(10/82)

Telephone Software Connection, Inc.
PO Box 6548
Torrance, CA 90504
213 516 9430

Teleram Communications Corp.
2 Corporate Park Drive
White Plains, NY 10604
914 694 9270

Telesensory Systems, Inc.
3408 Hillview Ave.
PO Box 10099
Palo Alto, CA 94304
415 493 2626
348352 TSI PLA

Teletype Corporation
5555 Touhy Ave.
Skokie, IL 60077
312 982 2000
TELEX 25 4051
TWX 910 223 3611

Terrapin, Inc.
380C Green St.
Cambridge, MA 02139
617 492 8816

Texas Instruments
Inquiry Answering Service
PO Box 1443
M/S 6404
Houston, TX 77
also
Texas Instruments
8600 Commerce Park Drive, Suite 100
Houston, TX 77036
713 776 6511

Software Toolworks
14478 Glorietta Dr.
Sherman Oaks, CA 91423
213 986 4885

Trantor Systems, Ltd.
4432 Enterprise St., Unit I
Fremont, CA 94538
415-490-3441
Trantor makes a hard disk unit for
the Osborne I computer. (11/82)

Threshold Technology, Inc.
1829 Underwood Blvd.
Delran, NJ 08075
609 461 9200

Tymnet, Inc.
Corporate Offices 10261 Bubb Rd.
Cupertino, CA 95014
408 446 7000

Ungermann-Bass
2560 Mission College Blvd.
Santa Clara, CA 95050
408 496 0111

Unicorn Systems
30261 Palomares Rd.
Castro Valley, CA 94720
415 881 4490

United Software of America
750 Third Ave.
New York, NY 10017
212 682 0347
Telex 640055

Universal Data Systems
4900 Bradford Drive
Huntsville, AL 35805
205 837 8100
TWX 810 726 2100

Vanguard Data Systems
8696 S. Atlantic Ave.
South Gate, CA 90280
213 564 6402

Vanguard Systems Corp.
6812 San Pedro
San Antonio, TX 78216
512 828 0554

Vector Graphic
500 N. Ventu Park Rd.
Thousand Oaks, CA
213 991 2302

Verbatim
323 Soquel Way
Sunnyvale, CA 94086
408 245 4400
TWX 910 339 9381
Verbatim is a major manufacturer of
floppy disks. (11/82)

Vikor Company
51 Lake St.
PO Box 3123
Nashua, NH 03061
603 889 8530

VisiCorp
2895 Zanker Rd.
San Jose, CA 95134
VisiCorp, formerly Personal
Software, is the publisher of
VisiCalc and the other
Visi-products. (11/82)

Vista Computer Co.
1317 East Edinger
Santa Ana, CA 92705
714-953-0523
800-854-8017 (outside CA)
Vista sells a variety of low-cost
items, especially disk drives,
mostly for the Apple II. (11/82)

Vynet Corp.
2405 Qume Dr.
San Jose, CA 95131
408 942 1037

Wang Laboratories, Inc.
1 Industrial Drive
Lowell, Ma 01851

617 851 4111

Western Computer Systems, Inc.
PO Box 10191
Eugene, OR 97440 2191
503 485 4222

Western Digital Corporation
3128 Redhill Ave., Box 2180
Newport Beach, CA 92663
714 557 3550
TWX 910 595 1139

Western Union Electronic Mail, Inc.
1600 Anderson Road
McClean, VA 22102
703 821 5800

Westico, Inc.
25 Van Zant St.
Norwalk, CT 06855
203 853 6880

Whitesmiths, Ltd.
127 West 80th ST.
New York, NY 10024
212-799-1200

Williamsville Publishing Co.
PO Box 250
Fredonia, NY 14063
716 679 1434

Workman and Associates
112 Marion Ave.
Pasadena, CA 91106
213-796-4401

Xerox Corporation
Public Relations
701 South Aviation Blvd.
El Segundo, CA 90245
213-679-4511

Xedex
222 Route 59
Suffern NY, 10901
914-368-0353
Xedex makes the "Baby Blue" CP/M
upgrade board for the IBM PC.
(11/82)

Xerox Corporation
Office Products Division

1341 West Mockingbird Lane
Dallas, TX 75247
The Xerox Office Products Division,
headed by Don Massaro, once head of
Shugart Associates, puts out the
Xerox 820 personal computer, and
other products.

Yourdon Software Products Group
1133 Avenue of the Americas
New York, NY 10036
212 730 5840

Zilog
10340 Bubb Rd.
Cupertino, CA 95014
408-446-4666
TWX 910 338 7621
Zilog, an Exxon Affiliate, is a
semiconductor manufacturer best
known for the Z-80 processor. Its
16-bit microprocessor, the Z8000, is
not doing well in competition with
the Motorola 68000 and the Intel
8086. Zilog's Z8 is an interesting
computer-on-a-chip.

Ziyad, Inc.
30 Broad St.
Denville, NJ 07834
201-627-7600
Ziyad makes a sheet feeder for
letter quality printers that it
calls an "Intelligent Paper
Processor". Ziyad markets this
device through Lanier, Syntrex, and
other word processing companies.
(9/82)